This book constitutes a supplement to Alfred Marshall's *Official Papers*, which were edited by John Maynard Keynes for the Royal Economic Society in 1926. It presents material which Keynes did not include, along with editorial notes and introductions to the various pieces. It represents, therefore, a further step towards completing in published form the collected writings of one of the great modern economists.

Material included covers the following: Marshall's 1880 evidence as Principal of Bristol University College to the Committee on Higher Education in Wales and Monmouthshire; comments on a paper by J. S. Nicholson prepared for the Gold and Silver Commission in 1888; sections of the *Final Report* of the Royal Commission on Labour (1891–4) dealing with trade unions, irregularity of employment and other matters attributed to him by his widow together with selections of his questioning of witnesses who appeared before the Commission (including Sidney Webb, Charles Booth, Robert Giffen, Tom Mann); and last, by way of an appendix, the alleged first version of his famous Memorandum on the Fiscal Policy of International Trade prepared for the Chancellor of the Exchequer in 1903 (of which the final version of 1908 was included by Keynes in 1926), but which cannot really be ascribed to Marshall.

The contents facilitate the enhancement of understanding Alfred Marshall, the doyen of British economics in the nineteenth century and founder of the Cambridge School of Economics.

This book constitutes a supplement to Alfred Marshall's *Official Papers*. It focusses on the advice that Marshall, one of the founding fathers of modern economics, offered to the British government in the late nineteenth century. The topics covered include education, the role of women, trade unions, unemployment, public enterprise, the quantity theory of money, inflation and trade, the benefits of free trade and the dangers of protection. The material offers valuable insights into policy thinking a century ago, much of which has a surprising degree of relevance to the pressing issues at the end of the present century.

OFFICIAL PAPERS OF
ALFRED MARSHALL

A SUPPLEMENT

OFFICIAL PAPERS
OF
ALFRED MARSHALL

A SUPPLEMENT

EDITED BY

PETER GROENEWEGEN

University of Sydney

CAMBRIDGE
UNIVERSITY PRESS

FOR THE ROYAL ECONOMIC SOCIETY

Published by the Press Syndicate of the University of Cambridge
The Pitt Building, Trumpington Street, Cambridge CB2 1RP
40 West 20th Street, New York, NY 10011–4211, USA
10 Stamford Road, Oakleigh, Melbourne 3166, Australia

First published 1996

Printed in Great Britain at the University Press, Cambridge

A catalogue record for this book is available from the British Library

Library of Congress cataloguing in publication data
Marshall, Alfred, 1842–1924.
Official papers of Alfred Marshall: a supplement / edited by
Peter Groenewegen.
p.   cm.
Contains material omitted from original 1926 ed., which was edited
by John M. Keynes.
Includes index.
ISBN 0 521 55185 4 (hardback)
1. Great Britain–Economic conditions–19th century.   2. Currency
question–Great Britain.   3. Aged–Great Britain–Economic
conditions.   4. Taxation–Great Britain.   I. Groenewegen, Peter D.
II. Marshall, Alfred, 1842–1924. Official papers of Alfred
Marshall.   III. Title.
HC255.M387   Suppl.
330.941'081–dc20   95-30972   CIP

ISBN 0 521 551854 hardback

JK

CONTENTS

3b EVIDENCE

3C 'MEMORANDUM ON DISPUTES AND ASSOCIATIONS WITHIN PARTICULAR TRADES CONSIDERED IN RELATION TO THE INTERESTS OF THE WORKING CLASSES IN OTHER TRADES'

PREFACE AND ACKNOWLEDGEMENTS

This book is a by-product of my work on Marshall's biography. When I was writing its Chapter 11 on Marshall as adviser to governments, I came to realise the significant gaps in the collection of his official papers which Keynes had prepared. The suggestion to rectify Keynes's omissions, particularly by including some material from the voluminous reports of the Labour Commission (guided by advice from Marshall's widow which was rejected by Keynes) was put to the Royal Economic Society and to Cambridge University Press. These both showed encouraging interest in this project of a supplementary volume to Keynes's edition of Marshall's *Official Papers* which, in a New York reprint, is still readily available. I am especially indebted to Donald Winch and to Patrick McCartan in this context. Work for the volume was assisted by support from the Australian Research Council, and research assistance from Mark Donoghue, Susan King and Jack Towe. John Whitaker gave comments on a number of points, as did Rita McWilliams-Tullberg who encouraged me to reprint the education evidence. As usual, Valerie Jones prepared an excellent final manuscript. I am indebted to Peter Halls and Jacky Cox as successive archivists of King's College, Cambridge, for giving me access to the valuable material on this topic among the Keynes Papers; to Donald Ross and Rowland Thomas at the Marshall Library, Faculty of Economics and Politics at Cambridge University, who gave me access to the Marshall Archive when required. Permission to reprint the material from official documents was gracefully granted by the Public Records Office as was that for printing Marshall's formerly unpublished draft on trade unions by the Faculty of Economics and Politics at Cambridge who hold the copyright.

Peter Groenewegen

GENERAL INTRODUCTION

When Keynes edited the *Official Papers of Alfred Marshall*, he claimed that the volume contained 'the whole of Alfred Marshall's contributions to official inquiries on economic questions with the exception of his work on the Labour Commission'. Keynes explained the reason for this omission as follows. Because Marshall was a member of this Commission and not a witness, 'it was impossible in this case to identify or separate his contributions from those of the Commission as a whole'.[1] In this preface, Keynes was mistaken on various counts, in some respects, wittingly so.

While Keynes was still in the process of editing the material for publication, he was advised by two knowledgeable correspondents that the plan on which he was working was partly flawed. Professor T.E. Gregory wrote Keynes in September 1925 that some papers which Marshall had prepared for the Gold and Silver Commission had not been included in the printed *Report*. Two of these Keynes subsequently included. The first was a Memorandum on the Relation between the Fall of the Exchanges and Trade with Countries which have not a Gold Currency, dated 13 January 1888. Secondly, Keynes printed the preliminary Memorandum in which Marshall had answered a number of questions put by the Commission to academic and other experts. This was dated 9 November 1887. In between, Keynes inserted the transcript of Marshall's evidence over three days, and a further Memorandum prepared either late January or early February 1888. This had been written

---

[1] J.M. Keynes, *Official Papers of Alfred Marshall* (hereafter *OP*), London, Macmillan, for the Royal Economic Society, 1926, p.v.

to enable Marshall specifically to address evidence by Messrs Nisbett and Barclay as he had been requested to do by Thomas Farrar in the last question put to him while giving his oral evidence.[2] The third item mentioned by Gregory was not reproduced. This was a detailed comment by Marshall on Nicholson's paper for the Commission, dated 30 June 1888. It was very critical of Nicholson's position, which Marshall claimed misrepresented his own. It is of special interest because it very succinctly explains Marshall's highly qualified position on the quantity theory, seeing it at best as a very limited explanation of the price level.

The second correspondent who offered assistance in Keynes's editorial task was Marshall's widow, Mary Paley Marshall. She wrote Keynes on 22 March 1926 advising him on two matters in the editing of *Official Papers*. Her first advice concerned minor revision to the Memorandum on the Fiscal Policy of International Trade which Marshall had intended to make had he lived to have reprinted it himself. This was to substitute 'colonies' or 'dominions' for 'dependencies', terminology no longer appropriate after the First World War. This Keynes appears to have done, using the word 'colonies' rather than 'dominions' where appropriate.

More importantly, Mary Paley Marshall sought to give advice on what Keynes ought to do with the Labour Commission:

> As to the Report of the Labour Commission, I believe that the whole of VI, 'Irregularity of Employment' was practically his and especially its §3, pars. 227–244, and §7 of II on the effects of Trade Unions . . . I remember Alfred saying that he should have liked to reprint VI just as it stood, but that he thought he had no right to do so.[3]

Whether Keynes took up her suggestion that he should consult Balfour on the matter is doubtful. There is nothing in the file from the Keynes Papers to suggest that he did so. It may be noted also that when Marshall in the early 1920s had good reason to reprint some of this material in Book IV of *Money, Credit and Commerce*, he did not do so, perhaps for the reason Mary Paley Marshall reported to Maynard Keynes some years later. As R.C.O. Matthews[4] has argued, and Mary

---

[2] *Ibid.*, p. 169.

[3] Mary Paley Marshall to John Maynard Keynes, 22 March 1926 (Keynes Papers, King's College, Cambridge, RES/2/41).

[4] R.C.O. Matthews, 'Marshall and the Labour Market', in *Centenary Essays on Alfred Marshall*, ed. John K. Whitaker, Cambridge, Cambridge University Press, 1990, pp. 14–15, 17–18, 31–2.

Paley Marshall had done herself in 1924 when she prepared notes to assist Keynes in the preparation of his famous obituary, Marshall's hand is visible in the Commission's *Final Report* in these as well as in other sections.[5]

Other material associated with the Labour Commission can be directly associated with Alfred Marshall. Obvious examples are the questions he addressed to witnesses at the Commission's public hearings. Although these present Marshall's views in a different way from the answers he gave to Royal Commissions when he had appeared before them as a witness himself, his questions do often represent his views. This is particularly evident when his questioning is sustained, as was the case for a number of important witnesses whom he interrogated at considerable length when the Commission was sitting as a whole. Marshall's work for the Labour Commission is therefore further illuminated from his approach to the gaining of information from witnesses, information which later featured among the Commission's summary of this part of their work in the *Final Report*. Another item by Marshall, though not published by the Commission in any form whatsoever, can nevertheless be associated with his work for it. This is a twenty-one page hand-written Memorandum on trade unions, written sometime in 1893[6] and intended for use by the Commission in both the introduction and the conclusion of the preliminary, factual summary of the evidence of the *Final Report*. Its contents supplement some of Marshall's views reflected in the segment on trade unions of the *Final Report* attributed to him by Mary Paley Marshall.

Keynes's own bibliography of the writings of Alfred Marshall ought to have alerted him to a third omission.[7] This was the evidence Marshall gave in December 1880 before the Committee on Intermediate and

---

[5] Earlier, in the context of Keynes's writing of his obituary memoir on Marshall, Mary Paley had argued that Marshall's contribution to the *Final Report* of the Labour Commission included material on the minimum wage (Keynes's Marshall file, Keynes Papers, King's College, Cambridge, A24.1/27). And see below, introduction to Item 3, pp. 90–1.

[6] It is preserved in the Marshall Archive (Box 6 (6)), Marshall Library, and has until now not been printed. See below, introduction to Item 3.

[7] J.M. Keynes, 'Bibliographical List of the Writings of Alfred Marshall', described as an attempt to list those of Marshall's works 'extant in print' and with 'some permanent interest'. It appeared originally in the December 1924 issue of the *Economic Journal* and was reprinted in *Memorials of Alfred Marshall*, ed. A.C. Pigou, London, Macmillan, 1925, pp. 500–8. Item (1), p. 500, is the 1880 evidence on higher education Marshall gave to a government committee.

Higher Education in Wales and Monmouthshire in his capacity as Principal of Bristol University College. Although its limited economic interest may have made it unsuitable for inclusion in a collection sponsored by a Royal Economic Society, as Keynes suggested in the remark from his preface quoted in the opening paragraph of this introduction, its omission could have been explicitly justified. After all, its contents covered aspects of business education, a subject of some interest to economists, as well as aspects of the finance required for setting up new tertiary educational institutions. Moreover, the material provided a rare glimpse of Marshall's activities while at Bristol, a subject on which there had been relatively little in the volume of *Memorials of Alfred Marshall* which had appeared the year before.[8]

These three items are reprinted in what follows. Item 1 reproduces Marshall's evidence to the Committee on Intermediate and Higher Education in Wales and Monmouthshire from the Committee's official *Report*. Item 2 reproduces the four page Memorandum on Nicholson which Marshall had written during June 1888 for the Gold and Silver Commission. Item 3 reproduces material from the Labour Commission associated with Marshall. It is divided into three sections. Item 3a reprints two segments of the Commission's *Final Report*, namely Section II, §7 – 'Representations Made as to the Injurious or Beneficial Effects of Trade Unions' and Section VI, 'Irregularity of Employment'. These are the items which Mary Paley Marshall specifically claimed to be attributable to her husband. Item 3b reprints selected evidence from the Labour Commission as a representative sample of Marshall's questioning of witnesses on its behalf. Most of this comes from the evidence gathered while the Commission was sitting as a whole; only one example of evidence is included from Marshall's questioning as a member of Group B of the Commission concerned with issues of transport and agriculture. The rationale for this selection is discussed in some detail at a later stage,[9] but it may be indicated here that the witnesses chosen were all eminent persons within their fields hence enabling Marshall to ask a wide range of inter-

---

[8] This is confined to less than three pages of Keynes's Marshall memoir ('Alfred Marshall 1842–1924', in *Memorials of Alfred Marshall*, ed. Pigou), a brief reference by Marshall himself in his obituary to Jowett, and a reference by Marshall in a later letter to a friendship formed at Bristol.   [9] Below, introduction to Item 3, pp. 88–9.

esting questions. They were either well-known socialists or working-class leaders (John Ludlow, Henry Hyndman, Sidney Webb, Ben Tillett and Tom Mann) or prominent social investigators and statisticians (Charles Booth, Sir Robert Giffen and E.R.L. Gould). Item 3c presents Marshall's draft paper on trade unions he prepared for the Labour Commission in 1893, even though it appears not to have been used by it in any formal sense.

A fourth item included is associated with Marshall's 'Memorandum on the Fiscal Policy of International Trade'. Keynes reprinted this in 1926 as the last item in his collection of Marshall's *Official Papers*. This was its 1908 version, but the paper had been originally written, and printed, in 1903. More than fifty years later it was claimed[10] that the original 1903 version had been discovered in Treasury files and it was therefore decided to include this earlier, never published version to supplement the 1908 document as reprinted by Keynes. Closer study of the 1903 Memorandum reveals that it cannot be ascribed to Marshall, although he may have had some minor impact on it.[11] Item 4 therefore consists of a detailed discussion of the 1903 Memorandum on the Fiscal Policy of International Trade and its wrong attribution to Marshall. The Memorandum is, nevertheless, reprinted as an appendix because of its interest as a document in the 1903 tariff debate in which Marshall took such an active part.

All items included are accompanied by their own editorial introductions and detailed editorial notes. The last are particularly required in the reprinted evidence from the Labour Commission to place it in context. Material associated with the Labour Commission also forms by far the greater part of this collection, appropriate given the time Marshall spent on it and the value it had for his education as he later claimed.[12] The volume is therefore a genuine supplement to Keynes's original edition of Marshall's *Official Papers* since together they give easy access for sampling the whole of Marshall's considerable contribution to government inquiries over the period from 1881 to 1908 when he occupied the chairs of political economy at Bristol and Cambridge. For

---

[10] By J.C. Wood, details are provided below, pp. 304–9.   [11] See below, pp. 309, 312.

[12] See 'Alfred Marshall, Professor of Political Economy at Cambridge', in *Alfred Marshall. Critical Assessments*, edited by J.C. Wood, London, Croom Helm, 1982, Vol. I, p. 150; Alfred Marshall, *Industry and Trade*, London, Macmillan, 1919, Preface, pp. vi–vii.

Marshall scholars, the contents of this volume provide further insight into his life, his work and his ideas while more generally, its contents will be of use to persons interested in the late Victorian and early Edwardian eras.

ITEM 1

Evidence to the Committee Appointed to Inquire into the Condition of Intermediate and Higher Education in Wales and Monmouthshire by Alfred Marshall, given at Newport, 20 December 1880

INTRODUCTION

The Committee in question was set up in August 1880 to fulfil a promise made by the then recently re-elected Prime Minister, W.E. Gladstone, to the House of Commons. Its terms of reference were to obtain information and to give advice on:

1. The nature and extent of the existing provision –
   (a) Intermediate, and
   (b) Higher,
   Education in Wales, how far it is made use of, and what extension of it is necessary.
2. How far the benefits of that provision are limited by conditions which favour any particular denomination.
3. The best means of supplying any deficiencies under the foregoing heads, and how far existing endowments may be so applied.
4. That new contributions are needed to meet existing deficiencies; whether these can be found under existing endowments, or should be raised by other means; and for what objects such contributions can best be given.
5. Whether a University for Wales, with power to grant degrees (in arts) is necessary, or would tend to confer a real benefit on higher education in the Principality.[1]

The appointed Committee members were Viscount Emlyn, MP; Lewis Morris, Esq.; Professor John Rhys; H. Richard Esq., MP; and the Rev. Prebendam Robinson. The Committee was chaired by Lord

[1] *Report of the Committee Appointed to Inquire into the Condition of Intermediate and Higher Education in Wales*, London, HMSO, 1881, Cmnd 3047, pp. iii–iv.

Aberdare, while its secretary was W.T. Warry, one of the superior offi-
cers of the Charity Commission, the duties of which included involvement in the provision of public education as legislated for in 1870.[2]
Since the Committee was empowered to procure advice and information from 'individuals . . . conversant with the subject',[3] Marshall's presence as a person giving evidence is easily explained. In 1880 he was
Principal of Bristol University College as well as its Professor of
Political Economy, positions he had occupied from July 1877.[4] As senior
administrator of a newly established nearby higher education institution, he had the experience to inform the Committee on those parts of
its terms of reference related to higher education.

The Committee reported on 18 August 1881, its contents explicitly
noting Marshall's contributions to its fact finding on only one occasion.[5]
With respect to matters related to higher education, the Committee recommended as follows. Despite the somewhat adverse experience of
Aberystwyth, it proposed the establishment of more University Colleges
in Wales, in the first instance in Glamorgan, hence regardless of the
claims of towns such as Cardiff. It argued that £4,000 by way of a grant
in addition to incomes from fees would be sufficient to place such
Colleges on a sound financial footing, given the experience of the smaller
Irish University Colleges. The Committee also recommended that the
new Colleges should be run on non-sectarian lines and be open for education to girls and young women.[6] The *Report*, moreover, suggested a
power to confer degrees for the new Colleges, on the basis of examinations conducted by appointees of the ruling bodies of the Universities of
Oxford and Cambridge,[7] notwithstanding the opposing evidence

---

[2] *Ibid.*, p. iii. The membership therefore involved an academic, Professor, later Sir John Rhys
(1840–1915), Professor of Celtic Studies at Oxford and later Principal of Jesus College
(involved in the inquiry, *Report*, p. lxix); two Members of Parliament, a clergyman and Lewis
Morris (1833–1907), a Welsh poet and educationist, and, like Rhys, associated with Jesus
College, Oxford, where he was an undergraduate but not a Fellow. Lord Aberdare was then
Minister of Education.   [3] *Ibid.*, p. iii.

[4] See J.K. Whitaker, 'Alfred Marshall: The Years 1877 to 1885', *History of Political Economy*
4(1), Spring 1972, pp. 1–61; Peter Groenewegen, *A Soaring Eagle: Alfred Marshall 1842–1924*,
Aldershot, Edward Elgar, 1995, pp. 275–84.

[5] *Report*, p. xxxiii. It repeated Marshall's objection to an expanded college system as a degree
giving body because he regarded 'the growth of examinations as an evil, and foresaw a difficulty in providing for these multiplied examinations [from lack of] a sufficient number of
qualified examiners' (cf. below, pp. 30–6, 59, Q. 18,214–29, Q. 18,353–4, the answer quoted in
the text is from Q. 18,229).   [6] *Report*, p. lxvii.   [7] *Report*, p. lxviii.

(including that of Marshall). The whole *Report* was brief and, apart from three minor dissenting opinions on particular topics, a majority one.

Marshall's evidence was given relatively late in the proceedings, on 20 December 1880, presumably because his heavy administrative duties at Bristol made it difficult for him to attend its hearing during term.[8] The few extant Marshall letters for November and December 1880 do not mention the fact he was giving evidence to the Committee, and there appear to be absolutely no contemporary references from him on the experience.[9] He did, however, occasionally make reference to the arguments he had presented at that time, most strikingly in the context of the debate over women's degrees at Cambridge in 1896–7.[10] It is surprising that he did not use his plea for practical education given to the Committee when preparing material in support of the Economics and Politics Tripos during 1901–2, although he did remember to invite his former businessmen friends and colleagues of the Bristol University Council, Lewis and Albert Fry, to comment on the business education implications of the proposal.[11]

Marshall's evidence to the Higher Education Committee has only been rarely commented on. It is ignored in Keynes's famous Memoir of Marshall and therefore did not feature in the *Memorials of Alfred Marshall* a year later.[12] As indicated earlier, it was excluded from

---

[8] Whitaker, 'Alfred Marshall: The Years 1877 to 1885', esp. pp. 7–10; Groenewegen, *A Soaring Eagle: Alfred Marshall 1842–1924*, pp. 276–7.

[9] *Correspondence of Alfred Marshall. Economist*, ed. by J.K. Whitaker, Cambridge, Cambridge University Press for the Royal Economic Society, forthcoming, Letters 85–9. These mention invitations to Foxwell to stay with the Marshalls in Bristol over the festive season and an invitation from Jowett for the Marshalls to stay with him in Oxford over Christmas, an invitation Marshall thought they should decline because of the pressure of his research work which had languished during term time because of excessive administrative duties. The Marshall scrapbook (preserved in the Marshall Archive, Marshall Library, Cambridge) misses all the early pages concerned with the Marshalls' Bristol experience, so can provide no guidance on the matter.

[10] Marshall quoted the evidence from Bristol in his flysheet to members of the Senate (on degrees for women), 1896, and in a speech to the Senate reported in *Cambridge University Reporter*, 26 March 1897, pp. 791–6.

[11] Groenewegen, *A Soaring Eagle: Alfred Marshall 1842–1924*, pp. 546–7.

[12] That book of biographical essays and reprints from Marshall's published articles, unpublished manuscripts and correspondence, edited by Marshall's literary executor, Pigou, therefore missed out on an important aspect of Marshall's work. It was included in Keynes's bibliography of Marshall's published material which was prepared with the aid of Mary Paley Marshall in 1924 during the months after Marshall's death in July of that year.

Keynes's edition of Marshall's *Official Papers*.[13] John Whitaker discussed it as part of his valuable essay on Marshall's experience in Bristol and Oxford between 1877 and 1885, drawing out Marshall's views on higher education and implicitly treating it as an exercise in Marshall biography associated with the Bristol period.[14] Another interesting use of Marshall's evidence was made by Rita McWilliams-Tullberg. She views it essentially as a foundation for her argument that the Bristol period provided, in ways difficult fully to explain, the rationale for Marshall's virtual regression to the 'angel of the hearth' model. She piquantly relates certain perspectives of Marshall contained in the evidence to the probable feelings of Mary Paley Marshall (Marshall's wife of by then almost three and a half years) because she would have read her husband's views given to the Committee when asked to assist in the customary proof reading and alterations permitted to the givers of official evidence.[15] This initial part of Marshall's manifold evidence to official inquiries has been used to a considerable extent in the only full-scale Marshall biography,[16] but despite its subject matter, Marshall's evidence has not been really used by the authors of books which report in considerable detail on his views of business and economics education.[17] This inadequate recognition of what is a valuable biographical source for Marshall's life and opinions justifies its reprinting in so far as that treatment was inspired by lack of knowledge about the existence and importance of the material.

The evidence by Marshall here reprinted is not only interesting for those concerned with Marshall biography. It contains fascinating

---

[13] See above, general introduction, pp. 3–4.

[14] Whitaker, 'Alfred Marshall: The Years 1877 to 1885', Appendix A, pp. 38–41.

[15] Rita McWilliams-Tullberg, 'Alfred Marshall and the "Woman Question" at Cambridge', *Economie appliquée* 43 (1), 1990, pp. 209–30, esp. pp. 216–19, the last page of which mentions the hypothesis about Mary Paley Marshall's feelings mentioned in the text.

[16] Groenewegen, *A Soaring Eagle: Alfred Marshall 1842–1924*, pp. 280–1, 497–8.

[17] John Malony, *Marshall, Orthodoxy and the Professionalisation of Economics*, Cambridge, Cambridge University Press, 1985, does not include Marshall's evidence in his bibliography; Alon Kadish, *Historians, Economists and Economic History*, London, Routledge, 1989, Chapters 4–6, effectively commences his account of Marshall's role from 1885 when Marshall returned to Cambridge as Professor of Political Economy, hence ignores the Bristol experience; Alon Kadish and Keith Tribe, eds., *The Market for Political Economy*, London, Routledge, 1993, hardly discusses the Bristol situation in economics education, hence fails to mention Marshall's evidence despite the frequent references to his views on economic education throughout the text.

perspectives on higher education issues from an experienced university administrator with two and a half years involvement in a newly created tertiary education institution and from an academic economist who by then had a dozen years of teaching experience at one of the old universities, and at a new university, to his credit. It presents views on the usefulness of examinations, the maintenance of standards in new institutions, scale economies in examining and in effective specialised teaching departments, running costs of newly established Colleges as well as issues of female education. The last topic makes Marshall's evidence valuable for those interested in women's studies. Moreover, the evidence contains interesting asides on business and vocational education, the role of part-time teaching and corporate sponsorship therein, a topic by then of growing importance in Great Britain, and one of continuing interest in the following century. In short, it is a social document of lasting interest for those concerned with the development of economics and of higher education in the United Kingdom from a historical perspective.

TEXT

Committee on Higher Education in Wales
and Monmouthshire,

Town Hall, Newport,
Monday, 20th December 1880.

Present:

Lord ABERDARE in the Chair.

Viscount Emlyn, M.P., Lewis Morris, Esq., Professor Rhys,
Henry Richard, Esq., M.P., Rev. H.G. Robinson,
W.T. Warry, Esq., Secretary.

PROFESSOR ALFRED MARSHALL, M.A.,

EXAMINED.

18,161. (*Chairman.*) You were a Fellow of St. John's College, Cambridge? – Yes.

18,162. And you are now Principal of University College, Bristol, and professor of political economy there? – Yes.

18,163. You have been good enough to attend in order to supply us with some information as to the college over which you preside. Will you be kind enough to do so? – University College, Bristol, began work in the year 1876, a meeting having been called in 1874 to consider the plan on which it should be founded. The college was founded as a college for the West of England and South Wales; and among the governors of the college were the mayors of all the chief towns and the heads of one or two educational establishments in South Wales. The council was nominated partly by a meeting of the governors, partly by the vice-chancellors of the three universities of Oxford, Cambridge and London, by the London company of Clothworkers, and by Balliol and New Colleges, Oxford, all of which bodies contribute to its funds. The council has from the first included Professor Jowett, Master of Balliol; Professor Henry Smith; Dr. Percival, who was then headmaster of Clifton College, and is now President of Trinity College, Oxford; Professor Smart, Dr. Caldicott, the headmaster of the Grammar School, Bristol, and other persons eminent in education. The college was founded to provide for those above the ordinary school age of both sexes a liberal education. From the first it succeeded well; in fact, it pioneered the way of the movement that is now extending largely in England of giving higher education to the two sexes conjointly. It was the first college in England in which that experiment was worked on a large scale; and the experiment may be said to have been thoroughly successful. We have now seven professors and six lecturers, who give about 40 separate courses of lectures in the day time, and about 24 separate courses in the evening. The courses in the evening are designed to meet the wants of those who are engaged in the day and who have small means; and the fees are very low. The number of students attending the college is rather over 500, of whom about 160 come in the day and the rest in the evening. Rather more than half the day students are men, and about two-thirds of the evening students are men, the rest being women.

18,164.   Is there any difference in the fees paid for the day courses and for the night courses? – Yes; the fees in the evening are very low, quite nominal, 10s.6d. for two hours a week for two terms. The fees in the day are much higher; they vary for different courses, but the standard fee is 5*l.* 5s. for a course of three hours a week for three terms.

18,165.   That is to say, for a year? – Yes. People representing all social orders come to the college. The women who attend the day classes are chiefly the daughters of the best families in the town. The male students in the day come from nearly the same classes, but not quite, because the tendency is for the sons of the richest inhabitants of Bristol still to go to Oxford and Cambridge. The fact that Bristol has two singularly excellent schools, Clifton College and the Grammar School, has prevented us from having as large a share of the education of the young men of the upper classes as we otherwise might have had. On the other hand they have helped us, as we have helped them, by making Bristol an admirable centre for anybody to live in who has a family to educate. The men students may be classed under three distinct heads besides the miscellaneous element of those who are seeking a general education. Firstly, the Baptist students; there is a very important Baptist college in Bristol under the management of Dr. Gotch, who is a member of our council, and an arrangement has been made between his college and ours by which all his students receive their entire secular education with us, while they get their religious education at his college.

18,166.   How many of those are there? – About 20. Under the second head come the students in the engineering department. That department has been successful in consequence of the willingness of a good number of important iron manufacturers, among whom I may mention two firms in Wales, the Isca Foundry and the Usk Iron company, to receive into their works, during the summer months, students of the college who receive their theoretical training at the college during the winter. This plan has enabled us to get students from a distance. A case occurred a little while ago of a Welshman, I believe he was from South America, who went to an eminent London engineer to inquire as to engineering schools, and was sent by him down to Bristol is consequence of our having this arrangement. Other schools are endeavouring to obtain a similar arrangement, and I think it may become a very important feature in engineering schools.

18,167.   How many such students are there? – There are about eight or ten; we have only begun to work that plan recently.

18,168.   When you speak of those two works in Monmouthshire receiving during a portion of the year those who devote themselves to engineering studies during the rest of the year, in what capacity are they received? – As articled pupils, I am not sure whether as a matter of fact there are any who are engaged at those two Welsh firms, but those two Welsh firms are on the list that is given in the calendar of firms who are willing to receive students under this arrangement. The method pursued is this: a student coming to us is recommended to select for himself some one firm in whose works he will spend his summer months. We give him all the information we can as to the nature of the work of the firms, the character of the locality and other considerations, among others the expense, for fees charged by the different firms vary very much, and we leave it to him to take one or the other. We have nothing to do with the pecuniary arrangement between the student and the firm; we simply give information.

18,169. (*Mr. Richard.*) You speak of articled pupils; whom are they articled to? – To the firm.

18,170. (*Chairman.*) That is not the system pursued in the larger iron works of the country? – I believe it is exclusively done in connexion with our college. The Yorkshire College at Leeds in their calendar published the year before last expressed a very strong wish that they could do the same at Leeds, but I believe that they have not been able to get the manufacturers there to consent.

18,171. In fact this system seems to have been pursued by these two companies for the purpose of co-operating with the college in combining a practical with a theoretical education? – By those two companies and others, viz., the Avonside Engine Company, Bristol; the Bristol Wagon Works Company, Bristol; Messrs. Bush and De Soyres, Bristol; Mr. Howard, C.E., Bristol docks, the Isca Foundry company, Newport, Monmouthshire; Mr. Christopher James, C.E., Bristol; Mr. John Lysaght, Bristol; Messrs. Lysaght and Scoones, C.E., Bristol; Mr. Thomas Morgans, Bristol; Messrs. Newall and Ogilvie, Bristol; Mr. Richardson, C.E., Bristol, Severn Tunnel; Messrs. G.K. Stoddart and Co., Bristol; Messrs. Stoddart, and Pitt, Bath; the Uskside Company, Newport, Monmouthshire; Messrs. John Watts and Company, Bristol. I have laid special stress upon the engineering department, because we hope not only that our engineering instruction may be as good as the corresponding instruction in the Universities of Oxford and Cambridge, but that it may be better, and there is no other department with reference to which we can hope that. Besides the Baptist students and the engineering students, a third distinct class is found in the chemical department, to which a great deal of attention has been given, and which I hope will grow; but there has been a change in the heads of the department, and its growth has not been so rapid yet as we hope it may be in future.

18,172.   How many students are attached to it? – Last session there were 21 attending the class on inorganic chemistry in the day and 33 in the evening, and there were 24 students in the laboratory.

18,173.   (*Professor Rhys.*) 24 besides the 21? – Many of them would be the same. Looking at the instruction given in the day as a whole, it may be said to cover the whole of what is generally understood under the term liberal education. It is rather hard to define it exactly, but it covers the subjects of the ordinary examinations in arts and science in the London University, or any other university. We have a large and growing medical school affiliated to the college, and the number of students I gave just now does not include those of the medical school. There are 60 students in the medical school exclusive of those I gave before.

18,174.   Those are day students? – Yes.

18,175.   Are there any girls among that number? – No. The medical school has its buildings on the college ground; the buildings are in fact supplied by our council; but it has a separate governing body, though our council is strongly represented on the governing body. So far I have been speaking of the day students at the college. The evening classes in the college (there are none in the medical school) are attended partly by people belonging to the upper classes of society who are engaged in the day and cannot come in the morning, partly by people engaged in the lower ranks of business, and partly by teachers. Perhaps, that is as good work as any we do; we teach the teachers of many of the neighbouring schools, not of course of first grade schools, but of second grade schools, in the evening.

18,176.   (*Chairman.*) And of elementary schools also? – Yes. The Latin, Greek, and Mathematical classes are largely attended by teachers. I wish to say something with regard to the district for the wants of which the college is intended to provide. It is a college not only for Bristol, but also for the west of England and south Wales. But in its first years it has drawn its students chiefly for Bristol, for this reason: if a student has to live away from his home it makes comparatively little difference as regards expense whether he goes 50 miles or 100, and when Bristol college was a new and comparatively untried institution (an institution of which nothing could be certainly promised, the only guarantee of its real success being the list of eminent people on its council) it was not to be expected that very many students would come from a distance. Those who lived in Bristol, and who could conveniently go to it, of course came in some numbers, but very few came from a distance. I have no satisfactory means of finding out how many Welsh students there are in the college, but I know of seven who actually live in Wales.

18,177. From what part of Wales do they come? – Chiefly from the south. I may mention that our first scholar, Pepyat Evans, is a Welshman, he lives near Cardiff.

18,178. When you say your first scholar, what meaning do you attach to that? – We have a scholarship examination every October, and the student who comes at the head of the list gets the first scholarship.

18,179. Who founded that scholarship? – It is given by the college. There are some scholarships for women, founded as a memorial to Miss Catherine Winkworth, who took a leading part in the education of women.

18,180. (*Professor Rhys.*) How many of those scholarships are for women? – Two.

18,181. (*Chairman.*) Have those seven Welsh students come of late years, or have you had some of them from the very first? – We have had some of them from the very first, but unfortunately our college returns are not made with a view to this inquiry; we have only the postal addresses of the students. They give the addresses in Bristol at which letters would find them, and we have not their home addresses; but as the result of some inquiries, which were conducted in rather a hasty way, I find that there are seven students whose parents actually live in Wales; six others born in Wales, but whose parents do not now reside there; and seven others whose parents, or one of them, were born in Wales. Judging by the names, there are an immense number of students of Welsh extraction, probably nearly half the names on our books are Welsh names.

18,182. A large part of the population of Bristol is either Welsh or of Welsh extraction, more or less remote? – I believe so. As a further evidence of our connection with Wales, I should like to mention that the college has given several courses of lectures in Wales. It received a grant from the Gilchrist Trustees in the session 1877–78, in consequence of which it delivered a course of six lectures upon heat in each of five towns, one of those being Newport.[1]

18,183.   The other four being in England? – Yes, one of them being Bristol. The same thing happened in the next session 1878–79, when six lectures were given on water, one of the towns in which those lectures were given being Newport. In last year, 1879–80, we gave some more lectures without the aid of the Gilchrist trustees, Swansea being one of the towns in which the lectures were given. We gave five lectures there.

18,184.   How were these lectures attended? – Very well. I think there were from 300 to 500 present at each lecture. The Town Hall was as full as it could be almost.

18,185.   That, in fact, was doing much the same work[2] as Oxford and Cambridge have been doing in various towns? – Yes, but rather less systematically. I do not know that that work has been done so much by Oxford. It has been done, I think, chiefly by Cambridge.[3] The work done by Cambridge has been more systematic, because the courses have been longer, they have been given generally by one

---

[1] For a discussion of the Gilchrist Lectures, see Whitaker, 'Alfred Marshall: The Years 1877 to 1885', pp. 24–5; Groenewegen, *A Soaring Eagle. Alfred Marshall 1842–1924*, pp. 292–3. Marshall himself gave one of the Gilchrist Lectures on water, 'Water as an Element in National Wealth', reprinted in *Memorials of Alfred Marshall*, ed. Pigou, pp. 131–41.

[2] This is a reference to the Extension Movement which had commenced during the early 1870s; at Cambridge, to be more precise, during May 1873. This development owed much to the initiatives of James Stuart, a Fellow of Trinity College, Cambridge, and a member of the Council of Bristol University College (above, pp. 14–15, Q. 18,163). Marshall was not actively involved in the Extension Movement on the available evidence, though a number of his students (Moore Ede, Herbert Foxwell and William Cunningham) were, as were later Arthur Berry, Alfred Flux, D.H. Macgregor and Arthur Bowley. For a discussion, see Alon Kadish, 'The Teaching of Political Economy in the Extension Movement', in *The Market for Political Economy*, ed. Kadish and Tribe, pp. 78–110; and for Marshall's involvement, Groenewegen, *A Soaring Eagle: Alfred Marshall 1842–1924*, p. 274.

[3] Marshall was wrong here. Oxford and London also made important contributions, while University Colleges like Bristol during the 1870s were likewise engaged in evening and part-time educational activities closely resembling Extension Movement classes, of which the Gilchrist Lectures, mentioned in n. 1 above, are an example. In any case, Marshall's information on the subject after 1877 would have largely come from Foxwell, with whom he kept up a lively, and often rather 'gossipy', correspondence while in Bristol.

lecturer, and an elaborate syllabus of each lecture has been distributed beforehand among the class. The object of our lectures has been
not so much to teach people as to make them want to be taught. The
object of the Cambridge lectures has been chiefly to cause a desire for
a collegiate education in the places in which the lectures were delivered. Our object was a lower one than that. It was to let ourselves be
known, and to let people get an interest in education. But a course of
six lectures by six different people upon such a subject as water could
hardly be said to have any high educational value. A somewhat
higher educational value is perhaps to be attributed to one or two
separate courses, each course being given by one lecturer. Professor
Sollas has given two courses[4] of lectures in Newport and one in
Cardiff, and those have been more of the character of those given by
Cambridge.

18,186.   Have you any facts to give us as to the age of the students? —
Our minimum age is 16; students are admitted below that age under
certain exceptional circumstances. As a matter of fact, I believe there
are not more than half a dozen below that age in the college. Three-
fourths of those attending the day classes are between the ages of 18
and 22; and probably rather more than one half of those attending
the evening classes are of that age; but many of those who attend the
evening classes are well advanced in years. In my own class[5] I have
two men with grey hair. It has always been the case that men of
mature age who are engaged in business come to classes in the
evening.

[4] That is, W.J. Sollas (1849–1936), initially appointed as Lecturer in Geology at Bristol
University College in 1879, and as Professor of Geology and Zoology in 1880. He moved as
Professor of Geology to Trinity College, Dublin, in 1883, and to a chair in Oxford in 1889.
Subsequently, he was elected a Fellow of the Royal Society and, for 1908–9, as President of
the Geological Society. Marshall probably had met him at his own College in Cambridge
during the early 1870s. Sollas was then a student with T.G. Bonney, a Fellow of St John's and
friend of Marshall, taking a first in the natural sciences tripos in 1873. Sollas was himself
elected a Fellow of St John's, Cambridge, in 1882, two years before Marshall's election to the
Cambridge chair of Political Economy in 1884. Sollas's appointment to Bristol at the start of
his career, like the appointment of William Ramsay (who succeeded Marshall as Principal in
1881) is a sign of the quality of the appointments to academic posts made at Bristol during
this period.
[5] Marshall's evening classes at Bristol were largely drawn from mature age working students,
and not surprisingly would on some occasions have included grey-haired persons. See
Whitaker, 'Alfred Marshall: The Years 1877 to 1885', p. 18.

18,187.   (*Mr. Richard.*) Have you any limit of age? – We take students to any age above 16; we do not take them under 16, except in certain exceptional cases.

18,188.   (*Chairman.*) Have you any theological classes? – I should perhaps answer this question first by saying that the articles of association specify the class of objects for which the college was established. The articles declare that the object is: 'To found, establish, endow, maintain, and conduct in or near the city of Bristol a college or colleges, and by means of such college or colleges, or by such other means as the association may think proper, to promote the education of persons of both sexes, and the study and advancement of science, literature, and the fine and mechanical arts, subject to the following as a fundamental condition, namely, that no student, professor, teacher or other officer or person connected with the college or colleges or the operations of the association, shall be required to make any declaration as to his or her religious opinions, or submit to any test of his or her religious opinions, and that nothing shall be introduced in the matter or mode of education or instruction in reference to any religious or theological subject which can be reasonably considered offensive to the conscience of any student.' For a long time we had no religious instruction of any kind, and we have not in fact now, but we hope to have after Christmas. In the calendar for this year it was arranged that the classical professor should give a course of instruction in the Greek Testament, it being distinctly understood that he would have that article which I have just read in his mind, and that he would not say anything that could be offensive to the conscience of any student.

18,189.   Was it contemplated to give that instruction in consequence of a demand for it? – There has always been a feeling that it should be given as soon as we expected there would be a demand. The plans were half perfected a year or two ago for doing it, but they did not come to anything. There was a letter written by an eminent divine in Bristol that had something to do with this particular movement; but I am sorry to say the demand has not appeared, a sufficient number of students did not present themselves at the beginning of this term to make it possible to open the classes. I hope, however, that they will be opened at Christmas.

18,190.   At present you have no means of judging what number will be likely to attend? – No, there is no reason to believe that the number will be large.

18,191.   (*Mr. Richard.*) At the Baptist College the Greek Testament would be taught? – Yes, a great many of those coming to us are preparing for the ministry of some denomination or other.

18,192.   They would take the Greek Testament in their respective colleges? – There are many students who intend to enter the ministry who are learning Latin and Greek with us, and who are reading the Greek Testament presumably at home.

18,193.   (*Chairman.*) Are any prayers offered up in the college? – No.

18,194.   Supposing your hopes, which appear to be very reasonable, are realized, that the increasing reputation of the college will attract students from a distance, have you formed any plan as to the mode of meeting that increase; would you leave the students to find their own places of lodging, or have you ever contemplated putting up hostels or halls in connexion with your college? – The plan adopted with regard to students who come from a distance is this: In the calendar it is stated that I am prepared to give help to any student who wants to find lodgings.[6] I say nothing unless the student takes the initiative, but if he does ask me for such help, I talk to him and find out what his means are, and what sort of lodging is likely to suit him, and I endeavour to meet his requirements from a list of lodgings which I have. There are on the list a few lodging-houses proper, but the lodgings are chiefly in the houses of gentlemen or ladies, to a great extent widow ladies, widows of professional men who have told me that they would like to take in such students. I have the exact details as to the terms on which they would take them. I find it possible to get all that students can reasonably want for 25s. a week.

18,195.   What does that include? – Living with the family in a quiet and inexpensive way; it does not include alcoholic drinks; it includes, however, generally a fire in the bed room. I always make it a condition that there should be some quiet place for study; and in the letter

[6] This was one of many duties assigned to Marshall as Principal. For a discussion, see Groenewegen, *A Soaring Eagle: Alfred Marshall 1842–1924*, pp. 275–84, esp. pp. 276–7.

of inquiry which I send out I always find out all the circumstances of the family.

18,196. Have you estimated the number of out-boarding students attending the University College? – No, I do not think we could very easily find out. Probably a very great number of students who come from a distance, but who are not known to us as coming from a distance, reside with relatives in Bristol. I am continually finding out that a student say, of the name of Jones, living with a man of the name of Jones is not a son of his, but perhaps a cousin who has come to Bristol to study. We have not found out how many such students there are.

18,197. Have you found that system sufficiently satisfactory to induce you to postpone, at any rate for the present, the providing of any buildings especially for the purpose? – Certainly; it would be most inexpedient to provide money for buildings, a preferable step would be to get somebody connected with the college to take a large house; but I think it would be most inexpedient for the college to take any sort of responsibility of the kind.

18,198. Are you prepared to make any statement with respect to the financial condition of the college? – Yes, I can give you the necessary information.[7] I have here a printed paper which has been issued by the council with reference to its canvass for funds. It will perhaps be best that I should read a part of it. 'The local contributions to University College, Bristol, have amounted to about 21,000*l*., spread over five years, beginning from October 1876. In addition to this sum Balliol and New Colleges, Oxford, have each contributed 300*l*. a year and the Worshipful Company of Clothworkers 525*l*. a year for the same period.'

18,199. Were those contributions for any limited number of years? – Five years; but we have hopes that they will go on. As regards the

---

[7] For a discussion of the financial situation of Bristol University College, which was continuously deteriorating during this time, see *ibid*., pp. 279–80. Marshall later was to complain to Hewins that these financial troubles induced the type of duties as Principal he most intensely disliked. See Marshall to Hewins, 12 October 1899, in A.W. Coats, 'Alfred Marshall and the Early Development of the London School of Economics: Some Correspondence', *Economica* NS 34(3), November 1967, p. 412.

525*l.* which was contributed by the Clothworkers' Company, the greater part of that was spent on technical instruction in connexion with textile manufactures at Stroud; but the expenses which were involved in that education were so great that it is not intended to go on with it on the same scale. For the present we have suspended teaching at Stroud, and are teaching at Trowbridge. The Clothworkers' company have promised us 300*l.* a year for six years on condition that we give instruction of that kind. To continue my quotation from the paper issued by the Council: 'The working expenses of the College (excluding about 500*l.* a year which by the direction of the Clothworkers' Company have been spent on instruction in textile industries at Stroud) amount to somewhat less than 4,500*l.* a year, of which about 1,800*l.* are supplied by the fees of students. A general increase in the scale of fees would check the growth of the college and much diminish its usefulness, nor is it probable that the change would increase its revenue. It has therefore been necessary to take annually about 3,000*l.* from the contributions to the college to defray its working expenses. About 2,000*l.* were spent in apparatus and laboratory fittings and preliminary expenses. A site in Tyndall's Park has been bought for 3,250*l.*, and about 6,000*l.* have been appropriated to the erection of part of the permanent buildings required by the college, and of temporary building for the medical school. Even should the college continue to receive the assistance which has hitherto been so generously given to it by Balliol and New Colleges and the Company of Clothworkers it will, in addition, require a sustentation fund of from 1,500*l.* to 2,000*l.* a year, and a further expenditure of 10,000*l.* on buildings will be necessary to meet its present wants.' I have here the balance sheet for the last year, and I can give you any detailed information from it that you wish to have.[8]

18,200.   It would appear that you would require a considerable sustentation fund? – Yes.

18,201.   To enable you to meet your expenses without drawing on your capital? – Yes; that is one thing that I wish to lay clearly before you,

[8] Annual Reports of the Council, presumably prepared by Marshall as Principal, presented financial details of income and expenditure and balance sheets of the college. See Groenewegen, *A Soaring Eagle: Alfred Marshall 1842–1924*, pp. 279–80, and for a discussion of the building plans Marshall prepared for the college, *ibid.*, p. 281.

in reference to any proposals that may be made for founding colleges in South Wales. I hope they will ultimately be founded, but one of the chief things I wish to say to-day is that the difficulties of doing so would be very great, and it seems to me doubtful whether founding such colleges is the best step to take at present. I believe that our expenses have been cut down as far as it is possible to cut expenses down. To show how economically our college is conducted, I may mention the fact that we do not print any of our examination papers, we write them with our own hands with the electric pen and the collograph.[9] In consequence of the depression of trade the council has been unwilling to increase its expenditure. The number of the staff has been kept down as low as it is possible to keep a staff which is to do its work efficiently.

18,202.   There is another alternative which no doubt has been considered; that is the increase of fees. Have you ever considered how any increase in the fees would operate on the success of the college? – I told them what our fees were, and they said their colleges would be ruined if they charged fees as high as ours charged.[10]

18,203.   I see by your statement[11] that Owens College, which has altogether received an endowment of 350,000l., overspends itself by 10,000l. a year? – Yes, it has. I believe, about 10,000l. a year net income from the endowment and there is about 10,000l. excess of expenditure over fees. You are aware that Oxford and Cambridge have an income between them of 500,000l. for the education of 5,000 students.

---

[9] For a discussion of the electric pen, which allowed faster and neater writing and enabled the preparation of multiple copies of documents, including the examination papers Marshall mentioned in reply to this question, see Groenewegen, *A Soaring Eagle: Alfred Marshall 1842–1924*, p. 278 n.*. Samples of writing with this pen are preserved in the Marshall Archive. One is reproduced as an illustration (No. 56) in the reference just cited.

[10] Fees were in fact the only increasing income source of the College during Marshall's period as Principal, the result of the steady rise in enrolments the College experienced. For details, see Groenewegen, *A Soaring Eagle: Alfred Marshall 1842–1924*, pp. 279–80. Fees charged were £5 5s. for three terms, £4 4s. for two consecutive terms, £3 3s. for either first or second term, and £2 2s. for third term.

[11] Presumably the statement Marshall had earlier submitted to the Committee prior to his examination as witness. It appears not to have been preserved and in any case was not published as part of the *Report* of the Committee.

18,204. And for other purposes? — Yes. I ought to have said for the promotion of learning and the education of students. Perhaps I should say at once that what seems to me the most important need for Wales is the foundation of a certain number of trade schools and the foundation also of a large number of scholarships, which should be tenable at any of a certain selected number of colleges to which the student might care to go.[12]

18,205. When you speak of trade schools, do you mean schools exclusively devoted to the teaching calculated to fit boys for various industrial pursuits, or schools having a commercial side? — I think there might be a great amount of variation in detail, but it seems to me that we may assume that we have a tolerably satisfactory system of schools on the old academic plan; grammar schools and schools of the same general character as grammar schools. But there is also wanted in every such centre of industry as Merthyr, Cardiff, Swansea, and Newport something more like the trade school in Bristol. The trade school in Bristol was founded by Canon Moseley[13] and it is an extremely valuable institution in its way; it has always been admirably managed, and the students have had much greater success in the examinations of the Science and Art Department than the students of any other school in England. It seems to me that it would be a very great advantage if such schools could be started in such places as those I have mentioned; they would involve very small expense, because being pointed directly to the South Kensington examinations they are able almost to pay their own expenses by the very liberal grants obtained for results from that department.

18,206. (Mr. Richard.) Has the trade school at Bristol any relation to your institution? — No, it is quite independent of it. It is one of the defects in Bristol that our educational departments though working

[12] In 1879–80, the College offered three general scholarships tenable for one year and valued at £25, £15 and £10 respectively, one scholarship for chemistry students valued at £25 and four scholarships exclusively for women valued at £15 each. Bristol University College, *Calendar*, Bristol, 1879, pp. 8–9, and see Q. 18,355 below.

[13] That is, Canon Henry Moseley (1821–72), the natural scientist and cleric. He was Canon residentiary of Bristol from 1853 to 1872. He was also associated with normal education and the transmission of practical mechanics, hence an ideal founder of the Bristol Trade School. This subsequently became the Bristol Trade and Mining School and in 1909 the Engineering Faculty of Bristol University.

to a great extent in harmony are not organized in connection with one another.

18,207.   (*Rev. H.G. Robinson.*) The trade school is under Colston's Trust I think now? – Yes, and the Merchant Venturers are assisting the school.

18,208.   (*Chairman.*) That, though a most useful institution, is hardly consistent with one's ordinary notion of a school? – It consists of three distinct departments. The first is a school for boys differing from other schools in no particular respect except that it is worked with great energy and that an exceptionally good scientific education is given in it; secondly, there is a mining department which has been very successful; and thirdly, there are evening classes. It seems to me that the greater part of the people, that is, the adults, in a place like Merthyr, who would require education, would require other teaching in practical mining or evening classes. There would not, I presume, in places of that kind be a very large demand for expensive education in the day for adults.

18,209.   Such a system would in fact be very much like that of the science classes in connexion with South Kensington ? – Yes; this trade school is nothing more, so far as the evening classes go, than a well organised set of South Kensington science classes.

18,210.   That would hardly serve as a substitute for a second grade school, or a commercial school, or one of the county schools established in England? – Its evening classes are directed towards South Kensington, but one of its departments is a day school for boys.

18,211.   When you speak of founding a school at Merthyr, or at any similar place, and compare it with the school founded at Bristol, with the assistance of two powerful corporations like the Colston Trustees and the Merchant Venturers, we are not talking in *pari materia*? – No, I do not know what assistance the trade school derives from those two bodies. I am not on the governing body of that school, but I am informed that the salaries of the teachers in the day school come almost entirely from the grants that are got from South Kensington. I understand that the day school would not pay its expenses if it were not for those grants.

18,212.   You do not know what advantages it derives from its connexion with the two other bodies? — No; I have understood that they are not very important beyond the possession of the building. The Governing Body are inviting plans to be sent in for an enlarged building.

18,213.   All this would be of great importance to our large manufacturing towns, but it would leave a very large part of Wales, where the population is so altered, still unprovided for? — Exactly so, and that is the main reason that makes me think it is important to devote what money there may be available firstly to trade schools, and secondly to scholarships, rather than to founding colleges. It seems to me that there is not in Wales any town sufficiently large, and in particular not any town containing a sufficient number of well-to-do inhabitants to enable it to start, in the present state of popular feeling with regard to education, a properly equipped college. A properly equipped college is a thing pretty exactly to be defined. It is very much more difficult to keep the attention of a class of adults than it is to keep the attention of a class of boys. You can teach boys a text book,[14] you can make them learn it and cross-examine them upon it, and it is not necessary that the teacher should know very much more than his text book; if he has a clear head he can teach tolerably well by merely knowing his text book, but it is different with teaching adults. They will not listen with patience to having a text book taught to them. You have to teach adults by persuading them that you are teaching something that they could not easily learn by reading a text book; and, consequently, I think it is impossible for a class to be held together, except by a man who has devoted the greater part of his time to the subject he is teaching and who is a leading man in that department; experience seems to show that no one else can do it. Now when one considers the competition that there is on the part of the better schools for teachers one is brought to this conclusion, that unless the colleges are prepared to offer a salary of about 1,000l. a year for each of their professors they cannot get the best men, save on one condition, and that is

[14] Marshall was very opposed to teaching 'a textbook', as he wrote to Sir William Ramsay, his successor as principal at Bristol, in 1914. In this letter he mentioned that he 'would not give a halfpenny for [a pupil taught] by the man who dictated a textbook' (reprinted, *Memorials of Alfred Marshall*, ed. Pigou, pp. 488–9).

that they make the posts agreeable to them. A post which is agreeable to a man of that kind is a post in which he can carry on his own studies, that means a post in which he is to teach only one thing. So we are brought to this, that all the chief teachers in such a college must be men studying some one department of science or learning, and who are teaching that alone. The consequence is that you must have a great number of them. Our number of seven professors and six lecturers is the very smallest with which it can be done, and it would be a very great advantage if we could have a few more. In teaching adults it is necessary for the lecturer to prepare the lectures, and the amount of labour involved in an hour's lecture represents a great deal more than an hour's teaching in a school. Then lectures require room and apparatus. Thus, the *gross* expenditure of an efficient college must be very large. But next the *net* expenditure of such a college in Wales would probably be greater than that of our college. For our fees last year were 1,900*l*., exclusive of the medical fees, and those fees are as large as those got in any other colleges of the kind, except Owens College and the London colleges. I said just now that I was told at Owens College and Leeds College that the scale of fees we charged, 5*l*. 5s. for the full course, would ruin these colleges; that is, it would diminish the number of students very much. It has always been a question of doubt with us whether we should not increase our receipts by having lower day fees, we certainly should diminish our receipts if we raised our day fees; the reason we are able to charge such high fees is that there is in Bristol an exceptionally large number of residents who, though not rich are well-to-do people, with incomes of something like 800*l*. or 1,000*l*. a year.

18,214.   You have Clifton[15] at your back? – Yes, a large majority, I should think three-fourths of those who come to our day classes come from Clifton. It seems to me that if a college is started, say in Swansea (and I mention Swansea because, so far as my imperfect information goes, that has a larger number of well-to-do residents than any other town in South Wales), and if such a college is to be fully equipped it must have the same total expenditure as we had; and

---

[15] That is, the Bristol suburb into which the Marshalls had moved in 1877 after Marshall's appointment as Principal. Clifton was a well-to-do middle-class suburb, and hence a useful source of students for the type of general education the College provided.

it could not expect for a long time to get as much from fees as we get. You would therefore have to look forward to a deficit of not much less than 4,000*l*. a year. On the other hand, trade schools could be started in great numbers at a very small expense; 4000*l*. a year would enable a very great number of Welsh students to get an education at some of the other colleges at Liverpool, Manchester, Birmingham, Bristol, or Oxford or Cambridge. With regard to the question of a university for Wales, we have formed a very decided opinion that we ought not to be made a university; that if we were made a university the effect would be very injurious to education; and as we do not wish to be made a university ourselves, for the same reasons we do not think it is expedient that there should be a university for Wales. Our reasons for not wishing to be made a university are chiefly these: We have not, and cannot have for the next 100 years, I should say, a sufficient amount of diversity in our teaching body to enable us to conduct the highest examinations properly; at Oxford or Cambridge there are on every important subject from 20 to 40 or 50 experts,[16] and the decision of the plan of every examination is the result of the working together of a great many minds; that is to say, a great number of experts in each department, together with a certain number of people of general information. Now on our staff we have only one person to represent each separate department, so we could not expect to have the same facilities in organizing our examinations as the universities would have. But what is more important is that our examinations could not be so good, they could not be varied. Everybody has a groove which is perceptible to any person who chooses to study him, though perhaps not perceptible to himself. An able crammer, if you gave him 50 examination papers set on any subject by any one specialist could put his pupil through a course of study that would probably enable him to get 20 per cent. more marks in a paper set by that man than in a paper set by anybody else. That is a point that we must look to. College examinations would have less

---

[16] This is an interesting indication of what Marshall considered to be 'important subjects' in this context, presumably mathematics and classical studies. Economics at Cambridge had only three 'expert' teachers in 1880, namely Foxwell, John Neville Keynes and Sidgwick, and Oxford had even fewer. Cf. below, Marshall's answer to Q. 18,261 on the need of the Cambridge Special Board for Moral Sciences to borrow examiners from outside Cambridge University to examine in its tripos.

variety than university examinations. As I have said, in university examinations, in the larger subjects, there are some 50 men engaged from time to time, and at the London University the examiners are changed after intervals of two or three years.

18,215.   Has not the Victoria University made arrangements by which the board of examiners consists partly of their own men and partly of those drawn *ab extra* from the older universities? – I understand that something of that kind has been done, but I am not well informed on that subject.

18,216.   Considering the very laudable exertions that the older universities have made to extend their benefits outside their immediate area, do you think it unlikely that they would consent to assist in the examination of students of other universities? – No doubt individuals would be willing to receive invitations to examine, but the older universities seem to me to be still much stiffer than it is advisable they should be with regard to such examinations.

18,217.   The London University draws its examiners from men educated in every university in the Kingdom? – Yes.

18,218.   Why should not a local university in the same way avail itself of the assistance of persons who were not members of its own senate? – Chiefly on the ground of expense. There is no difficulty that I know of, except that the total number of people who are fitted to conduct first class examinations in England is limited; and if they were to be examining in a great number of local universities they could do nothing else, and the expense to the local universities would be very great. If the examinations are really not to be conducted by the university itself, but by people outside, why should it profess to conduct the examinations at all? I wish to be understood in this not to be making any attack upon the Victoria University. It seems to me that there was an adequate cause for founding the Victoria University, a cause which does not apply, and is not likely to apply, to making any other college into a university.

18,219.   What was the exceptional reason, in your view for the founding of that university? – That the older universities had developed from the standpoint of pure classics and pure mathematics a form of learning for its own sake, and though learning for its own sake should rightly be the main object of education yet there is another object, and that is learning for practical purposes. The whole tone of Oxford and Cambridge University life leads people, I think, to regard each item of knowledge as valuable solely in proportion to its educating power. A Cambridge examiner would just as soon set a problem with regard to the law of force of the twelfth power of the distance as he would with regard to the breaking of a beam; and there is wanted a university in which prominence will be given to such questions as the strains necessary for the breaking of beams in preference to hypothetical theorems. I had a good deal to do with mathematical examinations when I was at Cambridge;[17] and in thinking over the way in which engineering students should be examined in mathematics, I have got to see that something is required very different from what is in vogue, and is likely to be in vogue at Cambridge.

18,220. That is to say, a closer application of mathematics to such studies than would be desirable at the University of Cambridge? – I am not sure that Cambridge may not have something to learn in that respect; the examiners ought to consider not only whether the particular matter to which their examination is directed will train the mind in the present, but whether it will make the mind active in practice hereafter. The associations of Oxford and Cambridge are not such as to make them fit to pioneer the way in that direction.[18]

18,221. Do you think the degree likely to be given at the Victoria college will imply a smaller amount of theoretical knowledge than is given at the older universities? – I do not know. I would hope not. I think that, if I had to set mathematical papers now, I could set them so as to bring out intellectual activity just as much as the papers I

[17] This is somewhat of an exaggeration. Marshall had sat the mathematical tripos in 1865 and subsequently coached candidates for that tripos for approximately two academic years (1865–6 and 1866–7). From 1868 he taught moral sciences as a St John's College Lecturer, and worked on mathematics only in connection with his economics studies which began in the late 1860s. His College does not appear to have used him at any time for mathematics teaching or examining.

[18] This seems more soundly based on Marshall's own experience as a mathematics student in the early 1860s. For a discussion of these weaknesses in Cambridge mathematics teaching at the time, see Groenewegen, *A Soaring Eagle: Alfred Marshall 1842–1924*, pp. 80–7, and the references there cited.

used to set at Cambridge without dealing so much with things that do not exist.[19]

18,222.   Does not what you have just been saying imply that the creation of a new university like the Victoria University has been useful in suggesting new lines of study and examination? – It rather implies this I think. Among all the claims that the Owens College people advanced for their being made into a university it seemed to me that this was the most important; that the examinations to which they had to submit, viz., those of the London University, were chiefly conducted by people who disregarded the applications of science to practice; and it was right that there should exist one university in the country the examinations of which were conducted to a large extent by people who had lived amongst business men.

18,223.   Then I assume your opinion to be that the two Universities of Oxford and Cambridge, supplemented by the London University and by the Victoria University, do really cover all the present wants of the whole country? – I think so, provided Victoria University is compelled to throw its examinations open. I think that ought to be held *in terrorem* over it, if Victoria University should decide ultimately to keep its examinations confined to those who have affiliated themselves to it; it would then be very advisable that there should be some other university which would do what the London University is doing from a slightly different point of view.

18,224.   That is examine all who present themselves, but with a wider range of examination? – Yes.

18,225.   Not running quite into the same grooves? – Yes. In what I have just been saying I have been expressing my own views rather than speaking as a representative of the college; I may say, however, that the opinion, so far as I know, of the majority of the council is strongly against an increase in the number of universities; but the reasons which I have given are my own.

[19] Marshall was never an official examiner for the mathematical tripos at Cambridge, nor does he seem to have set college examinations for mathematics students at St John's. However, as coach for tripos students from 1865 to 1867 he may well have prepared *pro forma* trial papers for his pupils, to give them additional practice in speedily answering questions, one of the attributes required for those who wished to excel in this examination.

18,226. If you think that reasoning would apply to your college, you think it would apply *à fortiori* to the case of Wales? – I will not say *à fortiori*, but at all events as strongly. I can hardly understand what a university for Wales would be. Wales is so large a country, and so much of it is near Liverpool and Manchester, and other large towns, that I can hardly imagine the whole population of Wales setting themselves to directing their education to one university in Wales. No doubt the total population of Wales is larger than the population over which we may be said to have direct influence.

18,227. You have spoken of the great cost of such a university; do you know what the cost is of the university, apart from the teaching colleges, of the Victoria University? – No, I do not; but I understand, from the papers that were issued, and from some slight conversation that I had at Owens College, with reference to the examinations, that they want to connect teaching with examination. I venture to submit that there is a great mistake, though teaching ought to be connected with class examinations; the degree examinations ought not to be conducted by those who have taught the candidates. There is a rule at Cambridge that no person appointed to examine in a tripos may take students a short time beforehand.[20] I think that experience shows that when examinations are chiefly conducted by professors who teach, the result is that the students seek to obtain marks by finding out what, according to the views of their teachers, is orthodox and what is not orthodox on any matter of opinion. Besides studying their subjects they have to study their teachers a great deal more than is expedient I think.

18,228. You mean, for instance, that they not only have to acquire a knowledge of the history of philosophy, but they have to adapt their opinions to the known opinions of the professors? – I believe that is the case.

18,229. If my impression is correct, the examiners for the Victoria University are partly the professors of the university, in order to see that justice is done to their own particular lines of teaching, and

---

[20] This seems to have been the reason why Marshall himself never examined when he became Professor of Political Economy at Cambridge in 1884. For a discussion of this, see Groenewegen, *A Soaring Eagle: Alfred Marshall 1842–1924*, pp. 334–5.

partly examiners externally chosen. If that mode of selecting the examiners were adopted would not much of that danger to which you have just referred be obviated? – Yes, but it seems to me very much better still for the examiners to be entirely from without. Then arises the question where you are to get your supply of examiners. I think the necessary growth of examinations is becoming one of the great evils of the day.[21] I think a student who spends a week in an examination room may pass a very pleasant week, and it will do him a great deal of good, but for the examiner it is simply destructive of his intellectual power, and I think we ought to diminish that evil as much as we can, by making one examination do for many places. The subjects embraced under the two heads of science and literature are becoming so various and the higher examinations are becoming so numerous that it seems to me that it will be impossible without drawing too much on the highest intellect in the country to have a thoroughly good set of examinations for each of a large number of places. The natural science tripos at Cambridge which started with four examiners now has eight, and I am told that it is not a really satisfactory examination even now, that they want 16; and there are at Cambridge only about 20 or 30 students for it. At a local college there might not be in one year more than two or three who were really worthy of a high class paper, in another year there might be none.

18,230.   (*Mr. Richard.*) I understand you to say that you have spent about 9,000*l.* or 10,000*l.* upon your site and buildings? – Yes; that includes the temporary buildings for the medical school.

18,231.   Still you consider that your buildings are inadequate? – Our buildings are only a very small part of what will ultimately be required. We are now living in two buildings, one an old house at a nominal rent, which is to come down shortly, and the other a wing of the new buildings. The estimate for the completion of the buildings is 50,000*l.* The wing we have put up cost about 5,000*l.*[22]

---

[21] Marshall revealed the same anti-examination stance at Cambridge. See *Cambridge University Reporter*, 13 November 1900, where he is reported as explicitly stating, 'He did not care much about Examinations. He thought they counted for too much in university life.'

[22] Marshall presented extensive building plans to the College Council in June 1881, on which he was probably working at the time he gave this evidence. For a discussion of their content, see Groenewegen, *A Soaring Eagle: Alfred Marshall 1842–1924*, p. 281.

18,232. You require a sustentation fund, to go on at your present rate, of 1,500*l.* or 2,000*l.* a year? — Yes, that is independent of the aid we get from the colleges and from the Clothworkers' Company.

18,233. From what sources is it proposed to draw the sustentation fund for the future? — From the subscriptions of those interested in education, which are asked for on the same grounds as those which have recently been got for the Owens College.

18,234. You have no endowments at present of any kind? — None.

18,235. With regard to the character of the education given, there is a very large commercial community in Bristol; how do you manage as between the claims of classical and commercial education? — I think there is no exact plan, the education given is the result of compromise. On the council originally there were two distinct elements, the university element (chiefly Oxford) and the local element, which was chiefly a business element.[23] The college opened in 1876 with only two professors, and several lecturers. Gradually we have gone on increasing our range. The demand for science teaching is slightly greater than that for literary teaching; and, what is more important, a certain amount of teaching goes much less far in science than in literature; so that we have more teachers of science than of literature.[24]

18,236. Have you anything like the system of bifurcation which prevails in some of the high schools in Scotland, where the boys are educated in common up to a certain point and then they are transferred to the classical side or to the commercial side according to the particular pursuit in life for which they are destined? — No, we have not that system. So far as my own influence goes, I have tried to prevent the college being broken up into literary and scientific sides. I know there is in some colleges an arrangement by which a student has to

---

[23] The twenty member College Council had three nominees from Oxford, and one each from Cambridge and London Universities; there was a staff representative elected by the Principal and the professors, two representatives from the Medical School, with the majority of members (eleven) elected by the Governors of the College. Of the latter, more than half were local businessmen.

[24] There were seven teachers (of whom four were professors) in the sciences; five teachers (of whom two were professors) in the humanities. There were two professors and one lecturer in the moral sciences (including Alfred Marshall and his wife, Mary Paley Marshall, responsible for the political economy teaching).

declare himself either a student of literature or a student of science, and if reading for a science associateship his literary classes would not count for the science associateship. Our general feeling is that that is not a right thing to do. A student before being admitted to any day class must come to me to get authority for entering the class, and I make it a rule never to admit a student to the literary classes alone, without trying to induce him to take one science class also and *vice versa*, and that seems to be working well.

18,237.   Your education is extra-mural. You have no buildings where any students can be lodged? – No.

18,238.   Do you find any material moral injury arising from the fact of all students living outside? – No; a great majority of them live with their parents, many of the others live with relatives or friends. There are at most only one or two – I am not sure whether there is even one living in a lodging-house. The others are living with respectable people, widows of professional men, and so on.[25]

18,239.   Do you exercise any supervision over them at all out of hours? – No. No doubt when the number increases so far that it is impossible to have any personal acquaintance with the people with whom they lodge it will be necessary to do as Owens College has done, viz., to adopt the regulations of Oxford and Cambridge with regard to students in lodgings. Owens College has incorporated those regulations in its calendar.

18,240.   You say the amount charged for board and lodging is about 25s. a week? – Yes.

18,241.   To which you have to add the cost of tuition? – Yes.

18,242.   For how many weeks in the year is the instruction of the college carried on? – About 30.

18,243.   You have not considered the question of the advisability of building hostels? – Yes, we have considered it, but we feel that there

---

[25] This contrasts sharply with Marshall's view on the important educational value of college residence for students at Oxford and Cambridge, a perspective (as shown below in n. 42) widely shared at the time. See Groenewegen, *A Soaring Eagle: Alfred Marshall 1842–1924*, pp. 503–5, 639.

would be no advantage in it. We would very much rather spend the money upon the college buildings. A hostel is always an experiment, and there is a want of elasticity about a hostel. I know the case of a school that was very much injured by a boarding house being started, the person who had to manage it turned out not to be very well fitted for the work. Under our present system we have perfect elasticity. Anybody that chooses may come forward and say 'I should like to take students.' Certain inquiries are made, and if the result of those inquiries is satisfactory the person is put upon the list. A man who had a very good private school in Bristol, and who has since given it up, is very glad to take in a few students.

18,244. Are you aware that in Ireland, in connexion with the Queen's colleges there, they have hostels, and that they have answered the purpose very well? – I was not aware of that; but I believe they have more money to spare there.

18,245. You have been making a very interesting experiment, which may be of great use to us in Wales, of combining the regular college instruction with instruction by evening classes. Do you require the young people who attend your evening classes to come prepared with a certain amount of education? – We perhaps shall ultimately have an entrance examination, but hitherto we have had none. There is this sort of indirect selection, that if a student finds that the teaching is above him he ceases to attend the college. That selection is always at work. Every now and then students come whom we think quite unfit to benefit by the instruction at the college, and after a time they cease to attend.

18,246. Is the education given in the evening classes mainly scientific or classical? – It is almost a perfect reproduction, on a smaller scale, of the teaching in the day.

18,247. As to the persons who give instruction in the evening classes, are they the same professors as are working in the day time? – Yes, with one exception. There is one teacher of French who does not teach in the day.[26]

[26] It should be added that from 1878–9, Marshall taught his political economy classes largely, but not exclusively, in the evening; his wife taking the main day class (see below, answer to Q. 18,250).

18,248.   That is not found to be too great a draught upon the strength
of the professors? – It is a very great draught upon it. When I said it
would not be possible for a complete college to be worked at less
expense than ours I might have added that the strain upon the health
of the professors is as great as it ought to be, and in some cases
perhaps a little greater.[27]

18,249.   You are making another interesting experiment, I think the
first in this country, of what is called co-education; will you tell us
what the result has been? – I think it has been eminently satisfactory.[28] I may say that it has been tried to a certain extent under advantageous circumstances: My wife was a lecturer at Newnham Hall,
Cambridge, and had got to know about women's education before
she came to Bristol,[29] and I am not sure that the college would have
worked so easily and with such perfect freedom from friction as it has
worked if it had not been for that. If there is anything wrong with
regard to the education of the women, if any woman has a difficulty,
she goes to my wife. I said just now that all students for the day
classes before taking a ticket are referred to me; as regards the women
they go always to my wife and she consults me in case of difficulty.

18,250.   Does she give any lectures? – She gives lectures on political
economy in the day.

18,251.   Are those lectures given to students of both sexes? – They are
open to both, but practically only women attend them.[30]

---

[27] Perhaps a reference to himself. In April 1879, Marshall had been diagnosed to have stones in
the kidney, then an inoperable ailment. It apparently ruined his health for close to a decade
and induced his effective resignation as Principal the following year after an earlier unsuc-
cessful attempt to resign in 1879.

[28] This contrasts with Marshall's later views on the subject with respect to Cambridge.
However, in 1877, the Marshalls claimed to have found the Bristol position particularly
attractive because of this experiment. For Marshall's views on women's education, see
Groenewegen, *A Soaring Eagle: Alfred Marshall 1842–1924*, pp. 501–7, and, for some examples of his treatment of women students there, *ibid.*, pp. 323–4.

[29] Mary Paley Marshall, who had successfully completed her moral sciences tripos in 1874
(without getting her degree or even a result recorded), joined the Newnham teaching staff in
1875. This aspect was stressed by an early woman student of the Marshalls at Bristol, Marian
Pease, in her reminiscences dated 23 February 1942, preserved in the Bristol University
Archives (typescript copy, esp. pp. 7–8).

[30] For the one year (1877–8) that Marshall taught the day class it contained one man and ten
women; subsequent years kept the number of men in this class at a similar low level. Marshall

18,252. Do the women attend all the classes? – All the classes are open to them, but in engineering of course there have been no women, in chemistry there have been but few. I have a paper giving the details of those attending each class and I will read some of the chief statistics with regard to them. These are the attendants on the day classes last session. No women in chemistry, 15 women in mathematics, 1 in experimental physics, 7 in a short course on sound and music, 4 in palaeontology, 7 in botany, 1 in geology, 9 in political economy, 14 in logic, none in law, 16 in modern history, 31 in English literature, 7 in Latin, 8 in ancient history, 7 in French, and 6 in German.

18,253. None in Greek? – It so happens that there are none in Greek in that particular session. The number varies. In one year almost all the good Greek scholars were women, that was in 1878–79.

18,254. You suggested that what would be suitable for some of the Welsh towns, take Merthyr for instance, would be trade schools similar to the one in Bristol? – Somewhat on the same plan.

18,255. Have you considered that you have already in Bristol ample provision for general education (which may be wholly wanting in Merthyr), in Clifton College and your own institution for instance? – I was assuming that there was already an adequate provision for education of what I may call the old fashioned type. Of course, if there is, not the first thing would be to provide it.

18,256. Did I rightly understand you to say that at any college that might be attempted to be established in Wales it would be necessary to have professors receiving 1,000*l.* a year? – No; only if you are to get the best men to teach and you do not give them leisure to go on with their own studies, if you are to buy them out and out with money, 1,000*l.* a year is the least you can buy them for, but if you buy them partly with leisure you may get them for 400*l.*[31]

later opposed the practice of using women teachers to teach mixed classes. See Groenewegen, *A Soaring Eagle: Alfred Marshall 1842–1924*, pp. 502–3.

[31] This probably reflected Marshall's own modest scale of values, but not the professorial salaries often in vogue at that time, which tended to range from £500 to £700. Nearly three years later, Marshall estimated the minimum stipend for a bachelor college fellow at £300 including £60 for four months travelling during the summer vacation (reported in *Oxford Magazine*, 18 November 1883).

18,257.   I have a list of the professors in Queen's College, Belfast, and
I find that taking the salaries they receive from the Government and
the class fees, and in some instances fees as examiners in the Queen's
University, there are none who receive much more than 500*l.* a year,
with the exception of the professor in the anatomy and physiology
class, in which the number of medical students is very large; but
565*l.* is the highest emolument that any one of the professors
receives. I suppose they are competent men? – Quite so. The ordinary salary for the professors in local colleges is 300*l.* a year and a
share of the fees. That is not the universal rule, but the general rule.
But these men are paid 300*l.* and a share of the fees, amounting altogether to something between 400*l.* and 500*l.*, on condition that they
are allowed to go on with their own studies. If the council were to
say 'you must do work that will not enable you to go on with your
own studies and you will be paid 500*l.* a year,' they would think
whether they had not better go to some large school where they
would get 1,500*l.* a year. The colleges have to compete with the
schools.

18,258.   The professors at Queen's College, Belfast, give nearly all
their time up to their duties, because in the list of the number of lectures given by each professor I find the Greek professor gives 268
lectures, the professor of modern languages 351, and Latin professor
285; so that they must give up nearly all their time to their work in the
college? – Nothing like the number of hours that a schoolmaster
gives up; the average number of hours in school would be between
20 and 26 per week, for not very much less than 40 weeks, about 800
or 1,000 hours a year.[32]

18,259.   Do you suppose that these professors occupy their spare time
in any other way that brings them emolument? – No; but a man who
accepts the position of professor may be desirous of still carrying
on his studies, and he is then ready to take a comparatively low
salary as a means towards study. If you say 'you shall not have any

---

[32] Nothing like the hours Marshall was to teach later at Cambridge as Professor of Political
Economy, which rarely exceeded 100 hours per annum. Marshall had experienced the work-
load of a good schoolmaster when he taught mathematics as a replacement teacher at Clifton
College during the first half of 1865.

time for study' you must give him more money.[33] A schoolmaster is supposed to give up all his time to teaching, and he has practically little time for study. Those men who wish to go on with their studies do not become schoolmasters if they can help it, and they are willing to take much lower salaries as professors, in which case they will have time for study, than they would be willing to take as schoolmasters.

18,260. In speaking of universities you, like most other gentlemen educated at one of our two large English universities, make them your ideal? – I will not say that.

18,261. Is it not possible to have institutions of a more modest kind, having power to confer degrees and thereby imparting a stimulus to the population in the midst of which they are planted, like the Scotch universities or the Queen's University in Ireland, that may fall short of your ideal, but which may nevertheless be very useful? – My opinion is distinctly not; my opinion is that teaching ought to be localized and examination centralized. Cambridge University with its income of 250,000*l.* a year is not a bit too rich for its work as a large teaching and examining body. To conduct your examinations you want 50 specialists in each department, which makes 200 or 300 specialists. I have been brought in contact at Cambridge with examinations in mathematics and moral science,[34] and I find that though in mathematics there is a sufficient choice of men, there is not in moral sciences. In fact, in no other subject except mathematics and classics does Cambridge afford anything like a sufficient choice of men. We have had to borrow men from Oxford, and once or twice from Scotland, and we have not enough variety in the choice of examiners to keep up a really high standard of knowledge in a variety of subjects.

18,262. What is the number of students at the two Universities of Oxford and Cambridge? – About 5,000.

---

[33] This reflected Marshall's major complaint about his Bristol position: the lack of time it provided for his own writing and research work.

[34] See nn. 17 and 20 above. On the record, he only examined in the moral sciences once. He was, however, involved in college examinations in the moral sciences during his period as College Lecturer at St John's from 1868 to 1877.

18,263.   Do you think that that adequately represents the number out of the enormous population of the United Kingdom that ought to be receiving higher education? – Certainly not; I think that education ought to be localized. There ought to be ultimately a college like that at Bristol in every town as large as Newport; but we are not ready for that yet. I think what we ought to do at present is to have colleges in all the largest towns, but while localizing education we ought to centralize examination.

18,264.   Would you have representatives of the two universities come down as examining bodies into all these localities and confer degrees? – The matriculation examination of the London University is held in the Bristol college every year, and we could have all the others if we cared to pay for them.

18,265.   You would not insist upon residence at the universities? – No.

18,266.   (*Professor Rhys.*) You are aware that many of the colleges at Oxford find it exceedingly hard to compete with the great public schools in the matter of getting able teachers. Would you say that it would be still harder in the case of a provincial college? – It would be still harder; but it is said not to be quite so true of Cambridge as of Oxford that there is a difficulty in retaining the best men.

18,267.   As to there being so much love of learning for its own sake at Cambridge, I would venture no opinion but would you really go so far as to deny that the great majority of the men who take up the study of the classics at Oxford, for instance, do it with a very distinct view to the social and pecuniary advantages to be derived from it? – Most certainly not. I believe more than half the men in Cambridge at present could have doubled their incomes easily by going elsewhere. Cases are continually occurring of headmasters of large schools offering posts which would in a short time be worth 1,500*l.*, a year to people who have just the means of living and who refuse the posts.

18,268.   Does that apply mostly to mathematical men or to classical men? – To all, I think.

18,269.   (*Chairman.*) I suppose the drain of able men is now very much greater than formerly, in consequence of the large number of first class schools that have been either established or greatly expanded in the last 20 or 30 years? – Yes; but, on the other hand, there has been a great change in the atmosphere of the universities. I was elected a Fellow at St. John's in 1865, and the number of fellows who were *bona fide* students then was not more than half what it was when I left Cambridge, 11 years after.

18,270. (*Professor Rhys.*) You mean that the number of students who love learning for its own sake, was on the increase? – Very largely on the increase.

18,271. With regard to the reason you assigned for the founding of Victoria University, do not you think that it was done partly in deference to the local desire to have a university in the north of England? – Certainly. There were a great many arguments urged in favour of a university there, which I did not think were strong, but I thought one was very strong; that, namely, which I have given.

18,272. That reason not being one that weighed with the people of the North of England? – I think it weighed with them. The Owens College people that I talked with complained of their students having to be examined by people who had no sufficient experience in education, for one cannot deny that many of the examiners for the London University though eminent men of science are men who have not had much experience in teaching.

18,273. (*Chairman.*) That argument was put strongly forward by the deputation that applied for the charter? – I believe so.

18,274. (*Professor Rhys.*) You think that the number of examinations is becoming a great evil? – Yes, they are beginning to be a great strain upon the examiners. If you have to conduct an examination it breaks up a week of your time; everybody who takes part in examinations ought to be a teacher, and a week out of the little spare time he has is a very perceptible loss. Though I think the objection to admit outsiders to the examinations at Oxford and Cambridge is a great deal stronger than it ought to be, and though I do not sympathize with many of the arguments put forward in favour of such exclusiveness, there is that very valid argument that Oxford and Cambridge men are in danger of being examined away, and all their energy taken out of them by these examinations.

18,275. You would admit women to be examined for degrees in the same way as men, so far as they took up the same studies? – Yes, they should be admitted to all the highest examinations. In all the highest examinations they should go on the same footing with men. So far as the ordinary examinations go, I think the present arrangement quite satisfactory.[35]

18,276. Having regard to the population of Wales, and the present state of higher education of girls in the principality, would you say that it would be desirable to have a college for girls in Wales? – It seems to me that you cannot have such a college in Wales. The number of girls who can leave home, and who ought to leave home, is really very small, and those are already very well provided for by the four colleges at Oxford and Cambridge.[36]

18,277. (*Chairman.*) Are you of the opinion that any college for girls ought to be taken to some seat of learning where there would be an adequate supply of professors in all branches of knowledge? – I see no reason why the education of girls, except perhaps a very few, should not be conducted in a place like Bristol. There are perhaps two or three in 100 who ought to have the very highest and the most specialized kind of training, and that cannot be given anywhere but at a university.

18,278. You carry on female education, but at a very great cost; you are living on your capital; you have an uncertain future as to the means by which you will be able to carry on your work. In the case of the colleges for ladies that have been founded at Oxford and Cambridge, they have been taken there not only for the purpose of getting the best education, but also of getting it upon the most economical terms. What is your opinion with reference to the possibility of establishing such colleges for women in a country like Wales, not very largely supplied with professors of the first eminence? – My impression is this: if you start a really good college in any one town

---

[35] This was a view to which Marshall adhered for all of his life: he was opposed to similar qualifications (degrees) for women at Cambridge, because these conferred membership of the university on the degree holder.

[36] On the subject of this question, the subsequent ones up to Q. 18,282, and again, Q. 18,304–6, see McWilliams-Tullberg, 'Alfred Marshall and the "Woman Question" at Cambridge', pp. 209–30, esp. pp. 216–19.

you may expect to draw men from that town, and a considerable number from neighbouring towns, but you cannot expect to draw any considerable number of women from a distance.

18,279.   (*Professor Rhys.*) That leads me to my next question, whether the great majority of the girls attending your classes are not inhabitants of Bristol and Clifton, living within reach of the college? – Out of the 200 probably there are not more than four or five who are known to us as living away from their homes; but I should think that probably something like 30 or 40 more are residing with friends or relatives, cousins and uncles, and so on.

18,280.   It would probably add to the difficulty considerably if girls had to be sent a long way from home, in case no boarding houses were provided for them? – It would.

18,281.   You depend then mainly, as far as girls go, on the resident population? – Yes; we have no strong competition as regards girls' education, so we get all the best female intellect of Bristol. We do not get all the best male intellect.

18,282.   (*Mr. Morris.*) You said your college was intended for the purpose of giving education to boys and girls above school age, what do you consider to be school age? – According to our definition it is 16, but practically we have very few under 18. We admit no one under 16, except for some special reason.

18,283.   Therefore, I assume, in the case of a middle-class school you consider the education should end at 16? – 16 or later; it would vary. The general impression in the country is, I think, that the students at Owens College are chiefly young lads; the facts are not so.

18,284.   Your view would be this: That at the end of the school period, that is to say, when a boy or girl arrived at the age of 16 or 17, a higher sort of education ought to be furnished. I am speaking of boys and girls in the middle classes? – Yes; an education on a different plan. Some people of that age do not like to be put through their paces as they are in a school. I come across a good number of boys who feel that they would like to take up some one or two things and study them more or less after the manner of adults. At a school a lad must go through five hours' instruction a day, a good part of which may be uninteresting to him, whereas with us he can take up what he likes. I consider that when boys and girls arrive at the age of 17 or 18 it may in some cases be desirable that they should not be forced through a groove.

18,285.   They have then arrived at an age when they should be taught rather by lectures than by lessons? – Yes; and they should have a freedom in the choice of subjects.

18,286.   Therefore, whatever may be said as to the necessity for young men in first grade schools remaining at school till they arrive at the age of 19 because they are going to a university, that would not apply to middle-class boys? – No. The age to which students would remain at a school would depend very much upon the nature of the school. Clifton College and the Grammar School at Bristol being such excellent schools, they retain their scholars to a somewhat advanced age.

18,287.   In the particular circumstances of Bristol I suppose we may say that the Grammar School and Clifton College really drain away a large number of young men who would come to you? – No doubt they do.

18,288.   Therefore, there could be no well founded argument as to the success or non-success of your college which did not take into consideration the fact of the existence of those two institutions? – Yes; only I would like to repeat that while they diminish our number of students in one direction they increase our number in another; because a parent with no particular reason for living in one town rather than another, if he becomes acquainted with the facts relating to Bristol as regards the means of education for boys and girls from their early years till they are completely grown up, is likely to go there in preference to almost any other town.

18,289.   Do you think that practically affects the question? – I am sure of it. I know people who have said to me 'I came here because this boy can go to this place of education, and this boy can go to that, and this girl can go to that.'

18,290.   Therefore it is really an advantage that there should be different institutions in one place answering different purposes? – Yes.

18,291. What is the distinction you draw between professors and lecturers; is that a distinction analogous to the difference between professors and readers at a university? – No; the arrangement is that in some departments the professor has an assistant as a lecturer who is paid a lower salary.

18,292. What are your professors paid and what are the lecturers paid? – The professors are paid 300*l.* a year and a share of the fees; the lecturers are paid in a great many different ways; some by fees.

18,293. You really have a very good staff of professors and lecturers? – It is difficult to avoid blowing one's own trumpet; it has been said by competent judges that the staff is exceptionally strong.[37]

18,294. Therefore you have not found the difficulty which seemed to you fatal, that the best men are attracted by the schools where they get 1,500*l.* a year? – What I mean is this: if we had endeavoured to start the college with a few men who should divide up the subjects between them, each dealing with four or five subjects, we could not have got specialists, each of whom was a leading man in his own department. According to the general estimate of the staff, the peculiar social advantages and the physical scenery in Bristol are worth at least 50*l.* a year. It is the general estimate that people would rather have 300*l.* a year at Bristol than 350*l.* in a less attractive place.[38]

18,295. Then we might hope, as Wales is rather a beautiful country, that we might save at least 100*l.* a year each in the salaries of our professors? – The great attraction of Bristol is that it has so much beauty of natural scenery, and also that it is a large town.

18,296. It is a pleasant place of residence? – Yes.[39]

18,297. With regard to the examinations, the number of which you say is becoming so great and which cause so great a strain upon the

[37] See n. 4 above.

[38] Cf. n. 31 above. Marshall's argument on differential pay scales to reflect a university's locational advantages/disadvantages is an interesting one.

[39] Not perhaps a fully honest statement on Marshall's part. For a variety of reasons, which included his personal health, his heavy administrative workload, the lack of good students and personal tragedies such as the death of his mother in 1878, Marshall loathed his Bristol experience and both Marshalls felt it as a 'relief' to depart Bristol for Oxford when the opportunity came in 1883. See Groenewegen, *A Soaring Eagle: Alfred Marshall 1842–1924*, pp. 233–7.

examiners; do you consider the examiners have to be considered in the matter very much? — I consider it is most vital.

18,298.   Nobody is bound to examine unless he likes, I suppose? — Many people conduct examinations against their will.

18,299.   Who makes them? — The routine at Oxford and Cambridge. Many fellows at Oxford and Cambridge marry and lose their fellowships and they have to earn money somehow, and they earn it by examining.[40]

18,300.   You would rather them spend their time in research? — I would rather have them spend their time in extending the boundaries of scientific knowledge.

18,301.   You think they would do that if they had nothing else to do? — Yes; I think there has been a great change in the feeling at Cambridge the last few years.

18,302.   You have not a fixed curriculum at your college? — No, and we are strongly against making a fixed curriculum, we wish to have freedom.[41]

18,303.   How long do your students generally stop? — As long as they like; as a rule perhaps two years; of course we are a young college, probably three years will be the average after a time.

18,304.   There would be a certain normal time in which you could teach them all that they would require to know? — No; it depends on the wants of the individual, and how much he knows before coming. With regard to women (and this has been overlooked in the discussions with regard to colleges for women at Oxford and Cambridge), the best women generally speaking are women whose families

[40] Examples from Marshall's personal acquaintances were Foxwell and later J.N. Keynes, who supplemented their incomes by examining for London University. Marshall himself had resigned his St John's College Fellowship in 1877 on marrying Mary Paley, the reason for his move to the Bristol position.

[41] Marshall's views on freedom of curriculum expressed here contrast with his rather authoritarian interpretation of his duties as principal to include the scanning of all examination papers in order to maintain consistency in standards. This practice was successfully challenged by William Ramsay on his appointment to Bristol. For a discussion, see Groenewegen, *A Soaring Eagle: Alfred Marshall 1842–1924*, pp. 281–2.

require part of their time; generally they have duties to perform to their fathers and mothers and sisters and brothers that takes up some part of their time, and while a woman can give half her time for six years much more easily than a man can she cannot give her whole time for three years so easily as a man can.

18,305.   Are you speaking of women who have reached middle age, or approaching it? – No; I am speaking of women of the ordinary college age, 17 to 23. Many of the best women, from the very fact that they are the bright lights in their families, are unable to go away from their families for a long time together; of two sisters one may be unimportant to the family, and the other important, the former may go away to study, but the latter must carry on her studies at home, or not at all.

18,306.   You mean it is important to the family to enjoy her pleasant society? – The family like her to be at home because she makes home cheerful, and very often she educates the younger brothers and sisters. The point I want to call attention to is, that, so far as women are concerned, the tendency is for them to study to a less extent than men in a given time. Women do not, as a rule take so many classes as men, they study a little during a good number of years. They stay with us longer than the men do.

18,307.   What I was coming to is this: do not you think it would really be better that you should have a fixed course, and a degree at the end of it, suppose you felt confident that you could keep up a proper standard? – Our own view is that it would be most injurious to us if we were constituted a university to give degrees. College associateships are the nearest approach to degrees that I think we ought to grant. Every associate should have shown that he or she has attained a high standard of knowledge in a certain number of subjects.

18,308.   That would be only a degree under another name, an inferior degree, but still a degree, or diploma or certificate? – If you like to call it a degree under another name you may. We consider that we ought not to grant the B.A. degree.

18,309.   Suppose you lived in a country in which it was practically impossible that the great majority of students should through poverty or other circumstances ever go elsewhere, or would not go elsewhere, would you give them a degree at home? – No, I think they ought not to have more than an associateship.

18,310. Do you consider that any of your students who go through the long course would necessarily be able to pass the examination for the pass degree at Cambridge? – They would have attained, I hope, a much higher intellectual standard than would be required for the pass degree; still they might not be able to pass, because it might happen, for instance, that they had studied English literature, the English language, and some one or two sciences. No one can take a degree at Oxford or Cambridge without studying the special subjects prescribed.

18,311. Would not such a person be a person of higher intellectual attainments than an ordinary pass man at Oxford and Cambridge? – Of course there is a controversy between London and Cambridge with regard to the meaning of the letters B.A. My own view is that the B.A. of Oxford or Cambridge means that the man has had some opportunities for learning the amenities of social life and is not an absolute fool, but nothing more.[42]

18,312. But you would be able to say more than that of your most promising students after they had gone through the course of training at the college? – Yes; still we wish our students when they conveniently can to take degrees at one of the universities, to get the test of independent examiners.

18,313. If it were found that the B.A. degree of a college in Wales was really inferior to that of London, then probably Welsh students would proceed to London to take their degrees? – I think if the Welsh University were to offer the B.A. degree on cheaper terms than the London degree most students would, to their great detriment, take the Welsh degree.

18,314. We might hope it would not be on cheaper terms; suppose three colleges to be established with a board of examiners on which

---

[42] For an eloquent discussion of this quality of a residential university education, see Sheldon Rothblatt, *The Revolution of the Dons*, Cambridge, Cambridge University Press, 1981, pp. 174–5.

the whole university should be represented? – You have to regard examinations as a whole. If a body were to be started to give pass degrees without having honour examinations it would do its work badly, and I do not think really good honour examinations in all branches of science and literature can be managed by a body of less than 300 men, considering that learning is so large and increasing its area so fast.

18,315. You mean there must be a body of students 300 strong? – No, the body of men from whom you draw your examiners. I wish to say why I think that. Only a very short time ago there were only two triposes, classical and mathematical,[43] and almost anybody could undertake to do almost any teaching for either tripos. A small college with six able lecturers could teach people all that was required for either the classical or the mathematical tripos; but now we have a mathematical tripos which is really three or four different triposes rolled into one, and we have a classical tripos, which is two or three triposes rolled into one; then we have a tripos in moral science, in history, and in natural science, besides a law tripos and a tripos of theology. Then we have the Semitic and the Indian language triposes. Mathematics has now become so large a science that no teacher can profess to know thoroughly everything that a student may want to learn. The same is true of classics. In natural science it is difficult to get anyone to teach all of any one science. In chemistry one man is good on one set of subjects and another on another set of subjects, and we have for our triposes about 40 examiners every year; we ought not to have the same men every year, and we ought not to have anybody who is not young, that is, between the age of 30 and 50. Of course a few old men go on, but we cannot bring old men up from the country to examine.

18,316. Practically, you consider it is impossible to have an honour examination at any local college? – Impossible to have a thoroughly good sct of honour examinations at any local college.

18,317. Do you think that is so at Owens College? – It is impossible that they can do it without importing their examiners.

[43] That is, at Cambridge up to 1848 when the moral sciences and natural sciences triposes were introduced.

18,318.   Might you not import examiners into Wales? – Then my argument is this: if you are to have a good examination in natural science you must get eight of the most eminent students of natural science to act as examiners, and you must pay them a very great deal. The expense could not be less than 100*l.*, and it is very doubtful whether you would get more than two or three candidates, and you might get no one who was really worthy of so elaborate an examination.

18,319.   You are probably aware that natural science is taught with some success at Aberistwith at this moment? – Yes. I do not know very much of the detail of the teaching there.

18,320.   In the event of the establishment of a Welsh university, do you think the students at your college at Bristol would be likely to compete for its degree? – No I do not think so at all.

18,321.   (*Rev. H.G. Robinson.*) Am I right in assuming that it is your opinion that a provincial college like that at Bristol is in itself a desirable thing? – Certainly.

18,322.   You think the ordinary school education ought to be supplemented, wherever there was scope for it, by an institution of that kind? – Yes.

18,323.   You would admit young persons at the minimum age of 16? – Yes.

18,324.   And is it your opinion that for boys of that age, and above that age it is a great advantage to have the freer system of education which a college gives rather than the ordinary school routine? – I think it a great advantage for some.

18,325.   Is that because you think by that means a great taste for learning would be cultivated, and habits of study more easily formed? – That is partly the reason. Also there are some students who tell their parents that they are tired of school, and who object to going on with the drill of the school, but who rather like to come to college to work as hard as they would at school, but to work only in subjects in which they are specially interested.

18,326.   A college would give the student an opportunity of selecting their own subjects, and of devoting themselves to those subjects? – Yes.

18,327.   Suppose a boy at the Bristol Grammar School, which we call a
first grade school intends to go to Oxford at the age of 19, do you
think it would be better for him, with a view to his Oxford education,
that he should remain at the school? — I think as the Grammar School
is so singularly successful in its instruction, there would be not any
gain in going to such an intermediate place of education unless in the
case of exceptional circumstances, but outside the great public
schools[44] there is hardly any first grade school that would compare
with the Bristol Grammar School.

18,328.   So, in your opinion, the advantage of a provincial college is
rather to that very numerous class who do not contemplate going to
the older universities, but intend finishing their education at the
provincial college? — Yes, it is chiefly for them.

18,329.   The number of youths of 16, or below 16, that you have is
very small? — Very small.

18,330.   Do you find that the working of the college is in any way
affected by your having students of rather widely different ages? —
No.

18,331.   The young ones take their instruction along with the older
ones? — Yes.

18,332.   Is there any catechetical teaching at all in the college? — Yes,
there is. There was a rule of the council originally that every lecture
should be supplemented by class teaching, class teaching being supposed to be catechetical. It has been found that that rule cannot be
applied rigidly, and modifications have been introduced to suit the
exigencies of particular subjects, but the general principle still
remains in force. In mathematics the teaching is entirely individual
teaching. The professor goes about from one student to another, each
student working for himself. In chemistry, in the full course, there are
four lectures in the week and one class. In languages, the teaching is
chiefly catechetical.

[44] These great public schools included Eton, Winchester, Westminster, Charterhouse, St Paul's,
Merchant Taylors' School, Harrow, Rugby and Shrewsbury. Marshall himself had attended
Merchant Taylors' School from 1852 to 1861.

18,333.   In order to make the college efficient, and in order to secure that the students should benefit by the instruction given there, they ought to come to you in a very fair state of preparation? – Yes, but I do not think it would do, in founding a college, to pitch the standard very high. As regards Greek, we have taught several people their Greek alphabet. There is no reason why that should not be done in a college. I think a college should always have a class in which students can learn the Greek alphabet.[45]

18,334.   Would those who required that elementary instruction in Greek be advanced in other subjects? – No, very few of them; very often people between the ages of 20 and 30 come to learn the Greek alphabet.

18,335.   Not having any amount of attainment in any other subject? – No high attainment in any other subject.

18,336.   You would not contemplate the placing of a college of the kind you have at Bristol in one of the towns of South Wales as a substitute for an intermediate school? – No.

18,337.   You presuppose the existence of intermediate schools? – Yes.

18,338.   Would you say that, in your opinion, a college could not live and thrive without an intermediate school to feed it? – I would not go so far as that, but I would say that intermediate schools would strengthen it very much. Intermediate schools have their proper work to do, while colleges have their proper work to do.

18,339.   The college must rather be the coping stone of the edifice? – Yes.

18,340.   Is not it the case that the staff of such a college is far more expensive than the staff of even a high grade school? – Very much more. It is very much more expensive in proportion to the number of hours teaching. You can get something like 800 hours a year out of a

---

[45] At Cambridge, Marshall strongly opposed compulsory Greek in the Previous Examination (a qualifying examination before students could present themselves for degree examinations) both when he was a young fellow at St John's and subsequently as professor. He was particularly annoyed, as Mary Paley Marshall wrote to Jowett, when a vote to abandon compulsory Greek for the Previous Examination was lost in 1891. See Groenewegen, *A Soaring Eagle: Alfred Marshall 1842–1924*, pp. 59–60, 274, 691.

schoolmaster, and you cannot get that amount of actual teaching out of a professor.

18,341. Is not it the case that in a school it is easy to adjust the staff to the numbers, whereas in a college you must have a staff irrespective of the numbers? — That is true.

18,342. That makes one great element of expense? — Yes.

18,343. You say that in procuring your staff you have to compete with the schools who will give their assistant masters 1,500*l.* a year? — Yes.

18,344. The number of those schools is very limited, is it not? — Not very small in proportion to the number of the best Oxford and Cambridge men. You may say that a man who has taken a good degree at Oxford and Cambridge, and is not specially disqualified, can always get something like that if he chooses to give up study and live a hard life of teaching.

18,345. Am I right in gathering from what you have said that we must almost necessarily take it for granted that the fees of such a college as you have referred to would barely contribute one half of the expense of the college? — They would not contribute one half of the expense of the college in a town as large as the largest town in Wales. You could not calculate upon their supplying more than a quarter.

18,346. In order to come nearly to the half there must be 500 or 600 students? — It depends on the number of the day students. Our students are more than one half of the evening students, and their fees are merely nominal fees, they do not pay any considerable part of the expense of the instruction.[46]

18,347. Your college at Bristol is based on a very comprehensive plan, you take almost the whole range of liberal studies? — Yes; but I am convinced that it would be impossible for us to do our work at all if we tried to cut out one half of our subjects. Some colleges have been started as science colleges, intending to give no literary instruction at

[46] Although, as shown in n. 10 above, fees were relatively low, they played a considerable role in defraying total outlays of Bristol University College. For 1877-8, their contribution to total outlays was 16.6 per cent; for 1878-9, 28.5 per cent; and for 1879-80, 17.9 per cent, the last year's percentage affected by the sharp increase in outlays from the building programme then being implemented.

all, but they will not be able to keep their position. Our attempt to do without certain sciences was a failure. One of our best students is extremely good in classics and in geology. Perhaps there is not another student in England who takes that particular combination. You cannot tell beforehand what classes a man will want; and this happens continually. – A person comes and says 'I want instruction in' so and so, mentioning four different subjects. If we can give instruction in three of those things and not the fourth he will say 'I must go elsewhere'.

18,348.   At the same time if you had to provide for one of the South Wales towns, might you not consider what subjects would be most suited for the circumstances of that place; at all events might you not, in the first instance, limit the instruction given in the college to those few subjects? – You might; you might cut out a few things that we teach, but if you did you would hardly be founding what was bona fide a college, and it would be better to call it a trade school. It would be better to have a good trade school than a bad college.

18,349.   The difference between a trade school and a college is that a trade school is for boys, while a college is for adults? – Not necessarily. It might be advisable, according to circumstances, or it might not, to connect the adult teaching with the teaching for boys. It might be as at Bristol, where the same staff gives boys a general education with a scientific bias and teaches some men mining from a technical point of view and prepares a great many men for the south Kensington examinations, but if you exclude literary subjects, if your teaching has reference chiefly to the industries of the place, it is almost better not to call the institution a college.[47]

18,350.   Might you not introduce one or two branches of literature without giving instruction on such subjects on a very wide and comprehensive plan? – I think it would be very difficult. At present we do not teach Spanish, but we think that it would be a great advantage to those who are intending to be engineers to learn Spanish. I do not think there is anything that we do teach that we could go without, except at a very great loss. It is like a great railway with a number of

---

[47] On the subsequent association between the Bristol Trade School and Bristol University, see n. 13 above.

small feeders. The feeders may not pay their own expenses, but they pay by the traffic they give to the main line of railway.

18,351. If I am not mistaken, your solution of the degree question is to throw open the degree of the old universities to non-residents? — I wish they would do it.

18,352. You think if that were done it would solve the whole difficulty as regards degrees? — Yes; but I do not think the difficulty is very great. The London University is getting much more liberal than it used to be. The great complaint was that it forced men too much into the same many-sided groove, but it is giving much greater freedom in the selection of subjects — it is learning by experience what is wanted in the country. I am not sure that we shall not get along fairly well with the London University alone.

18,353. Your view is that Oxford and Cambridge, from their great resources, would be able to command far more efficient machinery for giving degrees? — Than any place except London, which, since it examines for the whole country, has a very large revenue from fees and can afford to pay very high salaries to its examiners.

18,354. If Oxford and Cambridge had a monopoly of examining, would not there be a danger of their giving too stiff and rigid a form to education throughout the country? — The tendency is for the old universities to be much more liberal than the new University of London. There is much greater freedom in the choice of studies to a man going to Oxford and Cambridge, and particularly Cambridge, I believe, than for a student going to the London University. Every student who takes the London degree has to get up a very great number of subjects, many of which he has no interest in at all. There is a tendency at Cambridge to push the compulsory part of the exam-ination into as small a compass as possible, and as far as possible to push it out of the university altogether. A lad who comes to Cambridge with these has only to study the one thing that he takes an interest in.

18,355. (*Viscount Emlyn.*) You mentioned that there were some schol-arships given at the college; what is the value of them? — The value of them is very small, the council cannot afford to give expensive scholarships. We have one general scholarship of 25*l*., another of 15*l*, and another of 10*l*. We also have a chemical scholarship of 25*l*., and we have the two scholarships for women, the Catherine Winkworth scholarships of 15*l*.[48]

18,356.   Supposing the college were able to give scholarships of any amount, what do you think the value of such scholarships ought to be? – I think it depends on whether they are intended to support youths away from their homes or not. I think 25*l*. is a very good sum for a scholarship for a person who lives at home; but if he is to be taken away from home I do not think anything like that is sufficient.[49]

18,357.   With regard to the accommodation that your college would be able to afford, how many will you be able to teach with your present staff when you have got your buildings completed? – Our existing buildings are sufficient to accommodate all applicants for admission at present.

18,358.   You may want to spend 10,000*l*. on buildings, as I understood you, to put yourselves in such a position as to meet your present wants? – Yes, but we do not exclude students.

18,359.   How many will you be able to teach comfortably when you have got the new buildings completed? – A very large number without any very great increase in the expense. In chemistry, for instance,[50] we could teach twice as many as we do with the same staff. In physics we could teach three times as many. In geology we could teach three times as many. In languages and mathematics an increase in the number of students would involve an increase in the staff, but not a proportionate increase in expenditure because we now have a late fellow of New College, Oxford, a first rate classical scholar,

[48] See n. 12 above.

[49] As a student who himself had financed his university education from scholarships and a loan, Marshall was well qualified to speak on this subject. For an indication of the cost of his undergraduate education as a Cambridge student, see Groenewegen, *A Soaring Eagle: Alfred Marshall 1842–1924*, pp. 89–91.

[50] For the special provisions for chemistry in Marshall's building plans for the Bristol College, see Groenewegen, *A Soaring Eagle: Alfred Marshall 1842–1924*, p. 281; these probably owed much to William Ramsay's suggestions, who had joined the chemistry staff as professor in 1880.

teaching people the elements of Latin and Greek.[51] In the course of time he will perhaps be given an assistant who will do that work.

18,360. Do you expect a large increase in the number of day students? – We hope to have such an increase.

18,361. Proportionate to the increase which you would have in evening scholars? – I should think the two would probably go together.

18,362. Supposing a college were to be established away from any large centres of population, do you think it would be able to hold its own? – It would be utterly impossible to start a good college away from a centre of population without an enormous expense in scholarships.

18,363. In the event of these colleges being established in Wales, I take it that you are of opinion that they should be put near large centres of population? – Yes; I have already said it would be better, from our point of view, that they should not be very near Bristol. I would rather have one in Swansea than Newport, because Swansea and Bristol would between them cover a larger area than Newport and Bristol.

18,364. (*Chairman.*) If you expect to draw from Cardiff and its neighbourhood, and if, as you say, an enormous number of scholarships would be necessary for the purpose of maintaining those who come from a distance where are the scholarships to come from? – I said that only with reference to a college started in a place in which there was not a large population. I believe that the number of people in Cardiff who have friends and relations in Bristol is very great; and as our college gets a greater name and fame we shall get an increasing number of Cardiff students who would come over to live with their relations in Bristol.

The witness withdrew.

---

[51] That is, Professor R. Farnshawe, MA, Fellow of New College, Oxford, who was appointed in 1880. He was also responsible for teaching logic.

ITEM 2

Gold and Silver Commission: note by Professor Marshall on Professor Nicholson's paper 'On the Effects of a Fall in the Gold Price of Silver and General Gold Prices' (dated 30 June 1888)

INTRODUCTION

On Saturday, 23 June 1888, Marshall wrote J.N. Keynes[1] to ask him to look over a comment he had written on a paper by J.S. Nicholson, so that they would be able to discuss its contents the following Monday. Marshall had been asked to write the comment by G.H. Murray, the secretary to the Gold and Silver Commission, for private circulation to its members to aid them in the preparation of their *Final Report*. John Neville Keynes duly recorded in his diary entry[2] for Monday, 25 June, that 'Marshall was with me nearly the whole of the morning talking over another paper[3] he has written for the Currency Commission. He has got into controversy with Nicholson.'

Marshall's paper was eventually published by the Commission, despite the original intention of its private circulation only.[4] However,

---

[1] Marshall to J.N. Keynes, 23 June 1888, in *Correspondence of Alfred Marshall*, ed. Whitaker, Vol. I, Letter 243.   [2] Cambridge University Library, Add. MSS 7827–67.

[3] Marshall had already written three other Memoranda for the Commission. These included a preliminary one dated 9 November 1887 answering questions posed by the Commission (reproduced in *OP*, pp. 19–31); a 'Memorandum on Currency Differences and International Trade', not dated, but written in the first half of 1888 in response to a request from Sir Thomas Farrar on the last day of three in which Marshall gave oral evidence (*OP*, p. 169) and a 'Memorandum on the Relation between a Fall of the Exchange and Trade with Countries which have not a Gold Currency', dated 13 January 1888 (reproduced in *OP*, pp. 170–90, 191–5 respectively).

[4] In his notes to the letter of Marshall to J.N. Keynes, 23 June 1888, Whitaker indicates that Marshall's note was published among the supplementary material with the Commission's *Final Report*, London, HMSO, 1888, Cmnd 5112 (*Correspondence of Alfred Marshall*, ed. Whitaker, Vol. I, Letter 243, n. 4). As indicated in n. 3 above, Keynes reprinted the other three Memoranda as well as the transcript of Marshall's oral evidence given on 19 December 1887, 16 and 23 January 1888 (*OP*, pp. 32–169).

John Maynard Keynes in 1925–6 decided not to include it in his edition of Marshall's *Official Papers* with the other material Marshall had prepared for the Commission. This omission is all the more surprising since T.E. Gregory during September 1925 had alerted Keynes to its existence while a copy of the 'note' was also preserved with Marshall's private papers at Balliol Croft.[5]

Short though it is, Marshall's paper itself is of considerable interest. As John Neville Keynes confided in his diary, it is yet another example of Marshall's controversialist proclivities aroused when he felt his position to be misrepresented as was clearly the case in his view in the paper by Nicholson complained of. More importantly, it gives one of the clearest statements of Marshall's views on the limitations of the quantity theory (below, pp. 74–75). These views he considered similar to the opinion of Professor Erwin Nasse of Bonn, whom the Commission had invited as one of a number of foreign experts to answer several questions raised by its terms of reference.[6] Other parts of the 'note' reiterate the contents of the previous Memoranda which Marshall had supplied to the Commission, particularly one prepared at the explicit request of one of the Commissioners on the final day of his oral evidence.[7]

Unfortunately, the paper by Nicholson to which Marshall's comments are explicitly addressed appears not to have been published by the Commission. This makes it difficult to provide clear reference points to Marshall's replies on specific points made by Nicholson. However, a collection of Nicholson's monetary writings, that is, his *Treatise of Money and Essays on Monetary Problems*, in the third edition of 1895, parts of which were written at a time when Nicholson's 'examination before the Currency Commission [was] fresh in [his] mind', can act as substitute source for some of the opinions and arguments which Marshall attributed to Nicholson in his

---

[5] T.E. Gregory to J.M. Keynes, September 1925 (Keynes Papers, King's College, Cambridge, RES File/Official Papers). The Marshall Archive, Marshall Library, Faculty of Economics and Politics, Cambridge University, now houses the surviving Marshall papers including a proof copy of the Note on Professor Nicholson's paper here reprinted.

[6] Published as Appendix VII with the supplementary material included with the *Second Report* of the Commission, London, HMSO, 1888, Cmnd 5248, pp. 257–63.

[7] That is, the 'Memorandum on Currency Differences and International Trade' (*OP*, pp. 170–90) and see n. 3 above.

note.[8] In addition, Nicholson himself had given evidence before the Commission on 29 April and 20 May 1887, though that makes no explicit reference to the paper in question[9] and in fact deals only infrequently with the specific issues which Marshall controverted in his note.[10]

The Royal Commission on the Value of Gold and Silver had been set up in 1887 as a consequence of the *Report* of the Commission on the Depression of Trade. It had recommended the need for a special inquiry into certain monetary matters which had been placed before it in discussing depressed economic activity and its causes. The terms of reference for the Gold and Silver Commission were as follows. It was to investigate 'the causes of the recent changes in the relative values of the precious metals' and more specifically whether these changes were caused by a depreciation of silver, or of gold or of both these metals. In addition, it was to address both the supply and demand factors involved in the depreciation of either gold or silver or both and to look at its consequences on practical business in India (a silver standard country) and Britain (a gold standard country), with special emphasis on effects on their domestic production and trade. If such consequences were found to be detrimental, adequate remedies had to be proposed, whose own consequences on the interests of relevant parties had to be kept in mind.[11] In short, it was an inquiry into the causes of changes in the general price level, as well as on the effects of price

---

[8] J.S. Nicholson, *A Treatise of Money and Essays on Monetary Problems*, London, Adam and Charles Black, 1895, preface, pp. vii–ix. The relevant material, which Nicholson mentions in the preface is an essay, 'Causes of Movements in General Prices', read before the Royal Society of Edinburgh, 30 January 1888 (*ibid.*, pp. 342–79), and a section of the second part of the *Treatise of Money*, also written in 1888, reproduced with the collection (*ibid.*, pp. 150–5).

[9] Nicholson's evidence is reproduced with evidence before the Gold and Silver Commission in *Parliamentary Papers, House of Commons*, Session 27 January 1887 to 16 September 1887, Vol. 22, 1887, pp. 198–213, 175–92. Q. 5714 from Commissioner Barbour quotes from a statement written by Nicholson, but whether it was for the Commission, or was the paper to which Marshall referred in his 'Note', is not clear (*ibid.*, p. 290).

[10] The evidence did controvert Marshall's belief of the importance of a tabular standard (Q. 5421, p. 276); and commented on the effect of the depreciation of silver on Indian wheat exports at some length (*ibid.*, pp. 285–6).

[11] *Final Report*, Cmnd 5112, pp. iii–iv. A more detailed discussion of Marshall's participation in the Commission, and other relevant background material can be found in Groenewegen, *A Soaring Eagle: Alfred Marshall 1842–1924*, pp. 344–53. Most of the evidence was included by Keynes, as indicated in nn. 3 and 4 above.

instability (both inflation and deflation) on trade, levels of economic activity and the welfare of special interest groups such as farmers, merchants (particularly those in, or trading with, silver countries), workers, manufacturers and those reliant on fixed incomes for their living.

The terms of reference of the Commission cover most of the aspects of the debate raised in the text of Marshall's note here reprinted. These included discussion of the validity of the quantity theory as an explanation of changes in the general price level; the factors influencing the value of the precious metals given the recorded increases in their supply from new mining relative to the work they were expected to do for the monetary system as well as for industrial and decorative purposes; the impact of recent changes in the monetary systems of various countries on this demand; the impact of changes in relative price levels on international trade; and the respective impacts of differential changes in the value of gold and silver on the trade of gold and silver countries, including specific complaints aired by domestic producers (wheat, textiles) about the effective bounty which the depreciation of silver had conferred on India to the disadvantage of British producers. The setting for the discussion was the deflation of price levels since 1873 as measured by the various price indexes which were then coming into use, hence implying a shortage of the precious metals for their monetary function at existing price levels, growing industrial activity and productivity, and more or less unchanged financial institutions and habits. Remedies discussed by the Commission in this context centred on the introduction of bi-metallism, a proposal supported by Nicholson but only indirectly by Marshall.[12] The latter favoured a symmetallist scheme, adapting the gold ingot plan formulated by Ricardo to encompass both gold and silver, together with the use of a tabular standard by which to facilitate the making of contracts at fixed real values instead of fluctuating money prices, in short, an early indexation proposal.[13] Marshall's evidence to the Commission, together with some of his contemporary publications, form the major published version of

[12] Groenewegen, *A Soaring Eagle: Alfred Marshall 1842–1924*, pp. 351–3; *OP*, pp. 28–31.

[13] Alfred Marshall, 'Remedies for Fluctuations of General Prices', *Contemporary Review*, March 1887, reprinted in *Memorials of Alfred Marshall*, ed. Pigou, pp. 188–211.

Marshall's monetary thinking so that its completion by the reprint of this note on Nicholson is valuable, particularly because of its clarification of Marshall's rather ambivalent attitude to the quantity theory of money.[14]

[14] Detailed discussions of Marshall's monetary theory and the important role of his evidence to Royal Commissions therein, are Eprime Eshag, *From Marshall to Keynes*, Oxford, Blackwell, 1963; Pascal Bridel, *Cambridge Monetary Thought*, London, Macmillan, 1987, Chapter 3; and David Laidler, 'Alfred Marshall and the Development of Monetary Economics', in *Centenary Essays on Alfred Marshall*, ed. Whitaker, pp. 44–78.

TEXT

I do not understand the first paragraph of Professor Nicholson's 'Note on the effect of a fall in the gold price of silver on general gold prices.'[1] He enumerates many causes which the older economists believed to be capable of exerting an influence on the gold price of silver, and he seems to imply that I deny that they can exert any such influence. If that is his meaning, he is mistaken, for, on the contrary, a great part of my evidence and of my memorandum is occupied with examining the effects of these and similar disturbing causes. Following, as I believe, in the lines laid down by the older economists, I contend that such disturbances cause re-adjustments of the international distribution of the metals; and that this distribution, taken in conjunction with, firstly, the demand of each several country for the precious metals as commodities, and secondly, the amount and methods of the business which it transacts by means of the precious metals, determines the gold prices of goods in gold-using countries, and their silver prices in silver-using countries; and I contend that the gold value of silver is constrained to move in accordance with the ratio which gold prices bear to silver prices. Thus, I regard local disturbances of the gold value of silver as being speedily merged in a general modification of the ratio of gold prices to silver prices, in such manner that the gold price of silver never departs appreciably and for any considerable time from this ratio.[2]

It seemed to me that the most effective method of proving this was to

---

[1] This note has not been found since it was not published by the Commission. For indications of duplication of its possible contents in Nicholson's other monetary writings, see introduction, above, pp. 66–7. These are used in the notes which follow.

[2] See for example, *OP*, pp. 170–1, 191–2.

start with the case of trade with a country using inconvertible paper. I examined the way in which if any 'external' cause such as political disturbance should lower the gold value of the rouble in London (and such external disturbances are at least as frequent in the case of the gold value of the rouble as in that of the gold value of the rupee, and much more violent) there would instantly be a re-adjustment of the exchanges which would compel that value to conform to the ratio which gold prices bear to rouble prices.[3] Next, I showed that, after a trifling allowance has been made for the effects which international movements of the precious metals have on the balance of trade, a change in the gold value of silver cannot have a direct influence on prices in England of any other kind than would be exerted by a change in the gold price of a rouble.[4] One purpose of this line of argument was to show that the position that gold prices of goods in England are governed by the gold price of silver involves the position that they are also governed by the gold prices of the rouble and the South American dollar, and Professor Nicholson's note showed no reason to the contrary. For indeed I find nothing in it but a repetition of those opinions which I had endeavoured to combat in my memorandum, without any attempt to show where my subject fails. It would be impossible for me to work over the whole subject without re-writing the greater part of the memorandum; but, after indicating briefly some points which Professor Nicholson seems to me to have overlooked, I will endeavour to re-state more carefully some parts of my general argument to which he refers.[5]

He begins his argument by referring 'to a fall in the gold price of silver of the kind supposed' and says that 'it follows that all commodities exported to silver-using countries will at once fall in price.'[6] I do not know what cause he has in view, but I will take what seems the most probable supposition, and assume that the cause is a great increase in the production from the American silver mines, which lowers the purchasing power of silver in the European market, but which does not,

[3] *Ibid.*, pp. 171–2.   [4] *Ibid.*, pp. 172–5.
[5] The particular points which Marshall claimed Nicholson had overlooked are not easily identified from his other writings. Marshall's Memorandum referred to is the last one he prepared for the Commission, that is, the one to which the previous three notes refer.
[6] Cf. Nicholson, *Money and Monetary Problems*, p. 361. Marshall's Memorandum (*OP*, p. 178) attributes the 'new doctrine' to the evidence given to the Commission by Mr Barclay and others.

immediately at least, affect the purchasing power of gold. Let us then suppose that cutlery is being exported to India and that jute is being brought back; then as there has been nothing to change the relative values of cutlery and jute in India, the same amount of jute will be brought back, and since gold prices in England have by supposition not yet altered, it will be sold for as much gold as before. It is a matter of no great importance whether the exporter of cutlery brings back the jute himself, or sells his bill on India to some one else who does. In the latter case he may have some slight trouble in finding a purchaser of this bill, but since whoever has the bill can buy jute, &c. that will yield the old gold price, there is no reason why he should sell it at any considerable reduction on its old price. The fact that some exporters are not importers does not prevent the general character of foreign trade from being barter. It seems to me that Professor Nicholson ignores every influence which affects the value of a bill on India except the market price of silver here; that is, it seems that he takes no account of the fact that the value of the bill will be influenced, to a greater or less extent according to the circumstances, by the power which it gives to its holder of important jute, &c. and selling them in England at the old English price. I infer this partly from his saying at the beginning of the para-graph that a new par of exchange would be 'established'.[7] That phrase seems to me misleading. I think that no disturbance of the gold value of silver can be properly said to have 'established' a new par of exchange until its effects on the demand for bills, and through that on the interna-tional distribution of the metals has had time to work itself out.

The next step of his argument[8] is that there will result a check to exports. I think he here makes a vital omission, and that he should have said, a check to exports other than silver. For, on his supposition, silver would at once begin to move rapidly to India, with the effect of raising the silver prices of goods in India and lowering the gold price of silver in England. And this would proceed till equilibrium is found at a point at which the gold price of silver is again in accordance with the ratio of gold prices to silver prices. The fact that there has not recently been any

---

[7] Cf. Nicholson, *Money and Monetary Problems*, pp. 358–79, for his general discussion of these issues. I have not been able to identify the precise point to which Marshall objected, for reasons indicated in n. 1 above.

[8] Cf. Nicholson, *Money and Monetary Problems*, p. 366. I have not been able to identify the precise point to which Marshall objected, for reasons indicated in n. 1 above.

violent exportation of silver to India is, I think, conclusive proof that there has not been any considerable divergence between the gold price of silver and the ratio which the gold prices of goods bear to the silver prices of goods; and therefore that there has not been any considerable opening for the action of those disturbing causes on general prices to which Professor Nicholson attributes so great results.

(In the above sentence I have assumed that a large influx of silver from Europe into Indian trading centres would raise the silver prices of international goods there. Knowing that there are some people who deny this, I have taken pains to make the main argument in my memorandum independent of it; but I have given (p. 25) reasons for believing that the assumption is justified).[9]

Thus, then, I fail to see that Professor Nicholson has shown any valid reasons for believing that the general prices of international commodities can be appreciably affected, even for a time, by a change in the gold value of silver. It is, however, true that whatever belief there is in the country that this can be the case rests, not so much on general reasoning as on the often-repeated statements that the prices of certain wares, and especially wheat, do fluctuate from week to week in sympathy with the gold price of silver. Professor Nicholson pays no attention to the many lines of statistical argument by which it has been recently proved that there is no ground for these statements. But I may here mention that since the end of the period to which the statistics in my memorandum[10] refer the price of silver has fallen greatly, and that of wheat and many other goods has risen.

Returning to Professor Nicholson's argument, I find him continuing; 'But it is important to observe that if for any reason neither of these events occurs the exportation of goods for the lower price of gold must continue.'[11] He does not say what 'reason' he has in his mind, but it appears to be one which would cause a glut of Western goods in Eastern markets. In any case the results produced by this disturbing cause are to be attributed to it, and not to the change in the gold value of silver. I have already argued [above, pp. 70–1] that the effects which changes in the gold values of foreign currencies have on the general course of

---

[9] Marshall seems to be referring to his remarks in the Memorandum reprinted in *OP* at p. 179.

[10] The data concluded with that for the week ending 31 December 1887 (*ibid.*, p. 186).

[11] Cf. Nicholson, *Money and Monetary Problems*, pp. 370–1, for the type of analysis to which Marshall seems to be objecting.

trade are much exaggerated, in consequence of the habit of attributing to them results which are really due to other causes.[12]

This brings me to consider the paragraph in which Professor Nicholson reaffirms his opinion that a depression of prices due to accidental causes would continue long after those causes had disappeared.[13] It would take too long for me to repeat the reasons which I have given in my evidence in support of the contrary opinion.[14] But I should like to take this opportunity of stating a little more carefully what I understand the Quantity theory of the value of currency really to be.

The Quantity theory, like every other theory which endeavours to summarise in a few words a very complex situation, is apt to get the credit for being much cruder than it really is. It is so tedious to be constantly repeating all the many conditions which are implied in it, that some of them are in danger of dropping out of sight. The Quantity theory, as I entertain it, is, I think, in substantial agreement with the views of such writers as Professor Nasse,[15] and admits that the general level of prices is affected by many causes besides the quantity of currency. We have to take account of (i) the volume of currency; (ii) population; (iii) the amount of goods produced per head of the population, and their wealth generally; (iv) the amount of business to which any given amount of wealth gives rise; (v) the proportion of these payments that are made for currency; (vi) the average rapidity of circulation of the currency (and under this head provision may be made for the locking up of money in hoards, in bank cellars, military chests, &c.); (vii) the state of commercial and political confidence, enterprise, and credit; and this last head might be again divided. (The influence of cost of production shows itself in the amount of the metals available for currency purposes; and the anticipation of a change in the cost of production is among the many causes which determine the amount of hoarding.)

---

[12] See the argument in *OP*, pp. 180–1, 187–9.

[13] Nicholson's remark cannot be identified for reasons given in n. 1, nor have I been able to find a similar argument in his *Money and Monetary Problems*.

[14] See Marshall's evidence in *OP*, pp. 34–41, and his Memorandum, in *ibid.*, pp. 176–7. The next paragraphs of the text expand on this position and elucidate it.

[15] A reference to Professor Erwin Nasse, from Bonn, who had been invited by the Commission to give his opinions on its terms of reference. See Royal Commission on Gold and Silver, *Appendix to Second Report*, London, HMSO, 1888, Cmnd 5248, Appendix VII, esp. pp. 258–60.

Now since the general level of prices is determined by all these seven elements acting together, it is quite possible that one or more of them may be tending to move general prices in one direction, while yet the net result of all the forces acting on prices is to move them in the other. I do not then regard the theory as leading us to expect that an increase in the amount of currency would always or even generally cause a rise in prices, but only that it will cause prices to be higher than they otherwise would have been if all other changes of the time had gone on as they have done, but the volume of currency had not increased. For instance, a change in the proportion of business which is done for currency may exert as great an influence on general prices as a large addition to the volume of the currency. And, if it were true that a diminution in volume of the currency immediately called forth an increased use of cheques, clearing-house certificates, &c., then, indeed, the net effect on general prices might be very slight and very slow. But there is no evidence that this is the case. On the contrary, history seems to show that the periods in which banking facilities of various kinds have increased most rapidly, have been those in which the metallic currency has been increasing in volume and not those in which it has been diminishing. And when the matter is closely examined, it will, I think, be found that this historical result is just what might have been expected *a priori*.

The most potent in practice, and the most troublesome in theory, of all the causes which may affect general prices are movements of general confidence, enterprise, and credit. They are the creatures of opinion, And the prevalence of the opinion that a fall in the gold price of silver will lower prices may certainly cause such a fall, when it occurs, to check confidence, enterprise, and credit, and may thus somewhat lower the average level of prices.

But concessions of this kind do not make me the less inclined to require a rigid proof that the fall in the gold price of silver (or what I maintain are on almost the same footing for this purpose, the gold price of the rouble and the South American dollar) can create and maintain a lower level of prices than would 'directly' otherwise have existed; 'directly', that is otherwise than by its action in modifying one of the seven elements which I have enumerated under the quantity theory.

I do not understand that it is seriously contended that the fall in the gold price of silver has itself permanently injured general credit and commercial confidence; if it had done so, that, no doubt, would have been a *vera causa* of a fall in general prices. But I can discover no reason for thinking that it has done so. Of course, if the fall in the gold price of silver had lowered general prices, that might have weakened credit; but this will not help us to reason backwards, and attribute the fall in general prices to a fall of credit, which is attributed to a fall in the gold price of silver. It might, I think, much more plausibly be contended that the fall in general prices is closely connected with the fall in the price of the rouble, for that fall is in a great measure the expression of political and financial anxieties, which have undoubtedly contracted commercial credit, and thus lowered general prices.

Prof. Nicholson further maintains that a fall in the price of those goods whose values are governed by the course of Oriental trade will lower general prices in England.[16] But on the contrary I contend that if for the sake of argument we suppose a fall in the prices of one class of goods brought about by causes specially affecting them, the immediate effect will be to set free purchasing power which will raise the price of other goods. For instance, it is a well-established fact that in times when the cost of bread was a larger part of the working man's expenditure than it is now, a fall in the price of the loaf set shopkeepers in general to increase their stock-in-trade, knowing that there would be more money to spend on other things and that there would be a rise in prices.[17] Perhaps the popular way of stating the change was not strictly accurate; but the result was in accordance with the scientific doctrine that, other things being equal, a fall in the value of some classes of goods diminishes the volume of the currency that is required for transacting business with regard to them, and leaves more free for other business, and therefore raises the prices of other goods. I do not deny what Prof. Nicholson says about the general tendency of wages in different trades

[16] Cf. Nicholson, *Money and Monetary Problems*, pp. 362–72; the reference to those 'who hold that Ricardo and Mill said the last word on the theory of international trade' (*ibid.*, p. 371) seems to be a reference to Marshall who had defended the doctrines of the older economists on several occasions before the Commission (*OP*, pp. 170, 176) and even in letters to *The Times* (15, 30 January 1889).

[17] Marshall's argument cannot be found in his evidence given to the Royal Commission but it relies on the income effect of a price change in a staple commodity he later discussed in the *Principles of Economics*, London, Macmillan, 1st edn 1890, 8th edn 1920, as inspired by a hint from Giffen. A full discussion is given by Michael White, 'Invention in the Face of Necessity: Marshallian Rhetoric and the Giffen Good(s)', *Economic Record* 66 (192), March 1990, pp. 1–11.

to seek a common level, but it is obvious that this is a comparatively slow process, slower than that which I have just dealt with.[18] The result, I hold, is that this process, so far as it operates at all, will act in the opposite direction to that which he attributes to it. For the sudden fall in the first class of goods having set currency free to raise the prices of other goods, the levelling tendency which he describes is likely to raise the prices of goods which enter into Oriental trade, and bring back the general purchasing power of gold to that level which is indicated by the relation which the volume of the English currency bears to the volume of the business which it has to do, account being taken of the prevailing habits and methods of payment and of business transactions generally.

30 June, 1888. ALFRED MARSHALL

[18] I have not been able to trace Nicholson's reference to this issue in his *Money and Monetary Problems*; however, it was standard theory at the time and also held by Marshall as a long-run proposition. However, the time taken for such a result to be achieved in the labour market was far longer than the adjustments Marshall tended to assume in the value adjustments associated with international monetary transactions. For example, he argued that 'the gold price of the rouble will adjust itself almost instantaneously to the ratio which gold prices bear to rouble prices' (*OP*, p. 773).

ITEM 3

Material associated with Marshall's work for the Royal
Commission on Labour 1891–1894

INTRODUCTION

On 27 March, Marshall received a letter from Arthur Balfour, the nephew of the then Conservative Prime Minister, Lord Salisbury, inviting him to join the Royal Commission on Labour.[1] The setting up of the Commission had been announced by the Prime Minister during the previous February, because of a need to investigate a number of important issues in labour relations which had come into prominence during the late 1880s. Many of them arose from what is now described as the 'new unionism', that is, the replacement of the older, skilled craft unions with their generally conservative outlook on self-help and industrial disputation with the more militant, strike prone unskilled labour unions, of which the dockers were an outstanding example. The Commission's *Final Report* in 1894 concisely summarised the issues with which it was concerned in the following way:

(1) What are the leading causes of modern disputes between employers and employed; out of what conditions of industry do they arise; and what are the effects upon them of organisations on their side?

(2) By what means of institutions can they be prevented from arising, or if they do arise, can they be most pacifically settled without actual conflict in the shape of strikes or lock-outs?

(3) Can any of these causes of dispute be wholly or partially removed by practicable legislation, due regard being had to the general interests of the country?[2]

---

[1] Arthur Balfour to Alfred Marshall, 23 March 1891, Marshall Archive 1/2.
[2] Royal Commission on Labour, *Fifth and Final Report*, London, HMSO, 1894, Cmnd 7421, p. 8.

The reasons why Marshall was invited are not difficult to guess. He was a Professor of Political Economy at a leading university, an authority on labour questions[3] and, moreover, one sympathetic to the worker's cause in many respects. The last was not unimportant, since the twenty-seven Commissioners appointed included seven trade unionists from both the new and old side of the spectrum, and the selection of Commissioners was designed to achieve as balanced a cross-section of the community as possible. The reason why Marshall accepted the invitation has been succinctly put by Pigou. As a 'tireless collector of realistic detail' Marshall would have 'eagerly welcomed the opportunity of serving on the Royal Commission on labour, on which he came into close personal touch with many representative work people and employers of labour'.[4] Marshall himself, in correspondence and elsewhere, later described his work on the Commission as one of the greatest educational experiences he had ever enjoyed[5] though little of the direct impact on his work is apparent.[6]

Although Marshall devoted a very substantial amount of time to the Labour Commission by attending a substantial portion of its sittings[7] and by undoubtedly reading much of its massive documentation, there

---

[3] In December 1889, Marshall had initiated discussion on 'How has the Power of Trade Unions to influence rates of wages and hours of labour been affected by the social and economic changes in recent years', at the London Political Economy Club, a meeting which Balfour had also attended (see *Political Economy Club, Minutes, Members' Attendances and Questions*, London, 1899, p. 30). Earlier that year, Marshall had addressed the Cooperative Congress with a speech sympathetic to working men to which much publicity had been given in the press. Publication of the *Principles* in July 1890 and the reviews it received clearly established him as the leading British economist at the time, if that had not been established before.

[4] Pigou, 'In Memoriam', in *Memorials of Alfred Marshall*, ed. Pigou, p. 85.

[5] Alfred Marshall to Benjamin Jowett, 20 October 1891, to F.W. Taussig, 4 October 1895, to Edwin Cannan, 21 April 1906; Marshall, *Industry and Trade*, preface, p. vii; 'Alfred Marshall: Professor of Political Economy at Cambridge', in *Alfred Marshall. Critical Assessments*, ed. Wood, Vol. I, pp. 148–51.

[6] For a discussion, see Peter Groenewegen, 'Alfred Marshall and the Labour Commission', *European Journal of the History of Economic Thought* 1(2), 1994, pp. 288–92

[7] Marshall's attendance record at sittings was almost the perfect median, twelve commissioners attended more, thirteen fewer sittings than he did. He attended a grand total of sixty-two sittings out of a possible total 151. He attended all seventeen sittings of the Commission as a whole; thirty-eight out of forty-six sittings of Group B (devoted to transport and agriculture and to which he had been appointed) and four and three sittings of Groups A and C respectively. A detailed summary of his attendance record is given in Groenewegen, *A Soaring Eagle: Alfred Marshall 1842–1924*, p. 362 and n.*.

have been only very few studies of his work in this area. Keynes, in his memoir, largely ignored this part of his life. The one small paragraph devoted to it notes the Labour Commission as an interruption to writing Volume II of the *Principles*; an opportunity for Marshall to gain contact with 'the raw material of the subject' and, following Mary Paley Marshall, Keynes indicated that Marshall had 'played a big part in the drafting of the Final Report. The parts dealing with Trade Unions, Minimum Wage and Irregularity of Employment were especially his work'.[8] Since then, Ray Petridis has looked at the influence of Marshall's service with the Labour Commission on his attitudes to trade unions,[9] Robin Matthews included Marshall's work with the Commission as a significant part of his centenary evaluation of Marshall and the labour market,[10] while this editor has systematically discussed Marshall's contributions to the Commission both in a specific study devoted to the topic[11] and as part of his treatment of Marshall's role as adviser to governments.[12]

The general introduction to this collection has already stated that Keynes deliberately omitted material from the Labour Commission because Marshall being a member of the Commission rather than a witness, it was impossible to identify or separate his contributions from those of the Commissioners as a whole.[13] This is undoubtedly true in a formal sense. However, as he indicated in his memoir in the passage quoted in the previous paragraph, and as Mary Paley Marshall advised him while he was editing Marshall's official papers,[14] there were some parts of the Commission's *Report* to which Marshall had a special claim, even though Marshall himself believed it could never be exercised. Furthermore, even though as Commissioner he was unable to present

---

[8] Keynes, 'Alfred Marshall 1842–1924', in *Memorials of Alfred Marshall*, ed. Pigou, p. 52.

[9] Ray Petridis, ' Alfred Marshall's Attitudes to and Economic Analysis of Trade Unions', in *Alfred Marshall, Critical Assessments*, ed. Wood, Vol. III, pp. 480–507, esp. pp. 487–8.

[10] Matthews, 'Marshall and the Labour Market', in *Centenary Essays on Alfred Marshall*, ed. Whitaker, pp. 14–43, esp. pp. 14–15 and n. 1, 17–18, 31–2, 41.

[11] Groenewegen, 'Alfred Marshall and the Labour Commission'.

[12] Groenewegen, *A Soaring Eagle: Alfred Marshall 1842–1924*, pp. 360–71.

[13] *OP*, preface, p. v.

[14] Mary Paley Marshall to J.M. Keynes, 22 March 1925: 'I believe that the whole of VI, "Irregularity of Employment" was practically his and especially its §3, pars. 227–244, and §7 of II on the effects of Trade Unions . . . I remember Alfred saying that he should have liked to reprint VI just as it stood, but that he thought he had no right to do so' (Keynes Papers, King's College, Cambridge, RES/2/41).

his own opinions to the Commission in public,[15] he was able to get his name into the record by the diligence of his questioning. Keynes's problem about including Marshall's work for the Labour Commission can therefore be partly resolved by taking those parts of the *Final Report* which Marshall privately to his wife had claimed substantially as his own and by reprinting his questions to witnesses together with the answers they elicited. It is this approach which has been adopted, and the remainder of this introduction is devoted to a discussion of the material selected from the vast mass of material of the Labour Commission volumes.

MARSHALL'S CONTRIBUTIONS TO THE COMMISSION'S *FINAL REPORT*

Preparation of the *Final Report* by the Commission was a collective affair. Recommendations were prepared after the vast amount of evidence the Commission had gathered was reviewed in stages. This involved sub-division of the material into eight topics into which the review part of the *Final Report* is divided. These were: conditions of labour; associations and organisations of employers and the employed; relations between employers and the employed; conciliation and arbitration; limitations of hours of work by legislation; irregularity of employment; a labour department and labour statistics; and the employment of women. Apparently these reviews were initially drafted by Lord Devonshire as Commission Chairman undoubtedly with the assistance of the secretariat and the summaries of the evidence it had already prepared. These drafts were then, from time to time, submitted to the Commission as a whole, discussed and amended by the Commissioners, and then revised 'to make them as far as possible impartial statements of the facts, opinions and arguments with which they were intended to deal'.[16]

---

[15] Presumably, like Tom Mann, who was both commissioner and witness, Marshall could have presented himself as an expert witness on the subject. His private input would have come in deliberations over the wording of the *Final Report* and in discussions with fellow commissioners on recommendations at the conclusions of sittings.

[16] Royal Commission on Labour, *Final Report*, p. 7. The extent of the objectivity this method actually achieved was admitted in the *Minority Report* signed by four trade union commissioners, and almost certainly drafted by Sidney Webb.

Marshall was undoubtedly involved in the drafting process at this stage. However, on Mary Paley Marshall's recollections, Marshall had particular responsibilities with respect to a sub-section of Part II on trade unions as to their general consequences, and for the whole of the topic of irregularity of employment, which became Part VI of the review.[17] Given his recognised expertise on these topics as shown in his published writings,[18] Lord Devonshire may have easily assigned their preliminary drafting to Marshall, with the assistance of the Commission's secretariat. Such a division of labour was perhaps also practised with other Commissioners having special expertise on specific topics to which the work of the Commission had been devoted.

The two segments of this part of the *Final Report* specifically identified as written by Marshall by Mary Paley Marshall when she was advising Keynes in his editing task of *Official Papers*, are reprinted here. The first of these is quite short and deals objectively with claims about the advantages and disadvantages of trade unions as put to the Commission by the employer and employee representatives who appeared before it. The final paragraphs contain opinions with a specific Marshallian flavour. In paragraph 87, the distinction between community concerns and the concerns of individual trades, and the defence of the Commission's concentration on the second because it was more amenable to 'thorough' analysis and avoidance of superficiality is

[17] Keynes's addition of material on the 'minimum wage', which was mentioned previously, refers to only a small contribution in terms of space but significant in terms of outcome. On this topic, the *Final Report* is exceedingly brief in stating its opinion: 'We do not think that it has been seriously maintained on either side that the remuneration of work or rate of profit, or maximum and minimum wage rates in the general field of labour, should be fixed by law' (*Final Report*, p. 104). In the *Principles*, Marshall subsequently endorsed this Commission's view, largely on practical grounds, and because the only experience with minimum wage legislation was in Australia (see Marshall, *Principles*, 8th edn, 1920, pp. 714–15 and n. 1). However, some discussion of minimum wages occurs in the material on trade unions attributed to Marshall, and is reproduced below (pp. 95–6).

[18] On trade unions, these included the chapters in Part III of *Economics of Industry*, London, Macmillan, 1879, and the final chapter devoted to trade unions (Book VI chapter III) of the then newly published *Elements of the Economics of Industry*, London, Macmillan, 1892. As Ray Petridis has argued (in the reference cited in n. 9 above) Marshall had prepared a draft on the subject for the Commission, preserved in the Marshall Library, but ultimately this was not used by it. It is reproduced here as Item 3c. Marshall had discussed irregularity of employment and remedies thereto in evidence prepared for Royal Commissions in the 1880s (especially to the Gold and Silver Commission, in *OP*, pp. 90–7) and in his well-publicised Address to the Industrial Remuneration Conference in 1885.

typical of Marshall as is the explicit spelling out of the dangers this
method implied.

> In order to take a complete view of the whole question it would be nec-
> essary to consider not merely the effect of the action of trade unions and
> employers' associations upon the workmen and employers engaged in
> particular industries, but in addition, the effect of a highly developed
> system of such organisations upon the interests of the community at
> large and upon the wage-earning classes generally, whether unionists or
> non-unionists.[19]

The appeal to competition in the subsequent paragraph as a safeguard for
maintaining industrial efficiency is likewise a Marshallian touch on the
topic.[20] Prior to the publication of the *Final Report*, Marshall had prepared
a Memorandum on trade unions (which is reproduced below as Item 3c)
which he evidently hoped would be incorporated in the *Final Report*.[21]

Part VI of the *Report* on the Irregularity of Employment is also not
difficult to ascribe to Marshall. He had a long-standing interest in the
topic, discussed it before the Gold and Silver Commission and had published an address and an article on it during the 1880s.[22] Section 1
(reproduced below pp. 98–104) on causes of the irregularity of unemployment, in particular the segment on causes of business fluctuations,
reflects much of the content of these earlier contributions by Marshall
though other parts reflect the evidence before Committee B and, more
generally, the Commission sitting as a whole.[23] The special case of

---

[19] See below, p. 96. Marshall later attempted such a broader assessment of trade union consequences in the final chapter of the *Principles*, 8th edn, 1920 (esp. pp. 706–14).

[20] Marshall's strong belief in the virtues of competition as a regulator of anti-social behaviour is
a noted feature of his work, despite his equally forthright criticism of aspects of competition.
See, for example, *Principles of Economics,* 1st edn, 1890, Book I, Chapter I, pp. 5–8; 8th edn,
1920, pp. 5–10; 'Social Possibilities of Economic Chivalry', in *Memorials of Alfred Marshall*,
ed. Pigou, p. 342.

[21] Below, pp. 287–95, especially the introductory draft covering note by Marshall (p. 287).

[22] In particular, Marshall's Address to the Industrial Remuneration Conference in 1885 which
specifically dealt with remedies for irregular employment, and his paper, 'Remedies for
Fluctuations of General Prices', published in the March 1887 issue of the *Contemporary
Review*. His evidence to the Gold and Silver Commission in 1887 likewise discussed problems
of unemployment and their remedies (*OP*, pp. 90–7), as had the earlier Memorandum (1886)
written for the Royal Commission on the Depression of Trade (*ibid.*, pp. 8–11).

[23] The causes of business fluctuations associated especially with the credit system had been
addressed in Marshall's *Economics of Industry,* jointly written with his wife, paragraphs of
which Marshall reproduced in his evidence and some other writings. He likewise raised such
questions when examining witnesses, for example, below, pp. 153–4.

riverside labour in London on which much evidence was taken before both Group B, of which Marshall was a member, and the Commission as a whole, can also be ascribed to him. Marshall himself questioned Mann on some of the aspects of his plan, its similarities with that provided by Charles Booth, and would have been very capable to draft this section of the *Report*.[24] Section 3, as its paragraph 227 suggests, follows the pattern of Section 1, and many of its remedies acceptable to the Commission are similar to those proposed by Marshall in some of his earlier writings.[25] Other of its paragraphs are also typically Marshall, as, for example, the reference to 'chief element of mischief' in paragraph 233. This section also deals with minimum wages as part of the possible remedies to irregular employment in certain trades (paragraph 239), hence bringing it within the ambit of the subjects attributed to her husband by Mary Paley Marshall. Likewise, the discussion of municipal socialism as a remedy for unemployment was a topic in which Marshall was well versed, and which he strongly criticised when seen from this perspective only.[26]

MARSHALL'S EXAMINATION OF WITNESSES

Item 3b reproduces Marshall's questioning of a number of selected witnesses, together with their answers. Marshall's questions were, after all, his own work, and in style and tone often exhibit much of the man. His approach to witnesses also varies considerably, as illustrated in the friendly, very sympathetic and almost deferential treatment of Ludlow (below, pp. 129–32), of Giffen in his treatment of the American statisticians (below, pp. 239–44) and of fellow Commissioner, Tom Mann, on the connection between the eight-hour day and increased employment (below, pp. 159–71). The degree of freedom in this questioning appears to have only been constrained by a pre-arranged division of labour

---

[24] Below, evidence taken from Tom Mann, especially Q. 3202–8, pp. 153–4.

[25] See his 'How Far Do Remediable Causes Influence Prejudicially (A) the Continuity of Employment (B) the Rate of Wages', in *Report of the Industrial Remuneration Conference*, London, Cassell, 1885, pp. 176–9.

[26] See Royal Commission on Labour, *Final Report*, HMSO, London, 1894, §246 (below pp. 119–20), and some of his questioning of witnesses, for example, Ben Tillett Q. 3508–603, 3658, Sidney Webb, Q. 4342–5; below pp. 213–14, 282 respectively.

among the Commissioners present to concentrate on topics within their field of experience in the examination of the more important witnesses. Moreover, as is general practice in the conduct of Royal Commissions, the Chairman for the day commenced the questioning of each of the witnesses and also, as Marshall himself recalled,[27] occasionally intervened to calm an examination when it became too heated or to put frustrated witnesses at ease again.

The selection of witnesses needs some explanation. It has concentrated on witnesses who appeared before the Commission as a whole rather than the specific industry witnesses who appeared before the three Groups into which the Commission had divided its work. Ben Tillett's examination (below, pp. 275–86) is the only example of the latter included, and that only because of the range of issues covered by Marshall's examination, the prominence in labour history of the witness (one of the leaders of the 1889 Dock Strike) and his earlier association with the Marshalls.[28] Much of the evidence Marshall extracted from other witnesses before Group B tended to be more narrowly focussed, seeking out specific points on topics within the Commission, and, not infrequently, his own terms of reference.[29] Space constraints made it therefore necessary to omit this part of Marshall's questioning even though its inclusion would have been able to shed light on the truth in Beatrice Webb's charge that Marshall tended to intimidate working-class witnesses to get them to say what he wanted to hear.[30]

---

[27] Marshall wrote about this to Benjamin Jowett, 4 November 1891, saying how excellently Lord Derby kept the witnesses within appropriate bounds; a matter confirmed by Tom Mann in his later *Memoirs* (London, The Labour Publishing Co., 1923, pp. 100–1).

[28] Marshall had entertained Ben Tillett at home for dinner on the occasion of his talk on the Dock Strike to the Women's Social Discussion Society at Newnham College (November 1889). Tillett's later *Memories and Reflections* (London, John Long, 1931, p. 160) indicated Marshall was 'anxious to assess the economic meaning of our great struggle', that is, of strikes and the resort to them under the new trade unionism.

[29] Examples are his questions in relation to women's work on barges, and his interest in women's labour more generally. See Peter Groenewegen, 'Alfred Marshall – Women and Economic Development: Labour, Family and Race', in *Feminism and Political Economy in Victorian England*, ed. Peter Groenewegen, Aldershot, Edward Elgar, 1994, Chapter 4, esp. pp. 89–91.

[30] Beatrice Webb, 'The Failure of the Labour Commission', *Nineteenth Century* 36, 1894, pp. 17–18, in which Marshall, Balfour and Pollock are presented as academic 'dialecticians' who tried to lead working-class witnesses 'by skilful questions into some logical inconsistency'. Her private diary (entry for 24 December 1892, *The Diary of Beatrice Webb*, ed. Norman and Jeanne McKenzie, London, Virago and London School of Economics, 1983, Vol. II, 1892,

The seven witnesses appearing before the Commission sitting as a whole whom Marshall questioned were, in the order in which their evidence given to Marshall is reproduced: J.M. Ludlow, the Christian socialist and labour historian; Tom Mann, the dockworkers' leader and fellow Labour Commissioner; Sidney Webb, the Fabian socialist writer and member of the London County Council; Charles Booth, the businessman and social investigator; E.R.L. Gould, the American statistician; Sir Robert Giffen, the statistician and economist; and H.M. Hyndman, the socialist writer and leader of the Social Democratic Federation. Their questioning by Marshall was selected for inclusion on the following grounds. First, as eminent witnesses, familiar to Marshall through their work and often personally as well, their answers have a general interest beyond their particular expertise. Secondly, they are representative of the type of witnesses the Commission attracted: working-class leaders (Ludlow, Mann), socialist theorists (Webb, Hyndman), leading statisticians (Gould and Giffen) and social investigators and reformers (Charles Booth). Only employers' representatives, of whom a substantial number appeared before the Commission, are excluded from the sample. Thirdly, Marshall's questioning of many of these witnesses tended to be prolonged – that of Mann and Webb is in fact by far the longest – thereby giving a greater degree of continuity to the material which, after all, are only extracts selected from a very substantial mass of oral evidence. Last, and most importantly, the issues covered by the witnesses sample many of Marshall's special interests and areas of expertise in that they deal with minimum and fair wages, the eight-hour day, irregularity of employment, progress, competition and productivity, working-class improvement, adequacy of labour and industry statistics, municipal socialism, women and child labour, the views of the classical economists, the desirability of government intervention, housing policy, industrial disputation, conditions of work, conciliation and arbitration and cooperation, to name the more important. They therefore form a representative sample of his questioning by capturing the spirit of that questioning over fairly prolonged periods when dealing with very articulate witnesses.

pp. 25–6) added Leonard Courtney, her brother-in-law, to the 'dialecticians' on the Commission. This contrasts with Marshall's own account of the treatment given to working-class witnesses by the Labour Commission in evidence he gave to the Aged Poor Commission (*OP*, p. 209, Q. 10,202).

The context of the questioning is clarified by the extensive editorial notes to the evidence. These provide cross-references to evidence reproduced and not reproduced, documents presented to the Commission by the witness or, when appropriate, references to their writings. Interruption of Marshall's questioning by other commissioners sometimes including the chairman for reasons mentioned earlier, are likewise clearly indicated in the degree of detail required. Enough information is hopefully provided in this way to allow readers to enjoy this significant sample of Marshall's ability as Labour Commissioner in gathering information from witnesses.

AN UNPUBLISHED DRAFT FOR THE *FINAL REPORT* OF THE LABOUR COMMISSION

The Marshall Library at Cambridge contains relatively little of direct relevance to Marshall's work with the Labour Commission. Exceptions are some of his correspondence and this one draft Memorandum on 'Disputes and Associations within Particular Trades Considered in Relation to the Interests of the Working Classes in Other Trades'.[31] The paper, originally housed in Box 6(6), is undated, but its explanatory introduction (below, p. 287) suggests it was written during the drafting of the Commission's *Final Report* some time in 1893. Given the references to an already fairly well-defined structure of the *Report* and the incorporation of extracts from it in proof, Marshall's document was probably prepared in the final months of 1893, after his return to England for the October term from summer holidays spent in Europe (Colfosco in the Tirol). Whether it was actually submitted for this purpose is not clear. There are no annotations on this draft apart from those he made later.[32]

The document itself is sub-divided in paragraphs identified by letters

---

[31] A scrapbook of newspaper cuttings dealing with Marshall (prepared by his wife and preserved in the Marshall Library) ignores the Labour Commission despite the fact that the work of the Commission, sometimes with special reference to Marshall, was frequently reported in *The Times* and *The Economist*, both of which the Marshalls read regularly.

[32] These are indicated in the notes, below, for example nn. 7, 9 and 10 (below, pp. 291–2). At the conclusion of the MS he wrote (dated 11 October 1923), 'I am not likely to make a new study of Trade Unions; and without it any considerable use of this paper would be unwise.'

rather than numbers, the manner of identifying paragraphs in the sub-sequent 'Fiscal Policy of International Trade' (see below, pp. 306–7). Its topic falls firmly within the terms of reference of the Labour Commission: labour disputes and their consequences and the role therein of associations such as trade unions. Its reproduction here seems useful since it is a clear adjunct of Marshall's official work for the Labour Commission which so far has not been published. Once again, editorial notes assist in placing it in its specific context, partly to show its status as a supplement to Marshall's involvement in the drafting of the Commission's *Final Report* cannot be in doubt. As Petridis[33] has pointed out, it also adds to our knowledge of Marshall's all too few written views on the relative merits of trade unions.

---

[33] Petridis, 'Alfred Marshall's Attitudes to and Economic Analysis of Trade Unions', pp. 487–8.

TEXT

II

ASSOCIATIONS AND ORGANISATIONS OF EMPLOYERS AND EMPLOYED

7. Representations made as to the injurious or beneficial Effects of Trade Unions.

84. The employers who have given evidence have usually recognised a legitimate province for trade unions in bargaining as to wages and hours and watching over the general interests of their members, and admitted that strong organisations, acting within those limits, tend on the whole to improve industrial relations, and to make their members act in a better informed way and a more reasonable spirit. This is a subject which will be considered more in

detail in the following part of this Report.[1] But the view has also been put forward, even by those who hold these opinions, that the action and rules of trade unions have been in some respects prejudicial to the efficiency of production and to the industrial prosperity of the country.[2]

85. The allegations upon this point are as follows:

(1) That trade unions have a growing tendency to interfere with details of business, and so to take away that concentration of command which is necesary for successful management, and hamper employers in carrying on their business according to the methods which they believed to be best.

(2) That trade unions often misjudge the true position of affairs, and by ill-timed and excessive demands, as well as by placing employers under apprehension of these, discourage enterprise and further investment of capital in this country, to the detriment of all concerned, including ultimately, if not immediately, their own members. As a proof that trade unions have done less than is frequently believed in the way of raising wages, it is contended that wages have in many cases risen as much and as fast in unorganised as in organised employment. It is urged that the extension of machinery in manufactures, and the development of railways and steam navigation, are the main causes of the increased demand for labour and consequent advance of wages during the last half century.[3]

(3) That though organisations may tend to diminish the frequency of industrial conflicts, they extend their range; and that such conflicts on a large scale, especially in industries which supply raw material, are far more injurious to associated and dependent trades than are more frequent conflicts on a small scale.

(4) That workmen with a powerful union behind them are apt to become too confident as to their position, and to think that they cannot be discharged or punished, and so are likely to become

---

[1] *Final Report* of the Labour Commission, §90–2 (not reproduced here).

[2] Marshall's draft Memorandum for the *Final Report* of the Commission, 'On Disputes and Associations within Particular Trades Considered in Relation to the Interests of the Working Classes in Other Trades', reproduced below, esp. pp. 293–5, had dealt with this topic.

[3] This was a view also reflected in Marshall's *Principles* in the final chapters dealing with 'progress', present from the 1st edition onward. See 8th edn, 1920, esp. pp. 671–8.

indolent, careless or insubordinate, especially in cases where the foremen are unionists with divided allegiance.

(5) That the action of trade unions has a tendency to bring about a uniformity of wages and hours, both as between individual workmen and as between different localities; and that by insisting on a minimum wage which, in effect, determined the standard, and by seeking to abolish overtime and piece work, they are reducing workmen to a dead level of enterprise, discouraging work of more than average merit, and taking away from individual workmen the motive power of ambition and self-interest. A few independent workmen, in evidence, concurred with this view, which was put forward by many employers in trades where the unions are most powerful. It is further alleged that the uniformity of wages and hours which trade unions sometimes enforce as between different localities, tends to injure localities possessing less natural advantages in favour of those possessing greater ones, because the former places can only compete with the latter by means of lower wages (usually compensated for by lower cost of living) or longer hours.[4]

(6) That trade unions injure trades by the rigidity of their rules. It was said, for instance, that if, at the commencement of the iron ship-building industry, the workmen had enforced their present rigid limitations on apprenticeship, the industry, for want of sufficient hands, could never have developed to its present dimensions. It is also pointed out that the rigid organisation of the different trades in some cases gives rise to a too complete division of work, which prevents men from doing work for which they are qualified and which would at times conveniently fall to their lot, thus occasioning bad economy in production. This was the cause of the recent 'demarcation' disputes between various trades in the North of England. In the case of some trades connected with shipbuilding, it was alleged by representatives of 'unskilled labourers' employed in them, and admitted by those of the skilled workmen, that the organisation of the

---

[4] This is one of the issues addressed in Marshall's preserved draft for the *Final Report* reproduced below, pp. 290–3.

latter, as a rule, makes it difficult for those men who start in the lower classes to rise to the higher kind of work, even if they have acquired sufficient experience and skill. The rule or practice of refusing to work with non-unionists may also be mentioned under this head.

86.   The representatives of trade unions claim that, even supposing it to be possible to prove some drawbacks, the existence of these societies is essential to preserve the independence of workmen and to protect their interests. In proof of the benefits of trade unionism they point to the position of workmen in various trades before and after these associations were formed, and maintain that the action of trade unions has secured improved wages, hours and conditions of labour not only directly for organised workmen, but indirectly for those not organised. The refusal of unionists to work with non-unionists is often justified on the ground that the latter without cost to themselves have reaped the benefits secured by the sacrifices and exertions of the organised workmen.

These witnesses deny that their organisations tend to enforce a dead level of wages, except with regard to 'minimum rates', and represent that in almost every trade there are found many men in receipt of wages above what is known as the 'minimum of the trade', in consequence of their being better workmen. They deny, then, that these organisations take away the motive of self-interest and therefore diminish the energy of the individual workman, but they allege that, in the interests of large bodies of workmen, it is necessary to some extent to restrain by rules the natural desire of the individual workman to work overtime, for the sake of higher wages, and other modes by which he might seek to benefit himself at the cost of his fellow workmen as well as of his own health and strength, or that of his offspring. This action is not, they maintain, injurious in the long run to the general interests of industry, inasmuch as association raises the '*morale*' of the employed, disciplines and educates them, and by rendering their work more intelligent, increases its value. It is necessary, they say, that their rules shall place a check upon the natural temptation of the employers to excessive competition with one another at the expense of the employed, by way of cheapness of goods and speed of production attained by overwork and under-pay, but on the whole, and in the long run, these rules by their steadying effect, are good for the trade of the country. They allege that the action of strong trade unions is beneficial even to employers by preventing them from destroying each other through unlimited competition. It is usually admitted on both sides that strong organisations have been proved by experience to be almost a condition precedent to the success of voluntary methods or institutions of conciliation and arbitration, so far as these institutions extend beyond the limits of a single establishment to a whole trade or district, and will be no less essential for the purpose of any further development of such institutions, whether voluntary or created by the action of the State.

87.   We have not lost sight of the fact that the concern of the community, as a whole, with regard to the strength of organisation of employers and employed, and the agreement between them which it may be possible to obtain, is not limited to the effect of such strength or agreement upon the interests of these classes. Our attention has chiefly been devoted to the interests of employers and employed in particular trades, not because these interests are the only ones which need to be considered, but because such a course appeared to be most in accordance with the special reference made to us, so far as it went, than that it should cover a very wide area. Even when thus limited our task remained a very heavy one. It should also be observed that specific evidence can more easily be obtained with regard to the interests of particular industrial groups than as to the general interests of the public. In order to take a complete view of the whole question it would be necessary to consider not merely the effect of the action of trade unions and employers' associations upon the workmen and employers engaged in particular industries, but in addition, the effect of a highly developed system of such organisations upon the interests of the community at large and upon the wage-earning classes generally, whether unionists or non-unionists.[5]

88.   We have thought it desirable to call attention in a concise manner to the fact that agreement between a strong combination of employers

[5] This conformed to the Commission's own view of its role with respect to trade unions. Since working men wanted to organise in such unions, the Commission's recommendations should ensure that such organisations 'be rendered most conducive to public policy' with special reference to the maintenance of industrial peace (*Final Report*, §66, not reproduced).

on the one side, and workmen on the other, may possibly be attained, in some cases, by measures which tend to repress individual energy and freedom of industrial experiment. One result of such agreement may be to place difficulties in the way of new men endeavouring to work their way into a trade by means of methods of production not sanctioned by the existing trade custom. Such changes, though not immediately convenient to the employers and employed already engaged in a trade, have often, in the end, by enhancing the efficiency of production, conferred important benefits upon the public, and have contributed to the ultimate prosperity of the trade itself. The danger is not great in those trades which produce chiefly for foreign markets, nor, again, in those which are subject to intense foreign competition in the home market, but even in these trades, the growth of international combinations may make it possible to subordinate public to private interest. In the numerous trades in which foreign competition does not exist, or is not very keen, the pressure and the support of a strong union of workmen may give cohesion to associations of employers. Hitherto such associations have seldom been able to impose their collective will upon all the employers – engaged in a trade. There appears, however, to be some danger that, under the pressure of, and in alliance with, strong combinations of workmen, such associations might obtain virtually the same power with regard to fixing prices and determining the methods of production that similar associations have derived in earlier times from legal monopolies.[6]

89.   It must further be pointed out that unskilled labour, which it is more difficult to organise, may eventually suffer if skilled trades become close corporations, and, in any case, it is clear that a complete combination of employers and employed in any one great trade for the purpose of raising prices to an artificial level would, if successful, not only impose a tax upon the public but upon those engaged in related and dependent industries. It is obvious also that, where unionists are very strong, their refusal to work with non-unionists may altogether deprive the latter of employment; especially if they are for one reason or another unable to earn the minimum wages fixed by the trade union.

---

[6] This issue was addressed in Marshall's preserved draft for the *Final Report* reproduced below, esp. § C, D, pp. 289–90.

We desire to point out the existence of these various disadvantages which a very complete organisation of industry might involve, without expressing any opinion as to the proximity of dangers of this kind. Having called attention to the existence of such dangers we are free to pass to an examination of the influence which associations of employers and employed exert upon relations of these classes, and of the methods by which questions arising between them are settled.

VI

IRREGULARITY OF EMPLOYMENT

1. CAUSES OF IRREGULARITY OF EMPLOYMENT
2. SPECIAL CASE OF RIVERSIDE LABOUR IN PORT OF LONDON
3. PROPOSALS AND OPINIONS WITH RESPECT TO PREVENTIVE REMEDIES OF A GENERAL CHARACTER, INCLUDING THE EXTENSION OF EMPLOYMENT BY PUBLIC AUTHORITIES

1.   Causes of Irregularity of Employment[7]

211.   The subject with which this branch of our inquiry is concerned is irregularity of employment and the means suggested for preventing it so far as it is due (1) to industrial fluctuations affecting a trade, or trade district as a whole; (2) to chronic excess of the supply of labour over the demand for it in particular industries; (3) to the ordinary vicissitudes of work in a normal state of trade. It must not be forgotten in considering this question, that although the distress due to want of employment is often very visible and very deplorable, the great mass of the working classes have fairly regular employment. There are many who think that irregularity of employment is on the whole less in proportion to population now than in earlier times, although manifested on a more striking scale in particular localities, and rightly attracting a larger share of public notice.

---

[7] The subject matter of this section of the *Final Report* was later treated by Marshall in his *Money, Credit and Commerce*, London, Macmillan, 1923, Book IV, Chapter 2.

212.   Our attention was specially called to the evils resulting from the great oscillations between activity and stagnation to which many of the trades of this country are subject. The demand for products of many kinds is sometimes so considerable as to put in motion all the productive forces and cause new capital to enter into production, and at other times so slack as to throw a large part of such productive forces into partial idleness, although the proportion of the increase or decrease to the normal demand may be found on examination to be comparatively small. The alternating periods of brisk and dull trade are felt alike by skilled and organised workmen and by the comparatively unskilled and less strongly organised classes who are employed under skilled artisans in manufacturing processes, and also in the transport of goods by land and water. In the case of skilled and well organised workmen slackness of trade makes itself felt in the form of increased pressure on the out-of-work benefit funds of their trade societies, of short work, and ultimately, it may be, of reduced wage rates. In the case of the unskilled and less organised men it takes the form of increased competition for employment and low wages. In both cases the total earnings of the men in the trade are smaller, and, except in so far as the situation is met by working short time, more of them are out of employment.

213.   Fluctuations of trade in this country are due to a variety of causes, the chief among which may be briefly indicated here.[8] The majority of these periodical changes are connected in some way with the state of commercial credit, and the willingness or unwillingness of business men to embark on new ventures. The state of credit in every country depends each year more and more on the general conditions of business throughout the world. Great Britain is specially sensitive to these international influences, because so much of her capital is invested abroad, and in ships trading to foreign countries, and because so many of her most important industries depend largely on foreign demand. When credit is good and loans are easily obtained, much of the capital invested abroad goes to pay for orders to manufacturers in this country. The result is that production is

---

[8] As shown in the introduction, this topic had been systematically treated by Marshall in his *Economics of Industry*, Book III, Chapter 1. It was later discussed in *Money, Credit and Commerce*, Book III, Chapter 3, which reproduced segments of the earlier treatment.

greatly stimulated, especially of those things which are needed for the extension of railway, shipping, building, and manufacturing businesses. On the other hand, contraction of credit causes an immediate falling off of foreign demand; and any considerable falling off of foreign demand, especially if it takes producers by surprise, tends in turn to weaken credit. A shrinkage in the demand for our manufactures from particular quarters may of course have its origin in events not connected with the state of international credit, such for instance as wars, revolutions, failure of crops, the setting up of hostile tariffs, and so forth, and these events may of themselves bring about fluctuations of trade in this country. But the most formidable industrial fluctuations are those which are caused by the action and re-action of the state of credit on foreign demand, and of foreign demand on the state of credit. The industries which are most immediately and markedly affected by those alternating movements of confidence and distrust are (1) those concerned with ship-building and the manufacture of machinery of all kinds; (2) iron and steel smelting and working; and (3) the coal-mining industry, which is intimately connected with those above mentioned. Less directly, but seriously, a diminution of profits and wages in these great branches of industry must, of course, affect most of the trades which produce for home consumption.

214.   Seasons and weather are in some industries a cause of continual fluctuation of employment. Wet or frosty weather, the amount of which is variable in this climate, affects work which is carried on in the open, such as dock-work, building, brickmaking, shipbuilding, house and ship painting, and agricultural operations. Some kinds of work in England are also affected by the closing of the Baltic and Canadian ports in winter. Gas-making is an instance of work which gives much more employment in winter than in summer. Many industries connected with clothing and small luxuries are much more fully occupied at some seasons than others, by reason of change of temperature, or national customs, such as holidays and festivals.

215.   In some industries, chiefly those connected with clothing, the sudden changes due to the caprices of fashion are responsible for serious fluctuations of work. More than one experienced witness stated before the Commission that the desire for novelties both at home and in all parts of the world was an increasing difficulty, and

that manufacturers are no longer able to 'make to stock' as they used to do. Changes in fashion are so rapid that orders are withheld to the last possible moment and then come with a rush. This is a fruitful cause of alternate slackness of work and over-work, and one from which some of the weakest and most unprotected classes of workers suffer severely.[9]

216.   Another source of fluctuations of work, which seems at present to be growing rather than diminishing in importance, is the extent and duration of modern trade conflicts. When these conflicts occur in industries that supply raw material, such as coal, the dependent industries are reduced to a partial idleness for which they are in no way responsible. Strikes or lock-outs in a particular branch of industry may have a similar effect upon the remaining branches of the same industry.[10]

217.   Some industries are affected by the competition of foreign products in the home market; others by the competition of other countries in foreign markets, or by that of other districts in this country possessing greater natural advantages; or again by the introduction of new and more efficient processes. Changes due to these causes, although resulting in the displacement of labour, are often of too permanent a character to come under the head of fluctuations proper. Agriculture is in this country the most conspicuous instance of an industry in a condition of long-continued depression.

218.   The distinction between irregularity of employment due to trade fluctuations, and that which arises from chronic excess of the supply of labour over the demand for it in particular industries, corresponds to a distinction between temporary and permanent excess, and to this extent is a question of degree. Depressions of trade produce a relative superfluity of labour for a longer or shorter time, which, however is re-absorbed again when trade becomes good; and in the meantime a powerful trade organisation can do much in the way of tiding its members over the slack period by means of funds accumulated during the previous busy period. Where an industry is declining without any

---

[9] Marshall himself raised this issue with witnesses, for example, below p. 154, Q. 3208.

[10] This issue was also addressed in Marshall's preserved draft for the *Final Report*, below §G, pp. 290–1.

apparent hope of recovery, the temporary condition passes into the permanent. In such an industry the supply of labour may be permanently in excess of the demand, unless it drifts away in equal measure elsewhere. The latter qualification is an important one and is closely connected with a distinction which may be drawn, as respects superfluity of labour, between unskilled, and more or less skilled, occupations.

219.   Certain of the so-called 'sweated' industries cannot be classed as unskilled, and yet suffer from a permanent over-supply of labour, not so much by reason of competitors for work pressing in from outside, as because in the case of these industries all methods have to a great extent been superseded by others, and the workers are competing by an obsolete system of work against new and improved processes. Work at reasonable rates of remuneration is no longer to be had in them, and the workers as a body are too shiftless and too feeble to abandon the occupation to which they are accustomed and seek employment elsewhere. Such occupations are generally local, carried on at home or in domestic workshops sometimes under insanitary conditions, and are often more or less hereditary in a family. In some cases the state of workers in these trades is aggravated by the competition of a very poor class of alien immigrants, content with a still lower standard of living; but apart from this, the inflow of competitors from other occupations does not appear to be the main source of the over-supply of labour in them.[11]

220.   On the other hand an industry may be in a state of permanent depression, and yet not suffer from any superfluity of labour, simply because the workers in it drift away to other occupations as rapidly as the area of employment contracts. In such a case the pressure will be felt not in the declining industry itself, but in other occupations into which the workers dislodged by this or other causes overflow, competing with those already engaged in them and perhaps compelling them to compete in their turn with workers on a yet lower level. Agriculture affords a striking illustration of this. The demand for

---

[11] The Commission had heard evidence from Charles Booth on the 'sweated' industries when sitting as a whole (*Fourth Report*, Whole Commission, pp. 369–88); Marshall's part in this is reproduced below, pp. 214–20.

agricultural labourers continues to diminish, yet there has been a concurrent diminution of the supply in most rural districts. Instead of staying in the country they come to the towns, where, by their superior physical or moral capacities, they often displace the town-born labourers, and drive them down to lower and more precarious modes of existence.

221.   While unskilled workmen have not the resource afforded to many classes of skilled workmen by the accumulated funds of powerful trade organisations, it is on the other hand in some respects easier for the ordinary unskilled labourer than for the skilled artisan as such, to find other employment when work fails him in one district or branch of industry. In fact for some purposes unskilled labourers may be classed together as belonging to a single industry. This circumstance, however, cuts both ways, for while it makes it easy for a vigorous and efficient labourer to find a job, it also makes it easy for the less vigorous and less efficient labourer to be displaced and forced to compete for employment on a lower level. The result is that all unskilled labourers being as it were in possible competition with each other, the most incapable in body or feeble in character (and these include many who have once belonged to a skilled trade but from helplessness or incompetence or misfortune have been unable to maintain themselves in it) get sifted down, and crowd into certain ill-paid occupations at the bottom of the scale, in which their mere superfluity of numbers renders employment irregular and precarious. Lower still beneath this class of the casually employed and largely recruited from it, comes that of the unemployable.

222.   The third cause of irregularity of employment, namely, the ordinary vicissitudes of work in the normal state of a trade, has this characteristic mark, that it implies no superfluity of labour at all, whether temporary or permanent, in relation to the demand of the trade as a whole, but only a failure to bring together the employer seeking workmen and the workmen seeking employment. Even in skilled and highly organised industries, and in good times, there will always be a margin of unemployed workmen looking out for a job, and at the same time work waiting to be done if they only knew where to find it. Many trade unions act as effective agencies, so far as their own members are concerned, in helping them to obtain employment, not

only by supporting them while temporarily out of work, but by assisting them in their search for work.

2.   Special Case of Riverside Labour in Port of London

223.   We received much evidence, to which it is desirable to make special reference, with regard to one most striking case of employment made irregular by a combination of all the three causes already enumerated. This employment, at once fluctuating, insufficient, and industrially ill-organised, is that of the labourers employed in riverside work in London, more especially those employed by the Board of Directors, usually known as the 'Joint Committee', which controls some of the principal docks, including those in which there is the largest proportion of entirely unskilled labour. It is fluctuating partly on account of the weather, and also to a considerable extent owing to the fact that the import of some raw products, such as wool, food stuffs, or timber, is much larger at one season than another. It was, and in a less degree is still, uncertain and insufficient, by reason of the great excess of applicants for work in relation to the work to be done. And lastly, its irregularity is yet further increased by the difficulty of directing labour to the places where it may be required, consequent upon the great space covered by the docks and wharves, and the number of different managements.[12]

224.   Recent reforms at the London docks have done something to mitigate the evils complained of so far as these result from the excessive competition for employment. Under the old system prior to the strike of 1889 there were in the various docks a certain number of men permanently employed, or with a preference as to employment, but the greater part of the daily labourers were engaged at the dock gates to meet the daily fluctuations of trade. This was done by the contractors or the foremen of the companies, and still is done by the foremen to the diminished extent to which such casual labour is required. These casual labourers were employed and paid by the day, or rather by the hour; for, before the strike of 1889, there was no guarantee that a man would be taken on for even so short a space as four consecutive

---

[12] Some of this evidence is reproduced below, notably that by Tom Mann (pp. 136–40, esp. Q. 2275–93) and Ben Tillett (pp. 275–86, Q. 3642–70).

hours. No attempt was made to organise the work by drafting labourers systematically after finishing work in one dock, to begin new work elsewhere. The plan was to allow them to look for 'jobs' on their own account. It was to the convenience of contractors, foremen, and superintendents to have, as a rule, at the gates of the docks a much larger number of men than could certainly be employed on any day, so as to leave a safe margin for contingencies. Even after some improvements for the better had been made, one witness of experience (Colonel Birt) estimated that on the morning of the day on which he gave evidence (3rd November 1891) there might have been some 5,000 or 6,000 persons who had tried and failed to get employment at the gates of the various docks.[13] We believe, however, that since that date there has been considerable further improvement in the regularisation of labour at the docks. The evils of this casual system, which have been compared to those of gambling or indiscriminate poor relief, were vividly depicted by many witnesses. It was contended by some that much of this class of work was done by men incapable of steady and consecutive labour; that at the same time the irregularity of the work itself bred irregularity of habits, and that a vicious circle was thus formed. It was represented on behalf of the employers that the evils of the system were partly due to customs or prejudices among those employed; to the rule, for instance, that stevedores should work at loading but not at discharging ships, and to other divisions of labour enforced by the trade organisations or the custom of the port of London. It is, however, alleged, on the other hand, that the task of loading certain classes of cargo requires much more skill and judgment than that of unloading, and that the division is not altogether an arbitrary one. It was also stated that the difficulty of moving men from dock to dock to meet the exigencies of employment was due, in part, to the reluctance of the men themselves to fall in with such arrangements. In a like manner, an experienced witness attributed much of the evil of the London riverside system to the custom of paying wages by the day instead of by the week, and thus attracting to the work persons of casual temperament; but added at the same time that the custom

---

[13] Reported in minutes of evidence, Group B, Vol. I, Cmnd 6708–V, 1892, Birt's answer to Lord Hartington, Q. 7100.

was so strong that it could not be departed from, even if employers desired it, without the greatest difficulty, although in Liverpool payment to dock labourers of exactly the same class is made by the week.

225. The great strike in 1889, and the public attention excited by it, had the effect of calling the attention of the Joint Committee to the evils of the existing system. Subsequently the directors have taken steps to extend considerably an organisation of workers into (1) permanent labourers, (2) labourers having a preferential claim to employment. There is some conflict of opinion as to the extent to which it may be possible to carry this system, but there seems to be no doubt that the reform, so far as it has gone, has tended to diminish the former evils and to convert London dock work into something more of a regular occupation. In some London docks, and in some other ports, dock labourers are hired and paid, not by dock companies, but by the shipowners. In such cases, looking at the matter in connection with regularity of employment and apart from the questions which have arisen between unionists and non-unionists, a useful part may be played by such institutions as the 'free labour office' created by the Shipping Federation in the Albert and Victoria Docks for the registration of the names of labourers who desire employment. A witness, who superintended the labour at these docks, suggested (1) that wages should no longer be paid by the day; (2) that shipowners should in each place ascertain the number of dock labourers required, and keep a bureau of registry whereby men could be obtained by any shipowner desiring them for a day's work and half-pay when out of work. The witness said that a system of permanent engagement of this kind would 'pay the shipowner better, and be more satisfactory for the men', and, if thoroughly carried out, would 'free the docks from casual labour, and that is where all the difficulty and trouble is'.[14]

226. Mr. Charles Booth, whose elaborate inquiries have made him the chief authority upon this and other subjects connected with labour in East London, expressed in evidence the opinion that no legislative

---

[14] An example is Ben Tillett's evidence reported in minutes of evidence, Group B, Vol. I, pp. 137–58, esp. pp. 137–8, 153–7.

intervention was required in the matter, but that it would be possible for a committee of practical men to devise a scheme by which a system of transference of labour from one department of the docks to another according to the vicissitudes of work might be established, with the result of more completely, if not entirely, substituting permanent for casual labour.[15] A scheme of a larger kind proposed by Mr. Mann for the creation of centralised docks for the port of London under public management is printed as Appendix VI. to this Report.[16]

3. Proposals and Opinions with Respect to Preventive Remedies of a General Character, including the Extension of Employment by Public Authorities

227. We have now to consider the various remedies of a general character which were advocated in the course of the evidence submitted to us as likely to remove or modify the causes of irregularity of employment. Some of these remedies are of comparatively limited scope, and in dealing with these it will be convenient to follow as far as may be the classification of causes already adopted. There will still remain to be noticed the more ambitious and comprehensive views of those who hold that the true remedy, not only for irregular employment, but for other evils supposed to be inherent in the present system, is the extension of State and Municipal employment in the sphere of productive industry; and the substitution, more or less gradual, of public authorities in the place of private employers competing with one another for profit.[17]

228. Granting that it is out of our power to control the foreign demand for our manufactures, or to regulate seasonal variations, and

[15] That is Charles Booth's evidence to the Commission, Committee B on 26 January 1892; 2 August 1892, minutes of evidence, Group B, Vol. III, Cmnd 6894–VIII, 1893, Q. 24727–5030, esp. Q. 24,853–5,030; and Appendix 155 appended to that Report, pp. 562–88.

[16] Mann's scheme, 'State and Municipal Control of Industry', was reported with the *Final Report*, Appendix VI, pp. 178–85, esp. pp. 184–5, which contained his specific proposals.

[17] This was essentially Mann's position, both in his Appendix to the *Final Report* of the Commission (see n. 16 above) and in his evidence. This opinion was also reflected in the evidence given by other 'socialist' witnesses, such as Webb (Q. 3869–71, 4318–46, 4392–7) and Hyndman (Q. 8428–32, 8437, 8446–62), some of which is reproduced below, pp. 209–14.

the caprices of taste and fashion, it is not denied that failure to forecast changes of demand may and does aggravate the industrial fluctuations which they produce.[18] Accordingly there is one remedy which,
so far as practicable, is strongly advocated by men of all shades of
opinion, viz., that Government Departments or other public authorities should do more than is at present achieved in collecting and
spreading information, enabling both manufacturers and workmen
to forecast, better than is now possible, the course of trade and
coming demands in this and other countries. Proposals for the
improvement of the present machinery for the collecting and publishing of statistics will be considered in a subsequent part of this
Report. It has also been suggested that public authorities, imperial
and local, might, without prejudice to the public interest, so regulate
their purchases as to give employment to clothing and other trades
during the dull seasons.

229.   Again, so far as industrial fluctuations are the results of strikes
and lock-outs, it is clear that anything that will tend to obviate trade
conflicts, especially trade conflicts on a large scale in industries that
supply raw material will *pro tanto* help to remove a cause of irregularity of employment.

230.   Another class of remedies gives rise to wide differences of
opinion. Some contend that much of the evil of industrial fluctuations is due to excessive competition between private employers, who
in their haste to make money are inclined to be over-speculative
when trade is brisk, to work overtime, take on new hands, enlarge
their works, or open new ones, and, generally speaking, to produce
with feverish rapidity beyond the extent of the actual demand. Thus,
the work which might have been spread over a long period is con-
densed into a short one; the markets are flooded with goods, and this,
of itself, tends to bring on a collapse of credit and stagnation of
trade; works have to be closed, and men discharged, and the chief
effect of the period of lively trade, so far as workmen are concerned,
may have been to call into the industry more hands than it will, on the
average, support. It is on this view that the action of trade unions in

---

[18] This reflects Marshall's position on non-remediable causes of irregular employment in his
Address to the Industrial Remuneration Conference, Report, pp. 176–9.

restricting overtime, piece-work, and the admission of apprentices to trades, is often defended. Such action, it is maintained, tends to make work more constant and regular, to cause the demand to some extent to adjust itself to production, and to prevent too many additional hands being drawn into industries in prosperous times. Reasons of a similar kind are also urged in favour of the limitation of hours of labour by law.[19]

231.   Others, however, contend in opposition to these views, that the activity of the legitimate speculator, whose interest it is to make excess in one place compensate scarcity in another, tends on the whole to diminish trade fluctuations; that to prevent production by artificial hindrances from adjusting itself with as much elasticity as possible to the variations of demand would injure British industry, and in the long run be contrary to the interests of the workmen themselves; and that the stringency of Trade Union rules in connection with piece-work and overtime tends to increase irregularity of employment for reasons already indicated.[20]

232.   Abolition or restriction of overtime and piece-work, rules as to apprenticeship, and legal limitation of hours of labour are, it has already been pointed out, advocated not only as tending to diminish the violence of trade fluctuations, but also as distributing the work to be done at any given time more equally among the workmen engaged in any particular trade, and so diminishing the number of men out of work in that trade. This view, which is very commonly held by trade-unionists, is, no doubt, open to considerable criticism upon the lines indicated in the previous parts of this Report already referred to.[21] Those who oppose the view, contend that it is by no means clear that such a policy will ultimately benefit even the workmen in the industries where it is adopted; and that though it may bring an immediate advantage to existing workmen in particular

---

[19] Some of these issues are reflected in the evidence given by Tom Mann reproduced below, pp. 133–72, some of which was strongly contested by Marshall in his questioning (esp. Q. 3209–301, pp. 155–69).

[20] This was addressed by the Commission in §21 (not reproduced here). It addressed the issue of overtime which it depicted as bad for the employee's health, an encouragement to uneven employment, and a possible means of exploiting labour in depressed times.

[21] That is, *Final Report*, Section 2, §14–23, esp. §22 (2) (3).

trades, it may also, by limiting output, diminish the demand for the work of other industries, and so lessen both real wages and the amount of employment in the country taken as a whole.

233.   We are brought in connection with this matter to the consideration of the case of those occupations in which there is, independently of trade fluctuations, a large habitual excess of supply of labour over the demand for it. This has already been indicated as being the second chief cause of irregularity of employment, the first chief cause being that of trade fluctuations. It has already been pointed out that the occupations which suffer from chronic superfluity of labour fall into two classes; the first consisting of certain 'sweated' trades, not indeed requiring a high degree of skill, but yet not wholly unskilled; the second comprising unskilled occupations, requiring no special strength, ability, or steadiness, of which ordinary dock labour may be taken as the typical case. Of the sweated trades there are some which perhaps could not afford to pay the workers sufficient wages for a reasonable maintenance, even if they were less crowded, because to increase the cost of production would be to destroy a demand which lives only on excessive cheapness. Even where over-supply of labour is itself a chief element of mischief, it is in these trades due in a comparatively small degree to influx of workers from outside, except in particular employments which suffer from the competition of alien immigrants.

234.   It has often been suggested of late years that the immigration of destitute aliens should be prohibited altogether. Mr. Charles Booth,[22] however, expressed the opinion that such a measure would not do very much towards relieving the pressure of competition in the 'sweated' trades generally, and that the best hope of dealing, by any definite action, with the problem that these trades present lay in applying increased pressure of administrative sanitary requirements to the owners and occupiers of the places where they are carried on, in such a way as either gradually to transform their character, or else slowly to squeeze them out of existence with as little hardship as possible to those who are engaged in them.

---

[22] In his evidence to the Commission sitting as a whole (*Fourth Report*, Whole Commission, 30 November 1892). Prohibition of immigration of destitute aliens was, however, proposed before the House of Lords Committee on 'sweating', as indicated in the summary of this evidence prepared for the Labour Commission and appendix to the *Report* (Appendix 85, p. 171).

235.   The problem of over-supply of labour in the lowest grades of quite unskilled employment is of a different character. These occupations are constantly recruited from those who have failed to maintain a position higher up in the scale. The workers in them are to a great extent the shiftings down of the whole industrial population. Misfortune is sometimes the cause of their failure; and especially hard is the case of the honest and industrious workman whom want of employment deprives of proper nourishment, and want of proper nourishment renders incapable of efficient work, and who is thus dragged down lower and lower within the vicious circle of an ever-increasing physical and moral degradation. But large numbers of the casually employed are where they are, because they do not possess the qualities or the training required to keep them in a better position.

236.   The spread of education has already done something, and may be expected to do still more, to reduce the numbers of this class and of the 'unemployable' class below them; and of course everything which increases the demand for workers in the higher grades of industry will also benefit those in the lower. Emigration may be a remedy in certain cases, but one serious objection to it from the present point of view, is that the shiftless and incapable are not fit to emigrate, and if the emigrants are to be drawn from a better class, this is in effect to remove the more capable in order to lighten the pressure of competition on the less capable. Another suggestion is to attack the evil by legislation tending to keep rural labourers on the land. The position of the agricultural labourer will be considered in a subsequent part of this Report.[23]

237.   The last-mentioned proposal aims at removing the pressure of competition which comes from above. Another plan is to try to remove it from below, in other words, to limit the number employed in any over-crowded occupation by eliminating the least capable among the over-numerous competitors for employment. This is the essence of the reform already mentioned as having been adopted at the London docks.[24] The effect of such a reform is to give more regular work to a limited number of men, but at the expense of

---

[23] This was done in the *Final Report* (§354–62) and in a separate review (prepared by Little) and printed on pp. 195–253 of the *Final Report*.   [24] Above, pp. 104–7, §223–6.

throwing others upon the general labour market. For this reason not all the witnesses on behalf of the dock labourers were fully agreed to the value of these changes to the class taken as a whole; and some of them were led by this line of thought to advocate compulsory limitation of hours of labour, so that work, and consequently wages, may be shared more equally, and to demand such institutions as municipal workshops, in order to give work to those thrown out of employment. In the special case of the London docks the balance of gain certainly seems to lie on the side of a smaller number of men being employed in a regular manner, instead of a larger number in a casual manner. But the general issue (which in its broader aspects, concerns skilled trades as well as unskilled) is one of no small difficulty, and raises (among others) the important questions (1) how is the limitation to be effected; (2) how far can it be applied without doing more harm than good; (3) what is to be done with those who are eliminated and deprived of their former means, precarious though they might be, of earning a livelihood?

238.   As to the first of these points it must be observed that in the particular instance of the London docks, the limitation of numbers was effected by the action of the employers. The history of the struggle at the London docks, and of the events which followed it, is instructive in many ways. Among others it affords an interesting illustration of the difficulties which have been indicated in a previous part of this Report,[25] as besetting all organisations of workers in occupations where the supply of labour is habitually in excess of the demand, and is, moreover, being constantly recruited from outside. It is natural that any union that may be formed in such an occupation should seek to secure regular employment and steady earnings for its members by restricting the number of the men employed. But it is powerless to effect this unless it can both limit its own members, and at the same time exclude non-unionists from employment altogether. The very large number of those who would have to be excluded in these circumstances would seem to make the policy hopeless of success. An attempt of the kind appears actually to have been made at one time by the Dockers' Union; but it failed, and was speedily abandoned and

---

[25] *Final Report*, Part II, Section 3, 'In What Industries Trade Unions have been the most successful and the reverse', esp. §77–9 dealing with unskilled labour.

disavowed. The Union did indeed secure, as one of the terms of settlement at the end of the strike of 1889, an undertaking that no man
should be engaged for less than four consecutive hours. But the yet
more important reform of organising the labourers into classes of
permanent men, and men with a preferential claim to employment,
was the work of the Dock Companies themselves, acting, no doubt,
more or less under the pressure of public opinion. Had the attempt of
the Union been successful, the right of labour at the docks would
have become the monopoly of a close corporation. The system actually adopted, though it creates privileged classes of workmen, leaves
their privileged position dependent on continued efficiency and good
conduct, and does not relieve them entirely from outside competition, though it considerably diminishes the amount of casual
employment.

239. The number of workers engaged in an occupation might be
restricted by indirect as well as by direct means. Thus it is contended
that the proposal to establish a minimum legal wage, advocated by
one or two witnesses, would, if it could be enforced, and if the
minimum were fixed high enough, have the practical effect of limiting the number of those employed in low grade occupations at the
cost of depriving of employment such as were incapable of earning
the minimum. And similarly, in the skilled trades, a powerful union
which included a large majority of the workmen in an industry, and
was strong enough to exclude non-unionists from employment, to
abolish piece-work, and to insist in every case upon payment of a
minimum standard wage, might probably control the numbers in a
trade even without placing any restriction on the admission of
apprentices.

240. This brings us to the consideration of the second question: how
far the limitation of numbers in individual trades can be applied as a
means of obtaining better employment for those in it without causing
even greater harm to those excluded from it, and to the community
generally? If the most skilled trades limit their numbers, and push
down large numbers into the grades below, and these again push
down others into a still lower grade, and so on, then there must be left
an ever-increasing number of persons struggling for employment in
the lowest grades, and the average wages of the whole body of the

working classes must be lowered. If the process of 'squeezing out' is applied to the lowest grades also, the number of unemployed will be largely increased.

What then are the principles that should guide public opinion and public policy in reference to particular cases in which this question arises? Without committing ourselves to a definite expression of opinion on this point, we think the following view worthy of mention. Any limitation, it is argued, of the numbers in a trade, which causes the same amount of work to be done by fewer men, is a public gain, provided it does not overtax their energies. For the men who are not wanted can produce other goods, or meet other wants of the public; and the working classes will receive their share of the increased national income. But if the limitation of numbers in the trade does not lead to increased efficiency on the part of those who remain, and simply raises the price of work in that trade by making it scarce, the result can hardly fail to be a public loss. More generally, if the limitation of numbers in a trade is effected by requiring a high standard of efficiency in it, the public will get more and better work in return for increased wages, and there will be a general gain. But if it is effected by preventing people from doing work which they are able to do, or would easily learn to do, the public will lose more than the trade will gain.

In the case of the docks, the smaller number of men working more regularly, and probably better fed, seem to have done the work quite as well as the larger number who had more regular employment before the great strike, many of whom were no doubt men of weak physique or character, unfitted to do good work in any trade. But if the reverse had been the case, and the real cost of labour had been increased, this would have meant injury to the public interest, and (inasmuch as the amount of employment available at a given time is not a fixed quantity, but bears a relation to the real cost of labour) the exclusion from employment of men for whom work might have been found.

241.   The third question, viz.: What is to be done with those persons who are eliminated from overcrowded industries, practically forms a branch of the general question of the 'Unemployed'? Whatever may be the advantages to the working classes or to the public generally of

the reorganisation of any industry with a view to the reduction of the number of persons employed in it, whether such reorganisation be the effect of the action of employers or of trade unions or other agencies, the immediate result of the operation will be to add to the number of persons who have little or no employment a certain number of persons who have hitherto earned a precarious livelihood by more or less casual employment. As we have already stated[26] we do not consider that, strictly speaking, the scope of our inquiry extends to the problem of the best methods of dealing with the effects of want of employment, closely allied though the problem is with the subjects with which we have had to deal.

242.   One of the methods most frequently advocated is that of the employment of the class of labour in question by municipalities or other local authorities, in productive industry in municipal work-shops or on agricultural farms. It is urged that even if such institutions could not be made self-supporting, work of this kind would, at any rate, be better than poor law relief or objectless labour in work-houses, and would afford a possible means of training and regenerating the class in question. In order to prevent confusion with regard to the way in which we have treated the matter, it must be observed that the extension of direct employment by public authorities has been advocated by different witnesses upon different grounds. It has been advocated by some witnesses chiefly with a view to the organisation and relief of surplus unemployed labour. It has been advocated by other witnesses upon the ground that, for the more general reasons hereafter indicated,[27] it would be better that, so far as possible, even that labour which can usually find employment, subject to temporary irregularities, in the ordinary course of industry, should be employed by public authorities rather than by private individuals or companies. It is necessary for the purposes of our inquiry to distinguish these two aspects of the question. The employment by public authorities of ordinary labour in necessary work does, in our opinion, fall within the scope of our inquiry, in view of the fact that it is advocated as a

[26] In the introduction of the *Report*, p. 8, the Commission indicated that it believed detailed examination of schemes for the employment of the temporarily employed 'lay outside their terms of reference and was more a subject associated with extension of modification of the existing Poor Law'.   [27] *Final Report*, §248 (reproduced below, pp. 121–3).

remedy for evils existing in the relations between employers and employed. We shall therefore proceed in the sequel to examine the arguments adduced for and against such a policy.

But the employment by public authorities of surplus labour, for the produce or services of which there is no existing demand, is so closely connected with the subject of the Poor Law and its administration that it seems to be excluded from the scope of the inquiry with which we have been intrusted.[28] We think that, if an investigation of the practicability of municipal workshops or agricultural home colonies with this end in view should be considered desirable, it should be undertaken separately in general connection with the subject of the reform of the Poor Law. We may point out that much valuable information upon this subject is to be found in the 'Report on Agencies and Methods for dealing with the Unemployed' recently issued by the Labour Department of the Board of Trade (1893).[29]

243.   The part played by many trade societies in meeting the irregularity of employment due to the ordinary vicissitudes of work in a normal state of trade, by helping their members to find vacant places, has already been mentioned. In the opinion of some witnesses, irregularity of employment might be greatly reduced if public authorities were to undertake a similar function by organising and supporting local registries and offices in connection with a central office, for the purpose of directing labour of all kinds to the points where it is most required.[30] We received evidence with regard to some of the labour registries promoted by local and philanthropic effort, which appear to have worked with success in obtaining employment, especially for such workmen as possess any special aptitude or skill. One such registry has been opened by private enterprise at Ipswich, another at Egham, a third in London by the Chelsea vestry; and others have recently been established by various municipalities. The evidence tended to show that up to a

---

[28] See n. 26 above.

[29] This dealt with the provision of labour registries as a method of transmitting information about vacancies and those looking for work.

[30] The Commission gathered a great deal of evidence on their operation in Britain, the Empire and in Europe. It likewise received considerable documentation on the subject.

certain point such institutions may do good service; but that great results are not to be expected from them. They seem least useful where the urgency is greatest, that is to say, in times of depression, and in the case of the less competent workmen. The suggestion was made that their value might be materially increased, if a network of such offices could be established all over the country in organic connection with each other, and perhaps with a central institution in London, and placed under public control. One reason given for thinking that such registries should be under public control, and that their cost should be defrayed out of the rates, was that workmen will not put confidence in institutions governed by capitalists or employers, and employers will not put confidence in institutions governed by trade unions. This difficulty might be met, in some cases, by registries formed and controlled by joint committees from chambers of commerce and trade councils, but most witnesses seemed to think that the better plan would be that of municipal registries. Some of the most serious and violent of recent industrial conflicts have been those arising between seamen and dock labourers and shipowners from the alleged attempt of trade unions to monopolise the supply of labour, and the counter movement on the part of the shipowners associated in the Shipping Federation, to establish registry offices of their own through which to obtain a supply of men independently of the unions. The recent strike at Hull turned upon this point. It is open to consideration whether local offices under the control of public authorities, not connected with any special industry but forming part of a general system, and carefully guarded from any undue influence on either side, might not be of some avail to obviate quarrels arising from this cause, while securing the advantages of registration for employment. In this connection it should be observed that the Labour Exchange (Bourse du Travail) in Paris, which was established in the year 1887, with a view to bringing together employers in search of workmen, and workmen in search of employment, appears to have fallen into the exclusive possession of a labour party of advanced views, by whom it was used for political purposes, with the result that the Government of France felt it necessary in the summer of 1893 to suppress it, at any rate for the time being.

244.   We have lastly to notice the proposals put forward by those for whom the only thorough-going remedy, both for irregularity of employment and for dissensions between employers and employed, lies in making an end of the present competitive organisation of industry, and substituting for it a 'collective' organisation based on public ownership of the means and instruments of production, and the control and management of industrial operations by public authorities. It is necessary to draw a distinction between the ultimate aim of those who hold these opinions and the actual measures advocated by the more cautious among them for present adoption.[31] The realisation of the entire collectivist programme would involve a reconstruction of the whole fabric of political, social, and private life in this country, and we do not feel that any practical purpose would be served by an attempt to consider it here. But so far as the immediate programme is confined to a tentative extension of State and municipal activity in fields of industry now wholly or partially occupied by private enterprise, it may be desirable to indicate in a general manner the arguments that have been urged for or against such an extension, especially in respect of their bearing on the subject now before us.

245.   Socialists will naturally be inclined to regard with favour any step which appears to constitute an advance in the direction of their ideal; but it is possible that others, who by no means believe in the Socialist ideal, may nevertheless hold that State and municipal employment of labour and control of industry may be usefully carried further than as at present. They may hold this not merely on the ground that certain kinds of work would be better done under public than under private management (which is universally recognised as a valid argument so far as the contention is admitted), but also for the reasons urged by socialists, that greater regularity of employment, and improved conditions of labour will thereby be secured for the workers. It may be added that many, even of those who do not look with approval on the further extension of municipal undertakings in the sphere of productive enterprise, would yet think it right that as much responsibility as possible should be thrown on local bodies, and

---

[31] Probably a reference to the evidence given by Hyndman and Sidney Webb, some of which is reproduced below, pp. 172–214, 266–74.

that they should not be needlessly prohibited from making such experiments as they desire.[32]

246. The policy of extending the field of public employment, not in order that the public may be better served, but for the sake of the workmen employed, and of the working classes generally, though by no means new in unofficial discussions of the subject, for the first time becoming an important factor in practical politics.[33] Such industrial undertakings as are now carried on by central departments or local authorities have hitherto been entered upon because it appeared on general grounds to be more desirable that they should be carried on directly by such public authorities, than indirectly through contractors, or by private enterprise. The matter has usually been considered from the point of view of the national interest, in the case of dockyards and arsenals, or the interest of the local community in the case of gasworks and waterworks. The central government at present carries on no manufacturing industries except those in connection with government dockyards and arsenals. The manufacture of gas and the supply of water are now undertaken by a good many municipalities, but apart from this they have not hitherto employed much labour of the ordinary industrial kind as distinguished from the labour involved in the maintenance of markets, parks, and public institutions, or that employed on roads, pavements, and sewers. Huddersfield is an instance of a municipal authority working a tramway. It is understood that the municipal authorities of Plymouth and Blackpool also now work the tramways. Bristol is the only instance of such an authority owning and managing docks. The administration of docks by public trusts is dealt with *post*.[34] Both the Huddersfield Tramways and the Bristol Docks have for some years shown an annual loss on working. But in the case of the Bristol Docks it was alleged that their acquisition by the Corporation was necessary, in order to save the commerce of the city from decay; while in the case of the Huddersfield Tramways no company could be formed to lease and work the lines which the Town Council had constructed. On this account the Town Council obtained a private

[32] For a detailed discussion of Marshall's views on this subject see Groenewegen, *A Soaring Eagle: Alfred Marshall 1842–1924*, pp. 593–5.   [33] See n. 17 above.
[34] *Final Report*, §250, below, pp. 126–7.

Act in 1882, empowering them to work their own tramways, subject
to the condition that they should lease them to a company, if one
could be found to take them over upon such terms as the Board of
Trade should approve.[35]

247. The evidence submitted to us cannot be said to show that the
workmen employed in the Government dockyards and arsenals, or
by municipalities, in the manufacture of gas, the supply of water,
tram work and dock work, are markedly, if at all, better off than
those employed in similar work in well-managed private establishments. Permanence and continuity of work are, indeed, admitted to
be greater in the Government dockyards and arsenals, especially in
the case of skilled artisans, (though some contend there are special
reasons to account for this); but complaint was also made that the
workmen in these departments received lower rates of wages than
they might have obtained for the same work from outside employers.
As regards the employment of labour in the manufacture of gas, the
supply of water, and on roads, pavements, sewers, and building operations, there seems little to choose between municipalities and private
firms. In 1888 the Huddersfield Town Council reduced the hours and
increased the number of men working on their tramways, making
some but not a proportionate reduction in their pay. It was pointed
out, however, that the wages were distinctly low, 26s. a week for
engine-drivers who had to do their own stoking. The Corporation of
Glasgow insisted, as a condition of renewing the lease of their
tramway lines, upon certain stipulations as to hours of labour and
other matters connected with the treatment of the men employed
being inserted in the lease. It appeared, at the date when the evidence
was given, that the Company had refused to take the new lease upon
these terms, and that the Corporation proposed to obtain powers
(which it is understood they have subsequently received) to work the
tramways themselves, when the old lease came to an end. For the
present the matter rests there. On the whole it may be confidently
affirmed that extension of public employment for the benefit of the
working classes seems to be advocated, not so much from experience
of the way in which public authorities have acted as employers of

[35] These municipal enterprises featured in the evidence of Sidney Webb as questioned by
Marshall, below pp. 211, 213–14, Q. 4325–30, 4342–5.

labour in the past, as from anticipation of what they may be inclined, or compelled by the electors, to do in the future. In this connection the action of the London County Council, in paying their park-keepers and gardeners considerably more than the market rate of wages, is a new departure, commended by some, and equally condemned by others.

248.   On behalf of the general policy of extending the sphere of public employment, arguments to the following effect were laid before the Commission:

(1)   Public authorities depending for their position on a popular vote will be largely responsible to the working classes. In this way these classes will indirectly have a share of desirable control over the conditions of employment. Moreover, such authorities being more open than private employers to the influence of public opinion, are likely to treat those whom they employ with greater consideration; and, not being biassed by desire for high profits, are able to take a more just and impartial view of the claims of labour. The result will be better treatment of the workmen employed by them, in respect of wages, reduction of hours, and increase of their number, with the effect of absorbing some unemployed labour.

(2)   There is reason to think that, if undertakings were brought under the control of public authorities it would be more possible to avoid trade conflicts. For many causes of dissension would be removed, especially the ill-feeling which arises as to the way in which the receipts are divided between different classes of citizens, viz., profit-receivers and workmen, and the latter would, like the civil service, have other means than strikes of representing their grievances and obtaining remedies.

(3)   The consolidation of rival establishments in the hands of a single authority will extinguish the mischievous competition which, by tempting to speculative over-production, aggravates the violence of industrial fluctuations; and will also put an end to the ruinous under-selling of each other by competing employers, which is often carried on at the expense of the employed.

Such consolidation would also make it more possible to

organise and control the supply of labour, and to convert it in some cases from labour of a casual character into one of permanent and continuous nature. It would be possible to know more exactly than at present what the amount of work is, and where labour is required, and to draft labour from one point to another. This was one of the chief arguments urged by Mr. Mann in support of the scheme which he laid before the Commission[36] for the creation of more compact and consolidated docks in the Port of London, to be under the control of public authority.

(4)   The enterprises (most of them in the nature of local monopolies) which would first be brought more generally than at present under public control, such as gas and water works, tramways and docks, employ a class of labour which is composed to a great extent of the less skilled and trained labourers. It is precisely this class which is weakest and least able to organise and protect itself, and which suffers most distress from fluctuations of employment, and sends most recruits into the ranks of pauperism. It would, therefore, be in many ways a public benefit, and even a public economy in the long run, if men of this class were, to a much greater extent than at present, directly employed by public authorities. The great necessity of the day seems to be to find continuous and permanent employment for this class, so far as practicable, and thereby to raise its social standard and self-respect.

(5)   The extension of employment by public authorities would be economically advantageous. The State or municipalities engaging in industrial enterprise, and borrowing on the security of taxes and rates, could raise capital more cheaply than would be possible for private employers; they would also need less to start with so far as private enterprise is hampered by expenses in connection with company promoting, and the obtaining of concessions and parliamentary powers where these are required. A smaller portion of the profits of the undertaking having to go in interest, a larger part would remain to be applied to other purposes, including better treatment of the *employés*. Lastly, the

[36] See n. 16 above.

transference of industrial enterprise from private to public management would save the loss of an immense amount of capital now annually wasted in hopeless undertakings, in struggles between rival establishments, and in litigation.

249.   It must be observed, in connection with the statement of arguments on the other side, that the case of those who desire to extend the sphere of employment by public authorities was placed before us much more fully than the answer to it. We did not think it necessary to hear much evidence in support of those principles of public policy which have hitherto been usually accepted and are well known. It may be sufficient to call briefly to mind the considerations commonly urged in reply to the arguments just summarised:

(1)   A large extension of direct employment by the State or by municipalities would tend to introduce into national and local politics a dangerous element of corruption. It is difficult for public authorities, whose position depends on the result of a popular vote, to combine with success the parts of direct employers of labour and custodians of the public purse. They are, always exposed to the temptation, if they are the employers of a large, and perhaps, the most politically active part of their constituents, to bid for their votes by undertaking to over-pay them at the expense of the rest. It is not desirable that such matters as the wage-rates or hours of work of public *employés* should become decisive questions of politics.

The more just and impartial view of the claims of labour, expected to be taken by employers who are under no necessity of making a profit, might too often come to mean, in practice, the taxing of the community for the benefit of the particular classes of workmen who happened to be in the public service. What was given to them would be taken from others; and the result would be discontent on the part of the less fortunate men in private employment, an increased tendency on the part of labourers to flock to the great centres of population in the hope of sharing the good things that were going, and a demand for ever fresh additions to public works in order to satisfy ever-growing claims.

(2)   It may be conceded that strikes would not be likely to be very

frequent in public establishments in which the conditions of employment were distinctly better than those prevailing in private establishments. No doubt, too, any disputes that did arise between employers and employed would take a different form under Government management. But this gain also would only be secured at the expense of incurring the dangers mentioned in the last section. The record of dockyard constituencies is not of favourable augury for the proposal that coal mines and railways should be 'nationalised' and worked under State management.

(3) Monopoly, either public or private, extinguishes the evils of competition; but with them its benefits also. Single control too has some undoubted advantages in the facilities it gives for the organisation of labour, though even where desirable, it does not follow that the single control should be that of a public authority. But it may be doubted whether a further extension of the work now undertaken by public authorities would provide any real remedy for irregularity of employment. The greater continuity of employment at present enjoyed in Government works is caused partly by their giving only the overflow to private works, thus increasing the irregularity of employment in private trade. Public employment is not generally more regular than that of private firms which have similar work to do; for instance, it is about equally regular in the case of gasworks, waterworks, tramways, and railways. Any additional constancy of public employment obtained by securing a man against dismissal when he becomes idle or negligent is not in the public interest.

(4) The argument that local authorities in taking over the management of gasworks, waterworks, tramways, and docks, would be enabled to provide more employment for just the class that stands most in need of help, seems to overlook the fact that the more capable among unskilled labourers have as a rule little difficulty in finding employment. The class of men who could be advantageously employed as gas stokers, and in connection with waterworks and tramways, are probably able to look after themselves fairly well. A large proportion of dock labourers stand no doubt in a different category. But a municipality would not be

able, any more than private employers, to overcome the hard truths that where the supply of labour is greatly in excess of the demand, regular work is only to be secured for some at the cost of refusing even casual work to others, that a rise in the real cost of labour tends to narrow the field of profitable employment, and that to improve the conditions and increase the remuneration of labour in a poorly paid occupation beyond a certain point, is to expose the very class whom it is desired to help to the competition of better men whom the improved conditions attract from other occupations. It would appear that the extension of public employment for the sake of the employed has as its natural complement the right of every citizen to demand employment from the public at wages sufficient for a maintenance. But to concede this right would be to place the national welfare in jeopardy.

(5) Lastly, the allegation, that employment by public authorities in fields now occupied by private enterprise would be economically advantageous, is strenuously denied, and the contrary maintained. Although capital may be borrowed upon public securities at a lower rate of interest, a definite charge must be provided for the redemption of capital, or such changes as the substitution of electricity for gas or a transfer in the current of trade might leave a community saddled with a debt without corresponding income-producing asset. Moreover, it is contended that the credit of the State and of local communities is good only so long as their debts are small relatively to their resources, and that it would probably suffer material damage if such a policy were carried out; while even now the interest gained by investments in good English railways is very little higher than that obtained from Consols. And though it is doubtless true that private undertakings are much handicapped by the exceptionally heavy legal and parliamentary costs which are levied in England, yet this fact, it is argued, points not to the intrusion by the State into fields of work for which its fitness is doubtful, but rather to the concentration of its efforts on that work of simplifying law and administration, which it alone can perform, and now performs inadequately.

It is further contended that, whatever may be the loss through wasteful forms of competition, the wastefulness of competition is not to be compared to the wastefulness of the inertia of Government Departments, when grown a little old and escaped from the prying eye of public criticism.

If it be proposed that public authorities should undertake works involving the use of a large plant and expensive machinery, it is urged that, in this case, the system would have great disadvantages as compared with one of private enterprise. The motive of self-interest compels the ordinary manufacturer or contractor to use his machinery to the greatest effect, and to search continually for improvements by which it may be made to work more economically. A public body having rates and taxes to fall back upon, is under no such pressure, especially if in possession of a monopoly Wherever competition is removed there is great danger of stagnation taking its place.

It is not denied that public authorities can utilise the progress made by others. New plant put up at the public expense is always up to date; but thence-forward neither officials nor electors are eager to replace it by better plant. Thus it is almost always easy to prove the efficiency of government experiments that have been tried only a few years. But they soon fall behind, and by diminishing the area from which inventions can come, they retard progress in private industry.

250.   Some of these considerations apply with less force to the management by public authorities of a class of undertakings like gas and water works, tram ways, and, perhaps, docks, in which industrial procedure is simple and not much machinery is required, and which naturally lend themselves to local monopoly, than to the management by such authorities of skilled work involving the use of elaborate machinery, and exposed to the competition and vicissitudes of the open market at home and abroad. Others again only apply in any strong degree to public authorities directly elected by popular franchise, and would be less applicable to mixed bodies in the nature of public trustees, some of whom might be nominated by State officials, and others by town councils or county councils or other bodies. Thus it might seem that public trustees of this kind, being independent of

votes, would not be consciously or unconsciously influenced by the desire of obtaining them, while at the same time they would be under a sense of public responsibility and not influenced by motives of private interest. On these grounds it has been represented that docks, for instance, are best managed neither by private enterprise, nor by municipal bodies, but upon the principle of dock trusts. At Liverpool, Glasgow, Dublin, Belfast, and Swansea, the docks are controlled by the Dock Trusts, representing various official, commercial, and local interests. The Liverpool Mersey Docks and Harbour Trust, which is a good example of these bodies, consists of 28 members, of whom 24 are elected by parties who pay annual dock dues to a certain amount, and the other four members are appointed by the official conservators of the Mersey. On the other hand there are some who contend that public trustees are in some respects even less fitted than public officials for managing a great business for long periods together with probity and energy. They consider that such bodies as the Liverpool Dock Board are under exceptional conditions. That board is really in a position of trustees, not for the public, but for the shipping community, and there are special causes which make their work efficient. But the instance chiefly relied on by advocates of the principle was that of the Commissioners for the Victorian railways. The greatest expectations were formed of this Board at the time of its appointment; but in a very few years it was found necessary to abolish it.

251. We must not omit to notice, before concluding our remarks on this part of the subject, the increasing practice on the part of public authorities of inserting in contracts for the execution of works, stipulations as to the wages and hours of the workmen employed, or other provisions for their protection. This practice was to some extent sanctioned by the resolution which was passed by the House of Commons in February 1891, 'that, in the opinion of this House, it is the duty of the Government, in all government contracts, to make provision against the evils recently disclosed before the Sweating Committee, to insert such conditions as may prevent the abuse arising from sub-letting, and to make every effort to secure the payment of such wages as are generally accepted as current in each trade for competent workmen.' It was stated in evidence by a witness

from the building trade,[37] that this resolution had 'brought about quite a revolution in the system of tendering for contacts for the Government', and had exercised a considerable indirect effect upon other contracts and work. In the contracts of the London County Council the principle, it is stated, has been carried still further, inasmuch as the contractor is required not only to pay the recognised rate of wages, but to observe the recognised custom as to hours of work. The Commission were urged by the witness in question to recommend that this last observance should also be required in government contracts. Cases have occurred in which public authorities, insisting upon provisions of this kind, have been unable to obtain satisfactory tenders, but a judicious use of this method of control may possibly be a desirable *viâ media*, in many instances, between the plan of mere business contract, and that of direct execution of works by the public authority. There would appear to be a growing feeling, with which we sympathise, that central or municipal authorities, whether they employ labour directly or indirectly should recognise that low wages are not necessarily economic wages, and, without departing altogether from the test of the value of labour in the open market, should act in the spirit of the most generous employer under existing circumstances. It must not be forgotten, however, that the principle of insisting on liberal wages for all workers, irrespective of efficiency, is liable to abuse, and that, if carried too far, it will not only have the effect of taxing the community for the benefit of the more efficient members of the working classes, but will also increase irregularity of employment for the less efficient, and deprive them of work which might otherwise have been open to them.

[37] Evidence, Group C, Q. 17,405.

3B EVIDENCE

Minutes of evidence taken before the Commission as a whole

Marshall's examination of J.M. Ludlow, CB, 28 October 1892

[Following the questioning of Mr Abraham.]

PROFESSOR MARSHALL

1850. I think you have made a careful study of the conditions of the working classes in England for a longer time than anybody has now alive? – I think I have gone more round the social question than anybody now living, although many persons are far better informed as to particular branches of it.[1]

1851. I think, in conjunction with Mr. Lloyd Jones, you wrote a book on the progress of the working classes?[2] – I did.

1852. That I think was the text book for the subject in all countries for a long time, and might I ask you to give the Commission your general impression as to the changes in the condition of the working classes during the time of your observations? – I think the condition of the working classes has changed immensely, but not so much I am happy to say, as the change in public opinion on the subjects relating to that class. I find now that boys and girls almost fresh from school are at a point of advancement in relation to this question at which in 1884 we could not bring grown-up people to, and were considered heretics and revolutionists for trying to bring them to. I think the change in public opinion on that subject has been something perfectly marvellous. I cannot express it sufficiently. The working class also has developed enormously in intellectual acquirements and habits of business and largeness of outlook, though perhaps they have lost a little of that enthusiasm and spirit of generous aspiration which I think distinguished my working-men friends of the earlier days.

[1] Marshall's high regard for Ludlow was recorded by some working men who visited Balliol Croft in 1901. See Mary Paley Marshall, *What I Remember*, Cambridge, Cambridge University Press, 1948, p. 41. 'He [i.e. Marshall] was enthusiastic about Ludlow and valued his work highly.'

[2] That is, J.M.F. Ludlow and Lloyd Jones, *History of the Progress of the Working Classes, 1832–1867*, London, 1867.

Now the black spots in the country may, I think, almost be counted on the fingers. In former days it was very nearly all black with but a few white spots.

1853.   I understand you to hold that the condition of the working classes has improved very fast, but not so fast as public opinion has as to the proper standard of the condition of the working classes? – I think that is so.

1854.   You divide the progress of the working classes into material and moral progress? – Yes.

1855.   Would you give us generally an account of the material and moral progress they have made. May I ask you to give first the artisans, and secondly the labouring classes? – The material progress of artisans if you ask me for the figures —

1856.   No, not figures. I do not ask for them? – The intellectual progress of the workers has been very great.

1857.   Take the material side first, and speak to the producing power of the wages of artisans? – I have no doubt that the wages have increased very considerably indeed throughout the country. As I say, there are only a few districts in town or country where they are very low indeed. I take, for instance, as one instance, the very vast improvement of the whole class of riverside labourers. I remember the time when in the ballast heaving trade the gangs were contracted for by the publicans, and a sober man had not the least chance. That has been all swept away. In those days also there was a tremendous struggle at the dock gates, which was put a stop to within the last few years by the Dockers' Union.

1858.   When you first knew the working classes, is it now a fact that the question of having merely sufficient wherewith to buy bread was a very important question for them? – I hardly know how to answer your question. I was a member of the Anti-Corn Law League for that matter, and in that respect I certainly went into it, because I thought the price of bread was too high.

1859.   I meant when you first knew the working classes, were not they compelled to spend a very large part of their income on the mere purchase of bread? – Yes; my chief experience of the working classes dates from 1846 for the beginning, but chiefly from 1848. At that time the Corn Laws had been abolished, and I do not think there was that struggle which you speak of.

1860.   Your experience begins later perhaps? – Yes, a little later.

1861.   Do you think that the material improvement has been the more marked in the artisan class or in the unskilled labouring class? – Very remarkable in both, but what is the most cheering feature has been the approximation between the two. At the time when I first knew the artisans there was a broad line of demarcation between them and the labourers, and there was a sort of tacit coalition in many cases between the employer and the labourer; the artisan was equally opposed to both. But since then we have seen the very cheering spectacle (I say this quite apart from any personal characterisation of individuals) of members of the aristocracy of the trade, as it is called, the engineers, coming forward in the most manful manner to lead the unskilled labourers. Mr. John Burns and Mr. Mann, for instance.[3] I can hardly express my sense of the value of that fact in bringing together the different sections of the working classes. Then to go to another instance of the wearing away of petty jealousies: the first working man who was ever a member of a Royal Commission, Mr. Applegarth,[4] who was at that time the secretary of the Amalgamated Society of Carpenters and Joiners, was, I was told, worried out of his place by sheer jealousy, because instead of the working men being proud of having him on the Commission, they were all jealous of him. But at the present day the present Commission is an instance of the total disappearance of that feeling, and the presence of so many working men upon it, shows the better view which has been

[3] John Burns (1858–1918) and Tom Mann (1856–1941) were both leaders of the London dock-workers, after an initial training as skilled metal workers (engineers). Tom Mann was a member of the Labour Commission and appeared as a witness (see below, pp. 133–72). Both were acquaintances of Marshall, who entertained them at Balliol Croft.

[4] That is, Robert Applegarth (1834–1924), one of the leaders of the British Trade Unions, Secretary of the Amalgamated Society of Carpenters and Joiners, member of the Council of the First International, which he left after the Paris Commune; he served on the Royal Commission of Inquiry into the Contagious Diseases Acts, the first worker to serve on a Royal Commission.

adopted by the working men. That, I think you will also see from the proceedings of the Trade Union Congress from year to year.

1862.   You have been speaking of the growth of moral sympathy between the labourer and the artisan classes? — Yes.

1863.   Should you say that the differences between the prosperity of the labouring classes are greater than they were, should you say that the difference between the income of the two classes is as great as it was then? — I have no figures at my disposal to enable me to form an opinion upon that.

1864.   Could you add anything more to the general history of the working classes during your experience; you have spoken of the intellectual improvement? — Yes.

1865.   But could you give a further instance of their advance? — The workmen take a much greater part generally in all social questions, you find them everywhere; you find them in the magistracy, you find them in the town council, and the London County Council, and so forth. They have risen and are rising on every side of the social scale.

1866.   Could you tell us anything of the amusements of the working classes when you first knew them? — I can tell you this, that a vast number of them did not know how to amuse themselves in the least, and during our experience of the Working Men's colleges, amongst other things, we were quite surprised at the inability of many of the genuine working-men to understand fun — literary fun — at all. If something very humorous was read to them they did not take it in the least, and they really had to be educated into the sense of humour. That, I believe, was in a great measure owing to the very depressing circumstances under which they had been brought up from childhood. I am speaking of the time before the repeal of the Corn Laws.

1867.   Do you say they had less humour before the repeal of the Corn Laws than at any other time? — I should think so.

[Examination of Mr Ludlow continued by Sir John Gorst.]

Marshall's examination of Tom Mann, 14–16 November 1892

[Following the questioning of Mr Thomas Burt.]

PROFESSOR MARSHALL

2257.   You say that your position is substantially the same as Mill's with regard to socialism?[5] – Yes, I think so.

2258.   Do you think that he and you lay quite the same stress upon all the different sides? – Perhaps not, I dare not say so much. He would probably be much more cautious than I am.

2259.   The point of agreement was this, was it not, that if mankind could be governed entirely by public spirit, there would be no longer any use in private property? – I think that fairly states his position.

2260.   But that until that time has come we must be careful not to cut off any of the springs of activity? – Very careful. He emphasises that very strongly, and I should like to say that so far as I am able I desire to appreciate it equally strongly.[6]

2261.   Do you think that he would have endorsed your statement, that inventions are more likely to be made under a collective *régime* than under an individualist one? – I could not reply to that with a definite 'Yes' or 'No', but reading most carefully as I have read and thought over that which he has stated, especially in this volume I now hold in my hand which is his autobiography, then it seems to me that what I ventured to say is quite warranted by what is here stated.[7]

---

[5] J.S. Mill's chapters on socialism written during 1869 were printed in the *Fortnightly Review* in 1879, six years after his death, at the request of its then editor, John Morley. These were the major writings on the topic by Mill, but he also wrote much on the subject in addition in his *Principles of Political Economy* (in *Collected Works*, Toronto, Toronto University Press, 1965), and, to a lesser extent, in his *Autobiography*, London, Longmans, Green Reader and Dyer, 1873, to both of which Mann also referred in his evidence. Marshall's own tendency to socialism owed much to Mill. See Groenewegen, *A Soaring Eagle: Alfred Marshall 1842–1924*, Chapter 16, esp. pp. 570, 580–1.

[6] A good interpretation of Mill. See in particular, J.S. Mill, *On Socialism*, New York, Prometheus Books, 1987, Chapter 4, esp. pp. 119–29.

[7] Mann was perhaps thinking here of the eulogy to socialism Mill provided in his *Autobiography*, pp. 231–2, preceding the remarks he quoted in answering Q. 2264.

2262.   Can you find there or anywhere else in his writings any support
for the opinion that inventions would be more likely to be made under
a collective *régime* than under an individualist one? – I do not think I
could point to any particular paragraph where he expressly states that;
but unquestionably the general conclusion to be drawn from a perusal
of this is that he favoured the development of the common control of
industry, and believed that men would gradually learn to work for the
common good as effectually, as thoroughly, as honestly, and as
earnestly as they now do for their personal and private good.

2263.   I think that could not be challenged if the word 'gradually' is
interpreted to mean spread over many centuries. Do you take the
word 'gradually' in that sense? – I will take the word 'gradually', but
not quite in that sense of centuries. I am quite willing to take the
word 'gradually'.

2264.   I mean as representing Mill's opinion; Mill did not expect that
this 'gradually' represented a progress that could work itself out only
in the course of centuries? – If I might be permitted to quote the particular passage that weighs very strongly with me, and which seems
to be supported by the general context, I will do so. After stating that
very short passage that I quoted this morning concerning the desirability of all participating equally in the benefits of combined
labour,[8] he then says: 'We had not the presumption to suppose that
we could already foresee by what precise form of institutions these
objects could most effectually be attained or at how near or how
distant a period they would become practicable. We saw clearly that
to render any such social transformation either possible or desirable
an equivalent change of character must take place both in the uncultivated herd who now compose the labouring masses and in the
immense majority of their employers. Both these classes must learn
by practice to labour and combine for generous, or, at all events, for
public and social purposes, and not as hitherto solely for narrowly
interested ones.'[9]

---

[8]   *Ibid.*, p. 232. Mann quoted this in answering the question (Q. 2249) which had been addressed
to him by Mr George Livesey.
[9]   J.S. Mill, *Autobiography*, p. 232. The 'we' in the quotation refers to J.S. Mill and Harriet
Taylor, the person whom Mill regarded as having strongly influenced him on human progress
and the role therein of socialism.

2265. Does not that very passage show that he thought a change in human character had to come before it would be safe to move much in the collectivist direction? – It does.

2266. With regard to the tendency for inventions to grow under Government management, have you watched whether it is the practice for private works to copy their new ideas for machinery from Government works or whether the practice is the other way? – I should say it is the other way.

2267. And therefore so far the world would not be ready to trust its inventions by Government departments? – At the present time, no.

2268. You gave as one suggestion that ultimately I suppose the Government should suppress literature that was not likely to promote the public well-being? – I think that properly falls within its province.

2269. That has been tried before in the history of the world, has it not? – Yes.

2270. By the Inquisition, for instance? – Yes.

2271. And by Autocratic Governments, the Government of Russia, for instance? – Yes.

2272. I believe it would be rather difficult to get your memorandum,[10] for instance, into Russia? – Yes, I believe it would.

2273. Do you think it is quite certain that the suppression of what is thought injurious literature may not come to be the suppression of that literature which would have turned out to be the most important for the future? – It might be so; but it is not probable that it will be so. The kind of Government of course that I favour is that kind of government which should be properly representative of an educated people. The cases that you have quoted have not been Governments representing an educated people. The democracy in those countries is very far from being educated, and might properly be covered by the term used by Mill, 'An uncultivated herd',[11] which

---

[10] Possibly a reference to Mann's Memorandum on 'State and Municipal Control of Industry' which he had submitted to the Commission. It is reprinted as Appendix 68 to the *Fourth Report*, Whole Commission, pp. 115–23.

[11] Used by Mill in the passage quoted in Q. 2264 above.

perhaps is largely true of the workers of this country but less true than formerly, and will be still less true in the future; find when that time arrives then the Government will be proportionately improved.

2274.   Do you not think that by the time we are so far improved as to be able to know what literature to suppress, we shall be so far improved as of ourselves to abstain from writing improper literature? – I think it is very probable, and I recognise that that undercuts what I have previously said; but having previously said something concerning this it still served my purpose.

2275.   Now, passing to the special question of the docks, I think the changes that you have proposed would have two advantages, a geographical re-distribution of work and a re-organisation of employment?[12] – That is so.

2276.   And the two really stand on quite different grounds? – Quite different grounds.

2277.   It would be possible to have either without the other to a certain extent? – Yes.

2278.   Taking the geographical distribution as it is, supposing that it should be found impracticable to cut the new canal, you have followed the evidence given by Mr. Booth and Mr. Hubbard,[13] and others, and I think you are of opinion that it would not then be practicable, even if everybody wished, to make labour dovetail in with the present arrangements? – It would be partially practicable, but we could not make a good job of it, and therefore tackling the proposal, I am, of course, identified with those who would like to see a thorough good job made of the business if we once take it in hand.

---

[12] Probably a reference to Mann's discussion of the 'Struggling condition of the Docks, Wharves and Warehouses of London', part of his Memorandum of 'State and Municipal Control of Industry' (*Fourth Report*, Whole Commission, Appendix 68, pp. 120–3, esp. 'The Proposal', pp. 122–23).

[13] This was the evidence given by Charles Booth to Committee B in January 1892 (Q. 11,364–92) and again in August 1892 (Q. 24,727–25,030) and that by W.E. Hubbard (Q. 4581–918) in July 1891, minutes of evidence, Group B, Vol. I, Cmnd 6708–V, April 1892; Vol. II, Cmnd 6795–V, June 1892; Vol. III Cmnd 6894–VIII, February 1893.

2279. I wanted to get from you more clearly what you thought were the difficulties in the way of Mr. Booth's proposal.[14] You mentioned the need of allowing a free pass by the railway, would there be any great difficulty in that. Would it not be a very small commercial transaction to give to all the dockers free passes along the railway to their place of work? – That in itself would not be a very large proposal to carry out, but I question the advantage that could arise from trying to carry it out. I have previously stated that occasionally practically the whole of the men are required, very rarely; but still occasionally practically the whole of the men in the port are required to do the work of the port, and if that should happen once or twice a year it upsets the whole contention.

2280. I do not quite see how. Was not Mr. Booth's proposal that the work should be arranged for a number of men who would do a moderate day's work during the greater part of the year; and that in times of special stress, and only those, they should work a little overtime and a few outsiders should be got in? – That fairly states the position taken up by Mr. Booth as I understand it.

2281. And what are the objections to that? Why is that impracticable? – Less because of the actual location of the docks and wharves than because of the sectional interests from the employers' side.

2282. But do not you think much may be done by the employers getting to look at employment from the point of view of the *employés* under the influence of growing public spirit and growing public opinion? – I think considerable good could be done in that direction, but I am not anticipating that it will be done in the immediate future; and even then the same spirit would prompt them to take the matter in hand in a more complete fashion.

2283. Do you not think that the path of least resistance at present is to try to bring public opinion to bear upon employers in this and other industries to consider employment as a public function and not as a private affair merely? – I consider that part of my personal duty and every day of my life I try to carry it out.

[14] These were spelled out during Mann's questioning of Charles Booth, the previous August, particularly Q. 24,948–50 with reference to train travel.

2284. Do you not think this is an easier way towards that route which you and Mill alike desire than the complete taking over the management of industries by Government? – I could certainly lay equal stress upon it, and I do not believe that the taking over by Government authority would be very effective, unless that spirit permeated the average man.

2285. So that whatever route we go, we must largely wait on the improvement in human character? – Largely, yes.

2286. Then turning to this question of the geographical distribution of dock work, I think that the matter has been already discussed between you and Colonel Birt rather at length before Committee B., has it not?[15] – Not at length. It was inferentially referred to, but not with any grasp.

2287. I think in question 7021, Committee B., you asked 'Do you consider it no disadvantage to have the number of lighters going up and down the river, which are now going, and the consequent handling of the cargo, putting it from the dock quay into the lighter, and then gathering it and then putting it out of the lighter on to the wharf quay?' and he answers, 'You cannot put your ship, which has 50 descriptions of cargo, alongside a warehouse suitable for each of those articles; you must lighter them, put your ship where you will. In our docks, for example, goods are stored in the dock; we lighter a very large proportion of them; we cannot put the ship where you will. In our docks, for example, goods are stored in the dock; we lighter a very large proportion of them; we cannot put the ship where the room is. But even if we had one central dock you must lighter them. Say the ship is from Calcutta, she has jute, silk, sugar, tea, all sorts of stuff on board. The jute must be stored in one place', and so on. I think you rather would desire to meet that objection, that you have something to say in answer to that? – I admit that this is fairly weighty, and that it is really an objection to the contention that I have

---

[15] This refers to Mann's questioning of Colonel Birt, before Committee B on 3 November 1891 (minutes of evidence, Group B, vol. I, April 1892, Cmnd 6708–V, pp. 348–52). Mann's recollection was better than that of Marshall: his questions dwell inferentially on the location of the docks mentioned, but not in any detail. See esp. Q. 7019, raising an issue about 'the position of the docks collectively' (*ibid.*, p. 349).

put forth that a ship should be brought right alongside the warehouse
to receive the special cargo that she has, and that there should be no
secondary or unnecessary handling. So far as this statement is a
truthful one that it is impossible to overcome the lightering it min-
imises my contention, but as one who is fairly familiar with the operations that go on at the various docks and wharves, I am certainly of
opinion that nineteen-twentieths of the unnecessary handlings,
according to my interpretation, which now take place could be
renewed, although I admit the truthfulness of the general lines of
this statement of Colonel Birt.

2288. Colonel Birt did not seem inclined to admit that anything
approaching nineteen-twentieths could be avoided, did he? – He did
not for the dock that he is responsible for, but he is only responsible
for the Millwall docks, and although you skipped one little line, I
wish to be allowed to note. In reply to me he commences, 'Of course
if you could obviate that it would be better.'

2289. I did not notice that I had omitted that? – That is in direct reply
to my question. He says, 'Of course, if you could obviate that it
would be better'; that is, if you could obviate the lightering so much
the better; and then he proceeds to show that it would be very difficult to obviate much of the lightering. My reply to that is, 'Yes, I
admit that there is some lightering that could not be obviated, but
nineteen-twentieths of that which I am calling unnecessary is really
unnecessary.'

2290. But you did not get him to agree with you, I am afraid? – I do
not think I succeeded in imparting to him a correct notion of what I
was driving at. For instance, I am not sure which particular question
it is,[16] but I addressed a question to him to this effect: I said, 'What
about Tilbury; have they the requisite warehouse accommodation',
in effect, I said, that I well remember, and he said, 'Yes, they have
splendid warehouse accommodation', the fact being that they have
not one single warehouse. The very next day I received a letter from
a dock director, one of the joint committee, saying, whatever did you

---

[16] That is, Q. 7041 (minutes of evidence, Group B, Vol. I, p. 350). The precise wording is 'Has
the Tilbury Dock any warehouse accommodation? – Grand warehouse accommodation, but
unfortunately they have never anything to store.'

mean by your question to Colonel Birt concerning warehouse accommodation; he said, do you not know that we have not a single warehouse at Tilbury. He had misunderstood the drift of my question, and corroborated my own position by saying, as a director, that they have not a single warehouse, nor have they; they have nothing but transit sheds.

2291.   Does it not go on at question 7042, where you say, 'Or have they transit sheds'? – That is the question.

2292.   Does he not there say that the transit sheds are so made that they can be used for warehousing anything even silk? – He does so reply, and all I can say to that now is this, it was not for me to make a statement then, that they have not one single warehouse or shed where they can work cargo. The working of cargo means this, take tea, for instance; tea is commonly discharged in fact is now being discharged at the Tilbury docks, the working of tea means, if it is Indian tea, as the bulk of it is, that the tea is first put out of the chests, or bulked, and the chests are repaired by tea coopers. The tea is mixed to equalise the quality, that does not take place with China tea, but it does with Indian tea, and it is Indian tea that we get principally. Then the working of that, and the weighing of that, and the housing of that, and the piling of it and delivering of it requires very large warehouse accommodation. They have not one single warehouse where they can do a little bit of that at Tilbury. Therefore it all has to come up to the up-town warehouses, or to the wharfingers.

2293.   What do you think of Colonel Birt's opinion that tea must be brought right into the centre of London, and that it would not do for it to be warehoused at their docks? – I do not think he said it would not do to be warehoused at the docks; he said, the nearer you can get to London Bridge the better, which I thoroughly admit, but these would be sufficiently near, I am contending. He did not say it would be sufficiently near, he says the nearer you can get to London Bridge the better.[17]

---

[17] That is, Birt's answers to Q. 7020, 7045, 7052 before Group B, in which Birt argues first generally and then with respect to tea, 'with certain goods it is better to be as near London Bridge as you can get them, the nearer you can get to London the better' and 'much nearer London Bridge than the suggested docks would be' (minutes of evidence, Group B, Vol. I, pp. 349, 351.)

2294. Did not you think he implied that in his case the Isle of Dogs would be too far off for warehousing under such conditions as those? – Possibly he did. I could not say. I do not think he caught what I was driving at and I was rather dissatisfied with the general replies, and with my own questions on that occasion.[18]

2295. He seemed also to think that the growth in the size of ships would render it increasingly difficult for them to come up even to the Albert Docks? – That certainly is the case, and I replied to that this morning[19] by saying that even the largest ships now, such as the 'Cunnarder' recently launched, of 600 feet in length, and 9,000 tons without machinery, could not come up to the South-West India Dock for instance, because they were dredging, and I am proposing that we should dredge, and I say that by straightening the course of the river, the natural scour could largely contribute to the cleansing and deepening of the river, and we should overcome that difficulty with considerable ease, because that difficulty has been met by the Clyde, by the Belfast people, by the Tyne, and by every important port. Practically the Clyde has been created by that. It was a mere ditch prior to the Commissioners taking it in hand, and they have made it a grand place. It is a real qualified port now, where the smartest liner can now be run in, and with the least effort we could do the same here.

2296. I do not like to ask you questions on engineering on my own authority; but might not the result be to diminish the scour instead of increasing it, because the amount of water that now comes up past the lower reaches must be sufficient to raise up some 20 feet of whatever it is, the water that goes round the Isle of Dogs. When the course was shortened there would be less water at every high and low tide flowing past Gravesend? – No there would be the same water, but it would go a little faster.

2297. But surely there would not be so much wanted, because the length of the upper part would be lessened? – Yes, but nature will supply it to us whether we want it or not. I think that is the rule. I think the natural forces will send it up.

[18] Mann may have been thinking of Q. 7019–21, but he may also be referring to the greater part of his questioning of Birt, which, after all, came very early in the day, being the thirteenth day of sitting of Group B. [19] That is, Mann's answers to Q. 2173, 2225–7.

2298. Have you considered at all the expense of this dredging? — I have.

2299. Have you given an estimate for it? — I have not submitted an estimate. Pardon me for one moment there, if you remember I gave two estimates this morning.[20] When pointing to the map on my right now, that is the one allowing for the canal, I stated that to construct that channel and to build up the foreshore, as shown on that map, the engineer's estimate was 4,000,000*l*., but turning to this other map, and dealing with the construction there as shown, and the building up of the foreshore, and allowing for the excavation of the basin, and also allowing for the excavation of two tunnels and new dredging, which I did not previously allow for, then the estimate was 6,684,000*l*.

2300. Do not you think it is possible that enough may not have been allowed in that sum for dredging? — The engineer who gave the estimate is thoroughly conversant with dredging and wall-building. It is the same engineer that I quoted from this morning.[21] We spend an enormous sum on dredging now every year. I have the dock company's balance sheet, which will show what they have spent themselves, and I would just like to quote it. I forget what the sum is, but I have the balance sheet, and I will just quote what they have spent. For the half year ending 30th June 1892 the dredging comes to 16,469*l*. That is the one dock company, and that is for the half year, and it is 33,000*l*. for one company, for one year, as apart from what the Thames Conservancy do, and apart from the other companies.

2301. Do you think that is any considerable part of what would be required for dredging under your scheme? — I do, and I think very much of that would be rendered unnecessary in the future by the additional scouring.

---

[20] That is, Mann's answer to Q. 2179 gives the engineer's estimate at £4 million, his answer to Q. 2232 raises it to £6 million to cover the additional work which Mann mentioned in answer to Marshall's question.

[21] That is, in his answers to Q. 2176, Mann named the engineer as Mr Cheesewright of the Haymarket, as the person responsible for the cost estimates referred to in his answer to Q. 2299 (and see n. 20 above).

2302.   I think that the Government, as a producer of printed matter, have chiefly occupied themselves with the production of blue books and ordnance maps. Do you apply your socialistic scheme to the Government management of ordnance maps? – Their development and production?

2303.   Yes, I mean do you think that the ordnance maps are as much up to date as they would be if the management were in the hands of private persons? – I think not, and whatever effect that may have on my general contention, I certainly say from my point of view it is a disgrace.[22] If that detracts from my own argument I am prepared to stand by it.

[Marshall's questioning is here interrupted for a series of questions (Q. 2304–3142) by Mr Gerald Balfour, and several other Commissioners, Sir Frederick Pollock, Samuel Plimsoll, Jesse Collings, Anthony Mundella, Leonard Courtney, David Dale, George Livesey, William Turnstill and Henry Tait, which dealt with collectivism, hours of work and the determination of wage rates, the Australian eight-hour day – which carried over to 16 November. Marshall's questioning then resumes, partly to follow up the questioning by Balfour, Dale and Livesey.]

3143.   I have some questions to ask you with regard to points similar to those on which Mr Balfour has examined you, but I will endeavour to avoid, as far as possible, raising just the points which he has raised. Perhaps, as he asked, your views as to what would happen on certain special hypothesis, it would be well for me to take the other line, and to ask what your views are as to what actually would happen. I have here a short statement of what I suppose to be your opinions, and I would like to ask you whether I have got them right as a basis of discussion. Your starting point is that there is a surplus population of about 10 per cent, which cannot find employment under the present conditions of industry? – Yes, I need not fix the percentage particularly.

---

[22] In his morning evidence, in reply to Q. 2173, Mann had used an ordnance map of the dock area, nearly twenty-five years out of date and, as he put it, 'not a good recommendation of State control'.

3144.   No. The reduction of the hours of labour to 48 per week would have different effects in different trades you say? – Yes.

3145.   And in some trades it would not diminish the output? – I would not like to say that of any trade immediately, but in a very short period the output would be equal to what it is now under the nine hours.

3146.   In others it would be diminished? – Yes, or what would be equivalent to the output there would be less work done.

3147.   Yes, I use the word 'output' for a short phrase, as meaning that? – Yes.

3148.   In so far as it diminished the output it would absorb the unemployed you say? – Yes.

3149.   And you say in so far as it did not diminish the output, it would not absorb the unemployed? – Yes, generally I say yes to that.

3150.   You further say that the result would be that in the trades in which a man did eight hours' work, there would not be less done, because the unemployed coming in would fill the vacant places, and would turn out as much as before? – Yes.

3151.   So that the production would remain about where it is now? – Not quite that; production would be stimulated by the increased demand, which increased demand would be brought about by the purchasing power given to those who would be absorbed.

3152.   There is, I think, a vital point in the statement of your opinions, which is that there would be an increased consuming power? – That is a vital point.

3153.   You hold also that the absorption of the unemployed would tend to diminish unsteady habits of life? – I do.

3154.   And that that would tend to diminish the unsteadiness of production? – I do.

3155.   And you also hold that consequently we should have gradually through the increased wages and production a greater aggregate of production? – Yes.

3156. And that in some way that I do not quite understand this would accelerate improvements in the art of production? – Yes, shall I forthwith make it clear in a brief statement?

3157. Yes; will you state merely your opinion, not giving it controversially because we can discuss the question afterwards? – I take it for granted, judging from past experience that the increased cost of production which would ensue immediately it was applied, would stimulate invention, stimulate the application of improved methods of production.

3158. Thus, there would be a double increase; there would be increase; because of the improvement in the arts of production, and there would be an increase in the total work done? – Yes.

3159. From causes before mentioned and from others in addition? – Yes.

3160. And then after a time there would be again a surplus of labour? – That is so.

3161. And then a further shortening of the hours would be both possible and advisable? – I think so. I did guard myself there by saying either a further shortening of the hours, or if the capacity to consume on the part of the mass of the people developed to such an extent that they desired to consume an equivalent to their increased capacity to produce they might then still continue to work the old hours.

3162. Now the simplest of these two cases is that of a trade, in which the reduction of the hours of labour would not diminish the output? – Yes.

3163. We might get them out of the way therefore. So far as those trades are concerned, the result I gather would be to do them neither harm nor good, but merely to make them hurry up their work and press more into each hour, is not that so? – Yes, and other incidental services would be rendered, which I feel you have in your mind, and which I need not trouble to emphasise.

3164. Now this is a side issue, but it is one which is of very great importance; your system as a whole depends on the change resulting in getting people out of their unsteady habits of work, and the getting people into steady habits of life? — I should not have felt it necessary to say that I am prepared to say yes to that, but I should not have felt it necessary to say that independently.

3165.   Anyhow you regard that as very important? — Very important, and highly desirable.

3166.   Do not you think that making a man do in one hour the work that, if left to himself, say as a peasant proprietor, with no master over him, he would have preferred to take an hour and 20 minutes over, has a tendency to increase feverish habits of life, which tend to undermine the social stability at which you aim? — Yes, there is a tendency, undoubtedly, in that direction. I should try to minimise that evil tendency by introducing forces that would have a counteracting tendency, and that should be stronger than the evil one. Taking away the manual labour might make them more able for continuous mental exertion or devotion to their work or to the application of an improved scientific knowledge.

3167.   Do not you think that men are very differently constituted, and that if two men have the same amount of work to do in a day, one will be happier if he gets it all done in 6 hours, and another if he takes 10 hours over it? — I fear that is the case; but that system which I should look upon as desirable, if realisable, I do not understand to be possible in an industrial community like unto this. We cannot have men with these different dispositions working in mills under a regimental system such as we have and such as we are likely to have even to a greater degree. Therefore, not seeing any hope for that elasticity that will allow some men to take 6 and others to take 10 hours over their work I am obliged to meet the difficulties in other directions.

3168.   Taking the special case of mining, has it not been said that, as it is, many miners hardly stop for their dinner at all, but go on with their work after a very short pause? — That is the case. That is commonly the case in the north.

3169.   Is not it generally the medical opinion that habits of that kind tend to undermine the stamina of the race, and to bring about those nervous habits that lead to unsteadiness of life? — I should certainly say yes to that.

3170. Has not it been said that in many mines, the way in which the eight hours' law would be met would be by the men giving up their dinner hour, and that many of the men would go on eating while at work and would go on working right through the whole of the 5, 6, or 7 hours that they have at the face? – Yes, I believe that has been said; and I believe that, therefore, but I think a question of that nature could well be left to those who are actually engaged in the trade, leaving it to their commonsense to work just as stiffly as they thought proper.

3171. Is not there, in fact, a great deal of movement, backwards and forwards, by men going from one place to another for employment. A man will try working in one place and finding he does not like the conditions, which another man would perhaps like better, and then he will go to some other place? – There are very considerable changes in these industries that cover the country.

3172. And if there were a six hours' day in some mines and an eight hours' day in others and a ten hours' day in others, would not the tendency be for each person to be working just about that number of hours which, taking account of his habits of mind and character, was the best for him? – With mines under relatively the same conditions, did you mean?

3173. No? – There the same amount of work per week could be turned out by men of the same capacity do you mean?

3174. No, I do not want to introduce that condition? – I do not see the desirability or advisability of encouraging such a system.

3175. Do not you see it would be likely to have a great effect on the health and vigour of the next generation. Do not you see, I mean, that forcing men to get through in six hours a day's work that they would rather have taken eight or nine hours over at the face, it would be likely to undermine the digestive faculties, and that, though that would not affect the present generation it would affect the vigour and working capacity of the next generation? – Certainly. I do not think such evil would ensue. I am not favourable, of course, to such a rushing system as would call from an average man as much work in six hours as ought to be done in eight. That ought to be dealt with under fair conditions, and I think that may be safely left to the men who are engaged in the industry. I am of opinion that the miners of the north, and I have some little knowledge of pit work, who are on a six and a half or seven hours shift would rather work right ahead for seven hours, and then have the longer time out than loiter about for an additional two or three hours, certainly I would. I would like to work effectively, sharp and smart, and then have leisure afterwards myself.

3176.   I should expect that of you, but many others would not. Do not you think they should be allowed to go their own way[?] – So far as that will fit in with the general well-being I would, but I do not think that that laxity suggested would tend to the general well-being.

3177.   Anyhow, so far as it goes, it is an argument against a uniform day of eight hours? – Yes, so far as it goes, it is an argument against it.

3178.   Connected with this preliminary point there is the question of the relationship between an hour of work and an hour of duty. Take the case, for instance, of a signalman who is on duty and must be ready to hear in case the electric bell rings, but who has no reason to suppose that the electric bell will ring for the next couple of hours. You said, I think quite fairly, that an hour of duty ought not to be counted as equivalent to an hour at work? – I do not remember saying that.[23]

[Mr Dale here (3179) interrupts to indicate he does not recall this point, Marshall continues.]

3180.   Not this morning the day before yesterday, I think?[24] – We were discussing this subject yesterday, but I did not express myself in that way. May I repeat what I think I did say?

3181.   Yes? – It was this. The question was as to the intensity of differ-ent kinds of labour, and I said I recognised the difference, and that it is reasonable to suppose that there should be different working hours. But I put the maximum at 48 a week for those who work under easy

---

[23] Perhaps a reference by Marshall to Q. 2609–10 from David Dale which used a porter and a signalman as the example, but not in the way Marshall here suggests.

[24] Marshall is wrong here, it was yesterday's questioning, as Mann correctly replies in his answer. See n. 23 above.

conditions, but urging that those who worked under more intense conditions should have a lower maximum.

3182. That is what I recollect exactly. You would propose then, that the maximum week should be 48 hours of duty, and not 48 hours of work necessarily? – Yes.

3183. And you think that a sort of scale should be made, not, perhaps, at once, but gradually, by which work should be graduated, an hour of work to count equal to an hour and a half of being on duty, or two hours, or an hour and a quarter, so that ultimately there would be for various trades 48 hours on duty, or in cases where the work was very intense, and, perhaps, for some, I think, you said there should be 36 hours per week? – Yes.

3184. That seems to be the only fair way of facing this fundamental difference between an hour of duty and an hour of work. But I want to ask you whether it would not be better first of all to clear the subject under discussion. We have had much said about 48 hours of work being as much as a man can do, and if after all what we mean is 48 hours of duty, we ought to have it more clearly made out, and see what it is we are proposing? – I do think so. I am not quite sure, whether, by replying 'yes' just now, I committed myself to this, that an employer might control a workman for six times 12 hours in a week.

3185. No. I understood you might control him for six times eight hours? – Yes.

3186. That what you think we should go for is not a week of 48 hours of work, but a week of 48 hours of duty, and when the work is of such a character as to involve a much greater strain than that of being merely on duty, then the number of hours should be something less? – Quite so, exactly.

3187. Do not you think it would be better as a matter of procedure to face the question of duty first and to decide the hours of duty, to discuss and decide first what is the maximum number of hours of duty that should be called for, whether it should be 48 or 60, deciding at the same time roughly that you would count, say, an hour down in the mine of actual work at the face as equal to an hour and a half on duty, and thus consider what was the right meaning of work and duty in that way? – I think that is desirable, and in one case, I think, I have done that by saying that eight hours or six times eight for the week should constitute the maximum, and then come down according to intensity.

3188.   Have you sufficiently separated your position from those who argue that the number of hours ought to be reduced, on the ground that 48 hours of hard work is as much as anybody ought to be called upon to perform? – Perhaps, I have not made that sufficiently clear, but I have for a long time always interpreted my own views, or tried to, on those lines, eight hours for the form standard, or to use your phrase, which, I think, is a very good one, duty as distinct from work.

3189.   All I am suggesting to you, and those who think with you, is that you should make more clear to the public what it is you are aiming at? – Quite so. I thank you for the suggestion.

3190.   Now we pass to those trades in which a diminution of the hours of work would diminish the output. That change you hold would absorb the unemployed, the unemployed being the surplus under the present conditions of industry? – Yes.

3191.   I think that is really the centre of the whole question? – Yes.

3192.   Whether there is a surplus or not? – Yes.

3193.   We will not take the condition of Ireland, that being different from the condition of England, and as so much of what we have said generally would not be quite true of Ireland, let us take the population as 30,000,000 on the whole? – Very good.

3194.   There are, of course, very great differences of opinion as to how many persons there are actually unemployed in normal times? – Yes.

3195.   You have given us your estimate, and we will take that estimate for the purposes of argument. According to your view then there is a population of 30,000,000, of whom, I think, you say 10 per cent is surplus?[25] – Under normal conditions I have stated 10 per cent is

---

[25] The figure of 10 per cent came from Mann's Memorandum re the 'State Regulation of the Hours of Work' (*Fourth Report*, Whole Commission, Appendix 71, p. 127), where it is stated: 'Some 10 per cent of the male workers are subject to casual, intermittent employment, or are out of work altogether, that is, about 800,000 in a normal state of trade as we now experience – and the remaining half, or 400,000 are entirely idle.' This was referred to in the previous questions by David Dale (Q. 2583–5).

surplus, or getting no work or only casual work, half of whom would be averaging two days a week, leaving 5 per cent entirely out of work. That is what is stated here in this paper. That would be so under our present day conditions. But probably it is not so good as when I wrote that.

3196. Shall we take 5 per cent of the 30,000,000? – It is immaterial, I think, for the argument.

3197. Take 10 per cent as the easier number to deal with. Then that would mean that, if there were not 30,000,000 in the country, but 27,000,000, all our difficulties would vanish, according to your view? – No, very far from that; because with the 27,000,000 there would be the same conditions.

[Mr Dale (3198) interrupts to ask whether it was 10 per cent of the population, or 10 per cent of the male workers? Marshall then resumes.]

3199. When you say you took 10 per cent of the male population you took off 10 per cent of the rest of the population? – Yes. I cannot endorse that argument that if we could emigrate 3,000,000 away all would be well. I cannot endorse that.

3200. I want you to define your position a little more. It seems to me that your argument would lead to this, that under the present conditions of industry there is work for the working part of the population of 27,000,000, and that the remaining 3,000,000 are surplus under the present conditions, and that we want to diminish the hours of labour, in order to absorb the workers belonging to that 3,000,000. You say that a diminution of the hours of labour would absorb them and from that I infer that if those 3,000,000 were instantly to emigrate we should all be employed fully, and that one of the causes of want of employment is the plethora of workers, and you say that by taking off 10 per cent you would destroy want of employment? – The effect, I should say of sending away 3,000,000 of the population would be to improve the conditions, temporarily, of those who remained behind, but immediately the old difficulty would begin to assert itself. To re-state how, I should have to again repeat what I have in effect previously said, that it is due to the methods under which the industries are now conducted, that in order to supply the demands of the community, trade is conducted on sectional lines, and thus the fluctuations that takes place, render it necessary for the employers to dispense with the services of a number of the workers, and then the effective demand of that portion who are dislodged ceases. Then that has a damping effect upon trade generally, and continues to have a damping effect till stimulated by some other means, and one of the ways to soundly stimulate it, is to make such a reorganisation as will absorb them again into the ranks of the workers.

3201.   Then when you say the population is surplus do you not merely mean that in this imperfect world it is not possible to make organisation so complete that every round man shall find a round hole just exactly to fit him? – I never did intend to say that if there was surplus population in this country, we should not make provision for them, or that we might not make an outlet for their energies. All I have intended to say is that under the present method of conducting trade there is this percentage out of work; but I do hold that this country could make use of many more than we now have, and I did not admit that in this imperfect world it is just the case that there must be disproportion because of our incapacity to organise trade. I believe that we might improve upon it. We might not make it perfect, but I am making this amongst other proposals by way of improving upon the terms of the trade and industry of the country, believing that thereby we are getting a so much nearer approach to perfection than we have had as yet.

3202.   I quite understand that you hold that we may improve gradually the organisation, but what I want to get at is how the reduction of the hours of labour would tend to improve the organisation of industry, except in that one point that I admitted, namely, that if a man is very much overworked he is likely to get into loose, nervous habits of life and to be an unsuitable worker; that point I have admitted, I do not think it comes to much, but I will admit that. Beyond that I cannot see that you have shown (and that is what I want to ask you to do now) how the diminution of the hours of labour would improve organisation. Perhaps I should begin by asking you what you consider to be the causes of the present irregularity of employment? – The one fundamental cause, from my point of view, is this sectional organisation of industry. To give a practical illustration as to the effects that would be likely to follow upon a re-arrangement, I would say that thousands of those who are now workless in London, and who, in consequence, have no purchasing power, many of whom are dying, and therefore are no good to the community themselves, might be absorbed by properly apportioning the work to be done in connexion with the tramway system of London. That is just by way of giving an illustration. I think that no one would be seriously interfered with, but that these men would be placed in a position in which, obtaining wages, they would possess purchasing power, to the advantage of themselves and their families and that would be a step in the direction of more effective organisation by putting a stop to the excessive working hours of those who are now doing work, and there would be a more proper and equitable apportionment of it between the total number.

3203. In what way would this shortening of the hours of labour improve, as you wish, the organisation of industry which would not result from a mere cessation to exist in the case of three millions? – The improvement would consist in this, that the men to-day who are doing the work are working what I think everyone in this room would call an unreasonable number of hours, and that is undesirable, and having other men available, it is desirable that we should minimise that which we now call excessive.

3204. Yes, but that does not quite answer my question, I think. Perhaps I may put it in another way, and ask you whether you admit the following to be causes of irregularity of employment that would not be directly affected by a shortening of the hours of labour: Would you admit that fluctuations of credit are the chief causes of fluctuations of employment?[26] – They are a chief cause.

3205. Do you see how a diminution of the hours of labour would affect that? – Only in an indirect manner by affording the workers more leisure for mental development enabling them to get a keener grasp than they yet have got of the basis of our present industrial system, and finding out how to improve it.

---

[26] This was, of course Marshall's own view, as indicated in several of his published writings. And see above, pp. 99–100 for the *Final Report*'s review of this subject.

3206.   There is nothing like leather; I think they ought to study more political economy? – I agree, saying that I should not allow that to be passed over in a light fashion, because to my mind that is one of the fundamental reasons why it should be advocated, and, although I also allowed it to pass over when you said 'It is the central point of the whole thing, is it not,' meaning the surplus, I said, 'Yes', and thought it was judicious to do so, but to my mind a man is actuated by the desire for intelligence all round, and I want these fellows to have a chance of getting that intelligence, believing that they will contribute most materially to the improvement of the present condition of things. Therefore it is no joke with me when I say let us have more leisure.

3207.   Then is not another cause, the uncertainty of how much of any particular thing would be wanted in a year? – I am sorry to say that there is considerable uncertainty due to this ineffective organisation.

3208.   Does not that depend particularly upon changes of season, as that of a cold season or a wet season affecting the demand for particular classes of clothes; and does not it also depend upon fashion?[27] – It does.

3209.   Would the diminution of the hours of labour affect those causes? – It would tend in the right direction; it would not directly affect them but only indirectly.

3210.   How? – On the same lines as I replied previously.

3211.   By improving men first? – Certainly, by improving men first. I am prepared to stick to that.

3212.   Then is not another cause, the uncertainty as to how much of total demand for any particular class of goods will fall to any particular firm? – That is very uncertain.

3213.   Do you see how to diminish that uncertainty; do you see how the diminution of the hours of labour would diminish that uncertainty? – No, I never proposed that it would.

[27] Another pet view of Marshall, mentioned in his writings on depressions and unemployment, and see above, pp. 100–1, for the Commission's *Final Report* on this subject.

3214.   Is not another cause the uncertainty of success on the part of employers, and of life and health and mutual agreement on the part of employers and employed in relation to industrial agreements? – Yes, that is another cause of dislocation itself.

3215.   Would the diminution of the hours of labour affect that? – Yes, I think so.

3216.   How? – Because many of the difficulties now take place in consequence of excessive hours and the evil consequent thereon.

3217.   You mean that there would be less things to contend about? – Yes.

3218.   But so far as the incentives to success on the part of employers go that would not be affected? – No, I do not say that it would.

3219.   Permanent employment was given to slaves because if there was nothing worth for them to do they were set to do something not worth doing? – I believe some such system did prevail.

3220.   But as soon as people began to be paid for work instead of being whipped to work, irregularity of employment began? – Yes.

3221.   I suppose you would admit that irregularity of employment exists in the most civilised nations? – I am sorry to have to say, yes.

3222.   And you would admit that on the whole it has steadily diminished through the course of history? – I am not prepared to say 'yes' to that, and I think the proportion is as much as it was. When I find a highly organised trade like that of the iron founders, for instance, issuing their monthly report for this month saying that they have 19.1 [per cent] of their members in receipt of benefit, it does not commend itself to me that there is much of a diminution.

3223.   It is a side issue, but perhaps I had better turn off on to that point. The statistics of the iron founders, which are the most handy trade statistics for this purpose, have been quoted so much that it would be advantageous if we followed the causes of want of employment amongst the iron founders? – The general depression is the cause given.

3224.   Are not the causes chiefly special to the trade? – I can scarcely say 'yes' to that, although corresponding trades in connection with the engineering industry do not suffer quite to the same extent. The pattern-makers is one of the contributory trades that do suffer equally, and they are suffering now.

3225.   Is it not a fact that the iron founders have suffered more from the introduction of machinery than any other important trade? – I do not think so.

3226.   Is it not a fact that at a time when more iron founders were out of employment than at any other time there was a notice in the Ironfounders' Monthly Report that unskilled Irishmen were earning 10s. a day for hammering away at machines in the foundry? – Yes, but there is very little work (I think I am correct in stating this) done by the members of the organisation that has been taken away from them.

3227.   Is not that contrary to the opinion of the members themselves? – I will not pledge myself to it. What I understand to be the case is that those men who have not been members of the organisation to which we are now referring are connected with that department of the industry where the machines were made use of most. Still I am not saying or intending to say that improvements in machinery have not contributed towards this large number being out; but taking the number that are now out of work and comparing it with the number that they have had out of work any time these 10 years, then the whole statement is a shocking one and one that will not warrant me in saying that matters are improving. When I find that an organisation like that has 17 or 18 per cent of their men unemployed, and in receipt of benefit, that does not justify me in saying that things are getting more hopeful.

3228.   So much has been made not only now but during the last 10 years of the history of the iron founders that it may be worth while to push the point a little further. Is not it true that the iron founder proper is a highly skilled artisan with very delicate instincts and generally very fine fingers; and is it not the fact that they have very careful and exact touch? – He is a very skilled man.

3229.   And is not it true that he would be physically incapable of doing the work by which the Irish navvies were earning 10s. a day? – Oh, no. He would not be incapable of doing it. He would not have the will.

3230. Are you sure that they do not themselves say that they could not do it even if they wanted to? – I will not be responsible for anything that they have said.

3231. I have heard them say that that is the case? – Yes.

3232. Is not it the case then that the position of the iron founders just at the present time is rather like that of the hand-loom weavers some time ago when the power loom was pushing its way? – If it should be thought, advisable I will leave the iron founders and take the trade I am connected with myself. I have had the pleasure of subscribing in order to keep 9,500 organised men out of work myself. That is not good business, and I cannot on the strength of that say that there is a very large diminution of the numbers of the unemployed.

3233. But many of those have grey hairs? – They are included in the superannuation, but I have not included them in the numbers I have given. The superannuated members are chiefly grey-haired men.

3234. Have not they more white hairs? – I will admit that there is a proportion of the 5,400 or so, which I have mentioned, who, because of their years are at a disadvantage, but that does not detract from the force of my statement because there are strong healthful young fellows in the vigour of life who are wanting a job and cannot get it. When they were absorbed it would be time to ask, is not the cause due to the fact that those men are getting on in years? But I say that as long as a young skilful fellow is there and cannot get a chance of work, it is no use talking about the elderly men being there.

3235. Is not it true that our opinion as to the want of employment is mainly or to a great extent derived from trades union statistics, and that the trades union statistics for comparative purposes are some-what vitiated by that fact of the rule with regard to the local minimum being more strictly adhered to now than before. A man whose hairs have just turned grey has a greater difficulty than he had before in getting employment? – A man whose hairs are just turned grey certainly has a greater difficulty, but I do not think that need affect our general contention whilst young men are out of work which is the case and has been the case any time within the last 10 years.

3236.   It affects it surely because the number of those who are out of work has increased? – I do not think it does because there are young men capable of doing it, and if they get a man at all it makes no difference to the number. If there is a man 45 years of age, he would be considered an elderly man in the engineering trade now, I am sorry to say, and when that is so, the employer says to him: the time has come for us to part, and a young man steps in his place; therefore the proportion is the same.

3237.   Yes, the proportion is the same, but is it true that there are a number of men who, were it not for this rigid rule that they have in the engineering trade now, that no concession is to be allowed for elderly men, since they would have the requisite knowledge and connexion with the trade, be able to use their hands and their minds in a useful way and get employment? – No, not unless they dislodged somebody else.

3238.   That is supposing that there is a certain amount of work to be done? – Yes, and it happens to be the case in a trade like the engineering trade.

3239.   I will not discuss that point now. But as to the trade union minimum, do not you think that if a large trade fixes upon a local minimum for every class of work, some of which is of a very elementary character, that the result must be for the wages to be fixed sufficiently high to tempt not a very high class of men in time of good work, and to throw them out of employment in times of bad work because though they were worth something they are not worth the minimum wages? – There is a tendency in that direction.

3240.   Do not you think that a considerable quantity of the present want of employment could be taken away at once by greater discrimination in the application of the trade union minimum? – No , I do not think it could, and I say that as one who ought to know exactly what is going on. I know the shops where this kind of thing is applied in various parts of the country, and I do not believe it would make half of 1 per cent difference, and I question whether it would make a quarter of 1 per cent difference because men of every degree of skill are available.

3241. But some of them may have something a little against them? – If so they clear out, and another man who has not that little something against him is there, always available. There is not an engineer's shop out of the 600 in London that cannot have a qualified man of any age today. There is not one of the 600 engineer's shops in London today who would be in want of skilled men to suit than in connexion with any department of their trade, and who could not get them at any age.

3242. He would not be necessarily accustomed to their special branches of work? – He would be sufficiently accustomed so that he could walk right in and never having seen the drawings used before, the foreman could place them in his hands and say, there is the drawing, work to it.

3243. We have been over the chief causes of the irregularity of employment, and we have your opinions as to the extent to which the diminution in the hours of labour would remove those causes? – Yes.

3244. I want you now to come back to this and to sum up, in what way do you think that a diminution in the hours of labour would permanently diminish the irregularity of employment? – It would not permanently diminish the irregularity of employment. I have never made such a proposal as that it would. On the contrary. In effect I said yesterday[28] and if I was not sufficiently explicit I will say it now, that immediately that step was taken, supposing it were taken, the old difficulty would begin to be created, and therefore I came forward with other proposals saying that both parties to the industrial system must try and approach each other with a view to neutralising the evil effects of want of employment and distribute the bad effect of declining trade over the whole of the persons engaged in the trade. That was because I was fully alive to the fact that a mere reduction of the working hours question from nine to eight would not meet the difficulty.

3245. We have got to this, we have assumed for the sake of argument that the reduction of the hours of labour would increase the employment for the time being, but yet it would not bring about a permanent

[28] This probably refers to his answers on Tuesday morning to questions by David Dale as chairman (Q. 2523–5).

diminution of want of employment or unsteadiness of employment? – Yes, I endorse that.

3246.   But only indirectly you say in so far as it acted on men's character? – That is so. That is, acting on men's character to qualify them to take other and further and more important action.

3247.   But you say that if it ended in itself without changing men's character, it would merely fill up the ranks temporarily and only would take away the unemployed for the present? – For the present. Its good effects would be temporary.

3248.   Yet the evils of regulation forcing people who might prefer to do their work more slowly, to work faster, these evils would be permanent though the benefit would be temporary? – By passing from one man to more you mean as I understand.

3249.   The evils that such a regulation of the hours of employment would inflict in forcing people who prefer to do their work leisurely to take it in a hurry would be permanent though the benefits would be temporary? – I should not like to admit that in every case where a man who desired, say, ten hours instead of eight, to do his work in it was always an evil. He should be encouraged to do it in eight. I think in many cases it would be desirable that he should develop a higher degree of efficiency, but he could develop that degree of efficiency without unnecessarily straining.

3250.   But still in so far as it was an evil that evil would be permanent while the benefits would be temporary? – Yes.

3251.   Then I should like now to get to understand a little more clearly in what way you think that a diminution of the hours of labour would temporarily absorb the unemployed. I think you took the tramway industry as one? – Yes.[29]

3252.   There is no doubt that if the hours of labour in the tramway industry were diminished no man could do very much more than he does now per hour? – Very little more.

---

[29] Marshall is presumably thinking here of Mann's answer to Q. 3202 (above, pp. 152–3) in which he gave the operation of the London tramway system as an example.

3253. And, therefore, if the present system of trams were maintained there would be a demand for more drivers and conductors? – Yes.

3254. But is there anything in the nature of the case to determine the number of journeys that are made for a given line of trams. Could not they be diminished? – I do not quite follow that.

3255. Would not it be likely that this change would make the tramway companies say: – 'It does not pay to run so many trams, so we will run fewer, and get those few to carry more passengers: but the wages have risen so high relatively per mile to the fixed charges that now we will run fewer trams'? – Yes. I think it is quite possible that such a pressure might be applied, and I should not object to it being applied.

3256. And would not Bills for laying down new trams before Parliament be many of them withdrawn? – I should not think so.

3257. Is not it a very close question in many cases whether it is worth while to make a particular tram line or not? – Yes, I believe it is.

3258. And would not this probable increase in the wages bill determine people in many cases not to proceed with them? – It might possibly in some cases, but I should say that there will be an increasing demand, and that this would, in the aggregate, stimulate that demand that the reduction of working hours brought about would contribute to the general good condition of the average worker who uses the tram, and there would be more likely to be an increased demand rather than a reduced demand.

3259. We will get to the increased demand, perhaps a little later, but for the present is it not true that an increase in the wages bill would be likely to make employers diminish the amount of work done for them in the tramway industry and in other industries? – That would depend upon the amount of profits made. As I have admitted in some cases in connexion with trams, there is a consideration whether it is worth while to lay down the line or not, and run it; but in some instances, and I do not think there are many, this might be the deciding point to cause them to decide unfavourably with regard to the establishment of the line.

3260.   Why do you think there are not many? – Because I believe that the average tram-line pays very well, or could be made to pay very well if it were properly conducted.

3261.   I thought you meant there were not many industries of that kind? – No.

3262.   Do you not know that there are many industries in which an increase in the wages bill would cause employers to fail in business? – No, I do not think there are many. I think there would be very few indeed when compared with the aggregate industries of the nation.

3263.   Could you give any reason for that belief? – This reason, that all the staple trades are paying fairly well. Many of the smaller trades are also paying well, and it is not at all probable from my point of view that the employers would withdraw in consequence of the slightly increased cost of production.

3264.   I am not talking of their withdrawing altogether, but of their abandoning production with regard to cases in which they are now in doubt as to whether it quite pays or not? – Quite so. Taking that phase of the question I do not think it would prevent them. I think there would be more industries stimulated and, in a sense, created, than there would be thrown out of gear.

3265.   I would rather keep to the question of increased demand off for the present. Do not you think there would be many industries thrown out of gear? – I do not. But I do not see how I can properly reply to your question unless I am allowed to take into consideration that increased demand that I contend would ensue. If you debar me from using that as an argument then I think I must say I think there is a considerable proportion that might be interfered with seriously.

3266.   Then we, perhaps, had better go to the increased demand. Why do you think there would be an increased demand? – Because I believe that the facilities for production would be enlarged considerably. I believe that production would be stimulated, the methods of production would be improved upon, and concurrently the capacity to consume would also develop.

3267.   Yes. But we have not got improvements in methods of production yet, have we? – I must get to that in order to reply to your question.

3268.   No doubt if any change would improve the methods of production it would increase the wages all round. But I do not see how you get there. We have got this, a diminution in the hours of labour in the trades of the tramway class – ? – Would you have me confine my remarks now to the aspects of the tramway class of trades other than those of production.

3269.   To trades in which it is not true that the output would remain stationary but would be kept up in spite of it? – Yes.

3270.   We shall want a name for them so we had better say industries of the tram class? – I shall understand that.

3271.   That is those in which a diminution in the hours of labour would diminish the output per man. I want now to know how such a diminution would increase the demand? – Such a diminution in that particular trade if cut off from the other trades would not —

3272.   From all trades? – If cut off from the industries of the nation generally and the people engaged in them, then I do not see that the demand would be increased. The demand would only be increased, therefore (I find a great difficulty in separating this class of trade from trades generally), by the greater capacity of the public generally to utilise these improvements.

3273.   I do not need to cut off any particular class of trade. I will ask you to consider what would be the results of a general introduction of the 48 hours' system per week in all trades? – In all trades?

3274.   Yes? – Then my reply is that because purchasing power would be given to many who have not purchasing power now, the tramway companies, in common with other companies would derive a share of that purchasing power.

3275.   Where would the purchasing power come from? – In many instances, I believe, it would come (speaking now of trades in the aggregate) from employers' profits. Possibly it would affect interest. In some cases it would affect rent, and in other cases it would be the direct outcome of more efficient production.

3276. Well, we will put off the more efficient production because we have not got there yet. Putting that aside I cannot see that you have indicated any increase of demand, but merely that certain workmen would, in your opinion, get more wages, certain profit-receivers less profits, the wage-receivers would buy more, and the profit receivers would buy less to exactly the same amount. Where is the increased demand? – The increased demand would be felt in certain circles in which it was not felt before, and to some extent it might be felt adversely where it had been felt and I think that re-distribution would be conducive to the general well-being.

3277. The re-distribution might be, but would it be anything more than a re-distribution; would it be anything more than taking off the demand, say, for some kind of velvet, and putting on a demand for some kind of rough cloth, say? – Yes there would be an increased demand.

3278. Why? – You are not debarring me from raising that point now, are you?

3279. No, that is the point I wish you to go into? – There would be an increased demand because of that latent demand that now exists on the part of the workless being made an effective demand.

3280. I still do not see it? – We are speaking of trades in the aggregate I think, not only tram trades and similar ones?

3281. Yes? – Therefore, I think that I have this morning said that the result would be that men would be brought into contact with the raw material out of which value is created. They are not creating value now and the re-organisation through the regulation of working hours would enable them to become wealth producers and therefore they could become wealth consumers.

3282. We have got this, the hours of labour diminished in a large class of trades, other men taken on to take their places, these new men getting wages which we are supposing for the sake of argument do not come partly out of the pockets of the old wage-receivers but come out of profits, the result, more demand on the part of wage receivers but since these extra wages have come from profits would there not be an exactly equal diminution of demand on the part of profit receivers? — I have not admitted that it would come entirely from profit or from land or from interest as I will emphasise and as I can and do again emphasise, the increased value that would be produced, the increased production by the workers being afforded an opportunity for exercising their energy.

3283. Will you say why the diminution of the hours of the worker would cause an increase in the aggregate amount of production. If it would, then, of course, I concede everything? — A decrease in the hours of work on the part of those who are now working, affording an opportunity for those who are workless to be brought into work, and their energies to be made productive it seems to me gives the answer to your question.

3284. But why would the stopping of one person's work cause another person not only to make up the deficiency but to go beyond it? — Because there would be an increased demand in consequence of the purchasing power being obtained by an increased number of persons.

3285. But in order to prove that there was this increased demand I was asking you to prove that, and now you give us as a reason that there would be this increased demand. Are not we arguing in a circle? — I will repeat the statement in another form, I will repeat the statement which I desire to emphasise. Workers are now workless; they cannot obtain an opportunity of creating value by the expenditure of the mental and physical energy they possess. The re-arrangement proposed in the shape of re-adjustment of working hours would afford them an opportunity of becoming purchasers because of the purchasing power created by their being brought into contact with the raw material, that is the point that we have to consider. If that is no point I shall be glad to learn it.

3286. What I understand is this: I will take the trams as an illustration, and it is as good an illustration as any other; you have no objection to the trams being taken as an illustration, have you? — No, that will serve.

3287. On a certain line suppose there were 20 men employed before the reduction of hours, and after the reduction of hours there are 30

888887

men employed; I think the old 20 get, on your supposition, as high wages as before? – Yes.

3288.   The new 10 do not gain at the expense of the old 20, that is your position, I think? – I have not said anything contrary to that, so that I am prepared to take it that that is so.

3289.   The new 10 are paid wages we will say 300s. a week in all, that is 30s. per head, or 15*l.* a week, which may come out of a rise of the fares; or if they are not raised, then out of the income of the tram proprietors? Take the case of the fares not being raised first. The fares are not raised. The 15*l.* now is taken out of the pockets of the tram proprietors, and they spend 15*l.* less. The tram drivers and conductors take 15*l.* more, therefore the demand is, from my point of view, unaltered. What is your view? – The demand is as it was. Confining attention to those trades I am prepared to say yes. The demand is as it was. It is simply a re-arrangement, but I do not admit that that would be the case when distributed over the productive work of the country.

3290.   I thought you did not object to the trams being taken as a representative industry, but I will take any other trade you like; take the cloth producers, or even your own trade? – Yes, I would consider several trades. I would suggest this, that if those who are workless today, perhaps some 70,000 say in London, the majority of whom possess the requisite qualifications for producing value, can be brought into contact with the raw material, a re-adjustment of the working hours will make it possible for them to be brought into contact with that raw material, and they will create value by their leisure. This will enable them to make an effective demand for furniture from the cabinet-makers, for clothing from Yorkshire, and ditto with regard to the provisions and as to household requirements, and in the same way they would affect the tram lines and every other means of transit.

3291.   I want to go over the same ground step by step. You do not like the illustration of trams, but take some other trade? – I like the illustration of trams to serve its purpose, but it cannot serve for a general purpose.

3292.   Then take another trade that you think not open to the same objections? – Take the baking trade, food.

3293. Very well; suppose that in any particular place 50 more baker's workmen are taken on in consequence of the reduction of hours of labour there, and they receive between them 70*l.* in wages, which is not taken from the wages of the other working bakers, but comes from the profits of the master bakers, these new working bakers spend 70*l.* a week more, and that is making a demand for tram fares and other things to the extent of 70*l.*, but the master bakers have lost exactly 70*l.* of purchasing power; wherefore there is a mere redistribution and no increase of purchasing power, is not that so? – A mere re-distribution and no increase showing again the unadvisability of dealing with that subject on sectional lines.

3294. But I am supposing the change to be simultaneous in all trades? – Then the argument is not applied in the same way.

3295. But that is what I want to show? – The argument loses its force, that is the one you have suggested by your question. It seems to me it loses its force when we cover the entire trades of the country.

3296. But I want to know where the particular point in that argument that I have gone on, is wrong. The working bakers get 70*l* a week more, that is to say, 50 more working bakers come in and get 70*l.* a week and spend it in making a new demand for goods, and that 70*l.* comes out of the pockets of the master bakers, and they therefore have to withdraw an old demand for exactly 70*l.* There is therefore, in my view, no change in the aggregate amount. At what step is there a change? – Again, it seems to me, I must repeat what I have said, but perhaps I can put it in another form. It is the same argument that I used when I said 'If this be no point then I shall be glad to learn it.'[30]

3297. I want you rather to point out what fallacy there is in that particular argument because it claims to be conclusive? – I want to see human energy get to work upon the raw material to create and give value, a portion of which value will come to those whose energies have been set free to engage upon it, giving them what they require, and allowing the requisite margin of profit and interest if need be, for we are under a condition of things in which profit and interest are allowed.

[30] Above, p. 165, Mann's answer to Q. 3285, last sentence.

3298.   But we are not supposing that more bread is baked? – Oh, yes. I want to suppose that more bread is baked. I must contend that more bread would be baked because of the increased demand, which demand is made possible by the opportunities of the workers for getting into contact with the raw material. That brings it to this again, simply an improvement upon the present methods of organising industry.

3299.   But do not you see that what we are trying to find out is whether a diminution of the hours of labour would cause an increased demand? – I may say distinctly, yes, because it would improve the present organisation of trade.

3300.   And what you say is, if I understand you rightly, that there would be an increased production, that increased production being to meet the increased demand; that seems to me to be arguing in a circle? – It may; but it seems to me to be perfectly sound. For instance, if by some means I was possessed of the requisite capital and could get in contact to-day with some of the workers in the east of London, I would tell this class to make furniture, and this class to make bread and other articles of trade, and to engage in other departments of trade. I would say 'Here is the workshop accommodation, here are the tools, and I advance what is requisite for your sustenance whilst you are creating value here.' If a man was creating value to the extent of 2*l.* per week I would say, then surely it is advisable to get that which he had created, leaving a margin for managerial expenses. There would be a new industry created, so to speak, and not interfering with and detracting from what other people had been doing before. It would be making their latent demand an effective demand. I may say that a readjustment of the working hours would practically do that without taking that special step that I have suggested might be taken.

3301.   I am afraid I must not stay longer over that point, but I will ask one question more only, and that is, you have said, I think that wages are governed by the organised demands of the workers; the total produce of industry goes to the owners of capital, and land after deducting those wages. Am I interpreting you rightly? You say the total produce of the country goes to the owners of capital and land after deducting those wages which are obtained and governed by the organised action of the workers? – Yes, or action corresponding to organised action.

3302. Supposing that trade is not organised and that an employer, by adding an additional man, can get something that he can sell for 20s., and supposing that for raw material and plant, and so on, the cost will only be 2s., will not it then be worth his while to offer either 8s. to that man or as much as will be left of 8s. after deducting a little for extra trouble, say 7s.6d.? – Worth the employer's while?

3303. Yes? – I think it would be, but he does not seem to think so, as a rule.

3304. But is not the whole of the employer's mind occupied with considering whether he cannot find out some way of employing people so as to get from the sale of their products just a little more than will replace his outlay in the way of profits? – The effect upon wages is this, according to my experience, that no employer, irrespective of profits, voluntarily advanced wages.

3305. I did not ask whether he advanced wages; what I meant to ask was, whether he is not on the look out for seeing whether he could not extend his industry profitably? – Yes. I believe his mind is engaged in that way, and it is one of the most startling anomalies in civilisation to my mind that he should make such a big mistake over the business, and I wonder why he should concern himself about people wearing a bit of linen in Africa rather than concerning himself about how to raise the purchasing power of the people here. By that I mean that I cannot quite follow why employers of labour, as a rule, devote their mental faculties to thinking out how they can extend their sphere of operations with advantage, and I cannot understand why they go so very wide of the mark, and that is one of the biggest anomalies I have ever met with, and it is difficult for me to understand.

3306. But if in consequence of the internal difficulties in the trade, or from any other reason, a particular trade is not organised and each man has to make bargains for himself, is it not then true that an employer who could see his way to getting for 5s. a man to produce an article which he could sell for 10s., out of which he would only have to pay 2s. for general expenses and raw material would say, I will have that thing made, I will go into the market as a bidder for labour? – Yes, if he was convinced that he would obtain the requisite value, or that he would purchase labour cheaply by paying a relatively high wage. Then independently of trade union action the voluntary action on the part of the employer would be the means of wages being raised, I quite admit that.

3307.   Is it not a fact that wages have risen nearly uniformly in organised and in unorganised trades. Is it not true that there has been very little increase on the average in the wages of organised trades relatively to that which has taken place in unorganised trades? – Yes, that is so, on the average, but that still leaves it true, according to my mind, that the organised effort first put itself forth and set the pace and made it easy for the others to follow and obtain similar advantages without actually organising.

3308.   Why? – Because it developed in them a spirit which enabled them to make application and to take concerted action, sometimes spasmodically, but at any rate making them agree to act together for the time being, which action immediately had the effect of organisation. But in nearly every case the organisation was the cause, the combined action was the cause.

3309.   Does what you say go any further than this, that if any race of workers are so spiritless as to take what is given them without question, it may be a good long while before capital comes into the trade to raise their wages to their fair competitive value? – It does not amount to very much more, I admit that, but the organisation is that which has shown the spirit, in this country that has been the means whereby the spirit has been exhibited.

3310.   But are there many trades which have been so entirely without spirit as to make no attempt to better their condition, because they are without organisation? – No effectual attempt.

3311.   No effectual attempt; do you think that is so? – I think there are many trades in this country, that there is a considerable proportion of workers in this country who have never been able to make anything like an effective demand for improved conditions.

3312. Do you think there are many trades in which, if it became clear, that the employers were getting rich at a very great rate, and paid 5s. for labour that was worth to them 7s. 6d. net; do you think there are many trades in which the men would not look out for other employers? – If it were not so, the shocking wages that are yet paid in this country would not be a fact. There are wages in this country now paid of so scandalous a character, that I do not know what other explanation to offer.

3313. But is the margin great in those trades between the wages paid and the net amount received by the employers? – Sufficiently great to warrant a very considerable advance in wages. I most thoroughly and earnestly believe that.

3314. You are an ardent co-operator, I believe? – Yes.

3315. Is not the way to make co-operation effective to apply it in production as well as in trade? – Yes, and they will go in for that undoubtedly.

3316. The engineers have tried it already, have they? – Yes, they have made a fairly good show.

3317. Yes, but have not they found the profits were in practice a little less than in imagination? – There are special reasons why they should be so. They have been handicapped as compared with employers who have had a training in running just one industrial machine, and having no other object in view. I still stick to the point I stated at any rate, that many groups of workers in this country are receiving a shockingly low rate of wages when the profits taken by the employers warrant a considerably higher rate of wages being paid.

3318. Do you think there is a large proportion of workers in this country under those conditions? – That is a very vague term, a large proportion, because I should call anything large if there were 200,000 or 300,000, I should say that was too large.

3319. But should you say if there were one-tenth working under those conditions that it was large? – Yes, quite so, unhesitatingly.

3320. I must not detain you longer with questions on the labour bureau and the arbitration scheme, but I may say, perhaps that I agree with very much of what you have said. I would like to ask you one thing, and that is whether what you have said with regard to the Government arbitration scheme is not likely to be a little misunderstood in regard to your use of the word arbitration. Do not you really mean 'mediation'. Do you really mean compulsory arbitration, or do you mean compulsory mediation?[31] – I mean conciliation, mediation, and if need be arbitration.

3321.   I am only asking now this question in order to get at what your opinion really is. Is not what you want that under certain circumstances (and you have detailed the circumstances) an authoritative inquiry should be made into the causes and circumstances of an industrial dispute, and an inquiry held in public, and the opinion of those who made the inquiry published. You said that opinion should not generally be enforced? – No.

3322.   You said the mere publication of it would often be sufficient? – I did say so.[32]

3323.   I entirely agree with you, but is not there a proper name for that, and is not it compulsory mediation? – Quite so. What I did not say, and perhaps ought to have said, and which I will take opportunity of saying, is this: that I wanted that that board should hold themselves prepared to arbitrate if called upon to do so.

3324.   Yes, but what you want is compulsory mediation? – That is so.

3325.   With voluntary arbitration? – Yes, with voluntary arbitration.

3326.   Arbitration only at the request of both sides? – Yes, that is so.

[At this point, the questioning is continued by Sir Frederick Pollock.]

Marshall's examination of Sidney Webb, 17–18 November 1892

[Marshall's questioning continues on from that of Mr Gerald Balfour.]

---

[31] A reference to Mann's answers to questions (Q. 2752–7, 2767, 2781) raised by Messrs Tait and Mundella the previous day.   [32] That is, Mann's answers to Q. 2777–81.

4069. You have proposed to leave to the Home Office a very complete authority over many aspects of industry, I think? – I have proposed to extend the authority which is given to the Home Secretary under the Factory Acts in any future amendment of the Factory Acts.

4070. You do that, because you think that the Home Office would be practically under the control of the people? – Yes, more than in any other way that I can at present think of.

4071. If you had lived 120 years ago, would you have had the same opinion? – No, my argument is based upon democracy.

4072. Do you think that the history that you have given of the changes in economic opinion has been rather misleading, because the conditions are now so different? – I certainly do not think they are misleading, but I might refer to the much more complete statement of Professor Ingram in the latter part of his history.[33]

4073. You are, I daresay, aware that the opinions of Professor Ingram on this particular point are not generally accepted? – I am not aware of that. I certainly do not admit that.

4074. You describe Adam Smith as having located a system of natural liberty?[34] – Yes, in brief.

4075. That is what you may call the popular position of Adam Smith? – Yes, only giving it this brief expression. Of course I am quite sure Adam Smith was not by any means so individualistic as many of those who came after him.

---

[33] That is, J.K. Ingram, *A History of Political Economy*, Edinburgh, A. & C. Black, 1888, conclusion, esp. pp. 243–6. These pages criticise *laissez-faire* and end on a plea for political economy to be directed 'to one great end of the conservation and development of humanity'. It was cited in Webb's *Socialism in England*, London, Swan Sonnenschein, 1891, p. 88 n. 1.

[34] A reference to Webb's answers to Gerald Balfour (Q. 3914) in which he mentioned Adam Smith's 'Theory of Natural Liberty'. Perhaps also reference to Webb's historical essay on the basis of socialism (*Fabian Essays*, London, Walter Scott, 1889) which describes Adam Smith as 'no complete champion of *laissez-faire*, though his great work was effective in sweeping away foreign trade restrictions and regulations, and in giving viability to labour by establishing the labourer's geographical freedom to move and to enter in the wage contract when and where he best could' (p. 44), or to his *Socialism in England*, pp. 81–2, which has, however, no direct reference to Smith.

4076.   You are aware, I suppose, that he made something like fifty first-class exceptions to the general principle of individual liberty?[35] — I am aware of that, and I am aware that those exceptions were slurred over — I mean quite honestly and unconsciously slurred over, by some of those who followed him.

4077.   You are aware that most of the modern tendencies of economics were to a certain extent anticipated by Adam Smith? — I think that is so to some extent.

4078.   I suppose it was the next generation of economists who in your opinion preached that a man's duty was to get rich. Those are your words, I think?[36] — Yes, they are. Of course it is a very popular and rough exposition of a very common form of middle-class training in this country 50 years ago, which was, I think, derived from the economists of the time.

4079.   That was a very common opinion amongst some of the middle class; it is a popular opinion that that had its origin in economic writings? — It is.

4080.   Are you aware of any economist who holds that opinion? — Certainly none to-day.

4080a.   But are you aware of any economist of that generation who said it was man's duty to get rich? — I am not aware I asserted that any economist said so; but I think — I do not know that my statement is of any authority on that point — that those who have examined the effect of economic teaching at the beginning of this century consider its effect was to intensify and strengthen that popular feeling.

4081.   If then you said it was a teaching of the old school of economists that man's duty was to get rich (and I think I took down your words exactly), it was not an expression of your opinion? — That is of course a very rough statement of what was the effect of their doctrines.

---

[35] Cf. Jacob Viner, 'Adam Smith and *Laissez-Faire*', *Journal of Political Economy* 35, April 1927, pp. 198–232, and the quotation from Webb's historical essay on the basis of socialism in n. 34 above.

[36] Such words are not from S. Webb, *Socialism in England*, nor from his earlier evidence. The sentiment is, however, reflected in these sources, as in the essay on socialism in the *Fabian Essays*, cited in n. 34 above.

4082. Do you believe the old school of economists did teach that man's duty was to get rich? — I really must ask you to break that question up. There were a great many old economists. I do not think it would be an unfair statement to make, for instance, of Nassau Senior and McCulloch.

4083. I will come to Nassau Senior presently as an individual. Your statement, I think, was that the old school of economists taught that it was man's duty to get rich. Do you adhere to that statement or not? — I say that certain of the economists who unfortunately came most prominently into public view did in effect teach that doctrine.

4084. What economists? — Of course I am not able without any books or anything to give any specific reference to any specific sentence; but I am giving the Commission for whatever it is worth, my own view of what was actually learned by the people from those economists.

4085. But as you speak as an economist, and as your opinion is therefore likely to have some authority, and as if true it would have a very important effect. I should like to know what economist you think did express this opinion? — I have already said that I think the general effect of the teaching of McCulloch and of Nassau Senior was to that effect.

4086. I did not ask you what the effect of their teaching on others was. I asked you whether they expressed that opinion? — I have already said that I cannot remember at this moment or cite any sentence which I could give you. I have not the books.

4087. I have read most of their writings, and I may say that I think I have not come across a single sentence that admits of that construction ? — That is interesting rebutting evidence which the Commission will doubtless be glad to have from you. May I ask you — I do not want, of course, to prescribe the questions, but I should rather be glad to give an explanation of, or to explain my views rather than to discuss this matter.

4088. I was going on to ask you whether you would be surprised by a statement that a person who has read these books has not found any statement which in any way bears out your general impression? — I should be surprised.

4089.   We now come to the Factory Acts. You said, I think, the economists opposed the Factory Act? – I was quoting, if I may say so, from Greville's description of the controversy which was caused by the Ten Hours Bill,[37] and he said, 'All the political economists are against it, of course.' One would not wish to pin him down particularly to the 'all', but I think that may be taken as the view of the House of Commons at that period.

4090.   Do you know in what sense he was using the words 'political economists' there? – I should be very sorry to interpret Mr. Greville.

4091.   You are aware that when the Spaniards invaded Mexico, and wanted the Mexicans to give up their gold and silver, they burned them, because they would not say where their gold and silver were, and because they should be converted to the Christian religion? – I am not aware of that interesting fact.

4092.   Do you think it would be fair to say that that action was the result of the teachings of Christianity? – I am not aware even of that.

4093.   That would be a somewhat similar case, I believe, to the action of certain persons in this case under the alleged authority of political economists? – This would be interesting evidence, I admit, I have no view on the subject.

4094.   I am asking your opinion as to whether you think that would be the case? – I did not know of the existence of the interesting instance which you gave.

4095.   Are you acquainted with Mr. Nassau Senior's history? – Not well acquainted.

4096.   Do you know what his chief occupation was? – No.

4097.   Are you aware of a celebrated statement of his with regard to the accessibility of political economy to people at large? – I do not remember what statement you are now alluding to.

[37] Earlier, in reply to questions from the chairman, Leonard Courtney, Webb had indicated that the leading economists, and especially Nassau Senior, had opposed the Ten Hours Bill (Q. 3608), but he did not quote Greville in this context. Greville's diaries are, however, quoted on this point in S. Webb and H. Cox, *The Eight Hours Day*, London, Walter Scott, 1891, p. 240.

4098.   I am alluding to the statement[38] that while in all other sciences a man required to travel long before he reached a point at which he could express a confident opinion, in political economy he had only to walk as far as to the end of his garden, and then he found himself quite at liberty to express an opinion. Do you know that statement? – I have heard a statement to that effect, an opinion which, I believe, is very largely held to this day.

4099.   And are you aware that the opinions which he expressed about effects of the Factory Acts on profits have been regarded by economists as a proof that economic doctrine is not quite so easily to be mastered?[39] – It has always been my impression from reading his writings that they were an instance of that.

4100.   Ought you not therefore to regard Nassau Senior's declarations as to the Factory Acts as opinions of a man who was not a representative economist? – I should be very sorry to say that Mr. Nassau Senior was not an economist.

4101.   Is there any other recognised economist who spoke against the Factory Acts? – I have in my possession an extremely virulent article from the writings of Harriet Martineau to the same effect.

4102.   Would you regard Miss Harriet Martineau as a recognised authority? – Miss Harriet Martineau was the source from whom a large number of the people of England derived their economic teaching, and still derive it.

4103.   Are you aware that Miss Harriet Martineau said that, when she wrote her tales, she would not read beyond the chapter which she was going to illustrate, for fear she should get her mind confused?[40] – It is an incident in Miss Martineau's life which I should be glad to remember.

---

[38] This resembles the discussion in Nassau Senior's lectures, arranged and edited by S. Leon Levy, *Industrial Efficiency and Social Economy*, London, P.S. King and Sons, 1928, Vol. I, pp. 32–6.

[39] Marshall himself had lectured on this topic in his 1873 'Lectures on Women', and had also studied Marx's account of the matter. See Groenewegen, *A Soaring Eagle: Alfred Marshall 1842–1924*, p. 272. Webb himself had earlier referred to Nassau Senior's role in the ten-hour debate in answering a question from Leonard Courtney (Q. 3608).

[40] Marshall disliked Harriet Martineau's economics intensely and recounted this story in a footnote to his *Principles* (1st edn, 1890, p. 63 n. 1; 8th edn, 1920, p. 763 n. 1, the version first introduced in the 5th edn). For a more detailed discussion of Marshall's views on Harriet Martineau, see Groenewegen, *A Soaring Eagle: Alfred Marshall 1842–1924*, pp. 516–17.

4104.   Are you justified, therefore, when I ask you what economists of position condemned the Factory Acts, in quoting Miss Martineau as an instance? – I would rather leave that for you to decide.

4105.   Putting aside Mr. Nassau Senior and Miss Harriet Martineau, can you mention any other economist who attacked the Factory Acts? – I am strongly under the impression that Mr. McCulloch opposed the Factory Acts. Had I known that the Commission were going to inquire into the state of economic feeling in the year 1840, I would have come down better prepared; but I in my ignorance rather thought that was outside the scope of this reference.

4106.   I am referring to this point merely, because so much of the evidence you have given has been devoted to indicating that the economists have rather been behind the age? – Perhaps I may say that it seems to me that there has been a change of opinion among the economists, but if Professor Marshall wishes to suggest there has not been any change, I shall be glad to withdraw that statement.

4107.   I am not suggesting that there has not been any change? – Then I do not understand you to contradict my statement.

4108.   I think you said that Mill held that the only businesses in which joint stock companies could succeed were those of banking and insurance?[41] – No, excuse me, I said, or meant to say, that he indicated those as the chief probable instances in which joint stock enterprises could succeed, and I pointed out that joint stock enterprises had now flowed over successively into innumerable other instances. Therefore I wished not to specify to what departments of industry other terms of collective action might be successively applied.

4109.   Was it not pointed out long before Mill that banking and insurance were the two businesses in which publicity was of primary importance?[42] – You are such an authority on economics that I should not wish to correct that.

---

[41] A reference to Webb's answer to a question by Gerald Balfour (Q. 3991) in which he stated: 'I have in my memory that John Stuart Mill and others attempted to do that for joint stock enterprises 40 years ago, and arrived at the conclusion that banking and insurance were the two subjects which joint stock enterprise could best take up.' And see Mill, *Principles of Political Economy*, Vol. II, p. 136, Vol. III, p. 685.

[42] *Ibid.*, pp. 136–7, when he states 'Another advantage of joint stock or associated management, is its incident of publicity.'

4110.   Is not that true? – I would accept it on your authority.

4111.   Is it not true that banking and insurance are businesses in which publicity is of special importance? – I accept your authority.

4112.   Is it not more possible for a banking or an insurance society to do a large business under joint stock management than under any other? – I am not well acquainted with banking, but I believe there are some private banks still surviving in the city of London who do a considerable amount of business.

4113.   But their number is diminishing? – I believe their number has been diminishing.

4114.   You are acquainted with Mr. Mill's writings? – Somewhat, yes.

4115.   Have you read his chapter on joint stock companies?[43] – I think I must have done.

4116.   Are you aware that he advocated the extension of the principle of joint stock companies in every direction? – I have not that recollection, but all I say is that it is not any contradiction to my statement.

4117–8.   I understood it to be a contradiction of what you had said.

   [Mr Courtney interrupts to ask: 'I think what you said was that Mill said that banking and insurance were best adapted to joint stock enterprise? – I used the instance merely as an instance of no importance, as a reason why one would be sorry to prophesy as to what industries other forms of collective control could or could not be applied.' Marshall continues.]

4119.   With regard to the Factory Acts, I think I understood you to argue that economists had opposed the Factory Acts, and were proved to be wrong? – That was my impression.

4120.   And that the opposition to an eight hours law was likely to prove wrong in the same way? – No. I said economists were singularly shy of committing themselves to an opposition to an Eight Hours Bill.

---

[43] Marshall is wrong. There is no chapter on joint stock companies. However, Book I, Chapter IX, 'Of Production on a large, and Production on a small Scale', devotes §2 to 'Advantages and Disadvantages of the Jointstock Principle'.

4121.   But did you not also say that the principles of the Factory Acts were similar to those of an Eight Hours Bill? – Really it depends upon what Eight Hours Bill. I suggested that the regulation and the shortening of the hours of labour was an extension of the existing principle already applied in the Factory Acts.

4122.   Is there not a fundamental difference in principle between the Factory Acts and the reduction of the work to eight hours? – It is not my opinion.

4123.   Take Mill's statement, for instance, with regard to the Factory Acts, 'Freedom of contract in the case of children is but another word for freedom of coercion'?[44] – May I ask whether you are under the impression that the existing Factory Acts apply to children only; does your question rest on that assumption?

4124.   No, my question does not rest on that assumption. Do you not think that it is important to observe that freedom of contract in the case of children is but another word for freedom of coercion? – I do very strongly.

4125.   And does not the Act apply directly only to women and children? – No.

4126.   Does not the Act, in so far as it limits the hours of labour, apply directly only to women and children? – That is so, but it applies to adult men in all sorts of other particulars.

4127.   We are now talking about the hours of labour. Was not the Act, in so far as it applied to women, defended on the same ground? – I am not aware. It was defended on so many grounds.

4128.   Does not Mill argue that women ought to be free from control by their husbands; but that so long as they are under the control of their husbands the Factory Act ought to apply to them for the same reason as to children?[45] – I remember that he does.

4129.   Is it not true with regard to women and children that if their hours of labour are shortened their leisure is sure to be used for the public benefit? – I should not like to say that.

---

[44] That is, Mill, *Principles of Political Economy*, Book V, Chapter XI, §9, p. 952.
[45] That is, *ibid*., pp. 952–3.

4130.   Is it not true that the hours the children are free from the factory are spent in school, or asleep, or in play? – Really I am not able to say how children occupy their hours. They occupy their hours so very differently, such children as I am acquainted with.

4131.   Do not they occupy them in such a way as to make them likely to be healthier and stronger? – I really do not know. I am no special authority in these points.

4132.   And women, when set free from factories after 10½ hours, are likely to attend to their domestic duties? – I should say it depended on the woman. I do not know.

4133.   And is not one of the great arguments against the rapid diminution in the hours of labour of adult men that it is not perfectly certain that they have yet learned how to use leisure well? – I believe that argument has been used.

4134.   Do you consider it an important one? – It all depends upon the meaning of the word rapid, and the class to which it is applied. I do not think any general answer can be given applicable to all classes of workers.

4135.   In the beginning of the century the Government was, I think you have said, not in the hands of the people? – That is my opinion from reading.

4136.   Therefore it was reasonable for economists to oppose legislation on the ground that it was likely to be class legislation? – I think that that was the motive which dominated largely a number of reformers of that time.

4137.   May it not be true that the change of opinion on the subject of socialism has been a gradual variation, owing to a great extent to the fact that now legislation is not likely to be class legislation against the people? – That is my case.

4138.   But is that quite consistent with your implying that economists have changed their position? – I really cannot judge. I am quite willing to withdraw the statement that economists have changed their position if you imply that they have not.

4139.   I do not imply that they have not changed their position at all, but have you not implied that they have changed their position fundamentally? – I should have thought a great number had. I did not say that all economists had.

4140.   Have you not implied that the economists of this generation hold a fundamentally different position from that held by economists 50 years ago? – I think I would say as much as that, but it depends on your definition of 'fundamental'.

4141.   Have you allowed at all for the fact that this Government legislation was less likely to be class legislation? – I have included that in my answer.

4142.   You have spoken a great deal about municipal tramways and gasworks and so on, have you not?[46] – Yes.

4143.   And about gasworks and tramways owned by the municipalities? – Yes.

4144.   Are you sure that any such things exist? – I should be quite willing to accept your assurance to the contrary, if you think that no such things do.

4145.   Can you tell me of any gasworks or tramways owned by the municipality? – I thought that was the case in Manchester.

4146.   Are you sure they have not borrowed? – I am sure they have not borrowed the gasworks or the tramways.

4147.   Where did they get the money from? – That is another question. I am quite sure that the Manchester tramways belong to the Manchester Corporation, and the Manchester gasworks belong to the Corporation, and that they are the legal owners of them.

4148.   But how did they get the means of obtaining them? – I do not know.

4149.   Did they not borrow them? – I really do not know. I believe they have a debt.

---

[46] A reference to Section 3 of the summary of Webb's socialistic and semi-socialistic schemes prepared for the Commission by its secretary (*Fourth Report*, Whole Commission, Appendix 73, pp. 136–8).

4150.   I must rather press this question? – If you will explain what you
are driving at, I should be able to tell you what my opinion is on the
subject, or give you the information for which you are asking me.

4151.   I am asking a definite question. How did the municipality obtain
the money which they obtained? – I am sorry I have not come prepared with the answer in this case. I should have been glad to have
looked it up, if I had known the Commission would want the information.

[Mr Courtney (4152) interrupts to ask: 'Is there any difficulty? –
Is it not the fact that the Manchester Corporation owe a large sum
of money to somebody or another in respect of a considerable
part of the gasworks? – Quite so. If that question had been asked
me, I should have been quite willing to answer it. If Professor
Marshall wishes any further information, I should be glad to give
it if it is in my power.' Marshall continues.]

4153.   Will you make the statement in your own words? – I believe the
piece of information which you desire I should give the Commission
is that town councils have borrowed sums of money. I should not
have thought myself of giving that information to the Commission.
But I gladly do so at your request.

4154.   Mr. Balfour asked you what property was owned by public
authorities some 50 years ago, and what property there is now?[47] –
And I told him I could not answer.

4155.   But perhaps you can answer certain general questions. The
property standing in the name of public authorities consists in
modern times to a great extent in tramways, gasworks, waterworks,
and so on; but is not a much larger part the roads and the ordinary
means of communication? – I am sorry I have no figures at hand as to
how much there is. The Commission can obtain that from the Blue
Books.

4156.   But you agree that the roads of the country are probably a very
important property? – I can form no idea of what proportion. I am

---

[47] A reference to Webb's answer to Gerald Balfour's question (Q. 3983) in which Webb brought
up the possibility of private enterprise being superseded 'during the past 50 years'.

It is in the Blue Books.

4157. You think that the roads are an important property? – I think they are important, yes.

4158. And is it not true that about 40 or 50 years ago a great deal of property was owned by the community without the need of having to borrow money from private sources to purchase it? – I believe it was so.

4159. Are you sure then on the whole there has been an increase of collective property in the last 40 years at all proportionate to the increase in private property? – Really, if information is desired on that point, I can only refer to Mr. Giffen.[48] I have not the figures. I am perfectly willing to give any information that I have, or to explain my position in any way; but I cannot give any information which I do not possess, and on which I am not an authority.

4160. What I am asking you is whether you are sure that the statement which you made was correct? – The interesting facts which you have given or suggested as rebutting evidence would of course make me doubt it.

4161. That which passes as municipal property – gasworks, water-works, and so on – is obtained by capital borrowed from individual savings, is not that so? – It may be so. It would depend upon the facts of the case.

4162. In forecasting the probable influence of collectivism on indus-trial progress, is it not important to recollect those agencies of indus-trial progress which have been collectivised in recent years are not the property of the respective corporations, because there is a mort-gage on them? – I defer to your statement; but I should not put it in that way. If there is any point connected with it on which I can give information to the Commisison I should be glad to do so, but I do not really know what I can add to your statement.

[48] The reference by Webb to Giffen is obscure. It does not refer to the Memorandum which Giffen had prepared for the Commission as a whole and which dealt with labour statistics and associated material. It may refer to Giffen's statistical data reproduced in Fabian Tract No. 5, *Facts for Socialists*, London, Walter Scott, 1890.

4163.   Do you not think that the general adoption of collectivism would be likely to retard the growth of those mechanical appliances on which industrial progress is dependent? – No, I do not.

4164.   Why? – I suggest that if I had said that I thought it would retard them I might have been asked why; but if I suggest no change would take place, it is surely for any other witness to say why it would take place.

4165.   Do you think it is possible that the motives for saving might be diminished? – It is of course conceivable, but not probable.

4166.   Do you not think it is probable? – No; I think on the contrary, the motives for saving would be increased.

4167.   Do you think it is not rather an indication of the importance of individualistic motives as a lever by which capital can be accumulated that municipalities have had to borrow from private concerns means of purchasing businesses? – It appears to me that your statement is an interesting example of the manner in which collectivism increases savings.

4168.   I do not quite understand why it illustrates it? – If you did not mean it to illustrate that, I will withdraw the statement.

4169.   I should like to know whether you can come to-morrow? – I should be delighted to come to-morrow at considerable inconvenience in order to give any information to the Commission, but I must venture to ask to be excused from debating these things. I should be very glad to debate the matter with any Commissioner at a proper time, but I cannot presume to take up the time of the Commission by debating questions and answers. I am prepared to give any information in my power, but not to debate or argue.

[An exchange follows with interventions by Mr Gerald Balfour, Mr Leonard Courtney and Sir Frederick Pollock about Marshall's questioning and the Commission's need to gain information on issues of municipal action in taking over public utilities (Q. 4170–4179). The sitting was then adjourned, with Marshall's questioning resuming the following day.]

[18 November 1892:] Mr. Sidney Webb re-called and further examined

(*The witness*) If the Commission will pardon me just for one minute, I feel that I owe an apology to the Commission for what I am afraid was a serious lack of courtesy yesterday.[49] I have been suffering from sleeplessness, and I wish very earnestly to apologise for what I am sure was a falling off of courtesy to the Commission, and especially to some members of it.

[Professor Marshall continues.]

4224.   I believe you take a moderate position as to the requirements of an eight hours law, and think it should not be a very rigid law? – Yes. I think I would prefer to say that I am very anxious that any law that should be passed should prove to be quite practicable in application, and I feel that no law which would be perfectly rigid and universal could be practically carried out.

4225.   It has been suggested to us by a railway manager that the law would be unworkable, because if a train were snowed up, or stopped by an accident or fog, it would be impossible to relieve the engine driver at the end of his eight hours. I suppose you would not consider that a difficulty under a law such as you propose? – I think it would be extremely important that any law should have some kind of provision for such exceptions as that. I think there is a precedent in the Austrian law limiting the hours of work in mines where there is an actual exception made in the case of snow, and I feel convinced that some such provision as that ought to be made in any law.

4226.   I think you also take a moderate position as to the effects that are to be attributed to the shortenings of the hours of labour in the past, holding that we must be careful not to attribute all the benefits that have followed these shortenings of hours to that shortening? – I think that is very important; that in no case can any single cause be given as the origin of the benefits.

---

[49] A reference to his answer to Marshall's question (Q. 4169, above, p. 185) and the subsequent remark by Balfour, 'Do I understand you to claim you may be excused from answering argumentative questions?', and the admonishing remarks of Leonard Courtney as chairman about Webb's willingness to answer questions (Q. 4174–5).

4227–8.   If I may venture to say so, I think that these two elements of moderateness in your book[50] on the eight hours day have contributed much to the service which it has rendered, and I find myself in agreement, both in reasoning and sympathy, with much that there is in every chapter. As, however, this is not the examination in chief, you will understand that my questions will be directed to those points on which I do not quite agree with you? – Yes.

4229.   I first want to ask you some questions as to whether you have quite sufficiently acted upon your principle of not attributing to shortening of the hours of labour favourable economic conditions that may be probably ascribed, in part at least, to other causes. I will first ask you with regard to Victoria. – Turning to page 101 of that book,[51] you say there, 'In Victoria the reduction in 1856 of the hours of labour of the skilled artisan to eight per day was not accompanied by any fall in wages. The continued prosperity of the capitalist interest in this wealthy colony indicates that the eight hours' day has not spelt ruin'; and in a note you answer Mr. Charles Fairfield's argument, 'that, in consequence of its socialistic legislation, Victoria is virtually insolvent', do you know what the wages in Victoria were before the introduction of the eight hours' day? – I am sorry to say I do not; but, of course, as it was at the period of what one may call the gold fever, the wages were very high.

4230.   Thirty shillings a day, I think, for artisans? – I have heard statements to that effect in particular cases.

4231.   Do not the special apologists of the eight hours' day in Victoria have to argue that though money wages have fallen, yet that the prices of commodities have fallen more in proportion, so that real wages have rather risen? – I believe they do argue that, but I should be sorry to say with exactly how much justice. I may say that my reference there was intended to be to what one may call the immediate effect of the reduction of the hours of labour. The whole course of

[50] That is, Webb and Cox, *The Eight Hours Day*, referred to in many of Marshall's subsequent questions.

[51] Webb and Cox, *The Eight Hours Day*, p. 101 and n.†. The authors answer Charles Fairfield's criticism made in his book *A Plea for Liberty*, ed. Thomas Mackay, London, John Murray, 1891, with the comment that Victorian government securities 'stand almost at the top of colonial securities' on the London Stock Exchange.

wages since 1856 in Victoria is of course a very complicated subject, and I should be very sorry to say what effect the reduction of the hours of labour had had upon the various changes which have resulted in those 36 years.

4232.   I think if you look at the passage on page 101 again you will see that you are bringing the history down to quite recent times?[52] – Pardon me, not with regard to wages, but with regard to the prosperity of the colony. I draw a distinction in deductive argument from attempting to assert that that which has followed a change has been due to that change, and pointing out that a change has occurred without actual injury following it. That does not of course assert that injury might not be caused by another such change in other circumstances.

4233.   Taking the whole course of Victorian wages, is it not true that their money value has fallen nearly as fast as the general fall of prices, so that it is rather difficult to prove whether real wages in Victoria are higher or lower than they were 30 years ago? – I believe that is so, but I understand that the hours of labour in Victoria in the staple trades have not varied during those 30 years.

4234.   Has not the real purchasing power of wages in England been increased by from 60 to 100 per cent during the same period? – I agree with Mr. Giffen's[53] statement to that effect as regards the large majority of industries, but I am afraid that there are a considerable number of workers whose condition, comparing class with the corresponding class of 50 years ago, has not materially improved at all – but that does not, of course, contradict the statement that in the great majority of the trades the wages appear to me to have risen to quite as much as Mr. Giffen states. I think Mr. Giffen's statement went first to money, and I also agree with him very largely in what he says as to the relation of purchasing power.

4235.   Is not the argument from Victoria that its history shows that 'the continued prosperity of the capitalist interest in this wealthy

---

[52] Webb is correct. The sentence following from the one quoted by Marshall (Q. 4229), reads: 'The continued prosperity of the capitalist interest in this wealthy colony indicates that the Eight Hours Day has not spelt ruin.' Marshall quotes this sentence in his Q. 4235 (below pp. 188–9).   [53] See n. 48 above.

country indicates that the eight hours' day does not spell ruin';[54] that is, I think, your argument. Is it not true that the wages of Australian workmen are to a very large extent made up of borrowed capital?[55] – I am afraid I cannot give a short answer to that. I do not believe that in the strict sense, wages are paid out of capital at all.

4236.   I did not mean to insist on any technical interpretation of the doctrine; I meant only to ask this: have there not been very large loans contracted by the Victorians in their individual and collective capacity, and have not these loans been spent to a large extent upon hiring labour to carry out productive and other works? – Certainly, and there has at the same time been a large emigration to Australia.

4237.   Do you not think that the English working people might get very good wages, whether they work ten hours or eight hours, or six hours, or even if they tied one of their hands behind them, if they had the security of some thousands of acres of good land per head on which they could borrow capital from foreign countries, spending that capital in hiring themselves out at high wages? – That is an extremely hypothetical question. I think, perhaps, I can answer it best by saying that I believe certain industries which are strong enough to combine, could get those good wages, but that other industries which, for various reasons, are not capable of protecting their economic interests by combination, would be likely to suffer considerably under those circumstances, as they do now, and I may say it has been shown by the recent Royal Commission in Victoria that they have suffered – even in Victoria itself.

4238.   Do you not think that every class of labour, even dock labour, might get high wages if every individual had at his back a thousand or two of acres of rich ground on which he could borrow, and employ the money in hiring himself out at high wages? – I am afraid I do not quite see your point, but I can answer to that that, of course, those circumstances would have a very favourable effect upon the labour market everywhere.

[54] See n. 52 above.   [55] This is not implied in Webb and Cox, *The Eight Hours Day*.

4239.   Have not the suspicions, too, of Mr. Charles Fairfield and others,[56] that the Victoria workpeople have been trusting too much to borrowed capital to keep their wages abnormally high for very short hours of work – have not those anticipations been borne out by the events that have happened since you wrote this book? – No, I do not think so. Or course, I am aware that there has been more or less what one may call a land panic in Melbourne, but I think that has happened more than once since 1850, and I should venture to suggest that these repeated commercial crises in Melbourne are due to more fundamental causes than the introduction of the eight hours per day in 1856, or than the high wages.

4240.   Still it remains does it not, that in spite of the great quantities of capital that have been lent to Victoria, there has been less progress on the part of the working people under the eight hours' day in Victoria than in England under what we may call a ten hours' day? – I should be very sorry to assert that, but also I should venture to suggest that I should be very slow to even hint at ascribing any such difference in progress, if it exists, to the difference in hours.

4241.   I am not quite asking you to go so far as that, but merely to say that *prima facie* the history of Victoria is rather against than for the proposition that a reduction of the hours of labour does not prevent a rise in wages? – No, I am afraid I cannot go that length. In my view the chief economic benefit of a reduction in the hours of labour is in the effect which I rightly or wrongly believe it will probably have upon what I may call the standard of life of the great mass of the people. I believe the fundamental prosperity of Australia is largely due to the high standard of life which the great mass of the people there have been able, through one cause and another to obtain, and I think that the shortening of the hours of labour in Australia is at once an expression, and if I may say so, a partial cause of this high standard of life.

4242.   Perhaps we may pass away from that subject, and take another historical illustration from your book. On page 97, with regard to the textile industries, and on page 99 with regard to the masons, you

---

[56] That is, Fairfield, *A Plea for Liberty*, ed. Mackay (the Charity Organisation Society Supporter), a work which also included Fairfield's *State Socialism in the Antipodes*.

contrast wages before 1850 for long hours with wages shortly after 1850 for short hours, is that not so? — Yes.[57]

4243.   I think you have not explicitly allowed anything for the clearing up of the railway panic, the passing away of the potato famine, the settling down of the revolutionary spirit that was shaking all thrones in 1848 and holding back commercial enterprise, the general adoption of free trade, the large opening of new markets to England in consequence of the 1851 Exhibition, and above all, the large influx of gold from California and Australia? — I should admit that if that instance had stood alone it would have been open to that criticism, although I have in words expressly guarded, in brief, against that inference, that it will be remembered that those instances of those dates are expressly compared and contrasted with instances of an analogous kind from all the dates which I have been able to obtain from the beginning of the century down to the present day, and at the end of the chapter I have repeated in a note[58] the warning which I endeavoured to give all through the chapter, that the fallacy of *post hoc ergo propter hoc* must not be fallen into; and I have summed up by saying that these instances can legitimately be quoted in disproof of the argument that a reduction of the hours of labour necessarily implies a reduction of wages. That is to say, I would not quote them as an argument proving that it involves an increase of wages, but I think those facts may be quoted against the correspondingly illegitimate, as it seems to me, argument on the other side, that a reduction in the hours of labour must necessarily be followed by a reduction in wages.

4244.   You have got just to the point I wanted. Do you think anybody maintains that a reduction in the hours of labour must cause a fall in wages? — Is not what they say, that a reduction in the hours of labour

---

[57] Although there are historical examples about effects of the reduction of hours on British textile workers and masons on pp. 97, 99, they do not exactly match the views posed in Marshall's quotation.

[58] If the chapter is that dealing with 'The probable economic results of an eight hour day', there is no such warning note. Such a warning is, however, given in the text at the start of the chapter: 'It cannot, of course, be inferred without further investigation that a reduction from ten to eight hours per day would have precisely the same economic results as a previous reduction from twelve hours to ten' (Webb and Cox, *The Eight Hours Day*, p. 94).

would cause wages to be lower than they otherwise would, that is, make them fall faster if they would otherwise have fallen, or make them rise slower or perhaps remain stationary if they would otherwise have risen; is not that the argument? – If I may say so, but I had thought it necessary to deal also with the arguments used by unreasonable persons, and it has been stated, I believe, more than once, that a reduction in the hours of labour must necessarily cause a falling off in the wages earned.

4245. But here we are specially concerned, are we not, exclusively concerned, with the arguments that are put forward by reasonable persons on either side of this controversy? – Certainly, in this room; but, of course, this book from which you are quoting was written to deal also with the arguments of unreasonable persons.

4246. Then do you not think that if the question under discussion is whether a reduction of the hours of labour caused wages to be lower than they otherwise would have been, a great number of the cases mentioned in your book, – I have chosen only some, I might have chosen, I think, several more – seem capable of an interpretation quite consistent with that opinion? – I think they are capable of such an interpretation but I imagine that in an economic inquiry as to the effects of a shortening of the hours, it would be wrong to rule out any fact bearing on the subject, although, of course, each fact should be accepted and used, with as far as may be, the caution which its circumstances require.

4247. One of these instances is that of the textile industries, and in this connexion I should like to ask, getting a little near to the subject we were discussing yesterday, whether you do not think that even a political economist of modern times might have thought that there was a great deal of force, I do not say in the extravagant positions of Mr. Nassau Senior, and Miss Martineau,[59] but in the position of those who held, as I think Mr. John Bright did, that so long as bread was at the extremely high price at which it then was, it was necessary to repeal the Corn Laws before reducing the hours of labour? – I think Mr. Bright was perfectly justified in attaching the most enormous importance to the repeal of the Corn

[59] See Marshall's questions on this above (Q. 4095–105, pp. 176–8).

Laws, and I think, probably, that by temperament and nature that was the work which he could best do; and it is an unfortunate result that the advocates of the particular reform are very often unsympathetically disposed towards other reforms which subsequent events may show to be of, perhaps, analogous importance, although it is difficult to say which at any particular moment is the more important.

4248.   Do you not think that a person in Mr. Bright's position at that time, not being able to anticipate all that series of events in the late forties or early fifties, of which I spoke, might think it much more reasonable than we, knowing these facts now, are inclined to do, to say that the Factory Act should be kept waiting for the repeal of the Corn Laws? – I am not quite sure that that would have correctly described the position; but assuming that that does correctly describe the position which he took up, I confess that I think Lord Shaftesbury took a view which is equally justifiable.

4249.   Quite so. I did not mean that it was not justifiable at all. I am not asking you to say that recent events have not shown that Lord Shaftesbury was wiser than Mr. John Bright. I am only asking you whether it was not possible to hold Mr. John Bright's position even from the point of view of modern economics? – I think that Mr. John Bright's position at that time was a perfectly natural one, and one which I think does his heart, at any rate, no discredit. What I do think it displayed was a certain lack of what I may call political instinct, which it is no blame not to possess in the fullest measure.

4250.   A reduction of the hours of labour as adult males is one of several ways in which we may, if we chose, turn to account, the increasing comment over production which the increase of wealth and of knowledge has given us? – Yes.

4251.   Do you not think that the advocates of this particular method of using up our increased resources, should pay a little more attention to the relative advantages of other methods, in particular to the extension of the Factory Acts in the direction of keeping children at school longer, and putting greater restrictions on such employment of women as prevents them from performing their parts as mothers and wives?[60] — If I may take that question in two parts; the question of the employment of children is one on which I feel very deeply indeed, and I entirely agree that it would be very desirable if those who are advocating reforms of the class to which we are alluding, would also especially press for a raising of the age at which children go into the factory, and for an extension of the period of instruction by half-time or otherwise. I have a little more difficulty with regard to the women, because there are difficult economic questions involved, but I have every sympathy with an extension of the Factory Acts in that direction and I think it would be very important if that could be pressed for in the way suggested.

4252.   You said yesterday that the economists of to-day have been very careful not to commit themselves one way or the other about the eight hours law? — That is my opinion, and I think they are right.

4253.   Might I suggest two causes of this caution. Is not one that they may think that the question of the relative advantages of diminishing the work of women and children, and of diminishing the work of those classes of men who already have a fair amount of leisure, has not been sufficiently discussed? — That may be so; I think there would be great reason for them to feel that.

4254.   May not another cause be in connexion with a statement made by yourself,[61] that the very best work is not done for pay. Perhaps I should explain; the very best work we are all agreed cannot be bought; nobody could have secured the writing of Shakespeare's works by offering to pay for them? — That is my opinion.

4255.   But is it not also true that though the best work cannot be bought, the best work must have as a condition freedom of initiative and freedom of action — so far as history shows — at least so far as we can judge from history? — I, of course, agree that those are extremely important conditions of the best work. Perhaps where I should not

---

[60] See Q. 4123–32, above pp. 180–1.

[61] That statement is not contained in Webb's evidence, nor in the summary of his published views appended to the *Fourth Report*. Cf., however, the following remark from the latter (p. 139): 'when all have learned to co-operate for the general good, the best endowed will seek their chief good in honourable social distinction, or rather, in the consciousness of having served worthily, and not in materialistic awards'.

agree with the thought that is there indicated, is in the comparative estimate of the conditions necessary for the formation of character. I believe that what I may call the *régime* of Collective Control would have good effects upon character, perhaps to a larger extent than is anticipated by those who do not take the same view with me. But I admit the very great importance of initiative and freedom, especially in various kinds of work.

4256.   It is difficult to prophesy as to the future, but looking at the past, is it not true that where bureaucracy has been established where the individual has felt himself tied by red tape at every turn; the energy that has made industry progress has vanished?[62] – I feel it extremely difficult to draw such a general conclusion, and especially for the reason that I think – I hope a great deal – a great deal of the bad effects of paternal government of the old kind can be connected by an extension of democracy. That is to say, I hope that bureaucracy under a real democracy, which we have hardly yet attained, to any-where, will be different – in degree certainly – and I hope different in kind in many ways to bureaucracy without a democratic *régime*.

4257.   I share those hopes to a considerable extent, but is it not rash to make a law when we can do without a law, so long as the history of the past, in so far as it does indicate the future, shows that where you have bureaucracy there you will not have progress? – I am afraid I cannot accept that statement. I should join issue on the statement. I entirely agree with the old position, that a law is an evil which should be avoided where it can be avoided without greater evil; but, of course, the case of those who ask for a legal shortening of the hours of labour is that the evil which will result without the law is greater than the evil which the law would cause.

4258.   I was suggesting that these two reasons, firstly, the fear that an increase of law might induce the stagnation of a bureaucratic *régime*, and secondly, the feeling that the relative merits of greater care for women and children and of greater care for the men had not been

---

[62] Earlier that year, when Marshall congratulated Beatrice Potter on her engagement to Sidney Webb (Marshall to Beatrice Potter, 22 January 1892, Passfield Papers, II i(ii) 205, British Library of Political and Economic Science) he mentioned that the line dividing him from the Webbs was that of bureaucracy versus freedom of variation.

sufficiently discussed, might be the causes why modern economists hold very much aloof from the eight hours movement; do you not think so? – I think they are; but I should have thought perhaps an even more important cause was the extreme difficulty of prophesying what would be the effect in economic relations of any particular alteration of this kind.

4259. Yes, I was rather taking that for granted. We will now then come to that; and first with regard to a point on which, I think, we are entirely in agreement; you, I think, lay great stress upon the influence of adopting double shifts as a means of raising wages. You have, I think, said something about it here, but perhaps you would kindly tell us what are the ways in which you think that the adoption of double shifts would especially help a rise of wages? – I forget at this moment in what place I have made any such statement. I do think that *prima facie* there would be an economic advantage if double shifts could be worked – I offer no opinion as to the practicability in various trades – if double shifts could be worked, especially in industries where a large amount of fixed capital is involved compared with the wage labour; but it would, of course, depend upon other circumstances how that additional economic advantage, which I think might in many cases be obtained in that way, would be shared among the classes contributing.

4260. Might we go into that matter a little more in detail. One of the advantages you would hold would be that the untiring machinery would be working long while man was working short? – Yes.

4261. That, consequently, machinery would be worn out by use rather than thrown aside as obsolete from the lapse of time. I mean that machinery would get through a greater amount of work before the progress of invention had had time to make it obsolete? – I think that is an incidental advantage.

4262. And that in consequence, machinery would be able to be improved faster and be kept more to date? – That also, I think, would be an incidental advantage.

4263. And that in consequence machinery would be more abundant relatively to labour, the supply of machinery would be increased relatively to labour, because one piece of machinery would do for two sets of workers? – Excuse me, I do not follow the argument. I think, probably, there would be an increase of machinery because it would mean that what one may call the economic cost of using machinery would be diminished in that way.

4264.   I did not mean that just then, though that, of course, is an important point. I mean this: since one machine would require two sets of men to attend to it, machinery would be running after men to work rather than men running after machinery to work on – the requisite supply of machinery would only be half as much, and, therefore, any given supply of machinery would be redundant, and this would force down the earnings of machinery relatively to labour? – I think that would be the *prima facie* effect, which, of course, would be very quickly counteracted by other tendencies to some extent.

4265.   On the whole, a less amount of capital would be required to keep going a certain amount of machinery, and therefore, with our existing capital there would be a tendency for capital to be redundant relatively to labour, and the rate of interest, therefore, would fall? – That is my opinion.

4266.   We are, I think, agreed on all these points. Does it not follow that *prima facie*, therefore, a reduction of the hours of labour from ten to eight without double shift would, for each one of these reasons separately, tend to lower wages? – It rather depends upon the meaning we give to the word 'tendency'. I think that the effect of a reduction of the hours would in a great many industries be so to alter the character of the work and the workmen, that in all probability the economic, the purely economic, effect would be comparatively small. I mean that the effect upon the product and upon the way the product was shared, would in a number of instances be comparatively small; but, of course, I should say that that must necessarily vary from industry to industry.

4267.   Passing to another point you sum up on page 121 of your book,[63] the probable economic results of an eight hours' day, as far as they

---

[63] Webb and Cox, *The Eight Hours Day*, pp. 121–2, sums up the theoretical argument in eight short sentences, of which Marshall in his question quotes the first, on a point he had contested heatedly with Tom Mann earlier in the Commission's hearings. Above, Q. 3283, p. 165.

can be discerned, I think, and the first result is 'a general shortening of the hours of labour may slightly decrease the average productivity per worker, but will, by absorbing a part of the unemployed, probably increase the total production of the community.' Will you kindly explain why it would increase the total production? — I may say that that is of course an extremely general statement, which has been deduced from the particulars in the preceding pages. I have endeavoured to give reasons for my belief that in a number of industries a reduction of the hours of labour would have practically small economic effects, other than the increase of leisure, and that in other industries, of which, of course, that of a night watchman is an extreme type, the service rendered per worker would necessarily decrease almost in exact proportion to the reduction in the number of hours. And accordingly if you place those two arguments together you might have on the whole of industry a slight average reduction per worker caused by this falling off in the services rendered by night watchmen, of railway signalmen, and that kind of industry coincidently with, putting it moderately, no increase in the productivity of the other industries owing to a shortening of the hours of labour. In that case you would get a general reduction in the average productivity per worker. But I have also endeavoured to show that the same reasons which would make the productivity of the night watchman fall off in almost exact proportion to the reduction in his hours, would almost necessarily involve an increase in the number of such persons, and I had come to the conclusion, tentatively, that that increase would almost certainly be sought for among the ranks of those persons in casual and intermittent employment, who are often spoken of as 'the unemployed'; and that accordingly the absorption of those into the ranks of these other workers would, as it seemed to me, maintain the total productivity in all probability by giving us, in place of these practically unemployed workers with their evil effect upon the standard of life of the classes near them, a disciplined and civilised body of men, such as our railway porters are. with, as I should suggest, their improving effect upon the standard of life of the classes near them. I rest the argument upon the improvement in the standard of life which I had hoped would be brought about in that way.[64]

[64] See Webb and Cox, *The Eight Hours Day*, pp. 106–10.

4268.   I then understand that you do not hold that the immediate effect of a shortening of the hours of labour would be to increase the total production of the community, but that that effect might be produced in the course of say, a generation? – No, I should not say that. I hold, whether right or wrongly, that the demoralising effect of these casual and intermittent workers is immediate in its operation, and that if one could remove, for instance, the condition of things which exists in East London, – if one could transform by some magician's wand the casual dock labourer and the home worker into as good citizens as the railway porter (who gets very low wages) you would have, as it seemed to me, an almost immediate increase in the services rendered by those people, and an improvement in the social efficiency of that part of the community.[65]

4269.   I understand the position to be that in certain industries the reduction of the hours of labour would diminish the output, per man, using the term 'output' generally, for all sorts of services? – Yes, quoting the typical case of the night watchman.

4270.   And that to make up for this deficiency certain of these who are now unemployed would be called in? – I thought so.

4271.   Then I understand you to go on that, immediately, these people who are called in to make up the deficiency would not only make up the deficiency, but, more than make up the deficiency? – Yes, I thought so.

4272.   Why should they be called in in a number sufficient to make up more than the deficiency? – That is a question of the relative proportion of such industries to the whole, and I feel that it is a question upon which there has been very little statistical inquiry, and upon which I feel very great uncertainty. I may say that the figure which I used[66] in connexion with the railway industry of 400,000 persons is, I think, erroneous, because that represents the total number of persons in railway employment; whereas I ought to have referred only to the traffic staff which is considerably less; but that and other industries,

---

[65] *Ibid.*, pp. 106–10.

[66] This is not given in the section on economic effects of the reduction of working hours on the railway industry in *ibid.*, pp. 129–32.

such as the tramway industry, would probably recruit their ranks to a considerable extent from the class which is now somewhat chronically under employed.

4273.   Perhaps it will fix the idea if we take a particular industry, the tramway; the hours of labour are reduced, and in consequence some of the unemployed are taken on to drive trams and act as conductors; there will be a greater expense, but I cannot see why then, there should be a greater productivity. Why should there be more trams running? – I am not sure that I have suggested that more trams would be run. That is not my opinion.

4274.   Then I do not quite understand where the greater productivity would come? – I am afraid the point at issue between us in the argument is our relative view of the effect upon the general social productivity of having these people in the condition in which they now are, and of having them in a condition, let us say, such as our railway porters. I have thought, perhaps incorrectly, that it would have a very marked effect upon the general industrial efficiency of East London if we could so improve the condition of those persons – that is to say, I hold rather strongly the doctrine that a rise in the standard of life of the people has a very great effect in the social efficiency of the work of the community.

4275.   I do not quite see how you connect that with this particular cause. The men at present at work will do less; there will be consequently a certain deficiency of work done; to make up that deficiency other people will be called in; I do not see how this deficiency on the part of some people causes other people not only to make up that deficiency but to go above it? – It depends upon our view of whether it does raise their standard of life as I should have thought. I am sorry I am not able to put it any clearer, but that is the basis of my argument. If, by reducing the hours of labour or by any other means, we can raise the standard of life of persons, especially those below what one would call a normal level of decent living, I had thought that it would have considerable and very prompt effects upon the general social efficiency of the labour of the country. I must admit that I am not able to prove it specifically, but that is what I have been driving at.

4276.   I would like to put it in my own words to see if I understand you. Is it that the people who are unemployed are capable of being turned into good citizens by employment being given to them, and that when once brought into employment they would become efficient workers and go on extending industry? – I believe that would be very largely the result.

4277.   In order to estimate how far this result would be likely to follow, we should of course want to know what is the real number of the unemployed, and what portion of them are ready and able to do a good day's work in return for a fair day's wages? – Excuse me – we have been using the term 'unemployed' as a kind of shorthand. I mean, of course, those classes of workers who are intermittently and casually employed in various occupations. I do not mean the local and particular unemployed owing to some seasonal or other cause.

4278.   But you are aware that there is a very great difference of opinion as to whether many of those persons could be made efficient workers by any change of condition? – I should be very sorry to believe that there are many people who think that no change could make those people into efficient workers.

4279.   Well, I would say the particular change of giving them fairly good employment for a certain time? – Of course it is part of my case that they have been extremely demoralised, partly by the conditions in which they have lived, and that, therefore, any measure of improvement would necessarily not be immediate, although I believe that it would immediately begin.

4280.   But you recognise that this part of your case rests upon a view of the character of the unemployed and casually employed classes which is far from universally accepted? – I am sorry that I did not know it was to any extent dissented from. I should have thought that regular and reasonably paid employment would have improved the character even of the most demoralised, though I should be far from saying that it would produce anything like a perfect character.

4281.   I think the question is not whether it would not improve them somewhat, but whether the fact that they are at present casually employed or unemployed does not indicate some deficiency on their part, in the large majority of cases, below the average standard? – I am afraid I should be sorry to say that. I think, of course, that other things being equal, the steadier and the more capable a workman the man is, the less he is likely to be unemployed at any emergency: but on the other hand, one knows, for instance that persons are often unemployed or that their trade is reduced from prosperity to one of casual and intermittent work by industrial changes. If I might quote a bygone case, about which there will be little doubt, I would say that it would have been a great gain if it could have been possible to have drawn off a number of Spitalfields handloom weavers in their long struggle against poverty; I am not saying that it would have been possible, but I am suggesting that it would have been a social gain if a number of them could have been induced to abandon their intermittent and dying work before they were actually and completely starved out to the extent they have been.

4282.   I think we should all agree with you, and I think we should all agree that any change, whether it be a shortening of the hours of labour, or any other, that brought the working members of society under some sort of training was a good one; but I think we should differ as to the extent to which this cause would operate, and I think we must agree to allow for it some quantity if not quite definitely settled? – I have scarcely asserted any more than that.

4283.   Making due allowances under that head, I want to ask you to consider the relation in which the doctrine that a reduction in the hours of labour would not lower wages stands to the doctrine of the extreme Malthusians; I say the extreme Malthusians – for, of course Malthus was a chief opponent of extreme Malthusianism – the extreme Malthusians hold, I think, that an increase of population by itself lowered wages much, and that other things being equal, a diminution of population raised wages much; is not that so? – That has been held.

4284.   And you do not agree with that? – I think it is only true with very wide qualifications.

4285.   Now I want to ask you another question which I have already asked here of Mr. Mann, but I should be glad to have your answer to it, because it really seems to me to be very important.[67] The

---

[67] Above, pp. 150–1, Q. 3193–7.

population of England may be taken to be 30 millions, supposing for the sake of argument, as we did then, that the unemployed, in the large sense of the term, be taken at 10 per cent in normal times, making 3 millions out of the 30 millions, do you hold that the wages would be very much higher than they are now, if all other things were equal, but the population were 27 millions instead of 30 millions? – I am afraid that hypothetical question requires me to consider which 3 millions would be dispensed with. I hold that it is one of the gravest dangers of an undue insistence on Malthusian doctrines that one may be diminishing the supply of just the classes whom the country can least spare. If one could dispense in some painless way with those 3 millions of unemployed, I think it is extremely probable that the wages of the rest, at any rate the real (as distinguished from the nominal) wages of the rest, would go up.

4286. No doubt, but I was taking the 3 millions drawn by lot? – I am afraid I have not considered that point. I do not feel able to say what the effect on wages would be.

4287. I should rather like you to consider it, if you would, because it seems to me to go to the root of the question with regard to the influence of the reduction of the hours of labour on wages? – It is very difficult to answer with all of the will in the world, because the withdrawal of one valuable servant of the community who, might happen to be one of those chosen lot, might so seriously affect the productivity of the community as to counterbalance any other possible effects.

4288. I did not mean to insist upon any particular change of that sort. I am supposing that the change had been made so as not to take away specially important people? – I think that a proportionate reduction of the population, of all classes and grades of efficiency, which is perhaps the fairest way of taking it, would have, as it seems to me, either no effect upon wages at all, or an effect which it would be very difficult to calculate. That is to say, bearing in mind the question of the position of the margin of cultivation of land which would have relation to it, and also the margin of utilisation, if I may so call it, of the existing stock of machinery and plant, I feel it utterly impossible to give any statement which would be at all useful as to the probable result of that.

4289.   But you have no special reason for believing that if other things were equal, but the population were 27 millions instead of 30 millions, wages would be much higher than now? – Assuming that the reduction is not from any special class, that is my view.

[Mr Courtney then interrupts with three questions (Q. 4290–2) indicating hypothetical cases of the reduction in labour in agriculture and mining and its consequences for the labourers, the farmers and others involved in the cultivation or exploitation of land. Marshall then resumes his questioning.]

4293.   I think perhaps it would be well for me to state again the doctrine that I am asking your assent to. It is, that if other things were equal, the land and the capital, and so on, but the population were 27 millions instead of 30 millions, then there would be a slightly higher level of wages, because labour would be less abundant relatively to capital; yet that, unless we accept the extreme Malthusian doctrines, we cannot hold that such a diminution of the population would raise the wages per head much? – I agree with you that we could not come to that conclusion, that it would raise the wages per head to an appreciable extent. I offer no opinion as to whether it would or would not, but I entirely agree that we could not deductively come to the conclusion that it would raise wages.

4294.   I am asking you only to assent to this, that to decide that it would raise wages very much would be to adopt extreme Malthusian opinions? – Yes.

4295.   And you do not adopt extreme Malthusian opinions? – Certainly not in that shape.

4296.   Now, would not a diminution in the amount of work done per head have just the same effects on the relations between the demand and supply of labour as an equivalent reduction in the number of workers, and would it not, therefore, have exactly the same results on the aggregate of wages paid? – I think the two cases are analogous, but as I am so uncertain about the one and equally uncertain about the other, I feel a difficulty in saying that it would be exactly the same result.

4297.   Would not the position of the workers, if their number were diminished, be better than if the hours of labour were reduced, in this way, — in both cases there would be the same aggregate wages to be divided out but with a diminished number of workers the divisor would be 27,000,000 and with the shortened hours of labour the divisor would be 30,000,000, and therefore the rate of wages per head, which could not be said to have necessarily risen as a result of the diminution of the population, might be said almost necessarily to fall as a result of the diminution of the hours of labour? — Excuse me; that seems to depend upon the assumption that the sum total paid in wages remained the same. Now, I do not hold that the sum total paid in wages will necessarily remain the same, even if the total productivity remains the same.

4298. Would not the effect on the relations of supply and demand between capital and labour of a reduction of the hours of labour be just the same as the effect of an equivalent reduction in the number of workers? — No, I am not able to assent to that. I think that that would be to leave out of account the alteration in the character of the workers, which I believe a shortening of the hours of labour will bring about.

4299. I knew that you would have that valid answer, and it was for that reason that I went to that point first.[68] We started, I think, by saying that a certain correction would have to be allowed for the training which this new employment might give to the lower ranks of workers: but subject to that allowance, eventually we should reach this result? — Again, not quite, because in addition to the potential results upon the casual labourer, henceforth to be a regular labourer, you have to consider also, as it seems to me, the effect upon the worker who is now working ten or eleven hours a day regularly, and who would henceforth only work a shorter number. I hold, in the strongest possible manner, that overtime work is costly and inefficient.

4300. Then ultimately the greater leisure will raise the standard and vigour of the population? — Yes.

4301. I think that answer is a good one, and I have no objection to it? — I should also say that in addition to that standard of vigour, the much

[68] Above, pp. 200–1, Q. 4275–80.

larger considerations which are included in the standard of life generally have to be taken into account.

4302.   There is one point of some importance though it is a minor point on which I am not in agreement with you, and that is the effect of an eight hours' day in those industries which are of the nature of a monopoly. I think it comes on page 132,[69] under the head of tramway and railway workers. Am I right in stating that your argument is that tramway and railway managers fix the fares at the amount which will yield the greatest gross receipts, and that therefore, if they had to pay more wages for work in consequence of the reduction of the hours of labour, they would have to bear that burden themselves, and could not shift it on to the consumers? – That is not quite what I said. I have said that according to the testimony of railway experts some of those opinions I have given, the charges are fixed, as they say, according to what the traffic will bear and that has very little relation therefore, in their minds to the actual cost which they incur in moving that traffic. But I have pointed out that that, of course, does not exclude from their consideration the increase in total working expenses which an increasing business may bring to them, nor the decrease in total working expenses which they may be able to effect, if there is a decrease in business. I have merely drawn attention to the fact that the total increase or decrease of working expenses is normally in much smaller ratio to the total increased receipts or decreased receipts than the whole percentage of working expenses. That is to say, that a railway company can carry a great deal more traffic, goods and passengers, without much increasing its working expenses, and that every increase in its traffic, up at any rate to a certain point, involves a diminution in the percentage of working expenses; and conversely.

4303.   Then I think I misunderstood you. I ought to have attributed to you the opinion that in tramway and railway business no very great part of the increased expense due to the eight hours day could be thrown on the public? – That is my opinion. I am told by some

---

[69] That is, Webb and Cox, *The Eight Hours Day*, pp. 129–34; p. 132 describes the case of tramworkers as 'closely analogous to the case of the railway workers'. The paragraph from which that quotation is drawn conforms to the gist of the remainder of Marshall's question. And see *ibid.*, p. 115.

railway experts that a certain part of the additional expense would probably be saved in better organisation and by more appliances.

4304.   Then, so far on immediate results, we are agreed; you go on also to admit, do you not, that such increased expense would prevent the rapid development of tramways and the rapid development of employment on them? – No, not quite. I have pointed out that an increased cost of working tramways might tend to militate against their extension on what we may call the margin of cultivation – that in some places it might just pay to run a tramway if you were allowed to work your men sixteen hours a day, whereas it would not pay, perhaps, to run that tramway if you were allowed only to work your men eight hours a day.[70]

4305.   I did not say it would prevent the development, but that it would prevent the rapid development. I think we were agreed? – No, I do not quite agree as to the total effect. I only said that there might be, and as it appears to me probably there would be cases on the margin of cultivation in which a tramway could not be made with an eight hours maximum when it might be profitably made with a sixteen hours maximum.

4306.   In all this argument it is very important, is it not, to make clear whether we are speaking of immediate or ultimate results? – Yes, and I have endeavoured to do so.[71]

4307.   Do you think you have sufficiently made clear that there are dangers to be feared, both immediate and distant, if a reduction of the hours of labour should cause any considerable diminution of output? – I have attempted to make it clear, but, of course, in my view, the dangers to be feared from not shortening the hours of labour are far greater.[72]

---

[70] This argument has not been found in *ibid.*

[71] Cf., for example, *ibid.*, p. 122 where, in the assessment of the economic effects in the reduction of work hours, 'time is said to be of the essence of the matter'.

[72] S. Webb and H. Cox, *ibid.*, suggest 'the possibility of maintaining the total amount of the product, not withstanding a reduction of working hours, however incredible it may seem, is proved by too much evidence to allow of doubt' (p. 104). The social evils attributable to excessive hours are demonstrated throughout, esp. pp. 139–52. And see above, pp. 197–9, Q. 4267–8.

4308.   Ultimately, I suppose, you would look to the emigration of capital and to a certain extent the lessened accumulation of capital as dangers to be feared? – No, I have endeavoured to explain why I do not think they are practical or serious dangers to be feared; they are possible consequences to be borne in mind.[73]

4309.   As regards ultimate results, I think you consider that the fear that our industries should be undersold by foreign competition is exaggerated – Yes.[74]

4310.   I should, perhaps, go part of the way with you there; but must you not take account of the fact that, so far as immediate results go, there might be a considerable disturbance and shock to credit, and in consequence, want of employment? – By a universal bill applying to all industries, I think if that were suddenly introduced and passed and effectively carried out immediately it might have those dangers, but I should venture to add to that that is hardly in contemplation, is it?

4311.   I did not quite understand you to say that? – That the carrying next session of a universal Bill fixing a maximum of eight hours per day for all industries whatsoever, and its being put into thorough effect promptly, is hardly in the contemplation even of those who advocate it.

4312.   I do not think you told us that before; do you think that the eight hours' day should be gradually introduced? – I think it is desirable that any change in industrial organisation should be gradual, and I think we have for some time been gradually moving towards the adoption of an eight hours' day.[75]

4313.   So that you would not advocate one sweeping Bill? – No, I have never advocated that.

4314.   Now, are you quite sure that the relative advantages of a little more leisure and of higher wages are not put somewhat differently by different classes of workers? – That is so. I, of course, wish to see

---

[73] Webb and Cox, *The Eight Hours Day*, p. 121.   [74] *Ibid.*, pp. 115–18.

[75] *Ibid.*, p. 122, where 'gradual and partial shortening' is the likely outcome in hours reduction forecast.

the raising of the standard of life – that is the basis of all my argument. Unfortunately it is just those classes who are debarred from
any decent standard of life who are very often least aware of the
desirability of the rise.

4315.   I should now like to take an instance of that by comparison of
two industries of which we have heard a great deal in Committee B;
one is the Huddersfield tramways, in which you have taken a great
deal of interest; and the other is the London Omnibus Company. Do
you know what the wages of the Huddersfield drivers are? – I believe
the drivers receive in Huddersfield 26s. per week.[76]

4316.   The drivers are skilled artisans. The tramways are steam
tramways? – Yes, I presume the drivers might be classed as skilled
artisans.

4317.   They would certainly be skilled artisans, would they not, quite
distinctly skilled artisans? – Of course they would not be members of
the Amalgamated Society of Engineers, but I would rather say they
belong to the new class of responsible labourers who have been so
much introduced during this generation.

4318.   But is not driving a locomotive steam engine a highly skilled
occupation? – I can only say it is a question of degree.

4319.   Should you say that it was a less or more skilled occupation than
driving a horse omnibus? – I really do not know at all, I am afraid I
could not do either.

4320.   An agricultural labourer could, I presume, get to drive an
omnibus much more quickly, or an ordinary person would get to
drive an omnibus much more quickly, I presume, than a steam
tramway? – Perhaps I might say that in my view the economic classification of skilled and unskilled is largely a matter of wages paid, and
I should rather inquire what the relative wages were before I
attempted to class my workers. Of course there is another meaning
to skilled and unskilled, and in that sense the agricultural labourer is

---

[76] *Ibid.*, p. 264, reproducing a Memorandum from the manager of Huddersfield Cooperative
Tramways dated 17 December 1890. This was made available to the Commission (*Fourth
Report*, Whole Commission, 1894, Appendix 73, pp. 153–4).

perhaps as highly skilled as the engineer, but economically it is not so.

4321.   But that particular method will hardly do when we are considering the effects of different modes of employment upon wages? – In Committee B, we were very much interested in the effect of municipal employment at Huddersfield;[77] we had a driver, and the manager of the tramways, and it is with reference to that evidence I am now asking you. Do you think it is a great result of municipal enterprise to give 26s. per week to a steam tram driver? – I think, perhaps, wages should be considered in relation to the place. For instance, I do not know what the wages of steam tram drivers in private employment in the West Riding of Yorkshire are, but I am able to compare the wages of tramway conductors, and the result is this: that at Huddersfield the tramway conductor gets for 48 hours work, 21s. per week, which viewed absolutely is small enough; and at Bradford, which is only a few miles off, the tramway conductor is getting under a private company, precisely the same wages of 21s. per week; but he has to work more than twice the number of hours per week. I assume from that, and from other general evidence which I have come across, that the wages paid by the Huddersfield Corporation are what one might call the wages current for those occupations in that district, and I would not ask the municipality, except as regards the minimum, to pay more than that rate.

4322.   We had the Bradford case before us, and we were not able to ascertain whether there were not exceptional circumstances accounting for that?[78] – I should be sorry to assume that there were any exceptional circumstances.

4323.   We have had great complaints of the wages paid under private management to the omnibus drivers in London.[79] Do you know what they are? – I am sorry I do not.

4324.   7s.6d. per day? – I think it is something like that.

---

[77] This evidence was reported in minutes of evidence, Group B, Vol. III, Q. 18,669–73, esp. 18,671 where 26s. was the wage indicated by the witness as stated by Marshall.

[78] This evidence was reported in minutes of evidence, Group B, Q. 18,669–73.

[79] This evidence was reported in the minutes of evidence, Group B, Vol. III, pp. 72–3, Q. 18,070–8. The wages there reported fluctuate from 6s. to 7s. a day.

4325. With a choice of working seven days or six days, as they prefer? — I believe that is so.

4326. Making the wages about twice as high as are paid to the Huddersfield tramway drivers? — As are paid in an altogether different town to an altogether different class of workers.

4327. A different class, but not, apparently, less skilled? — Upon that point I have no evidence. It is not to be supposed, of course, that if those Huddersfield men were employed in London they would not get the London rate of wages. The fact that there is a difference in the rate of wages, which may sometimes come — as between Keighley and Manchester, for instance — to as much as 10s. per week in the Amalgamated Engineers, must be borne in mind in comparing municipal enterprise in one town with private enterprise in another town.

4328. But is there a corresponding difference in the wages of locomotive engineers in Huddersfield and London? — Upon that point I have no particular evidence. There is a very large difference in wages generally between London and a town like Huddersfield.

4329. But a difference at all of this kind? — Yes, a difference of that kind.

4330. Of about 100 per cent? — I must demur to the comparison. You are, as I understand, comparing two different trades, and assuming that they are equally skilled. I have no information on that subject. I should not wish to admit the fact.

4331. Do you know that we have some London omnibus drivers before us, and that they expressed the strongest objection to a reduction of the hours of labour, if it involved, as they thought it must involve, a fall of wages?[80] — That is an extremely interesting statement of theirs, which I think is an illustration of your suggestion that different people took different views. I should not agree with them, of course, that it did necessarily involve a reduction of wages.

---

[80] This statement by Marshall is not easy to sustain from the evidence collected from tramworkers. Most, if not all, favoured reductions of hours and argued it need not be accompanied by reduced wages. E.g. minutes of evidence, Group B, Vol. III, Q. 23,716–19.

4332.   They were asked whether they objected, not only to an Eight Hours Bill, but to a reduction to eleven hours' work, if that should result in a fall of wages to 6s., and they expressed a strong objection to such a change? – I think it is very probable, but then I have given reasons to show that a reduction in wages is not so probable.[81]

4333.   Do not facts like this rather indicate that the advantages of increased leisure are not so highly prized by many people – whose occupation already gives them a great deal of variety – as is sometimes supposed? – I have already said that the advantages would be differently prized by different people. I prize them very highly in their effect upon the social well being of the community.

4334.   I suppose an intelligent agricultural labourer, with a little special training, could become an omnibus driver, even although he might not take to it at once; would you admit that? – I should think from the fact that the wages are at the high level that you have suggested,[82] that would probably not be the case, or else one would have supposed that those wages would have fallen.

4335.   I am afraid I must take that answer without analysing it, I would ask you only this, whether you are aware what have been the average wages of labour in pecks of corn throughout English history? – I am sorry I have not those statistics with me.

4336.   Has it not been proved that the day's wage of ordinary labour have oscillated about a peck of corn throughout the last 600 years?[83] – I believe that statement has been made.

4337.   That they have never, except in recent times, exceeded two pecks? – I have heard that.

---

[81] S. Webb and H. Cox, *The Eight Hours Day*, pp. 110–14, esp. p. 114, where it is stated 'On the whole, therefore, both experience and theory indicate that, so long as the aggregate amount of production be maintained, a reduction of hours can be made without any permanent fall in wages.'   [82] Above, Q. 4323–4.

[83] Marshall is here referring to T.R. Malthus, *Principles of Political Economy*, 1st edn, London, John Murray, 1820, Chapter 4, Section 4, esp. pp. 271–80, and see p. 284 where Malthus states, 'that during the course of nearly 500 years, the earnings of a day's labour in this country have probably been more frequently below than above a peck of wheat; that a peck of wheat may be considered as something like a middle point, or rather above the middle point, about which the market wages of labour . . . have oscillated'.

4338. Would not the wages of the omnibus driver be something like seven pecks? – I daresay; but I understood that statement to refer to unskilled labour.

4339. Yes, to ordinary labour. Is not that a great argument against disturbing that method of industrial employment, by which these results have been obtained, without a very great deal of consideration as to wages – ? – Excuse me – which results; the oscillation about the one peck?

4340. No, the rise from a mean of one peck for unskilled labour, to the seven pecks for labour requiring no more special training than that of driving an omnibus? – I must venture to differ. I do not think you can fairly compare the wages of unskilled labour, worked out by Professor Thorold Rogers,[84] for instance, in the middle ages, with the wages in corn to an omnibus driver in the 19th century, in a city where rents are so high. There are so many elements of difference. In the first place, the historical statement refers, as I understand it, to ordinary unskilled labour, but the omnibus driver belongs to a class to whom a capitalist company apparently feels itself compelled to offer far above the average wage even of many skilled trades I can only assume that they consider the omnibus driver to be what we should call economically a skilled labourer. In any case it would be difficult to compare the money, or even the food wages, of a man in London, where he has to pay large sums for rent, with the food wages of an agricultural labourer in the country districts in the middle ages.

4341. Of course, he would buy some things more cheaply and another thing more dearly now than he would then? – There would be so marked a difference in almost every respect, that I confess I am not able to offer any opinion as to the utility of the comparison.

4342. Passing to the Bristol Docks, are you sure that all the money which has been wasted at Bristol on docks was spent unwisely by private enterprise?[85] – I should be sorry to suggest that it was spent unwisely. There has been a considerable sum of money laid out on

---

[84] A reference to J.E. Thorold Rogers, *Six Centuries of Work and Wages, the History of English Labour*, new edn, London, Allen and Unwin, 1949, Chapter XIX, esp. pp. 538–40 (first published, 1884).

[85] A reference to Q. 4018 by Gerald Balfour the previous day indicated Webb thought money had been squandered by private enterprise in the Bristol docks.

docks in the case of the Avon much of which have become, as I understand, relatively disadvantageous, owing to other changes. It is difficult to say that the money was not spent wisely as far as could be foreseen at the time.

4343.   Is it not time that the Portishead and Avonmouth docks, though probably unwisely competing with one another, may yet be meeting the real wants of the times, so far as they go? – I am sorry to say, I do not know.

4344.   I thought you had special knowledge of that; I thought you laid stress on that? – No; I said, as I understood, the people of Bristol, as a whole, were of opinion that they had done wisely in purchasing these docks, even at a sum which caused an annual deficit to occur on the dock accounts taken separately.

4345.   But are you of opinion that the Bristol people think they were wise in spending something like a million pounds, which they did spend, upon improving their own docks, the Municipal docks? – That is another question upon which I do not think I have made any statement, and as to which I really feel I know nothing.

[Marshall's questioning is followed by that of Mr Abraham.]

Marshall's examination of Charles Booth, 29 November 1892

[Marshall's questioning follows that of Mr Austin.]

PROFESSOR MARSHALL

5592.   I suppose you regard the remedies[86] that you propose not as perfect remedies, but as remedies going a certain way for curing a very great evil? – Yes.

5593.   The objections that your plan would not be carried out perfectly would be in your opinion not fatal objections? – No.

---

[86] Booth discussed these remedies in answers to questions posed by David Dale (Q. 5417–19). They dealt with the need generally to enhance the standard of life of the unskilled worker to remove or reduce their 'helplessness', the need for control by extension of the Factory Acts, and the registration of workshops for the purpose of facilitating inspections.

5594.   Have you explained quite fully the ways in which you think it is likely that the improvement of factory and workshop legislation may tend to increase the evils of domestic work? – I have not.

5595.   Would you kindly say a little more on that? – It appears to me that any increased pressure put through the Factory Acts upon industries carried on under certain conditions to which those Factory Act regulations apply must have the tendency to drive work into other methods of production which are not so regulated and that would be an evil, and, in fact, seriously hamper the action of factory legislation.

5596.   You are in favour of increasing the stringency of factory and workshop legislation generally? – I think so, but I am first of all in favour of making it press evenly.

5597.   Yes, but you think that before we increase much the pressure of workshop or factory legislation we must put some pressure on domestic work? – Yes, I think you could not increase the pressure without first extending its area.

5598.   Have you considered the possible influence of the cheapening of electric power on the tendency of more stringent factory and workshop legislation to drive work into the houses? – I have considered it, but not at all exhaustively. It seems to me a most important point.

5599.   I am not quite sure that you did not change the use of the term employer in the course of your evidence. I want rather to get this cleared up. At the beginning I think you said that you would regard a man as an employer who was working with anyone save his own wife?[87] – Yes, there would be common employment which would have the same effect.

5600.   Later on you said, I think in answer to Mr. Tait or Mr. Austin, that you did not propose to make the employer responsible; you then had a different employer in your mind?[88] – Yes, that was so.

[87] See Booth's answer to Q. 5419 where employers are so defined, and Q. 5562 (addressed by Harry Tait) where employer is defined as the work-giver.

[88] The nature of the employer as the work-giver and the paymaster was further elaborated in the examination of Booth by Michael Austin (Q. 5568–72) in the context of assigning responsibility for the evil of sweating.

5601.   Is it that you would not make the giver-out of work responsible?
— Yes, that is the correct way of putting it.

5602.   You have spoken of the occupier and the landlord;[89] may there
not be three persons, the landlord, the tenant of the house, and the
person who has rented the room, or the part of the room, in which
this domestic work is being done? — Yes, but I do not think it would
be possible to recognise more than two, the receiver of the rent and
the payer of the rent. I do not think that you can recognise the sub-
letting of a room in a tenement, but that is a difficulty which I
perhaps have not sufficiently considered.

5603.   Then who would be the people whom you would choose, the
ultimate landlord and the actual employer or the tenant of the house
and the actual employer? — I am afraid I have not sufficiently thought
that out. The impression in my mind was the tenant of the house and
the person to whom that tenant paid the rent. I do not think I have
sufficiently considered that point; it is a difficult one.

5604.   They are all to be together responsible to the community, or if
we take only the two, the landlord and the ultimate employer, they
both are to be responsible to the community for the proper conditions
of work? — Yes.

5605.   Is it rather somewhat in this way, that one of them is to be in the
position of the acceptor of the bill, and the other in the position of
the endorser? — I think that is a very good way of putting it.

5606.   Might it be that the landlord was in the position of the acceptor
of the bill so far as sanitary defects go while the immediate employer
was in the position of the acceptor of the bill so far as the conditions
of the work itself went? — I think that exactly expresses it.

5607.   You have said that the present evils of the sweating system could
be much diminished by the spread of organisation among the
workers?[90] — Yes.

---

[89] Booth had in fact spoken of the landlord and the tenant, without distinguishing tenant of the
house or sub-tenant of the room. See his answer to Q. 5420–4, 5429, and Q. 5579, 5582.
[90] This was raised by Booth in his answer to Q. 5463.

5608.   Would you explain in what way; have you any particular ways in your mind? — No, I think I have not any particular way. The whole conditions of work, including wages, I think do depend largely on the organisation of the workers.

5609.   The point I meant was, do you propose to give the workers when organised a power of being something like amateur factory inspectorship through their officials, so as to get over the difficulty that an *employé* does not like to complain against his or her employer? — I should hope that something of that sort might act.

5610.   Things of this kind have rather been discussed, I think, on some of our committees. Do you think that this would be an effective way of bringing about thorough factory inspection without great cost to the State? — I should be hopeful of something of that sort happening.

5611.   You have spoken of inspectors; have you considered the necessity for inspectresses? — I have not. I did not wish to exclude the possibility of inspectresses.

5612.   Are you inclined to think that they are needed? — I have not really considered it.

5613.   Are you of opinion that a factory inspector spends a good deal of time now on clerical work? — I know he does, or else the necessary clerical work is not done, which is more the case.

5614.   So that if there were a clerical staff the clerical work probably would be better done, and also the inspecting would be better done? — Very much.

5615.   This complete registry of domestic workshops, as well as others, would involve a great deal of clerical work?[91] — Yes, a great deal.

5616.   You said that the material thus got together would go a good long way towards supplying us with an industrial census? — Yes; supplying the basis for an industrial census.

---

[91] Registration was discussed by Booth in answers to Q. 5439–46, in the last of which he conceded the need for 'an army of inspectors'.

5617.   I think you approve the suggestion that the givers-out of work should make a return to the persons to whom they do give out work? — I think it is a good suggestion that they should keep a list. Did you say make a return? — I think that may be very useful, but I had not included it.

5618.   But a complete register of all factories, workshops, and domestic workshops, and of all persons who take out work from givers-out (of course there would be many double entries), these together, if complete, would be a perfect industrial census, would they not. I should perhaps say a perfect census of occupations? — They would be the commencement of it, the basis of it. It would not be complete without a good deal of further investigation.

5619.   It would not be all we wanted without anything further, but the numbers would be all there, would they not? — Not necessarily, because the registration would not say definitely how many people were working in a workshop, but only how many it was registered for. I take it that a shop would be registered as a shop for four men, five men, or ten men; but it does not follow that four, five or ten men would necessarily be working there always, or at any particular time.

5620.   I ought to have said the registration taken together with the entry with regard to the registered workshop in the factory inspector's books because he always would have to enter that, would he not? — I conceive that to arrive at a census you would still have to enumerate, that you would still have not to inspect but to enumerate on the occasion chosen for the industrial census. You would have your list; you would have your addresses; you would know what the shops were and you would know about what they were intended to provide; but I think the enumerator would have actually to visit them as he now visits for the ordinary census and see actually how many people were working them on the day chosen.

5621.   But the factory inspector does have records, does he not of the number of people working in each factory? — I do not think he could do so with such multiplication of shops as we are speaking of. May I add in part response to what you have said I do think that the keeping of the list of the work given out by the employer would be of very great importance in assisting the clerical staff to find out whether all the shops were registered.

5622. I think you took part in the attempt, unfortunately futile, to get the Government to sanction the making of a special employers' census some time ago?[92] – Yes, I am afraid it was so. The suggestion was an employers' census to follow the numerical census of 1891, and it was not accepted.

5623. Would you kindly describe that suggestion a little more fully? – The suggestion was that after the ordinary census had been taken a selection of the picked enumerators should follow it by seeking out the numbers of the employed trade by trade; but I have felt that they would not have sufficient means of finding out where the employed were to be found unless they had such a list as this would provide. With such a list I think it can be done as a rider to the other census, adding a good deal of information, and especially throwing light upon the figures which are now got through what are called the occupation returns.

5624. I think the process of that inquiry tended to show that there were not in the Registrar-General's department a sufficient staff of persons with specialised knowledge to superintend work of this kind, as well as it could be done by the aid of the factory inspectors, and that the factory inspectors had a very valuable knowledge which was not possessed by the staff employed by the Registrar-General? – I think that is so.

5625. It would, therefore, be working towards the end which you had then in view, if this registration should lead the way towards an employers' census of the kind you then asked for, with the aid of and, perhaps, under the management of the factory inspectors? – I should not venture to say in what way it would be best done. It would be a combination between two Government departments, and in what way that combination would be best made, it would be beyond me to say.

[92] Booth referred to the desirability of a complete registry of factories as a considerable contribution to 'our industrial statistics' and 'as the starting point of an industrial census' (answer to Q. 5469).

5626.   I did not mean to go beyond this; that you think that the active co-operation of the factory inspectors would tend very much to make any industrial census thorough, and that it would be difficult to get any industrial census without that co-operation? – Yes, but I would follow some such extension of the sphere of the factory inspectors as we are now discussing.

[Mr Gerald Balfour and Mr Leonard Courtney then asked a number of questions (Q. 5627–8) dealing with sweated labour, and other aspects of domestic factory work, interrupted by the following, clarificatory question by Marshall, before Mr Courtney resumes.]

PROFESSOR MARSHALL

5720.   You used the term 'employer' again, I think? – I meant the giver-out of work.[93]

Marshall's examination of Dr E.R.L. Gould, 2 December 1892

[Apart from one clarificatory question (Q. 6650, not reproduced) Marshall's questioning follows that of Mr Austin.]

PROFESSOR MARSHALL

6690.   First one question arising out of what Mr. Plimsoll[94] said. You said that there were many people who thought that trusts were not unfavourable to labour; did you mean to labour in the capacity of wage receivers? – Yes.

6691.   You do not doubt that they are generally unfavourable to labour in the capacity of consumers? – Yes; I meant to labour as wage receivers.

---

[93] Above, Q. 5599–600 and nn. 87 and 88 above.

[94] This related to Q. 6683–4 addressed to Dr Gould by Samuel Plimsoll in the last of which he asked whether trusts were harmful to working people because of the high prices they generated, an opinion with which Gould agreed.

6692.   The experts of the Bureau have, I understand, all come to the conclusion that trustworthy information can only be collected by agents on the spot? – Yes, that is true.

6693.   Could you explain to us a little more fully all the advantages of that method over the method of collection by post? – I can explain by illustrating the experience of the Connecticut Bureau of Labour. I think it was the Connecticut Bureau from which were sent specially prepared blanks to the families of several hundred labourers, asking them to kindly keep accounts of what they spent for a month, I think it was, or two months, and to enter everything on the blanks. They found that a great many people started, but very few kept it up throughout, and this very curious reason was given. Some of the better paid labourers said, we did not continue it because we were afraid that our receipts being large, and therefore our standard of living being more comfortable, we would get too many of that side, and some of our poorer brethren who are less intelligent and do not get high wages, and do not therefore live as well as we, would not keep up the tabulation of these things, and thus we, or rather not we, but the whole labouring class, would be shown at a disadvantage in the State, that is, the manufacturers would say, 'Why, here the majority of the cases represented, which of course must be typical as this is a representative inquiry go to show that the people are living on a very high plane, therefore they can very readily stand a reduction of wages.' It is motives of that sort, which may or may not have any foundation of fact, added to the natural inertia of people to exert themselves to give such detailed statistical information as must be received to make a satisfactory report, on any subject, I do not care what it is, which make it thoroughly impossible to expect anything from the sending of schedules, except, perhaps, the entering of tabulations which already exist amongst the people who are asked to give information.

6694.   What is the feeling of the working classes with regard to the expenditure on the bureau; are they inclined to be stingy or not? – The working classes, are by no means stingy. Always you will find that each of the principal labour organisations in the United States has what it calls its legislative committee, that is a committee who go to the State capital from time to time, while the legislature is in session, and urge the passing of legislation in which they are interested. You will find invariably that part of the efforts of that legislative committee is bestowed on securing a good appropriation, even an increasing appropriation, for the labour bureau.

6695.   But you are probably aware that in this country the money to be spent upon labour statistics has been rather scarce? — I have understood so.

6696.   Supposing that our resources should not be increased quite so much as some of us would wish, what would you think were the relative advantages of many inquiries conducted by special agents? — It altogether depends on whether you will content yourself with undertaking a high class of statistical work or what one might call certain easy subjects of investigation. If, for example, you were going to make an inquiry into, say, the workings of the factory law, I can conceive at once how by a little co-operation with your factory inspectors you might arrive at a very valuable result by placing into their hands certain schedules of information which they could very readily fill out, and which would not cost them much effort. But if you are going to pass beyond the range of compilation in any degree, and to get into the range of original inquiry you will find that there is but one satisfactory method to adopt, and that is to the principle of sending special experts to get the facts on the ground.

6697.   I think you said something about the importance of combining census work with labour bureau work in order that there might be one set of high class workers rather than two less highly trained? — Yes.

6698.   You told us, I think, comparatively little about the census which was made by the Massachusetts bureau: could you tell us a little more of that? — I knew all about it at the time, but I cannot trust my recollection to give you a sufficiently general account. If you would care to ask specific questions, possibly I could recollect the facts.

6699.   Was the ordinary work of the bureau suspended for the time? — No, but certain sections of the census report which were made a speciality of, so to speak, that is, containing slightly added information which would make them more presentable, were made the subjects of annual report contemporaneously with the preparation of this census report. I may say that while being a separate report, it dealt with the same subject developed to a higher extent, that was all.

6700. But a good number of the permanent officials of the bureau were told off to do the census work? – Yes, they were; the census work was done distinctly by the bureau.

6701. So that they had not much force left for their ordinary work for the time being? – No.

6702. But their ordinary work need not be evenly distributed over different years; their ordinary work is of such a kind that it would be possible to do less of it in the census year? – Yes, that would be easy. For instance, in your statistics of manufacture, you are collecting statistics as to the nationality of the workers, and, perhaps, their social condition, the size of their families, the kind of houses in which they live, and so forth; those statistics can be very advantageously taken out and made into a separate report.

6703. The bureau, I think, choose every year some subject which they inquire into in detail? – Yes.

6704. And in the particular census year, of course, it would take either a light subject or no subject? – Quite so.

6705. One thing I did not quite understand, as to the choice of those subjects; you said first that the choice rests always with the Commissioner, but afterwards I understood you to say that Congress would make a requisition? – Yes, very true; but I distinguish between annual reports and special reports. The annual report must under the terms of the law be made every year, and the commissioner's discretion is only called into play for these reports. The Commissioner has the faculty of making special reports if he chooses, but as a rule, they are on subjects which Congress has asked us specially to inquire into. If I may be pardoned for the reference, one of my own reports, that upon Scandinavian liquor legislation for example, will come in probably as the first special report which our department has yet published. It was not ordered by Congress at all, and it is purely in the discretion between the Commission and myself.

6706. You are acquainted with the methods of inquiry pursued in England, as, for instance, by a Commission of this kind, with assistant sub-commissioners, to make inquiries upon special points; has that method been customary in America? – Obtaining information by correspondence?

6707. By a Commission, and by special sub-Commissioners? – Yes, that is the method adopted in some of the States, which have limited resources.

[Mr Leonard Courtney here interrupts to ask some questions (Q. 6708–11) about statistical inquiries by the United States federal government, with special reference to education and railways. Marshall then resumed.]

6712. Have you had the means of comparing the method of inquiry by Commissions with that by Bureaus of Labour? – We have had numbers of inquiries by legislative commissions or commissions appointed by the legislature, not necessarily from amongst its own members only, but including some of its own members and outside parties.

6713. Inquiries conducted very much on the same plan as this Commission is being conducted now? – Yes, receiving evidence and making a report thereon.

6714. And gradually a system of inquiries by Bureaus of Labour has grown up side by side? – Yes.

6715. Have they competed for the field of employment, and what has been the result of the struggle? – The Commission has been distanced.

6716. Can you give us any detail of that struggle for supremacy? – I do not know that we have had a great struggle for supremacy; but it has come to be generally recognised, even by legislators themselves, that they can much more quickly arrive at the facts through the accurate information which has been digested and put into presentable shape than is possible by taking up several large volumes of undigested testimony, and seeking for facts through contradictory statements without reference to any attempt at classification. I think one great superiority of the method on, what I may call, the technical side is that it gives information more readily accessible in better shape to be understood, and with a far greater assurance that it is accurate. In other words, it is a ratio of representative opinions or conditions rather than a series of opinions which may be entirely contrary one to the other. So much for the technical side. Then from the political side, the system has superiority over the system of inquiry by legislative commission in that it is absolutely non-partisan, and it has no purpose whatever to serve except to arrive at the facts; and its peculiar position is such that it would not dare for a moment, even though it could, to give any undue turning to the facts one way or the other, because in the future, when the other party came in, it would be a very bad thing for the bureau.

[Mr Gerald Balfour then interrupts with two questions (Q. 6717–6718) on the usefulness of the Commission in eliciting information. Marshall then resumed as follows.]

6719.   I suppose the fact that Washington is not the capital of the United States for all purposes, as London is of England, makes the working of Commissions a little more difficult than here. Is not that so? – Commissions do not necessarily sit at Washington.

6720.   Our English traditions, and the special facilities which London gives for inquiries by Commissions, would probably make us continue Commissions even though we had a labour bureau.[95] We, for instance, have appointed Assistant Commissioners? – I am not sure that I understand exactly what you mean. Perhaps we know them by a different technical appellation.

6721.   This Commission has appointed a number of gentlemen,[96] chiefly barristers, to travel over specified parts of the United Kingdom, and make reports as to agricultural conditions in those parts, and especially as to the conditions of labour in those parts. Are you of opinion that that work, for which people have to be got with no special training, would be better done by the trained officials of a bureau? – Decidedly,

[95] Later, in *Industry and Trade* (p. 143) Marshall defended the role of Commissions as a means of generating 'helpful knowledge'.

[96] Marshall omits to mention the fact that the Commission had appointed four Lady Commissioners to investigate specific issues of women's labour.

I would not hesitate to say so, no matter in connexion with what industry or what it is impossible to do on limited means.

6722.   With our English habit of Commissions would you regard it as a proper function of the labour bureau to take over from the Commissions' special inquiries? – Provided you endowed it with sufficient resources, so that its work might be made a success, and not kill it in the beginning by asking it to do what it is impossible to do on limited means.

6723.   I will now ask you with regard to the question of the difficulties arising as to business secrets. Are your agents generally able not merely to get reports from firms, but actually to go over their books? – Speaking from experience, no facts that were published in connexion with the Cost of Production from the continent of Europe were taken from any other source, and I have personally had the books in my hand and gone over them carefully, and abstracted the facts therefrom, and in connection with wage statistics my assistants have done so.

6724.   That implies that the manufacturers know that they are dealing with men of professional honour? – To be sure. On the continent of Europe especially our department is known not merely amongst professional men and scholars and publicists, but even among business men (some of the more notable ones, to be sure) as having conducted these inquiries in the past without any detriment whatever to the persons giving the information, and they have been willing to respond: but, of course, one must not jump to the conclusion that everyone who was asked liberally responded. I should think my own proportion of successes in ratio to failures, after a very great deal of effort, would perhaps be 2 to 10. But then you must understand that we are doing pioneer work, and that this was the most delicate of all subjects that we could investigate.

6725.   And also that the professional reputation of the bureau has not yet had many years to grow? – Not many years. The professional reputation of the national bureau is largely due to the personal reputation of Mr. Carroll D. Wright,[97] its chief, who had successfully

[97] That is, Carroll D. Wright (1840–1909) Commissioner of Labour for the State of Massachusetts (1873–88) then Head of the National Labour Department in the United States (1888–1908). In 1882, he published an Essay, *The Relation of Political Economy to the Labour Question*, Boston.

carried on such inquiries before in Massachusetts, and who, so to speak, educated public sentiment up to the point when they would confide in them.

6726.   May not the information that a business firm could give be divided into two classes; that is information which he would usually and generally be able to keep secret from his rivals in the same trade, and information which people in the same trade would be sure to possess? – Quite so.

6727.   And there would be no reason for refusing to give information as to the latter? – No, I should think not.

6728.   But you must not introduce a single item of the former class in that inquiry? – No. One must be careful, of course, especially in the beginning. These things are largely a matter of education. I remember, in one instance, I received all the facts that I was seeking in relation to cost of production from one of the very largest iron and steel works in existence in the country of which I speak. After it had been given the Director-General told me that he had never given such facts to any of his directors, nobody except the president of the company knew them; and furthermore not even the chief of the subordinate department knew them.

6729.   Now I want to get back to the question of the relation between the census and the bureau. You are aware, perhaps, that the English use of the word 'census' is much narrower than the American sense? – Yes.

6730.   The function of the Bureaus is to seek types, I think you said?[98] – Yes.

6731.   And to examine them carefully? – Yes.

---

[98] A reference to Q. 6518 by Leonard Courtney about the Census Bureau which elicited Gould's answer: 'we never attempt any census statistics; I mean we never attempt to study everything in connection with any given subject. That would be impossible in a country so large as ours. We seek for types, and to get representative facts' (*Fourth Report*, Whole Commission, p. 444).

6732.   May it be said that their investigation is intensive while that of the census is extensive?[99] – Quite so. The one deals with ratios, the other with totals you might say.

6733.   Is it true that the value of these two together is very much greater than twice the value of either separately. I mean if you can get rough general statistics of the whole trade and exact minute statements of the types of trade you are more than twice as well off as if you had either half? – Yes.

6734.   Using the word 'census' in the broad sense you would, I suppose, think that printed forms should be filled up? – To a very large extent, yes.

6735.   And these might contain all that knowledge which a man has no reason to desire to hide from his rivals? – And which he has readily accessible. That is a very important consideration.

6736.   Would you say that outside of the population statistics it might be worth while for the English bureau to make some of its investigations by printed paper, such as the size of establishments, the number of *employés*, the rateable value, and similar things with regard to agriculture? – I should think those could be very readily answered by the use of printed forms especially in connexion with your taxation authorities, whoever they might be. Certainly I think a very great deal of valuable information which has not been accessible might be obtained in that way.

6737.   So that when you said that you thought all the inquiries, other than census inquiries, should be conducted by skilled agents on the spot, that I think arise, although I did not notice it at the time, from the fact of your using the word 'census' in the American and not in the English sense? – Yes, quite so.

6738.   As regards the expenses of the Massachusetts Bureau, 10,800 dollars, does that cover the expense of the annual report, and the

---

[99] Marshall may be here referring to the method of Le Play, which he described as intensive. See *Principles of Economics*, 8th edn, 1920, p. 116, where it is contrasted with the extensive method of 'rapidly collecting numerous observations'. In an earlier answer to the Duke of Devonshire (Q. 7000) Gould had referred to Le Play's method in estimating workers' budgets.

report on manufactures? – No, it does not cover the expenses of the report on manufactures. There is 6,000 dollars in addition for that.

6739.   And the census is an addition? – The census is an addition, yes: I may say that the manufacturing statistics have been required ever since the year 1886.

6740.   The range of inquiry of the bureau has been extended beyond labour questions in the narrower sense of the word, I gather? – Yes.

6741.   What are the reasons for that? – The primordial reason was that the bureau made such a success of the statistics of manufactures, that it was thought to be desirable to continue them, and to continue the principal elements of those statistics from year to year, instead of waiting every 10 years for the State, and every five years for the federal census.

6742.   May it be put in this way, that special subjects of inquiry, not strictly industrial in their nature, are handed to the department, because it is the most skilled investigating body in the States? – To be sure; you may very readily say that.

6743.   As to the three orders of untruth, a fib, a lie, and statistics,[100] do you think that public opinion is getting to recognise that there are statistics which do not belong to that class? – I am very positive of it. I am speaking of course now specially with regard to my own country, but I believe there is a general recognition of it elsewhere.

6744.   You hold that public opinion is an ultimate force by which that condition of things may be remedied? – I do.

6745.   I suppose hitherto public opinion has been dependent to a certain extent upon statistics supplied by writers in current literature? – Yes. Perhaps not so much so upon statistics supplied as by dogmatic assertions which have been made by writers, the mere mention of whose name in times past was sufficient to either condemn or to cause approval to be expressed on any subject. But my own personal opinion is that the days of the *doctrinaire* are numbered, whether he belongs to the socialistic or to the *laissez faire* type; that especially in

---

[100] A reference to Disraeli's famous remark about lies, damned lies and statistics. Gould had mentioned this in an answer to a previous question (Q. 6511).

these days, when the democracy is becoming conscious of its power, and is securing more and more influence in the State, we must be careful that it becomes intelligent and enlightened on matters of State policy, and the more so as we now have incessant demands in all countries for what may be called social legislation from year to year. I think, therefore, it is exceedingly important that the Government should furnish organs of enlightenment which may be able to put into the hands of the people, an exact statement of facts relating to the conditions which surround them, and which form in their minds to a large extent their subject of thought, because if you do not do that you may be sure that you will find in their hands sooner or later a socialistic catechism, or anarchist tract.

6746.   I suppose if people cannot get trustworthy statistics they will use untrustworthy statistics? – I think that is the experience. In statistical parlance we speak of two kinds of statisticians, the statistician proper and the statistical mechanic. By the statistical mechanic, we mean the man who has, so to speak, sketched out in his mind the edifice he wishes to construct, and who will then choose simply such bricks as will build the building he wants to have, while discarding others which will not fit. This type, unfortunately, exists to a considerable extent.

6747.   In this country we have to contend somewhat against the notion that statistics are apt to be false, and therefore it is not worthwhile to take much care about them. Would you hold with that, or would you not hold that since statistics are sure to be used, therefore, seeing how much depends upon them, it is essential that you should have accurate statistics? – I should decidedly. I think in all realms of social inquiry, all nations are going in the dark in matters of legislation, unless they are enlightened by well conducted statistical demonstration of facts.

6748.   You have had special opportunities of observing whether that movement is general, I think, in particular at the recent Statistical Congress in Vienna?[101] – Yes; unquestionably the movement for the development of labour statistics is taking a very wide extension

---

[101] The Statistical Congress, or more precisely, the Congress of the International Institute of Statistics was held in Vienna in 1891.

everywhere. I remember at the Congress, which was held in Vienna last year, the Congress of the International Institute of Statistics, the bulk of the more distinguished statisticians enrolled themselves as members of the committee on labour statistics. That was the first indication. The second thing which resulted from the Congress, was a resolution from this committee urging upon the attention of different Governments the importance of organising statistical agencies to deal, in a greater measure than hitherto, with labour and social questions, with the expressed conviction of opinion that that was the most satisfactory way in which we could approach the study of the subject. Since that time there have been called into existence commissions in Austria and in Germany to study the question, in order to find out in what direction they can best enlarge the study of labour and social statistics. I had a talk the other day in Berlin with Dr. Geheimerath Von Scheel,[102] who is the Director of the Imperial Statistical Bureau, Berlin, in which he said that they were now discussing the question, and that it was only a matter of a short time when they should have, if not a distinct bureau of labour statistics, at all events, a development on one side of his department which should consecrate itself solely to that work. I had a letter a short time ago from Dr. Inama-Sternegg,[103] who is the president of the Imperial Statistical Commission in Vienna, asking me for information in relation to the latest development of American labour statistics, saying that they were determined to extend the Central Statistical Commission in Vienna, by adding to it a section which should give itself to the study of labour statistics. Shortly before that I was in Norway, and in conversation with Dr. Kiaer,[104] who is the chief of the Royal Statistical Bureau of Norway, he told me that he was, on his own responsibility, without an increasing appropriation, giving himself now to the collection of labour and industrial statistics. The other day in Brussels, I had an exceedingly interesting conversation with Mons Baeerenaert, the Prime Minister

---

[102] That is Hans von Scheel, Director of the Imperial Statistical Bureau in Berlin and author of a *Handbuch der Statistik des Deutschen Reichs*, Berlin, 1879.

[103] That is, Dr Carl Theodor von Inama-Sternegg, President of the Imperial Statistical Commission in Vienna, and author of a compendium on the Austrian Statistical Commission.

[104] That is, Dr Anders Nicolai Kiaer, Chief of the Royal Statistical Bureau in Norway and author of a Statistical Handbook for the Kingdom of Norway published in 1871.

of Belgium, and Mons. Leo de Bruyn, the Minister of Agriculture, Commerce, and Industry,[105] and both of them told me that they were organising a distinct labour bureau, on the model as far as they could make it applicable to their country, of the Department of Labour of the United States. Still a little further back, I had the pleasure of assisting at the organisation of the French Office du Travail, and giving information before the superior council in somewhat similar fashion to what I am now giving you to-day. These things, I think, are plainly indicative of the fact that nations are becoming alive to the point which I have just been endeavouring to make, not to the experimental or possible benefit, but to the certain benefit, judging from the past utility of these organs of original social inquiry.

6749. Do you think it is a general opinion that half a century ago England led the world in the matter of the investigation of the condition of the working classes? – I should think very probably.

6750. Do you think that opinion is so general now? – You ask me a very pointed question, especially as you are extending to me such hospitality, but I must be frank and say I think the opinion is that England is a little behind on this subject, that is in the development of labour statistics.

6751. And if we were for long to remain as we are now, with no organised body of trained investigators, we should be alone in that respect among civilised nations should not we? – If you leave the matter two years hence, my opinion is you will be alone amongst the principal nations.

6752. With regard to the functions that a bureau should undertake, we have already discussed the census, and I think you have said that factory inspection might be, but in your opinion should not be, under the control of the bureau – I think that is the least objectionable feature to add to it. If you are going to add any I think the fewest objections could be raised to that, but my own opinion is that it is better not to add it.[106]

---

[105] That is, August Marie François Beernaert (1829–1912) , Prime Minister of Belgium (1884–94), and Leo de Bruyn, Minister of Agriculture, Commerce and Industry.

[106] This repeats his answer to an earlier question by Leonard Courtney (Q. 6517) in which he indicated that such additional functions tended to detract from the statistical work of the organisation.

6753.   You think that with the factory inspectors under a different department the labour bureau might be empowered to requisition them for certain information which they could easily supply? – Decidedly. That is the practice in France. The Office du Travail, considering the resources of continental countries, has not a limited appropriation; at the same time it is not a large one, and it is now making a very thorough and careful investigation into wages, in mines especially, and a cordial co-operation has been established between the mine inspectors, who belong to another section of the French Government, and the bureau, with the result that they are collecting their mine statistics at no cost to themselves through the mine inspectors, and as regards the factory inspectors they are using them in the same way. All this teaches that it is quite feasible for a cordial co-operation to be established between the *personnel* of factory inspection and the bureau, though the former belongs to an entirely different department. I say it is quite feasible that it may be established, and with very great utility.

6754.   But with regard to arbitration, mediation, and conciliation, you think it would be highly inadvisable that they should be combined with the work of the labour bureau? – I think decidedly it is inadvisable to make any legal requirement in the matter. I do not think it is always advisable for the head of a labour department to stand idle in any great dispute which goes on between labour and capital. On the contrary, I think it is better for him to take an interest in it, and if he should judge it opportune to attempt to mediate, to do so, but that his judgment of the circumstances must determine his action. I think you ought not to fetter him by any legal responsibilities in the matter.

6755.   You made just now a distinction between mediation and arbitration; would you kindly give what, as you understand it, is the distinction between the two? – I conceive arbitration to mean a judicial settlement of a difficulty which has already grown into an open dispute. I conceive mediation to be the good offices of an outside agency coming in to seek either to avoid a rupture, or if the rupture has once been actually made, to endeavour to smooth it over as quickly as possible, without assuming the responsibility of making a positive award. I assume arbitration to necessarily carry with it the idea of a judicial award one way or the other; whereas mediation and conciliation do not.

6756.   Is it true that mediation has been much more successful in America than arbitration? – I could not say positively that it has. My own opinion is that it has. I could not quote facts in support of that view, but my own opinion is strongly that it has been.

6757.   One of the chief functions of mediation would be to bring public opinion to bear? – Quite so.

6758.   Should a court of mediation have the power of summoning evidence? – No, I think not, I think that the power of summoning evidence should only belong to a court of arbitration, and that a court of mediation should operate rather on a moral than on a legal basis.

6759.   You said that the publication of the reports with regard to industrial disputes had had the effect of diminishing those disputes?[107] – Yes.

6760.   Would that be partly by making each side know that if they did things that seemed just only to themselves, other people would soon have the opportunity of forming an opinion on the matter? – I think unquestionably that they were made to feel that public opinion would have a better chance now to decide on the equities of the matter, but I do not wish to be understood, in speaking of these matters, that the bureau report only influences the strikers; I believe it exercises quite as much influence on the manufacturers, because the probability is that the number of cases where one is in the right, about equally balances the number where the other is in the right.

6761.   I carefully used the phrase 'industrial disputes' rather than strikes? – Quite so.

6762.   Is it the case that public opinion acts not only by making people willing to accept a reasonable solution of a dispute but also by

---

[107]   This referred to an answer to Leonard Courtney (Q. 6455) in which Gould indicated that the Commissioner for Labour after undertaking an investigation of strikes in the United States between 1881 and 1886 found that 'within 18 months after the publication of the report, strikes had practically ceased to exist.' He confirmed and elaborated this answer to subsequent questions (Q. 6543–44) from George Livesey.

making people unwilling to do things which would be a reasonable cause of dispute? – Unquestionably.

6763. Do you happen to be acquainted with the constitution of our Board of Trade? – In a general way.

6764. You know that it has several departments, a railway department, commercial department, and so on? – Yes.

6765. I suppose that the Washington Labour Bureau, being responsible directly to the President, could not very easily, so far as I understand it, be copied under the English Constitution? – No; I do not see that the exact organisation could be.

6766. It would be necessary that it should be in some way or another responsible to a minister? – Yes, I believe so, for the reason, would it not, that your ministers are responsible to parliament, and not primarily to the sovereign.

6767. Exactly? – Whereas our ministers are responsible only to the executive, and not to the Legislature, except that they may be impeached by the Legislature for malfeasance in office, but their relations are directly with the President, and through him with the Congress.

6768. Under these circumstances should you see any objections to the constitution of a ministry of industry which should on the one side take over the existing work of the Board of Trade, and, on the other side, should be a Board of Labour, that Board of Labour having several departments under it, one being for statistics, and another for arbitration, or rather mediation. Should you think that there was any harm in there being an arbitration department and a statistical department under the same parliamentary head, but each with its own permanent head? – I think there would be this objection, that as regards arbitration there might be a tendency for awards to be one-sided. Of course, I am not speaking with any particular country in mind. I think wherever you have a political head to any institution, who mixes directly in the affairs of a department, such as naturally the head of this new department of industry would, he has a policy to maintain, and that, therefore, if you give to him the functions of arbitrating in industrial matters, it might possibly be that in time it would resolve itself into an institution which operated to the benefit of the class which had the majority of influence in the political party that happened to be in power. I think that would be one objection purely from the political stand point. I think on the other side, as regards a ministry of labour, that the minister should not himself be the one who conducted the inquiries, or have anything to do with the inquiries except perhaps to name them, that there should be a responsible statistician who has a life appointment, is thoroughly competent, is thoroughly independent of everything, and whose reports will be recognised as not having the slightest political taint about them one way or the other. We have had proposals time and again in the United States to erect the Department of Labour into a ministry of labour, giving its head a cabinet position, and this has, of course flattered the *amour propre* of the unthinking men perhaps amongst the labouring people, but it has always been regarded as unwise by the more sober thinking people of all classes; because with a change every four or eight years as the case may be of the cabinet office, there would come in the minds of the public the view that the policy of the labour department would change with the change of ministry, that it was no longer a purely statistical agency, but it was meant to work in harmony and in co-operation with the political party that then seemed to be in power. Those are the objections which I have to it, and furthermore this objection, that I think it is unwise to give any judicial powers in relation to industry to a man who at the same time is a politician who is dependent upon the suffrages of the people for his public career.

6769.   But granting all that, if we take it as necessary under the English constitutional practice that the permanent head of the statistical bureau should in any case be responsible to a parliamentary chief, and that that parliamentary chief should be in the same cabinet and share collective responsibility with the parliamentary chief to whom the head of the Arbitration Bureau is responsible – If we assume that that could not be avoided, do you think there would be any great harm in having the permanent chief of the Statistical and of the Arbitration Bureau responsible to the same parliamentary chief? – Oh, not at all; but would it not be better since the English people are already accustomed to the name of the Board of Trade, and in the public mind certain functions are connected with that; instead of creating a new Ministry of Industry, say, where naturally the things which would strike the public would be these new and added functions, and therefore cause them to expect something from them – would it not be better to leave the name of Board of Trade as it is, and create two separate bureaus under the present Board of Trade with their chiefs, independent of one another – bureaus independent of one another, but accountable to the same responsible head.

6770. It leads, I think, only to a question of words? – Quite so.

6771. The proposal, as to which I was asking your opinion, was that the board should be called the Board of Industry, and that it should have two halves – the Board of Trade as it is now, and the Board of Labour? – Would you not give it any other functions? Did I understand you to say that this new institution would take over the existing functions of the Board of Trade?

6772. Yes? – Then there would be added functions, would there not?

6773. A Board of Labour would have new functions entirely, except that what little is now done for labour by the Board of Trade would be passed over to the Board of Labour? – What I mean is this. Aside from the Board of Labour and the Board of Arbitration, there would still be other bureaus or other boards which now exist, would there not?

6774. I was asking you not as to a Board of Arbitration, but a Department of Arbitration under the Board of Labour? – Yes. But would there not still exist other departments which now belong to the Board of Trade besides those two? Or do I understand you to mean that you would create a new Ministry of Industry which should contain only these two subordinate departments.

6775. The Board of Trade as at present constituted contains many departments? – Yes.

6776. The proposal was that all those Departments should remain there, except of course that the Labour Correspondent would be transferred to the other side? – Yes.

6777. On that point then the Board of Labour would have a Department of Statistics, a Department of Arbitration, and perhaps a Department of Agriculture, the first two at all events? – Personally, I think it would be better if you added the Department of Agriculture, if you are going to create a new Ministry, because I think my objections would hold good if you had simply the arbitration and the labour statistics with a responsible Minister at the head. The people in time would expect from it a certain policy, and that the policy would change with the change of administration; but if they are made under the existing Board of Trade two separate bureaus which are well endowed and are quite capable of undertaking these new duties, I do not see that it would matter very much.

6778. You understand that in the plan on which I am asking your opinion the parliamentary head of this board of labour would be responsible for a great number of things of which the department of arbitration, if there were one, would be one, and he would be responsible for the whole of the present work of the Board of Trade? – I understood you to say you were going to have in the new Department of Industry only those two bureaus.

6779. Yes, but the Board of Trade, including the whole of the Board of Trade as it is now, except the labour correspondent, that is including many departments, and then the Board of Labour, including such departments as might be constituted under it, of which two, at all events, would be a Department of Statistics and a Department of Arbitration? – Do you mean then that the existing Board of Trade should remain and that there should be added to it two functions.

6780. Yes? – I did not understand you in that way. I should say I think that is the only possible expedient you could have under your English constitution and practice.

[The questioning was continued by Mr Gerald Balfour.]

Marshall's examination of Sir Robert Giffen, 24 January 1893, 2 February 1893

[Apart from a single clarifying question on a quantitative estimate of the residuum provided by Giffen (Q. 6938, not reproduced) Marshall's questioning follows that of Mr Tom Mann and the Duke of Devonshire.]

7071. With regard to the statistics of wages published by the Board of Trade, these are the wages per week, are they not? – Both per week and per year. We have worked it out in all sorts of ways.

7072. But has there been any attempt in England to follow the American plan of finding out how much each individual earns in a year? – What American plan?

7073. The plan followed, for instance, in the United States Bureaus? – If you could describe the plan to me, I should be very much obliged. I have looked at many of the statements, and many of the American reports about statistics of wages, and what seems to me the one very material defect in a great many of them is that they do not describe what they have done. They put before you a great mass of figures and begin to discuss the lessons which are to be derived from the figures, but they do not tell you exactly how they got them, or what difficulties they met with in getting them, and you do not know where you are. If Professor Marshall would describe the plan to me in detail I should be very much obliged to him.

7074. I suppose I must take it that, in your opinion, they really do not succeed? – No, I think that really having referred to a plan, it should be capable of description in some way or other. If you describe a particular plan, I will tell you whether it could be followed or not, or how it could be followed, but if you refer me to American books generally, I ask what plan you mean.

7075. Do you think it is impossible to send round skilled agents to a considerable number of firms to get those firms to show the agent all their books, and to trace through the books the whole of the earnings on each particular day throughout the whole year of a great number of individuals? – Of course that would be quite possible, but that is exactly what you get already, only you get it by the week. I do not see any difference – I do not see any virtue in taking a particular day.

7076. Is not it urged that the English plan has the disadvantage of only showing you what is called the theoretical average, the average that would be got if people worked a supposed number of days, say 310, whereas the American plan shows you what they actually do get in the particular calendar year? – No, I think the American plan, as you describe it, does not show that any more than the Board of Trade plan does, because we do show the payments of wages over large groups of people in a particular calendar year, and we have been most particular in getting that as well.

7077.   You do not deny they claim that superiority? – I do not know exactly what they claim, because I am bound to say that one of the difficulties of the American books is just that – they do not describe with sufficient particularity the process by which they get the facts.

7078.   Do you think they describe with less particularity than the Board of Trade described it? – Much less. When they say that they sent an agent to a place to ascertain the facts and he comes back and tells you that he has ascertained the facts, that is not telling you any-thing about what the agent has done. I think, if Professor Marshall would permit me to say so, it is really a case where he ought to show in some way or other that he is able to describe a particular plan exactly which has been followed, and what it is.

7079.   What I understand is that an agent is sent with a very great number of printed questions in the most minute detail, which he fills up in the office of the works, the whole of the books of the works being put at his disposal, and that he makes returns in such detail, that unless he has distinctly invented figures out of his own head instead of copying them from the book, they must represent the exact amount of money received in any calendar year by any partic-ular individual in the employment of that firm? – I have not seen the statements in which that appears to have been done in the way that you describe, and it is quite obvious that unless one sees the ques-tions which the agent has got to answer, it is impossible to express an opinion upon whether he was likely to get the information or not. But many of the questions – I speak of some of the returns which I have seen which he is supposed to have found answers to, are them-selves so difficult that not even the employers themselves could answer, probably. I wish to know what is the sort of evidence upon which he is satisfied that he has got the correct answer, and as to that you get no information at all from the agents. That, for instance of taking the name of particular persons from the books, and finding

out what a man was paid by a particular firm in the whole year, does
not answer the question at all as to the average earnings of that man,
because you do not know what he may have got from some other
firm and really the putting of the question is to show that those who
instructed an agent to find out such a thing, hardly knew how to set
about the business because they must know that the same firm has
not the same number of people at work all the year through – not
likely – and I may say that on that very subject, the report of Mr.
Carroll D. Wright's department about railway labour[108] makes the
fullest confession as to the unsatisfactory character of the results
obtained by that very method, that it really is a ridiculous method to
follow.[109]

7080.   I was not at all endeavouring to prove that they could do all that
they have tried to do, or that their methods were in all respects the
best conceivable, but I was confining myself as far as I could to statistics actually published by the Board of Trade, and I wanted to know
whether you were not of opinion that some further information is
wanted than that which is called theoretical (I presume you are aware
that the Americans talk of returns similar to those made by our
Board of Trade as theoretical returns) whether it would not be advisable to attempt to get some more positive information as to the
amount earned and expended? – I think there is a great deal to be
done in that respect, only I do not think that what the Americans
have done is any example or any guide at all, because they have most
completely failed. I refer especially to that return about railway
labour. The most absolute confession of complete failure is to be
found in that report.

[The Duke of Devonshire then interrupts by asking four
questions (Q. 7081–4) on the derivation of unemployment
statistics, and the difficulties therein, which Giffen in his answers
confirms. Questioning is then resumed by Marshall.]

---

[108] Fifth Annual report of the Commissioner of Labour, *Railroad Labour*, Washington, DC,
1889.
[109] Extracts from this *Report*, mentioned in Giffen's answer to Marshall's question, were read
out by Giffen to the chairman, Lord Devonshire, the following day (Q. 8086–7); a more
detailed extract was included with the evidence as subsequently printed (*Fourth Report*,
Whole Commission, Appendix 76, p. 288).

PROFESSOR MARSHALL

7085.   But what would be an exceptional trade?[110] – I think the building trade is exceptional, because in point of fact you may assume that most employments are more or less continuous. The fluctuation is an element, but it does not extend to the fluctuation between nothing and the figures which you give. But that particular effort to find out from employment books what wages a particular man has got by following him up all through the wages lists is an absolute and entire failure, and I think Professor Marshall may take it from me that it is so. It might have been known beforehand that it would be so, but that it is so there is no doubt. The work cannot be done in that way.

7086.   I do not know whether I am quite prepared to take it from you, but I had better pass to something else? – I refer you to the railway report,[111] and I could show you the passages in which the confession is made.

7087.   I should like you to explain more clearly how you ascertain during what number of days you will take a man to be employed in order to find his yearly earnings? – That depends so much upon the particular trade.

7088.   But in general? – I would not like to say in general any more than I have done; I must refer you to the thing itself, to the report itself when it appears; I should not like to go into it in detail.

7089.   To what report? – The report upon these figures which will appear shortly.

7090.   That of the Board of Trade? – Yes. I may tell you this, for instance, with reference to seamen's wages, which are included in one of the tables which I have not referred to. We have various tables as to the employment of vessels which were drawn up some years ago, which throw a great deal of light upon the matter, and in addition to that we had a special report from the Registrar-General of Seamen, a confidential report on inquiries which he made as to what would be the number of seamen as compared with

---

[110] This refers to the question put by Lord Devonshire immediately before (that is, Q. 7081–4).
[111] See the references in nn. 108, 109 above.

the number employed at any one time, and the difference corresponding to that employed vessels return which we have is about 10 per cent, and we do know in that case that the seamen are employed and are paid for. There are other inquiries we have made of a similar nature.

7091. But you think that it is best to confine yourself to this class of inquiry, and not to have as a basis the knowledge of the exact amount, that is earned, say, by individual miners in certain particular localities? – Provided you could make a sufficient selection of individual miners to give you a proper statistical basis, and provided you could really ascertain in point of fact what they do get, and then ascertained the same for other employments (it would be a tremendous work, and what the Americans have done would be nothing to it, and what the returns have done would be nothing to it) then you would have some sort of statistical basis, but there is a great difficulty in getting the absolute fact itself for a sufficient number of people either from the employer or from the workman himself, because the employer, although he pays certain men all the year through, does not pay others all the year through, and the workman, as a rule, I think you will find as to most of them, could not tell you very exactly what they had received in a given year; it would be a matter of calculation for them, and not so easy to ascertain, and then if you are to ascertain it by means of agents who go and put down questions and put them to the workmen, and are satisfied, or say they are satisfied, that the man has given them a true answer, you are liable to the personal error of the agent, which may be serious.

7092. These difficulties are inherent in any method of obtaining statistics, are they not? – No, some of them give satisfactory results without all that supreme labour. You often take trouble to ascertain what you might know without taking all that trouble.

7093. That may be, no doubt; but you do not intend to suggest that the American officials have not fully studied all these familiar points? – I think I may say that there are no persons in the world whom I would trust with the kind of inquiries which some of the American agents make, nor would I take the results from them in the way that they give them. I should like more information about what they do, about the actual facts and the way that they get them, and what were the inferences which they drew from those facts, and why they drew those inferences.

7094. I think, perhaps, I had better follow your order of subjects. As regards the residuum, how large do you take that to be?[112] – I think without taking a special investigation, I could hardly say or put any figure upon it, but, comparing the figures we have been dealing with of those employed with the factory returns, we find that the element does not come into question.

7095. You put the total number of people earning independent incomes at 13,200,000?[113] – About that; but I think I said that that was subject to the observation that I had not seen the occupations of the last census.

7096. But are you clear whether the residuum are counted in or not?[114] – Yes, quite clear that they are not counted in; at any rate in very many employments they are not included.

7097. Under what form would the residuum be entered in the census? – I do not think I should go into the question of the census in that minute way but there is a large figure of unspecified people of no occupation or unspecified occupations, as I think you are aware.

7098. Yes, if you regard the residuum as a large number, then the question of where they are put in the census becomes of importance, does not it? – That would be important, no doubt, but I do not think it would be a very large number – not a case of 20 per cent, or 30 per cent, or anything of that kind.

---

[112] Marshall had asked an earlier question on this (Q. 6938) which, as indicated previously (above, p. 238), has not been reproduced. This attempted to clarify whether the residuum were included among the 13 million as the total number employed Giffen had mentioned earlier in response to Q. 6914. The residuum was defined by Marshall's *Principles* as those in 'extreme poverty' which burden the 'higher faculties' and who have no knowledge of the ordinary decencies of life (8th edn, 1920, p. 2).

[113] This was the precise figure given by Giffen's answer to Q. 6914 on the total number of workers in paid employment.

[114] This in essence repeated Marshall's Q. 6938 to which Giffen had replied in the same way as he did to this question.

7099.   No, but would not this 13,200,000 include nearly all those in the census who had occupations? – No, it does not include the unspecified occupations at all. For every one of those in the census a special occupation had been put down.

7100.   Including general labour? – Including general labour; but then that is not so important an element in our census as it used to be.

7101.   Then whom does it omit? – I do not include, for instance, the professional classes at all.

7102.   No, of course not? – And I do not include all those under the head of the industrial classes, or anything of that kind. I make various deductions for employers and for things of that sort.

7103.   But this is at the other end of the scale? – Yes, this is at the other end of the scale.

7104.   You think that the exclusion of the residuum is not a serious difficulty? – Not a serious difficulty, and at any rate, I think you must always keep in mind that it does not affect the rates of wages that we have shown, but only affects the building up of aggregate; it does not affect the rate.

7105.   It does not affect the aggregate, you mean? – It does not affect the rate. The numbers affect the aggregate, but they do not affect the rate.

7106.   But you said you were more certain about the aggregate than the rate?[115] – I think I did not say anything of the kind.

7107.   Then I misunderstood you; I thought you said that the aggregate you got confirmed? – It is confirmed in other ways.[116]

7108.   Then with regard to the information that the Board of Trade gives, bearing on fluctuations, are you satisfied that it would not be better for the Board of Trade to give more statistics with regard to production; for instance, the statistics of the kind which Mr. Charles

[115] Probably a reference by Marshall to Giffen's answers to Q. 6917–19 which, however, contain nothing about what Marshall suggests they did in his Q. 7106.
[116] That is, the aggregation of the classes of paid employed labour which Giffen mentioned in answering Q. 6917–19.

Booth[117] published with regard to the docks, do not you think that the Government ought to undertake the publication, as far as it is possible, of statistics of that kind? – Of fluctuations in employment?

7109. Yes? – I believe that now, under the new arrangements we are making at the Board of Trade, we may be able to do a good deal in that direction.

7110. With regard to season trades, for instance, is there not a great deal of information accessible, but not published, that the Government might collect that would be of use? – I think that is one of the things that we propose to take up, now that we have increased our staff a good deal. I think it is a thing we may take up a good deal more fully.

7111. I think you told Lord Iddesleigh's Commission[118] that the statistics of production and internal trade should, in your opinion, be published so far as they could be got? – I think that a good deal might be done to improve the statistics of internal trade, but I think it might be more convenient to us to answer the question by asking what particular improvements might be made, in Professor Marshall's opinion. There is so much done that is not utilised, that I always feel a difficulty when people are speaking on the subject as to whether they are not asking for something that is already done. I always feel a difficulty as to what it is precisely they are asking for.

7112. I read that statement of yours before Lord Iddesleigh's Commission,[119] and I should be glad to know what trades you referred to? – As to mining and various other trades a great deal is done, but as to other trades, such as the building trade, for instance, nothing is done. We do not know how many houses are built, or what kinds they are, and what value, and things of that kind; whether there would be means of ascertaining that particular thing mentioned, I

---

[117] That is, Charles Booth, 'Evidence on Waterside Labour', material provided to the Commission, Group B (Vol. III of minutes of evidence, Appendix 155, esp. Table on p. 552). It may also refer to his *Life and Labour of the People in London*, London, Macmillan, 1896, Vol. VII, Part V, Chapter 1, pp. 392–432.

[118] *First Report*, London, HMSO, 1886, Royal Commission into the Depression of Trade and Industry, Cmnd 4621, 1886, Q. 9–12, 139–40. Marshall himself had supplied information to this Commission, which is reprinted in *OP*, pp. 3–16.   [119] See n. 118 above.

really do not know, but I should like always when improvements are talked of (we have to look at it in detail and decide what improvements are done), to know what is specially in your mind at present.

7113.   I did not intend to suggest anything myself, but if I had suggested any trade I should have taken the building trade as one of the most easy and most important? – I should think it would be one of the most difficult to do in this way, that you would have to ascertain the value of what was produced, which might often itself be a matter of estimate. You have such people as speculative builders, who cannot tell very well how their speculations will turn out till they have sold the property, and found that they have either made a profit or been made bankrupt, they are not quite sure which. How you are to tell what the production of a builder of that kind is, I do not know. You cannot have a unit of quantity very well, and how you are to get a unit of value is really very difficult to follow if you give your mind to it.

7114.   Would not it be possible to get it sufficiently near for many trades? – I doubt whether you could get it within 10 or 20 per cent.

7115.   If you could get it within 10 per cent., would not that be nearly all you wanted? – You could get it with a great amount of worry and friction.

7116.   Is not it a common thing for other countries to publish statistics of the number of houses being built? – But that is also being done in this country. There is a statement in the census with regard to the number of houses being built.

7117.   Once in 10 years? – Every 10 years.

7118.   That would, of course, be of no value for my purposes? – In addition to that there is the return that we have in the income tax form, which might be the basis of forming some calculation of what the new builders' work was, and that is the assessment of houses under Schedule A.

7119.   But surely the assessment of houses does not bear upon it? – The assessment of the annual income must give you some idea of the increase of buildings from year to year. My difficulty is that it only gives one part of the builder's work, whereas the builder has got to do repairs and has got to renew houses as well as build them; it does not give you the value of all that he does.

7120.   No, but one might suppose that the repairs at one time would be very much the same as at another, might not they? – Yes, but that is making suppositions again instead of having the statistics.

7121.   Quite so, but are the statistics published by the Board of Trade which you have been explaining, based directly on exact figures? – Surely they are almost all based on figures, I should think. If you take the imports and exports, they are based upon actual statements with reference to every transaction of imports and exports. There is an actual document for every transaction.

7122.   But no one would be more able than you to tell us how much interpretation those figures require, is not that so? – No doubt even with data of that kind it is difficult, but to get it for the building trade you would have to invent a mode of getting the data to begin with.

7123.   But is there any reason why we should not have such a means of ascertaining the fluctuations of activity in the country, not for a 10 years to 10 years interval, but from month to month or quarter to quarter, such as would be afforded by a study of the general amount of building work being done? – That would only be one item out of a great many. My own impression is that you could not get that particular thing from month to month. You might get a statement of the number of employed in the building trade from month to month, as practically we get now from the trades union reports, but as to a statement of the value which the builders produce month by month, I do not believe that you would get it so that it would be of any use whatever, because it takes so long before they know what the value is.

7124.   I do not think I proposed to get the exact value; that would not be necessary, would it? – What would be the unit in the building trade except the value?

7125.   Then there might be units of the different kinds of houses, or there might be units of the opinion that builders put upon the value of the house exactly corresponding to the units of the opinion that an importer puts on the value of his goods, allowing for similar errors?

– Not very well. I think that you must not apply things of that kind unless you are pretty sure of a good and useful result; it would be imposing a great deal of labour for nothing at all. I should like, before going into a scheme of that kind, to have it exactly before me as if I were proposing it to a minister, so as to be able to say exactly what it was to be.

7126.   I did not come prepared to make proposals to a minister. I was asking questions in order to get your views? – But those are matters on which one has not exactly views, those are matters of business which have to be discussed as matters of business.

7127.   You have asked me to give instances: We as individuals can buy our boots and shoes whenever we like. It does not make much differ-ence to us whether we buy our boots and shoes in January or in March, but we might know beforehand that by giving employment in one month rather than in another we can steady a great trade. Is it not the fact that the boot and shoe trade is a very fluctuating trade. People interested in the trade know at what time giving out extra orders would tend to steady employment, but ordinary persons do not; and would not it be possible for Government to publish statistics of that kind? – I am not sufficiently acquainted with the boot and shoe trade to make a statement as to whether anything could be published in that trade, but I should doubt very much whether such a thing as you con-template is even possible to anybody in the trade at all.

7128.   You would be aware that there are recognised times in the trade at which the trade is more busy than at others? – But that applies to so many trades.

7129.   But taking this one you would be aware that there are times recognised in the trade (I have not them in my memory at present, but I have seen statements with regard to them) at which the trade is more busy than at others? – I suppose so.

7130.   And that the trade of producing is not busy at the time at which the selling goes on most rapidly, but some time before? – Well, sup-posing that to be so?

7131.   And that if uninstructed people were to guess, they would guess wrongly, and that therefore it is not possible for individuals to do what they could to steady the trade without such information? – But I should be inclined to say that even if they had the information people would buy according as it suited their own convenience.

7132.   That is hardly an answer to the question. That is taking another line? – You are suggesting that the information ought to be got in order to enable people to buy when it suited the trade, instead of buying when it suits their own convenience.

7133.   I asked you whether the Government has not the power of publishing statistics which would enable the consumers, if they chose, so to distribute their purchases as to make one trade that is now very unsteady become relatively a steady trade?[120] – And the answer which I give to it is, that I do not suppose that it would have any effect in making the trade less unsteady than it is, because people would buy when it suited them and not according to the information you propose to give. That applies to the essence of the whole thing. Besides, I do not think it could be done, and that it is a different point. I think I am bound to say, as a point of that kind has been mentioned, that the real way in which fluctuations of that kind are equalised, is by means of what is called the floating capital in the trade. Trades make for stock at one time, and they do not make for stock at another time, and really the floating capital is obtained so cheaply, that it is a matter of the utmost indifference to the steadiness of the trade whether people buy in three or four months of the year, or six or eight months, or whether they buy evenly over the whole twelve months.

7134.   I specially took this trade because I suppose you must be aware that the people in the trade say that it is not possible to do that in this particular trade? – That it is not possible to make for stock?

7135.   No, that it is a dangerous thing to do, to make very largely for stock? – I suppose it would be so in other trades as well, but that they do make for stock is quite certain.

7136.   But perhaps not to any large extent, and consequently when orders are slack they have to dismiss their men? – Would not it be

---

[120] This was a hobby of Marshall's, and part of his remedies to irregularity of employment by means of providing more information. See his Address to Industrial Remuneration Conference, 1885, pp. 176–9, and *Final Report*, §215 (above, pp. 100–1).

well anyhow, that that should be ascertained? – How much that is the case?

7137. How much that is the case and what the fluctuations are, and what are their causes? – I think it would be extremely desirable that more information should be got and published about what the fluctuations actually are; but between that and entering on the question of the Government publishing information monthly which would be of use for any practical business, there is the greatest difference in the world.

7138. What kind of difference? – Publishing information monthly as to production in all trades would plainly be a most formidable and expensive work, whereas it would be comparatively easy to ascertain in a general way what the fluctuations of the trade are, not from month to month, but in such a way as you can ascertain them by means of special reports.

7139. You laid stress[121] on the fact that Mr. Wright found that the average income in Massachusetts was 67 per cent. higher than in Great Britain? – That is the way he put it in his wages returns.

7140. But did not you rather imply that he gave us to understand that his figures meant something more than they really did mean? – No, I think that he is to some extent responsible for the assumption that he is comparing English and American wages. If he did not say so, other people have done so, and it is constantly spoken of as if he had compared English and American wages.

7141. You said 50 per cent. of the American people are engaged in agriculture?[122] – Nearly that.

7142. Could that be true of Massachusetts? – I do not know how far it would be true of Massachusetts; but in that case there is another question which arises: of what use could it be comparing the wages of a small place like Massachusetts, about the size of an English county,

---

[121] That is, in answer to Q. 6975 from the Duke of Devonshire, Gould had indicated that Wright when Commissioner for Labour in Massachusetts had indicated that 'wages in Massachusetts were from 60 to 70 per cent higher than wages in Great Britain'.

[122] That is, in answer to Q. 6975 from the Duke of Devonshire, Giffen had stated that 'in the United States very nearly half the people are agricultural labourers or peasant farmers'.

with the wages of a great mass of people like those in the United Kingdom?

7143.   Surely there would be much good looking at it from the point of view of the Massachusetts Bureau? — They ought to have taken into account a much wider range of industries in Great Britain, so as to make a proper comparison for the general purposes for which such comparisons are made.

7144.   But they did compare many industries, did they not, in Massachusetts? — About 24.

7145.   You say that the average income of the agricultural classes in the United States is very low; are you sure of that? — It looks to me low, according to their own returns.

7146.   But do not you think that the reason why the Massachusetts Bureau omitted the agricultural industry was that for the agricultural industry the incomes enter in another form, and do not enter in the particular form in which you look for them; that they did it in order to be able to make a fair comparison? — When I made the remark I was referring not merely to the Massachusetts Bureau, but to the American Bureaus generally, all of which seem to omit the question of the remuneration of the agricultural labourer and the peasant farmer in the United States, although they form half the people.

7147.   Speaking of American agricultural labourers, are there very many agricultural labourers there? — There are, in the census of 1880, upwards of three millions entered as agricultural labourers, and there is a note too, about another million of general labourers, saying that very many of these are agricultural labourers also. There is a large number, and I think that is the largest class of labour in the United States.[123]

7148.   But would they be chiefly in the Northern States like Massachusetts, or in the Southern States? — All over.

---

[123] When revising the proofs of his evidence, Giffen indicated the exact population data: 'agricultural labourers 3,323,000, farmers and planters 4,226,000. These covered males and females, males alone being agricultural labourers 2,789,000 and farmers and planters, 4,169,000' (note by George Drage, Commission Secretary).

7149.   When you got the average for agriculture, ought you not, when making an attack on the Massachusetts returns, to lay stress on the fact that they do not include so much black labour? – But I am not making any attack on the Massachusetts returns.

7150.   I understood that you did? – No, I merely point out that I have got certain figures to present to the Commission, and that I have got no other figures to compare them with.

7151.   But I thought you laid stress on the fact that these Massachusetts returns were not valuable because they did not take account of agriculture? – They are not useful for a comparison between the general wages of the United Kingdom and the general wages of the United States, because they took no account of the wages of half the working population in the United States, which is very obvious.

7152.   But if it refers only to Massachusetts, is that of very great moment? – But they have been used as if they compared the industries of the United States and the United Kingdom.

7153.   The Massachusetts Bureau is not responsible for that? – I think to some extent it is responsible, because, if my memory serves me rightly, I observed a reference in the report either of the Washington Bureau or of this Commission of Professor Franklin's[124] in which these wages in Massachusetts and Great Britain were referred to as the wages in the United Kingdom and in the United States respectively.

7154.   But that report is quite a different thing, is it not? – He is partly responsible for that too.

7155.   In the north, at all events, the agricultural class is chiefly a farming class, is it not? – I would not like to say minutely what it is in the north of the United States. If I had thought of it, I should have brought the United States census volume with me, and you should have seen it at once.

7156.   But you must be aware that statements continually were to the effect that the agricultural labouring class is small relatively to the farming class? – In the north?

---

[124] Not easily identified, but referred to in the *Report* as a person employed in a State Labour Commission in America.

7157.   Yes? – That is hardly so if the figures I have given you generally are correct, that in the United States census they account for more than four millions agricultural labourers out of eight millions, which was the figure in the census of 1880 – four millions out of eight millions odd people engaged in agriculture, altogether that is.

7158.   Anyhow, a very large part of the agricultural class, more than half of the agricultural class, are farmers? – That seems to be so.

7159.   Is not it generally believed that, except in times of agricultural depression in America, the farmer is accumulating wealth in various forms very rapidly? – I do not know that it is so. At one time of my life, not lately, but some years ago, I had occasion to make a continuous study of American agricultural newspapers, and their complaint of the condition of the small farmer was something much more bitter and aggravated than any complaint we have of the condition of agriculture in this country – continual complaint, which was echoed, as we all know, by the proceedings of the Grainger party[125] in the United States, which was really a proceeding rising out of the great and widely-felt distress.

7160.   But the aggregate wealth owned by the farmers, anyhow, in places where a little while ago there was no wealth, consisting of farms and stock and implements and buildings, after deducting mortgages, would amount to something like 600*l.* a farm, would it not, or more if you took only the Whites? – I should doubt that very much indeed. In any case, I should like really to go into that a little more carefully before answering as to what the accumulated capital of the farmers is per head, because there are really such extensive complaints of the mortgages in the United States that I forbear to have an opinion.

7161.   I may say that I made a rough calculation allowing for mortgages, and I came to the conclusion that it was about that, from 600*l.* up to 1,000*l.*? – Including the capital value of the farms as well as the capital value of the stock and other things?

---

[125] The Grainger Party (or Grange Party) flourished in farming communities during the 1870s with maximum support peaking in 1874 (800,000 members). See S.E. Morison, H.S. Commager and W.E. Lauchtenburg, *A Concise History of the American Republic*, New York, Oxford University Press, 1983, pp. 435–7.

7162.   Yes? – And deducting the mortgages.

7163.   Deducting the mortgages. Again, is it not true that the greater part of the land that has been sold at high prices to the railways – those made without grants – and for building purposes, has been bought of farmers, and that a farmer in making up his earnings, counts up naturally the chance of selling his land at a great price? – But surely of late years, you must be aware of the complaints which have been made that the land has not been increasing in value, and that in the Eastern States the people have been leaving the farms just as in England, and you have had something like a fall in value in the United States as well as here in many parts.

7164.   But you are aware that matter has been investigated very thoroughly indeed by the Illinois department, with the result that the popular belief has been shown to be inaccurate? – Illinois is not one of the Eastern States to which I refer.

7165.   No, but the reports have been made very much with regard to Illinois. Illinois is one of the States in which it had been stated there had been a depression? – I do not know the particular report you speak of, and of course I cannot speak about it; but I should not like to speak about any report of that kind without having examined it very carefully.

The witness withdrew

Adjourned to Thursday next at 11 o'clock.

Thursday, 2 February 1893: examination of Sir Robert Giffen (continued).

[After two introductory questions (Q. 8086–7) by the Duke of Devonshire to clarify Marshall's questioning of a particular method to obtain wage data from actual payrolls, Marshall resumes his questioning from 24 January.]

PROFESSOR MARSHALL

8088.   I have noticed, in reading the Report on Railroad Labour, the particular difficulty to which you call attention; and if you will recollect, you will find that when you raised your objection before I said nothing on the other side, but I admitted that the methods of the American bureaus were not such as I should be prepared to defend on all grounds. But is it not true that the objection by you raised against the American method is merely that they have not had time in this particular investigation to go far enough? – I think not; the same kind of thing necessarily exists in every trade, and it would, be quite impossible, except at an enormous expense, to trace out every individual, and find out the other pay sheets in which he ought to appear, and then ascertain what he actually had been paid.

8089.   My point was this: Is it not a fact that the Americans are trying to find out how much irregularity of employment there is in the country, that the task is a very difficult one, and that they have not yet done nearly all that is essential for solving it; but that in England we are not attempting it, and are merely guessing at the result? – I beg your pardon, we are attempting it very much in England, and I hope in the course of the next 12 months to be able to show a great deal more.

8090.   In your previous evidence,[126] you referred me to an unpublished Report of the Board of Trade, as regards the wages of certain industries; of course, I cannot tell what there is in that, but the Board of Trade has already published statistics of wages in several trades, and I have looked into them, since you were last here. To see whether I could find the specific information I wanted, and I could not find it; is it there? – I do not know exactly what you were looking for.

8091.   I am talking of the returns of wages in the textile trades, for instance. I wanted from those to get some sort of opinion as to what was the actual amount of want of employment in England? – I do not know exactly what you have ascertained.

8092.   I ascertained nothing. I am asking the question whether it is not true that taking these reports, the reports already published by the Board of Trade with regard to wages, the Board of Trade has not even attempted what the Americans have attempted, though I admit they have not quite succeeded? – I think you will find a very large amount of information upon the subject in those reports.

[126] Earlier in answers to Q. 7088–90 from Marshall (above, pp. 242–3).

8093.   Is there any exact information as to the regularity of employment? We know of course the number employed at different times,
the maximum and the minimum. From that we can guess, if we like,
the amount of want of employment; but is there any means of getting
information other than that of pure guess? – Surely the statement of
the maximum and the minimum ascertained in a certain definite way,
is a means towards the end which you wish to arrive at. I do not say it
is the entire information which you wish to have; but it is a definite
thing which has been ascertained in a definite way, and so far it is a
contribution to the subject. It does not pretend to be anything more.

8094.   So that I am justified in saying that the attempt to find out how
much want of employment there is in England has not yet been
undertaken by the English Board of Trade? – I do not know that I
would go so far as that, because we have a great deal of unpublished
information.

8095.   So far as the published information goes? – I do not publish it
until we have ascertained a great deal of what it is expedient to ascertain; but all those facts which you have been referring to, are certainly
contributions towards the end which you wish to arrive at.

8096.   In the report with regard to textile industries there was no indication that you were going to publish a supplementary report with
regard to regularity of employment? – But that is exactly what we
are undertaking now, not so much with reference to the textile trades,
as with reference to those trades which are known to be rather more
fluctuating than other trades are. That is now being commenced at
the Board of Trade; and all the information necessary, which has
been going on accumulating, will be available along with the other
information which we propose to obtain.

8097.   I understand from what you said last time, that the next report of
the Board of Trade, with regard to wages will move more in the
direction of supplying information with regard to the irregularity of
employment than the report with regard to the textile trade did? – If
you will say the next reports you will be quite correct in saying so.
That is clearly a very important point to inquire into. But, as I have
often remarked, you must take one thing at a time when you are
going into statistics of this kind.

8098.   Another question of the same kind. In your answer to question 6997, you compare the American method of ascertaining the income derived from capital with the English method.[127] Now, I am not going to suggest that the American method has yet attained completely the results at which it has aimed; but I should be much obliged if you would explain what the English method is. You refer to the income-tax statistics. I am not aware how you can get from the income tax statistics a statistical measure of income obtained by capital as separated from the income earned by the higher grades of professional labour? – But, surely, the income-tax returns supply a large amount of information.

8099.   They supply statistics from which you, and I,[128] and a great number of other people, have made guesses, but I am not aware that any of us has ever thought he was doing anything more than making a very random guess? – I think it goes much beyond a random guess; it goes to the point of making a tolerably useful estimate for many purposes. Take, for instance, the income-tax returns; you find one of the items in Schedule D is Public Companies. It is quite clear, as regards Public Companies, that you have a very definite figure as to the amount of profits that are earned. That is only one illustration. Schedule A is another illustration. Of course, it requires a considerable amount of pains and trouble to make anything satisfactory out of it; but it is an advantage which we have in England, that we have these income-tax returns, and other information of that kind, which they have not got in the United States.

8100.   When you stated that, should you not also state that they have property-tax returns, which we have not? – Yes, and also that they do know that their property-tax returns, as regards all property except real property, are not worth anything at all. That is stated in the census reports of the Americans themselves.

8101.   All such returns require much interpretation, even the English – but, the American more than the English? – There is no doubt they

---

[127] Giffen's lengthy answer to this question makes such a comparison on the basis of published reports.

[128] In the *Principles*, Marshall appealed to the practice of the Income Tax Commissioners in settling issues associated with the definition of income. For example, 8th edn, 1920, p. 77.

all require interpretation, that is to say, all figures are not easily handled. That is quite certain. But because figures are not easy to handle, you must not say that you have not got figures at all.

8102. My question is, what are the figures by which you obtain your statistical estimate of that share of the income of the country which goes to capital? — But I have made no estimate before the Commission.

8103. No, but in this answer you say,[129] 'therefore if you are to get in any way the relations between wages and profits, the only effective mode of studying it is in the way I have put before you, by comparing the aggregate income from wages and the aggregate income from capital in the best way that you can.' Now I want to know how you get the aggregate income from capital? — Surely that is a question that will take us a very long way indeed.

8104. I understood you to say that you got it from the income tax returns, and my question is whether, in order to get the aggregate income from capital from the income-tax returns, every English statistician, yourself included, has not been compelled to make a rather bold guess? — No doubt you must make estimates upon certain points, but I should point out very strongly that, as to a large amount of the income from capital, there is no doubt whatsoever, and the margin as to which there is a doubt is much smaller than the question of the total amount.

8105. On that opinions are rather apt to differ, are they not? — No doubt opinions differ; but if the Commission would wish to investigate the subject, I could get it up, and should perhaps occupy one or two days in going through the evidence upon the point.

8106. My interest in the matter is only because you have brought in these disparaging remarks with regard to the American statistics, with regard to which I want to point out that there is a good deal to be said from their side?[130] — I may say that I made no attempt to make what Professor Marshall calls disparaging remarks upon the American statistics at all, because undoubtedly they have this

---

[129] This is part of Giffen's long answer to Q. 6997, referred to in n. 127 above.
[130] Above, pp. 239–41, 243–4, Q. 7072–80 and esp. Q. 7093.

difficulty, that they have not the advantage of our income-tax returns and statistics of that kind. What I pointed out was that, in a question as between wages and capital, unless you get the aggregates, you only have isolated facts, and that is all you get by the American plan. They look into a particular trade, and they say, or they endeavour to say, that in that particular trade so much goes to wages, and so much goes to capital; but that does not carry you very far in any shape or form, because there is the most infinite variety in what goes to wages and what goes to capital in different trades; and before you can get any conclusion at all, you must put it into an aggregate form, and that the American figures supply you with no means of doing.

8107.   But is it not a fact that all that class of questions of which you have been talking now, has been discussed with a great deal more fullness and more scientific care in America than in any other country? – I think not; most decidedly not.

8108.   Now go to question 6975.[131] In what I cannot help calling your disparaging remarks with regard to Mr. Carroll D. Wright, you said: 'I think he maintained that his figures showed that wages on the average were higher in Massachusetts than in Great Britain by something like 60 or 70 per cent. That was the deduction which he got from his figures. I think the statement for the limited purpose, the limited area of the comparison which he made, was logically defective in many ways. For instance, he took 24 different employments, and he took the average wages in each employment and added these averages together and divided them by 24, without taking into account which of the employments were numerously occupied in Great Britain and Massachusetts respectively; and so he arrived at the conclusion that wages in Massachusetts were from 60 to 70 per cent higher than wages in Great Britain.' While that statement naturally supplied a good deal of amusement, ought you not to have stated that the Americans had pioneered the way in determining the true average wages in every occupation by finding out exactly how many there were in each particular trade, and at each particular rate of wages? – I think not.

---

[131]   That is, Giffen's answer in response to a question from the Duke of Devonshire.

8109. Is it not true that in the particular report from which you quote, that is done in great detail with regard to Massachusetts? – Will you let me see the report?

8110. (*Handing the '15th Annual Report of the Bureau of Statistics of Labour' to the witness.*) Have we not there hundreds of industries with the number of people employed at each particular wage? I will read at random where I have opened, 'bobbin setters, spinning, 22 in number, average wages $3; bobbin setters, spinning – of another class 22, average wages $1.16; bobbin setters, spinning – again, another class – 22 average wages $1.80; doffers spinning, 4, average wages $3.60,' and after those, other classes of doffers, and so on? – May I interrupt? That is really not the point; that is the statement of the average wages of those numbers, not a statement of the numbers at the trade. I should like to say that no doubt the development of this mode of stating wages statistics has occupied the Americans for a considerable period, but before that report of the Bureau of Massachusetts, there were statements in our Board of Trade Statistics of the proportionate numbers in different trades and different employments. The point was one to which our attention had been directed, and in the very first memorandum which I wrote, or the second memorandum, with reference to the work of the department you will see we started with the idea in 1886, at the very beginning, and I think we have developed it much more than it has been developed anywhere else.

8111. I would like to go on if I may; is it not true that his next step is to find out the number of people in every separate trade, and the average wages in that separate trade? – 'Average wages' again, but we are speaking of the classification of wages now as I understand.

8112. Does he not do that with the object of finding out what are the average wages of all the industrial population, and is it not true that when he comes to Great Britain he says he is now compelled to abandon this method because the statistics necessary for his purpose are not published in Great Britain, and is it not true that so far from having made the very elementary mistake suggested by you, he at the end, to provide against persons falling into the error of supposing his statistics mean more than they do, says, 'In making such comparisons', that is comparisons got by adding up the average wages in particular trades without reference to the numbers in them, 'after results are obtained reference should be had to the recapitulation table and text, in order to fully understand the basis of comparison, that is, number of employees, respective number of men, women, children &c., and whether day, piece, or day and piece workers'? – I think I may say with reference to that, that it does not touch upon the point which I have mentioned here. I say 'he took 24 different employments, and he took the average wages in each employment and added these averages together and divided them by 24, without taking into account which of the employments were numerously occupied in Great Britain and in Massachusetts respectively.'

8113.   Is that quite accurate? – That is quite accurate.

8114.   Is it not true that, so far from not taking account of the question, he took very careful account and was much disappointed at finding that he was not able to make his comparison thorough because of the want of proper English statistics, he having supplied there the necessary statistics for his own country? – I am bound to say that, having the information as to rates of wages which he was satisfied with as to ascertain employments in England, he would have had no difficulty in making an estimate of the comparative numbers in the different employments; and in any case, instead of adding up the 24 different occupations in Massachusetts, and dividing by 24, he might have given you what he thought was a true average. I do not think that the matter had advanced so far at that time as Professor Marshall would like to make out, but I must deprecate again what he imputes to me, that I am wishing to disparage the American statistics at all. I have pointed out that they are not available for certain purposes, and that is all that I have said.

8115.   The point that I wish to put is this: Is it not true that the difficulties which you suggested to us had been fully and carefully considered by him; only with regard to the question what was the best method of dealing with those difficulties, he has formed a different conclusion with regard to it than that which you have formed? – I think he has not formed a logical conclusion at all.

8116. You object to a comparison that is made here between the average wages in Massachusetts and the average wages in England on the ground that agriculture employs nearly half of the people of the United States. We went on afterwards to discuss the question how far that statement related to Massachusetts; but are you sure of your facts with regard to the United States? – I speak exclusively from the census of 1880.

8117. Are not these the facts, in the census of 1880; male 'persons occupied', 14,744,942; agricultural labourers, male, 2,788,976? – It is quite impossible for me to speak about the American census without the figures before me, but I should like to state that the figure which I have got here is male persons, all occupations, census of 1880, 14,744,000; employed in agriculture, 7,057,000; and there is a note that many agricultural labourers have been reported simply as labourers, and that that figure of seven millions ought to be increased. Of course, those seven millions are not all agricultural labourers, they are peasant farmers as well; but these are the figures upon which I base my statement, that nearly half the people in the United States are engaged in agriculture. Of course, if Professor Marshall had been kind enough to refer me to the figures of the American census which he wished me to look up, I should have brought the census tables with me. I have given the figures now in the answer to question 7147.[132]

8118. I understood that you had the facts before you last time so I supposed you would have them before you now? – I could not bring all the books with me, of course, but I put a note of one or two facts in detail which quite supported the statement which I was making to the Commission; but, of course, if you are going to examine me about the details of the American census, I should decline to speak without having the census tables before me, naturally.

8119. Your statement, in answer to question 7157, that four millions out of eight millions, odd, people engaged in agriculture are agricultural labourers, I cannot quite fit in with the statement in the report that the male agricultural labourers are 2,788,976?[133] – That shows

---

[132] Above, pp. 251–4 (Q. 7139–58), and see Giffen's subsequent correction in n. 123 above.
[133] Above, pp. 251–2 (Q. 7141 esp.) and n. 123 where Giffen rounded Marshall's extract figure to 2,789,000.

that it is quite impossible to go into a discussion of this kind without the census before us – quite impossible.

8120.   The particular point, however, was, that the Massachusetts statistics were untrustworthy because of the number of agriculturalists in Massachusetts, and, at question 7141, I called attention to the fact that your argument against attaching values to these statistics was based on the fact that '50 per cent. of the American people are engaged in agriculture.' I raised the objection that it did not matter how many of the American people were engaged in agriculture – the statistics related to Massachusetts. I asked whether that would be true of Massachusetts. You say: 'I do not know how far it would be true of Massachusetts'; but it is not important, considering that you are here lending your authority publicly to discrediting this report, to consider that Mr. Carroll Wright was statistically perfectly justified in what he did, because the total number of agricultural labourers in Massachusetts was only 22,490?[134] – I think I made it quite clear on the last occasion, that what I objected to was the use of a comparison between Massachusetts and Great Britain as a comparison between the United States and Great Britain.[135] I am not quite sure that I followed exactly the point which Professor Marshall wished to make as to its being a proper comparison between Massachusetts only and Great Britain, but the tenor of what I meant to say was undoubtedly that Massachusetts, being a small place, practically about the size of an English county, you could not properly compare such a place with a great nation like the United Kingdom. I think it is really to make an improper use of statistics altogether. That is a general observation, but I must really deprecate what Professor Marshall imputes to me, that I am wishing to disparage these American statistics. Really what I pointed out was that you could not use that comparison between Massachusetts and Great Britain as a comparison between the United States and the United Kingdom, and I think I must rather object to Professor Marshall wishing to impute to me some other opinion about it.

8121.   Is it not the fact that the Massachusetts report was a comparison made for the purposes of the Massachusetts people, by their own special bureau, and that for that purpose a comparison between

[134] Above, pp. 251–2, Q. 7141–2.   [135] Above, pp. 251–2, Giffen's answers to Q. 7142–3.

Massachusetts and England was a reasonable comparison to make? — I think not, because the two things are not comparable. You might have compared Massachusetts with a particular English county, or with London; but it was not fitting that you should compare it with a great and extensive area like that of the United Kingdom, with a great variety of industries, much more than in Massachusetts. That was an improper comparison altogether to make essentially.

8122.   Is it not true that there are some people who think that a comparison between Massachusetts and Great Britain is much more instructive than one between the whole of the United States and Great Britain, because the conditions of life in Massachusetts are approximately similar to those in Great Britain; while there is such a very large Negro population in the United States, and the conditions of life in the South are so different from those in the North that a statistical comparison between the United States, as a whole, and the United Kingdom, as a whole, is misleading. I do not ask you to agree with that, but is not that a tenable opinion? — What I should say to that is that you might make comparisons on different bases for different purposes; but then you ought clearly to state what is the drift of your comparison, and what is the line you are taking. What I objected to was that the comparison between Massachusetts and Great Britain was used as a comparison between the United States and the United Kingdom. That I do object to; and, in objecting to it, I am not saying anything at all to disparage the American statistics as far as they go. This is really a matter of principle.

8123.   Is it not a fact that everybody's statistics are used by other people for illegitimate purposes? — That happens very often, but then it is the business of some of us who know statistics to point out when they are used illegitimately.

8124.   Yes, but I think that in the form in which you gave your original account, when you amused us so by describing the way in which Mr. Carroll Wright had added together the average wages of unequal trades, you did not, I think, make clear that he was not responsible for this?[136] — But I think I stated quite sufficiently the different points I

---

[136] Possibly a reference to Giffen's answer to Q. 6975 and see above, p. 260, Q. 8108, where Marshall quotes part of this answer.

wished to make. I think that altogether that comparison, and the way in which it has been used, have been really most unfortunate, and I hope some good will be done by what I have said now in pointing out the limitations within which such figures can be used.

[Questioning of Sir Robert Giffen continued by Mr Gerald Balfour.]

Marshall's examination of H.M. Hyndman, 2 February 1892

[Marshall's questioning follows that of Mr Trow.]

PROFESSOR MARSHALL

8606. Am I right in supposing that you consider that the present capitalistic system is fundamentally bad on the ground, namely, that wages at present constitute but a small fraction of the value which the labourers' work costs – that improvements go mainly into the hands of the capitalists, and that in consequence of that the increase of wages is, out of all proportion, less than the value of improvements in production?[137] – That is my contention. I should not support the wage-earning system even if it were free from those disadvantages, but those disadvantages are the main ones that present themselves to me.

8607. You gave an instance of the cotton industry as an industry[138] in which there had been very great improvement in production? – Yes.

8608. As the result of that, you would expect to find the fact that the price of calico and raw cotton were brought near together? – It might be so.

8609. And that has happened? – It has happened.

8610. You kindly gave us a budget of a working man's family?[139] – I did.

[137] Hyndman later provided a detailed statement to the Commission to this effect. It is included in the *Fourth Report*, Whole Commission, Appendix 143, p. 311.
[138] In earlier evidence, in response to Questions 8410–11 from the Duke of Devonshire.
[139] In earlier evidence, Q. 8437–46, especially his answers to Q. 8444–6 which detail the specific working man's budget.

8611. And I would ask whether there has been, in any of the chief things which the working man buys, any increase in the economy of production approaching that in cotton. First, as to house rent – has there been any improvement in the method of making or putting together bricks at all similar to that in the cotton trade? – I should say yes, in regard to building large houses. I should think that you could build cheaper, not so much of course relatively as in other departments: but large buildings can be built to-day at considerably less cost owing to improved machinery compared with what could be done even 10 years ago.

8612. But in some branches of the cotton trade one man's labour will go as far as 1,000 men's labour once did? – Yes, 100 years ago.

8613. There has been no change of that sort in the building trade, has there? – No.

8614. In the price of firing has there been such a change? – No, there has been no reduction – no marked reduction.

8615. In light? – A very considerable reduction; enormous, but not at all in that proportion – not a thousand to one.

8616. In soap? – Very material, but not a thousand to one.

8617. That is in the manufacture, when you have once got the materials? – Yes.

8618. But a large part of the expense of soap is the cost of materials? – Certainly. Soap is very much cheaper to-day on the market.

8619. And more of it is used? – Happily.

8620. As to bread? – That is very much cheaper.

8621. There is no change in the art of ploughing at all similar to what there has been in cotton manufacture? – No, but the reduction of the average cost of wheat, if you take the present prices, the cost is less than half of what it used to be.

8622. Wheat and oatmeal go together. Now groceries? – There has been a very great reduction in regard to commodities.

8623. Butter? – Stationary I should say.

8624. There has been no fundamental change in the art of producing butter? – No.

8625. Flour may go as bread. As to meat – there has been no fundamental change in the art of producing meat? – No; but taking into consideration the Canadian and Australian producers, it is cheaper than it has been for some years.

8626. As to clubs – you put down a very large sum for that?[140] – It is so in that particular case.

8627. It is more than the average? – It is more than the average. I took it purposely, because I knew him to be a thrifty man.

8628. Vegetables and fruit?[141] – Cheaper.

8629. But no great revolution in the art of production? – No.

8630. Then we come to the complaint against the present order of society, which has been repeated so many times by those who advocate a great change, namely, that whereas in the cotton industry and the pen-manufacturing industry, and a great number of similar industries, one man's labour will produce from a hundred to a thousand times as much as it did before, one would expect a corresponding change in the real wages of labour; but is it not the fact that when we come to find out how wages are expended, very little of them is expended on industries with regard to which that statement is true? – Yes, but I do not see where that gets us to. I mean, if you release a number of hands from the cotton industry, or the woollen industry, or those other industries to turn to other occupations, it is perfectly clear that the economy of production is as great as though you had done it on the land merely. The whole of our machinery of industry in that respect hangs together.

8631. What I want you to do is to explain in what manner you regard the fact that the great improvements in the cotton and pen manufacturing industries have not brought about an increase in wages, and

---

[140] In earlier evidence, in his answer to Q. 8445, Hyndman had identified payments for clubs, together with union dues, sickness and death benefits (paid to friendly societies) at 3s. 3d. per week or 13.5 per cent of the total expenditure.

[141] In earlier evidence, in his answer to Q. 8445, Hyndman had identified spending on vegetables and fruit at 2s. 6d. or 10.4 per cent, a below average amount.

how that constitutes an indictment against the present system, when the fact is that the price of calico for the working man has gone down almost quite close to the price of raw cotton, so that he has his gains from the cotton improvements in that small item, but the great majority of things on which he spends his wages are things with regard to which it is not true that there has been a great improvement in production? – I think, on the whole, there has been some improvement. But suppose there was not – let us take it the other way. We have got to take the profits and the amount of returns to the non-producing class in the country – that is what you must estimate it by. Those large powers of production at the present time represent a very large return for which, in my theory, no reward is paid to the worker. For instance, take Schedule D. There are 620 millions odd which are paid to those who are associated with the profit-makers, and so on; and I say that that is an increase in proportion altogether outside the increase in wages; and even if there were a proportional increase, there is a very large amount of remuneration to the portion of the community which does no work.

8632. That is rather a different point; I would propose to come to that later on? – That is what I mean. I mean to say this, that here in each department upon which we depend for our supremacy – cotton, wool, iron, and the like – the powers of production have enormously increased, but the advantage of the community derived from the returns to these various industries, is not shared, I say, proportionally by the workers.

8633. I think you are introducing a good deal of new ground there, and perhaps I had better not follow you over it; but before leaving this, I would like to say I have noticed that in your opinion the purchasing power of money with regard to far the greater part of those things on which the workmen spend their wages has increased? – I think it has.

8634. And since we know that the average money wage has increased very fast – ? – I would not say very fast.

8635. Well, since we know that it has increased, and some of us think it has increased very fast, and since the purchasing power of each shilling has very much increased, therefore, so far the present system has been beneficial for the working man, and he has been free to work – that is since the repeal of the Corn Laws? – I am not so clear about that. In the first place, as you yourself have pointed out, or some other member of the Commission did,[142] the position of a man in London, or any of our great cities, with the various expenses that are entailed upon him, similar wages do not represent the same amount in the city that they do in the country, through the necessity of having to feed out of doors instead of at home, and from the increase of rent and other things which in my humble judgment very largely handicap that increase of wages on which we are called upon to rejoice.

8636.   Then going to your next main point, that wages constitute but a fraction of the value which the working man impart to the commodities, that is, I think, another way of saying what you said just now that the income going to the capitalist class is increasing rapidly? – With capitalists and their hangers-on, yes.

8637.   I am not quite sure whether I understand what you mean by hangers-on? – You must include in that class lawyers, domestic servants, and those with whom they divide it up. They all get it.

8638.   I do not quite understand about domestic servants. If a man buys bread from a baker, do you count him a hanger-on? – No. It is true there may be too many bakers, and so far there is a superfluous number of them, but I would not count him a hanger-on, but a domestic servant, certainly I would.

8639.   What you mean then, by this statement really seems to come back to this, that wages constitute but a fraction of the value which the labourers impart to the things on which they work. I want to know how you get at that. Take it in this way: a man ploughs a field, and he is perhaps paid two shillings for a ploughing that is worth to the farmer eight shillings, but do you consider that the ploughing is produced by him or by him and the horses? – If the horses are fed out of the eight shillings, that is a necessary part of the machinery of the business.

[142] Hyndman referred here to the Q. 8440 posed by Sir John Gorst which raised the issue of the different real value of a specific money wage for people in the country as against city workers.

8640. So that you would include as part of the necessary expenses of the business, all the outlay for keeping the machinery going? – Certainly.

8641. Deterioration? – Deterioration, fencing, and so on.

8642. The earnings of the people who superintend the labour? – That would depend upon the proportion that you consider they should have, but you know as well as I do that under the old system of production the superintendent got a less proportion than the man who did the work.

8643. But how about the interest on the capital invested in the horses and plough? – I should not calculate that, except as a portion taken out of the workers. I do not recognise interest in that regard.

8644. But if it is true that where there are no horses and plough the work would have to be done by the spade, with great labour, does not the person who lends the capital to the farmer, with which he buys the horses and plough, contribute his share to the production just as much as the ploughman? – I do not so consider.

8645. We shall not agree. I am afraid? – I should be most happy indeed, but we can meet at another time.

8646. The whole argument depends upon the assumption that the men who provide the capital with which the horses and plough are bought does not contribute to the ploughing in the same way as the plough-man does? – That is so; the horses and plough do, undoubtedly, but not the person who provides the money. They are two things on which deterioration only must be calculated in my opinion.

8647. Do you consider that if the person who saved the capital had spent it on temporary passing enjoyments there would still be the capital for the horses and plough? – No; if you throw champagne into your stomach, or into the gutter it makes no difference, it is unproductive employment, except in certain cases.

8648. But you admit the plough makes the work of the labourer more effective? – Undoubtedly.

8649. And that would not exist unless he had saved the money? – I say the labourer has carried out the ploughing; the capitalist has directed industry into that channel in place of another, and taken interest for doing it.

8650.   But you admit the plough would not have been there unless the man who had saved or some other man in his place, had foregone present enjoyments in order to get deferred enjoyments? – But how did he get the right to present enjoyments?

8651.   By working? – If he is a capitalist, it does not follow that he would work at all.

8652.   He may have? – That is a possible thing; but it would take more than 25,000 years to save a million sterling, at the rate of 4s. a day, and there are many capitalists who have that.

8653.   Anyhow he had it in his power to consume on the spot, or to delay it? – I do not deny it.

8654.   He did delay it, and, in consequence, production is more effective? – Instead of directing a further increase of the growth of champagne in France, he directed a man to make a plough in England. So far, yes, and he takes interest for it, which he would not take in the other case.

8655.   His interest corresponds to the fact that he has helped to render the work of the agricultural labourer more effective? – It may be so, but I do not know that he has. I mean to say that that would equally, if not more than, apply under a co-operative system, when the reward would go to the worker in place of going to the capitalist.

8656.   I must now go to a point that is not really very important in itself, but as you quoted a passage from a book of mine,[143] it would be better, in order to avoid misunderstanding, that it should be cleared up. You stated that the effect of living in town is that the children grow up without healthy play, and that they are generally not so strong as their fathers, and that the grandchildren are not as strong as the children? – That is my contention.

---

[143] That is, from the *Principles of Economics* (1st edn, 1890, pp. 253–4, 8th edn, 1920, in a modified form, pp. 195–200). Hyndman had quoted the passage in his answer to Q. 8404 and indicated it came from Marshall's *Principles* in his subsequent answer.

8657. But is not it true that the deteriorating effects of town life are much less strong now than they used to be under the old insanitary conditions? – I should say this, that a feebler people, to a certain extent, lives longer, owing to the improvement of the sanitary conditions.

8658. Is not the great change, not in the intensity of the evils of town life, but in the largeness of population that is subject to them? – That is almost putting it in the same way.

8659. That is, the intensity of the evil per head is not so great as it was, in consequences of sanitary improvements; but the number of people subject to it is a larger proportion of the whole population? – I think that is possibly true. I never considered that, but I think that is quite possible.

8660. Is not this movement common to all countries, including America and Australia; I mean the movement towards the towns? – Certainly.

8661. Is not it true that in Victoria more than half the population are in the towns? – Not more than half, but if you take Geelong and Ballarat and Melbourne, I should allow you about two-fifths or three-fifths, perhaps.[144]

8662. Is not that a tendency over which the methods of production have little control. Is it not mainly the growing desire of people for the special enjoyment of town life? – And association; yes, possibly it is.

8663. And is not it true that the evil is that without being deliberately selfish they sacrifice the well-being of their children (for it is the children that are hurt, and not the adults mainly) to their own comfort? – To a certain extent I think that must be admitted. I do not deny it. I think that must be so.

8664. And is there anything whatever in our present system to prevent our stopping that, when once public opinion has been aroused to its

---

[144] The 1891 Victorian Census reported 474,440 residents in Melbourne; 140,956 residents in other towns, out of a total State population of 1,130,463, an urban population of 54.4 per cent.

importance? – I think we might. In the present system there is a necessity for people living round the factories, and there is a necessity for some workpeople living near their work, but I should say that it is possible for the State to introduce free transit for 20 miles round our great towns, and in my judgment, you would do a great deal towards doing away with overcrowding in that way.

8665.   Are you aware that a proposal of this kind has been made by persons who do not wish to revolutionise society, that any person putting up a house in a district that has got as closely populated as is good, should be compelled to contribute towards providing free play grounds? – Very likely; that may possibly be. I do not say that there are no people at the present moment who sympathise with my opinions, who do not want to revolutionise things.

8666.   Is not your proposal or others of the same kind suggestive of burning down a house in order to roast a pig. Could not this aim of yours be attained more easily? – If you show me how it could be done more easily I should be happy to co-operate with you.

8667.   Do you agree in what I state? – Some portions I follow of what you state, but not other portions. If it is once admitted that their object is to substitute co-operation for competition, we are partially on the same ground.[145]

8668.   I go on the principle that the State may always interfere in the interests of children, and that since children cannot defend themselves, the doctrine of self-interest does not apply in cases in which children are not concerned?[146] – Quite so.

8669.   But these opinions are held by persons who are not socialists? – Quite possibly. I daresay many of the views which Aristotle held on the slave system are not being applied, but are held now.

[Marshall's questioning was followed by that of Mr Gerald Balfour.]

---

[145] For a discussion of Marshall's views on co-operation, see Groenewegen, *A Soaring Eagle: Alfred Marshall 1842–1924*, pp. 454–8, 601–2.

[146] That is, the position adopted by J.S. Mill in his *Principles of Political Economy*, Book V, Chapter XI, §9, pp. 950–3.

Minutes of evidence taken before Group B – transport and agriculture

Marshall's examination of Ben Tillett, 15 July 1891

[Following on the questioning of Lord Derby.]

PROFESSOR MARSHALL

3641. You have appeared here in a double capacity; firstly, as the chief secretary, and with the exception of Mr. Mann, the person best informed of the general condition of the dock labourers – giving us facts; and you have also appeared as a social performer of a very thorough-going character. May I appeal to you first in your former capacity?[147] – We have had a great deal of statistical information given by different branch secretaries, but between them I do not think they have covered the whole of the area; it has at least been impossible for us quite clearly to understand the geographical relations in which the docks stand to one another. Do you think it would be possible for you to prepare and give to the Secretary a rough map of the London Docks (Tilbury might be treated separately) showing the class of work done in each department, and then adding further statistics? – I will endeavour to supply that, with the assistance of the dock companies.[148]

3642. We have had a great deal of information as to the season trades, and we have had a great deal said about the difficulty of supplementing the employment in one season trade by working in another season trade. We have had a great many statements made with regard to the geographical difficulty and the difficulty of tides, but we have never had those put forward in a systematic way, and I do not think we clearly understand the question now. Do you think you could give us facts that would enable us to see a picture of the thing as a whole? – I will endeavour to do that.

---

[147] Marshall had probably first met Ben Tillett at a function organised by Newnham College Social Discussion Society in 1889, during which visit he dined at Balliol Croft. Above, introduction, pp. 88 and n. 28.

[148] The Appendices to the evidence of Group B do not seem to include such material as specifically supplied by Ben Tillett.

3643. As an instance of what I mean, you yourself mentioned as season trades – tea, timber, and wool? – And grain.[149]

3644. From what you said afterwards, as well as from other sources, I gather that there are several other season trades, for instance, jute, which I think you spoke of as a season trade. That is a question of great interest from the point of view of those who think that the irregularity of the work at the London docks tends to lower the character of London work as a whole. Might I then ask that you should give us a picture of the docks indicating what class of trade is a season trade, and if so at what seasons it comes in? – In a brief outline I think I can do that now. I will say in the first place that the Tilbury Docks undertake the discharge of colonial goods principally. A small number of coasting vessels go there, but a very small number. There is not a great deal of transhipment, but a fair share of transhipment goes on at the Tilbury docks. They employ of all hands on an average about 1,000 a day. The Albert and the Victoria docks do chiefly colonial work, and the Victoria especially a big amount of grain work. At the West India Dock there is a great deal of sugar work done. At the South West India Dock there are in seasons a large number of China vessels with tea, and also at the Albert docks. At the London and St. Katherine dock most of the wool and the fruit and the continental trade is done.

3645. I wish now to go to one small point which has recently come up, and that is with regard to the appointment of representatives of the men to overlook the accounts. I am not quite sure that there may not be some misunderstanding from your having used the word 'representatives' there.[150] You do not, I suppose, necessarily mean the revival of the old system of representatives, by which, there was a representative for each gang, but you would be satisfied with there being a limited number of representatives, and you refer rather, I presume, to a trade union official or somebody of that sort than to a representative as the term has been used in the evidence? – What I had in my mind was not a union official at all. We should not claim

---

[149] In earlier evidence in his answer to Q. 3565 from Lord Derby (minutes of evidence, Group B, Vol. I, pp. 138–9).

[150] In his answers to questions on the 'municipalization' of the docks, Tillett mentioned representatives of the men on several occasions, for example, answer to Q. 3577, 3603.

that any man in a gang at any time should go to the office and put them out of their working routine, as the whim took him. But we say, whether a union man or not, if those men select a man, and he goes there at the particular wish of a section of the men, and at a stated time which the shipping companies would know of, that man should be allowed to inspect the books without let or hindrance; not half a dozen men, but just one man; and not the same man every day, but just as they may choose him.

3646.   You do not necessarily want a separate man for each separate gang? – No; unless the work is a separate job. You see there may be eight men working together upon the co-operative principle, and another eight in another part of the vessel. The representative of the one eight would not be a representative of the other as well. Wherever any class of men, be it either two or 200, are directly interested in one particular job there should be a representative either for the two or the 200.

3647.   I should like to get more clearly your reasons for thinking that the number of unemployed is greater than is commonly supposed. You said[151] that the fact that when public work was offered by Mansion House relief committees, or others, very few men turned up who were willing to do a fair day's work: did not show that there were not many who would not do a fair day's work, and could not get it, that they were deterred by a notion that the work had a taint of pauperism? That is rather a new idea to a certain extent, and I should like to know what evidence you have of it? – The evidence we have is this. In the winter time, at any of our dock gates, a large number of men are to be seen. Some of them may not have been at work for a month or five or six weeks. Were we to go to that body of men and there may be 500 and only 20 men are required, it might be possible that any one of the 500 may be taken on, and there they are in that expectant state. That is one reason why they do not go away. Then another thing is, they look upon it as pauper relief; they do not look upon it as legitimate work. Then again work of the description offered requires the strength not of a man who has been hungry for five or six weeks, but the strength of an able-bodied, well-fed man;

[151] In his answer to Q. 3594.

and heaps of these men have neither the strength nor the food in them (which means lack of will) to undertake the work. But those same men who have been classed as idlers by a certain section of the public readily fall into their season work when it comes round; and if there are 50,000 idle, and if there was work for 50,000 in the natural channels, those men would readily fall into the work; but out of that 50,000, you would not perhaps get 5,000 that would accept charity work.

3648.   Do you think that the kind of work offered by the Mansion House Committee is the kind of work that it is less possible to do on an empty stomach than the dock work? – I should say so. Then there is another point. Among dock workers there is a spirit of communism, so that men who have been hungry, directly they get into work, with any chance of earning the money at the end of the day, are able to get food; and I believe the dock authorities will bear me out in this fact, that after a period of depression it takes about three days before the men get into anything like working fettle, which proves that they had had no food, and were not fit for it. But when work is offered to them by any charity they have not that means of helping each other, because all the men who go there are hungry alike, and plenty of those who get work with their mates at the dock very often share their dinner, if not, their pocket money.

3649.   I am aware of what you call the communistic system at the docks, which is a very bright spot in the dock work, and a thing which should never be forgotten; but still, perhaps it hardly sufficiently accounts for the difficulty I have suggested; because when people work for Mansion House funds, if they can prove themselves to be hungry, they generally get something to eat early. But without pressing that point, I would ask you whether you are aware that it is commonly said that the class of people who only get casual work at the docks are people who belong to a very peculiar class – being willing to work very hard for very high wages, for a short time, but for the most part unwilling to earn equal wages by work spread over a longer time. Do you think that is the case? – No. I think the exigencies of the trade and our present commercial system, are the cause of it. A shipowner, if he has a vessel that costs him 100l. a day does not want to have her in many days. Time is money. The shipowner offers a little more than the usual pay; and the men who get it, because they know a period of depression is coming on, earn as much as ever they possibly can to tide over the difficulty. It is not because they want it, it is not because they seek it, or ask for it. It is because they are forced to it.

3650. I wish rather to press you on this point, because the evidence you are giving is somewhat opposed to what has been said by a great number of people who have made rather a special study of the subject. Is not a man of what is sometimes called an extremely Irish temper, who is prepared to exert himself very much for awhile, but insists upon being paid highly while he is at work, and will not go through the drudgery of continual work through a whole week; is he happier according to his view of life with the not irregular work of the dock than he would be with regular work at 4d. an hour, even although it gives him much greater wages during the week? – You put it as a question of 4d. an hour. I say, providing you give the man a decent living, an Irishman would rather work three following days than he would work 24 hours right off if he got the same pay. The amount of pay earned in the hour at this kind of work is not an exceptional rate of pay at all. The highest class and the most inter-mittent labour is the grain work, where the men have practically to put in all they know and all the strength they possess because there are periods when they are unable to get employment. They do not do it because they love it. They would rather have the 30 hours stretched into three or four days than they would do it right off. I have a drop of Irish in my own composition, and I have seen a lot of Irishmen at regular work, and they have been most punctual and sober; but the same class of men when they get into irregular work do develop that spirit, and if they did not they would eat their hearts out. They have got to make themselves happy. Under proper circumstances an Irishman as much as anybody else likes regular work.

3651. I did not mean to imply that this fitful habit of work was not itself to a great extent the result of a bad system. I wanted you to tell me whether you do not think it is also, to a certain extent, the cause of a bad system; whether you do not think that, as a matter of fact, those who hang about the docks and do not get taken on by the foremen are not as a rule people who either from birth or education have got to be impatient of steady hours of work? — No, that is not the cause. Any unsteadiness of habit among them is a physical result. Many of them have had to put up with very little food three or four or five days right off and generally when they get into work they have to get things out of pawn, and their children share the money they earn. After they get over the first feeling of depression that comes from their being exhausted in consequence, not of work, but of privation and short-ness of food, then they become as steady as anyone, and steadiness of work means steadiness of habit and sobriety as well, but when men are unemployed for a dozen hours one day and then are three or four days without work bad habits are formed.

3652. Can you from your personal experience say that people who do get into irregular habits and who spend rather unwisely the earnings they have got by a small amount of work, change their habits rather rapidly if they get regular work? — They do change their habits rapidly.

3653. You think that is the general rule? — Yes, and I will give an instance in point. When working at the docks I worked in the tea warehouses. In the summer very little tea comes over, and these men go to the dock gates and get a job there. These men in the summer have a do-not-care look and feeling about them because their work is irregular; their habits are not steady; but within a month after getting regular work the whole appearance of the men begins to alter because of the regular work.

3654. It seems to me that the question how far that is true, and I have no doubt that it is true to a great extent, is one of the most important questions as regards the possible improvement of the condition of the working classes of London as a whole, and I should be glad of any distinct evidence that you can give bearing on it? — I would say in the slack season there are about 70 per cent of the men employed in the tea trade who have to look about for work as gardeners, and at harvesting, at painting, and so on. Those who can get regular employment keep up steady habits; but with regard to those whose employment is irregular (it does not matter what their education may be), and who have to struggle at the dock gates, and who go there morning after morning and meet with disappointment and go

without food, the first temptation that comes into their mind directly
they handle any money is to get something in the shape of food and
in all probability something to drink. This would not occur to them if
they knew that they were going to work that morning, and knew that
a certain amount of money would be given to them. Then they
would go home. They would give their money up to their wives, and
all would benefit by it.

3655.   You spoke of the dockers, when they could not get work at the
dock, going about as painters? — As painters' labourers or doing anything else.

3656.   Have you made any estimate of the amount of wages that they
are able to get in that way? — Of course in the painting trade they
would get as much as the average workman.

3657.   We have been told a good number of times that the average
wages in the docks are this or that, and I have pressed witnesses[152] to
say whether the wages so got were not merely got by adding together
the total wages paid in the dock, and dividing it up according to a
rough estimate, no allowance being made for the earnings outside the
docks, and I have not been able to get any estimate or indeed any
considerable allowance for the earnings that those people would
make outside the docks? — In the particular trade I am interested in —
the tea trade — which is a cleaner kind of work, we should get a larger
number of men who are painters who would be earning a good sum
of money, and some men out of the shoemaking, carpentering, and
the cabinet-making trades, especially when there is the mending of
tea chests. But that does not affect materially the numbers engaged,
because at the very outside there are not more than about 3,500
affected that way.

3657a.   Was the tea trade the particular part of the work which you
used to do before you held your present position? — Yes. On the other
hand the average earnings of the men are taken from the dockers
who follow up the docks. In the summer they may go morning after

[152] This was a bit of an exaggeration on Marshall's part. He had examined only a few witnesses
from the docks before the appearance of Ben Tillett. Q. 2454–71, 2651–64 are the only ones
that fit his remark.

morning as well as in the winter. Of course the number of applicants for labour increases in the winter whilst the work is correspondingly less; but these particular men that we would take as typical dockers are not the men that go into other trades. The typical docker is the man who looks to the docks for whatever livelihood he can obtain; and that kind of man has on the average very low wages.

3658.   Now I come to you in your capacity of a social reformer. I am not sure that you have not taken up two positions even with regard to that. In an early part of your evidence you said no reforms in the docks would be satisfactory unless a complete reorganisation of the industry of the country were made.[153] I am not sure that we did not think you a little more impatient than you really were because just now in answer to the chairman[154] you have proposed as a palliative scheme a board of arbitration which would be based upon the existing organisation of industry without any organic change? – What I had in my mind was this; that arbitration boards and other means of settling disputes are only trimming away the edges; the root of the thing remains there still.

3659.   You came here as the secretary of the Union as one of the persons who has an all-round knowledge with regard to the docks. It is not open to this Commission to recommend the country to change fundamentally the conditions of its industry. It is open to this Commission to make recommendations for diminishing the evils that exist in the docks, and I should have rather liked to have been able to disentangle that part of your reform which would properly come within the scope of our consideration, from that which would belong only to the councils of the nation after the glorious revolution of which several socialists have told us? – What you would like then is that I should say that these very moderate proposals are all-sufficient in themselves.

3660.   No, I want you to make it more clear what proposals you think are practicable without an organic change in the condition of industry? – The palliatives mentioned are only a contributory solution to the question, but the economic position would be just the same.

---

[153] In his earlier evidence, Tillett had expressed the wish for the complete regulation if not nationalisation of waterside dock employment (for example, answers to Q. 3558, 3568–77).

[154] That is, Tillett's answers to Q. 3615–40 preceding the questioning by Alfred Marshall.

3661.   I am asking you to say what changes in addition to the institution of this board of arbitration you would desire to recommend subject to the condition of there not being such as would involve an organic change in the methods of industry. What reforms are needed practically in the docks without an organic change of the general condition of industry? – I cannot see any possible. It is so bad that I should say that nothing but a good clear out will do, but it may be eased. If we are to have any satisfactory solution there will have to be an organic change.

3662.   I want you to tell me how it is to be eased; what things you would propose in order to ease; other than a board of arbitration, are there other palliatives which you as the secretary of the Chief Union of Dock Labourers would recommend? – The only palliatives that we have we have tried, and they have failed. It is just the measure of our strength, that allows us to determine any improvement or any good for the men; it is the measure and power of the employer that allows him to determine whether or no he shall employ just as he likes, without considering the ratepayers and without considering the lives of the employés.

3663.   You are giving reasons for thinking that the palliatives will not by themselves do very much; what I want to know is, is there any other palliative that you would desire to propose in addition to the board of arbitration? – I think I made it clear to Lord Derby that we would have an inspection of machinery; that we would have a regulation in the hours; nothing over 48 hours; and that we were to have some means of settling disputes. I also thought that all accounts should be open to inspection of the men who earn the money; that they should have more opportunity of selecting their associates when a co-operative system is allowed them, that the machinery should be well attended to; that proper numbers in the gang should be provided for; and that the men should not work beyond the proper hours. Those would be palliatives. Above all, if we can put a conscience in the employer and the employed, that is the great thing to aim at.

3664.   With regard to this diminution of strain, I do not think that we have it clearly before us how far the strain at certain parts of the docks is of a different character from the strain at certain other parts.

You spoke very impressively of the way in which men in the prime of life, picked men, were set to work so exhausting that before long they ceased to be strong men and became diseased. There is great misunderstanding among the public on this matter, because there is not a sufficiently clear distinction in people's minds between different kinds of work in the docks; and I should like to ask you how large a proportion of the people engaged in the docks are doing work such that it is impossible for them to lead the lives of good citizens. What proportion of them are doing work involving so great a strain that at the end of their work they are unfit to enjoy life except in the more rough and brutal ways which they are, so to speak, forced into? – From a rough estimate I gather that 25 per cent of the dock *employés* have a decent chance to live, 25 per cent. have to do this heavy work which means physical incapacity in the long run, and 50 per cent are not able to live a decent life.

3665.   The 25 per cent. that do this excessively hard work would include the timber workers, I suppose? – Yes, they would include the timber workers.

3666.   Whom else would they include? – The timber work and the grain trade is all heavy work. Colonel Birt, of Millwall and Mr. Griffiths of the Surrey, will tell you he has the finest set of men breathing, big busty fellows who do the very heaviest kind of work. I do not mean those, I should say that practically 75 per cent of them while they are at work work very heavily, but the corresponding wage and results to the workmen are much more satisfactory than at the other docks.

3667.   Will you specify the classes of men whose work is so heavy that they cannot be expected when their work is over to take any pleasure except in the coarser forms of employment? – There are plenty of very light industries in the docks, while particular parts of the work are very heavy. The piling and the loading is very heavy work in nearly all cases. If the packets are 20 lbs. in weight or 200 lbs. it seems very heavy work. The timber work is very heavy work. So is the grain trade, especially the backing. A couple of hundred-weight upon one's back, and the running all day means that one man practically carries close upon 90 tons, which is rather heavy for a nine hours day.

3668.   What is the class of people you have in your mind when you talk of work being such that if a strong man enters on it his strength soon leaves him? – I mean especially in the piling and the loading which would mean delivery work; that is in all cases very heavy, and so is the work for the gangs who take in work from wages or from ships. Those are very hard forms of work – the housing work and the delivery work. Of course, in all docks there is a great deal of rummaging to be done, that is, where particular parts of a parcel have been taken away. It means that the dock companies in order to economise their room have the whole thing re-arranged and put up in a corner so that they can take a larger amount of stuff in the space cleared.

3669.   The drift of my question is this, a great many people say they want shorter hours of work; but on investigation it is found out that their work is not of such a kind as to be injurious as it now stands. This has been said with regard to the docks. It has been found by many inquiries that much of the dock work is not of an exhausting character by any means, so that it would be possible for a man to work 10 hours a day, and at piece-work, without its being likely to injure him or to make him a bad citizen or a bad father. But I do not think the public in general knows that there are a very large number of people in the docks, who do work which necessarily makes them bad citizens and bad fathers, because they are so exhausted by their work that it is difficult for them to abstain from drink and other coarse forms of pleasure. I want to know whether it would be possible for us to get a more exact classification of that part of the dock work which is contrary to the interests of the public, because of its severity as distinguished from that which does not really injure the people? – I have endeavoured to clear your mind upon that point. I say that all round there are about 25 per cent. of the whole of the dock workers who have to do this heavy work, and as I said to Lord Derby just now, if these men were not specially selected as they are selected, they would be quite unfit for the work. If the class of labour going to the dock was more regular, and there was a stream of relays, so that all able-bodied men should take their share in certain heavy labour, there would not be those possibilities of spinal disorders or hernia and accidents that arise. The men who work at some of the piles for 10 hours take more out of themselves than an ordinary man would in 15 hours at a lighter employment.

3670.   Of course that would not be the only method of re-arranging the work? – But it would be one of the essential methods.

[Marshall's question was followed by Mr Jesse Collings.]

3C   MEMORANDUM ON DISPUTES AND ASSOCIATIONS WITHIN PARTICULAR TRADES CONSIDERED IN RELATION TO THE INTERESTS OF THE WORKING CLASSES IN OTHER TRADES

But I would suggest for consideration whether it might not be better to keep only §A in the Introduction and to transfer the remainder to the end of the descriptive portion of the Report.[1]

The present Part III 'Skilled and Unskilled Labour' seems to me, in its present form, not a good ending of that portion. The opening paragraphs of it are analytical, and are really wanted at an early stage: while much of the remainder is of the nature of a general conclusion and might be so called: and in that case the bulk of this memorandum might be worked in with it.

Or, if Part VII is to be retained in its present form, I think a new Part VII, General Conclusions, might be added.

Alfred Marshall.

§A.   It will thus be seen that the evidence taken before the three committees was directed almost exclusively to the interests of particular industries. Representatives of the employers and the employed in each industry explained clearly and instructively its internal troubles and remedies proposed for them, and they suggested ways in which the public acting through the government to promote peace within that industry or to confer other benefits upon it. But they did not generally undertake to represent in any special sense the other side of the question and examine[2] the influence for good or evil which the action of that industry might exert on the well-being of other industries and of the public generally. The witnesses who appeared before the Commission as a whole did indeed consider the interests of the community in general rather than of particular industries; but they did so carefully with regard to various movements, and they seldom touched more than incidentally the question how the organisation of particular trades would be likely to affect the [2] working classes in other trades.

---

[1] The *Final Report* as published had an introduction, largely devoted to procedural matters, into which §A of Marshall's draft could have been accommodated. The conclusion of the 'descriptive portion' of the *Report* probably referred to the conclusion of the intended first part which summarised the evidence under seven broad headings. See above, introduction to Item 3, pp. 90–1.   [2] 'or to consider in detail' is crossed out in the original MS.

This latter question comes under the inquiry into 'The conditions of labour which have been raised during recent trade disputes' which the Commission is directed to make; and it is no doubt one of very great importance and urgency. But it seemed to them best not to attempt to investigate it at length. For it was more important that their enquiry *should be thorough, so far as it went than that it should cover a very wide area, and even when thus limited their task remained a very heavy one. Again, specific evidence can more easily be obtained with regard to the interests of particular industrial groups than as to the general interests of the public.*[3] For while there are many persons who can speak with intimate knowledge of the facts; evidence of the latter would necessarily contain much of a speculative nature, which would best be discussed at more leisure than is possible in an oral inquiry.

It seems desirable however to indicate clearly the way in which [3] a study *of the action of trade unions and employers' associations upon the workmen and employers engaged in particular industries needs to be supplemented by a study of the effects of a highly developed system of such organisations upon the interests of the community at large, and upon the wage earning classes generally, whether unionists or non-unionists.*[4]

§B.   It will presently be seen how membership of a trade union and especially of one whose provident benefits make him independent when out of work or in ill-health, tends to increase a man's self respect, and sense of responsibility, how it enables him to bargain on more equal terms with his employer; and by preventing him from having to sell his labour on artificially disadvantageous makes the action of competition more healthy and more serviceable to the community as a whole than it otherwise would be. And we shall see further how the growing strength and experience of the chief trade unions, up to certain limits, tends to diminish the number of strikes and lockouts, partly because it smooths away many personal jealousies; and other causes of conflict which are so frequent in the history of weaver and less [4] high organised unions; and partly because it facilitates clear understanding between employers and employed, and the settlement of many difficult questions by concilia-

---

[3] The italicised material largely reprints material from what appears to have been a printed proof of some earlier draft of the *Final Report*, corrected in Marshall's hand to make it fit the flow of his argument.   [4] See n. 3 above.

tion and arbitration. So far their action may be, and generally is, almost entirely beneficial to the public as well as to their own members. For if trade unions of but moderate strength, acting either by itself or in concert with an association of employers, restrict production, the public will be able to defend themselves by getting from elsewhere what they want, or something which will serve in its place, the attempt to raise the price against the public will recoil on those who made it.

§C.   This is most clearly seen in the case of trades that are closely run [5] by foreign competition. In those trades the workers early learnt to welcome every improvement, even if it caused themselves some temporary inconvenience for they perceived that since goods made by the old methods would have to be sold against those made by the new, an adherence to the old would lower their wages or throw them out of employment. Thus, however strong may be the combination within that trade, so long as English calico is sold at home at the same price as for export, Englishmen have no reason to fear that they will pay in the price of their calico much more than is necessary to give a good wage or a fair profit to energetic and enterprising people making it by the best available means. In such cases, whatever promotes internal peace within the trade itself is likely to bring the action of the trade as a whole more and more into harmony with national interests.

[6] § D.   Nearly the same may be said of a trade in which though foreign competition is less strong, there is yet effective competition between branches of the trade in different parts of the country; and in which trade organisations are only of a local character. Any attempt to raise price against the public artificially is checked by goods coming into their market from outside. Sometimes local regulations as to apprentices tend to keep the supply of skilled labour below the needs of the public, but then the deficiency is not without great loss by the migration of labour into the place from others and partly by the migration of the industry itself from that place to another.

§E.   Until within the last years there have been no signs of the growth of trade organisations so strong and with so wide a range of actions as to have the power, even if they had the will, to pursue [7] their own advantage at the expense of a great injury to the public. But the evidence submitted to the Commission has brought out very clearly a tendency on the part of trade organisations to become more firmly compact and to extend the range of their action over a great part or the whole of the country, to enter into alliance with similar organisation abroad, and to combine together various trades, the services of one of which might have been substituted in case of need for those of another. By all these means they are lessening the control exerted on them by external competition and it is therefore important to consider whether such power is at all likely to be used to the public detriment.[5]

§F.   The question at issue is not a class question between employers and employed, or between rich and poor: it is mainly between the immediate interests of particular trades and those of all industries taken together. It is sometimes thought that this question [8] has no practical bearing; because if the policy of each industry benefits itself, then the aggregate effect must be good for all. But this seems to be an error. For if each of a number of swimmers tries to hold himself up by pulling his neighbours down, the policy as a whole will injure all, though each man's policy may tend to help himself.

The dangers to be considered are mainly of two kinds: – limitation of output, and adherence to uneconomical methods of production.

§G.   One form of limitation of output is the cessation of work during a strike or lockout. Now though an increase in the strength of trade organisation much diminishes the number of such disputes, it widens the area over which they extend when they do occur, and makes them last longer. The net effect of this change is probably [9] beneficial to those in the trade itself; but it is often injurious to the general public for when there was a local dispute in a trade, the contestants themselves were the chief sufferers; the public could generally get its supplies at a moderate rise of price from elsewhere while some of the employment that went past the local trade in this way, was lost to it for good. But now if the dispute spreads over a wide area and cuts off many sources of supply, the public has to pay a very high price for

---

[5] Marshall seems to have thought here particularly about the 1889 dock strike to which foreign unionists (such as those from Australia) had contributed funds.

short supplies and the aggregate loss to the public during the dispute is likely to be as great as the combatants themselves and when the dispute is settled the trade recoups itself for much of its loss, and may even gain more altogether than it had previously lost by very [10] full employment at very high prices; but still the public is losing. To take an example, a suspension of work on any one of the trunk lines from England to Scotland, would probably injure the combatants more than the public; but the chief loss of a suspension of work on them all simultaneously would injure the public more than the combatants, even though the railways were compelled to carry at the customary rates when they resumed. This peril was brought very near in one of these great recent trade disputes to which reference is made in the terms of appointment of the present Commission.[6] Again, a suspension of work in all the coal mines of the country would be very injurious to the public; but yet might increase the year's income of coal miners and coal owners, and perhaps also of middlemen in the coal trade.

[11] It may be conceded that as long as the dispute lasts the pressure on the combatants is generally more intense than on any part of the public. But this is not always so. If the work of the trades is needed to supply other trades with raw material, or to form part of the same joint product of service, those other trades may be compelled to stop work altogether, and if any of them happen to be less-well-to-do than that in which the hitch occurs, they may suffer more than it does. Hardship of this kind could seldom be very great so long as trade combinations remained merely local and could be circumvented: but their modern growth in strength and extension may raise such hardships to a prominent place in industrial history.

§H.   The evil caused by working short time, or lessening of output in other quiet ways, attract less notice than those caused by [12][7] a great conflict; but if much prolonged they may be greater in the aggregate. When a certain diminution of output is the unavoidable result of changes that are needed to relieve a particular trade from excessive or

---

[6] The terms of reference of the Commission included 'the conditions of labour which have been raised during the recent trade disputes in the United Kingdom' and see above, introduction, p. 81.
[7] Marshall subsequently wrote at the top of pp. 12 and 13 of the original MS, 'rewrite'.

unhealthy work; there is a gain to be set against the loss. The gain may be the greater; and in any case allowances must be made for it. But putting this gain aside, a very small permanent diminution of output would more than outweigh the benefits of a total cessation of industrial disputes. For as Mr. Giffen has shown[8] the direct loss caused by them only amounts to about one per cent of the total output.

Even when a restriction of output in any trade is temporary, the steadiness of wage which it tends to secure for it is often granted at the expense [13] of increased unsteadiness of wage or employment, or both, in other trades. For instance, when there is a falling demand for ships, an artificially steady price of coal and iron is likely to stop shipbuilding altogether; and by this checking to demand for coal and iron to compel the trade societies in the coal and iron trades to have recourse to measures still more stringent and still more injurious to the public in order to sustain their price.

§J.   Recent events have shown the moderation of the working classes; few of them would deliberately grasp at the opportunity of getting wages that were unreasonably high relative to the standard of comfort prevailing in their own class; and they are probably justi-fied in thinking that they set a good example [14][9] to other classes in this respect. But yet there are signs that a very strong union may drift, without any deliberate selfishness, into a course of action that may be very injurious to the public without bringing great gains to themselves. For if a high wage has brought into the trade more workers than can be employed during the full week without lower-ing the price of their product and thus jeopardising that high wage; they may feel themselves justified in stinting production with the purpose of obtaining a fair wage, or at least what is sometimes called a living wage, in return for much less than a week's work. As a temporary expedient this may possibly do more good to the trade than harm to the public. But such arrangements once made [15][10] tend to be permanent, when they add to the comfort of those who

---

[8] Presumably in the Annual Report of the Board of Trade on the strikes and lock-outs of each calendar year which had been published since 1888.

[9] Marshall subsequently wrote 'doubtful' at the top of p. 14 of the MS.

[10] Marshall subsequently wrote 'keep' at the top of p. 15 of the MS.

have the uncontrolled power of imposing them. And if they became general and permanent, the prosperity of the country would decline.

§K. It is true that in the past combinations to raise prices have proceeded from employers[11] rather than employés; but such of them as are not directly connected with the relations between employers and employés lie beyond the scope of our inquiry. All experience shows that associations of employers are seldom so firmly knit together as those of employés and the latter have announced with growing frequency their intention to lend some of their own binding force to the former to enable them to regulate trade in the interests of both. Should this movement extend much further, complete harmony within individual trades may develop a deeper opposition between the interests of [16] wider industrial groups, just as the incorporation of small States in larger is sometimes the beginning rather than the end of disastrous wars. This opposition is at present slight, but it is showing itself with increasing force.

It could no doubt be held in check by the transference of all means of production to a central authority; and many of those who desire this end on other grounds, regard with satisfaction the growth of trade unities which would at once prepare the way for a more thorough consolidation of authority and make its uses more apparent.

But those who are averse to this remedy must rely on the force of public opinion. That is an ever growing force; and acts with increasing quickness as regards any selfish action, the consequences of which obtrude themselves on general notice. It is thus very powerful against any [17] [attempts] to raise suddenly the price of any commodity which is largely consumed by the great body of the people, or is needed as a material in important trades. But it is almost powerless against the injurious tendency of a trade unity to discourage experiments, which might be inconvenient at the time and perhaps disturb the smooth working of its regulations but which, if successful would cheapen the production and lower the price of its products.

[11] Marshall had dealt with this problem in his 'Some Aspects of Competition', his Presidential Address to the Economics Section of the British Association for the Advancement of Science in 1890 (reprinted in *Memorials of Alfred Marshall*, ed. Pigou, pp. 265–272).

§L.   For instance the constant tendency towards the curtailment of the hours of human labour and the increased expensiveness of machinery is in many trades bringing nearer the day when there would be great economy in making one set of machinery serve for two shifts of workers; and such a change would probably do more than anything else to increase the share of the national income [18] which goes to labour and diminish that which goes to capital.[12] But the first introduction of the new method generally causes some trouble to the employés and much to the employers, and is often opposed by trade associations. If this opposition is strong, and an employer adhering to the old ways has little fear of being cut out by others following the new, it will need a rare force of will and public spirit to induce him to try to pioneer the new way.

The same may be said of the opposition to piece-work and other methods of adjusting payment to efficiency in those cases in which they would be on the whole advantageous. No doubt there are many cases in which the opposition to these methods is reasonable; on the ground that partly by putting the employés at a disadvantage in bargaining [19] as to their wages and partly in other ways they would injure those in the trade more than they would benefit the public. But the evidence received by the Commission gives reason to think that the opposition is not entirely confined to such cases even at present. And it might become almost irresistible, if an all embracing association of *employés* in a trade were working in harmony with a strong association of employers.

§M.   It is not likely that deliberate opposition would be made to adoption of well tested mechanical or other improvements. But it is known that when English manufacturers under the stress of competition throw out their old machinery, it is often sold to countries in which a protective tariff or some other cause enables the local trade to combine effectively if not ostensibly against the local consumer. Again those old trade unities which went by the name of Gilds,[13] were always found wanting when the time came for [20] changes to

---

[12] Marshall stressed this aspect of economic progress in the concluding chapters of the *Principles of Economics*, for example, 8th edn, 1920, pp. 690–6.

[13] Marshall tended to link trade unions and guilds. See his *Economics of Industry*, written jointly with his wife, Book III, Chapter V, pp. 187–8.

be made. They did not ruin the country only because trade went round them, and left them to ruin those particular places in which they had dominion. The experience of the past thus raises some fear that the trade unities extending over the whole of England might probably throw some additional obstacles in the way of those experimental variations, which, though often proving abortive, sometimes lead the way to important inventions. And it should be noted that the force of public opinion cannot well be brought to bear against such obstructions as this; for no specific evidence can be given of the loss which it inflicts. The dangers may not be very near: but it concerns a great matter. For indeed a very small check to the inventions of the last hundred years would have diminished greatly the wages of labour in all countries but especially in England.

[21] All these considerations tend to show that though the growing strength of a trade union up to certain limits is almost sure to benefit the community at large, no sure conclusion can yet be reached as to whether it is for the public interest that it should work in unison with an association of employers in the same trade.[14]

[14] This passage well illustrates Marshall's ambivalence on trade unions during the early 1890s, which appears to have grown from that decade onwards. See Ray Petridis, 'Alfred Marshall's Attitudes to and Economic Analysis of Trade Unions', esp. pp. 480–1, 498–9.

ITEM 4

Appendix: Treasury document: 'The Fiscal Problem',
25 August 1903

INTRODUCTION

On 2 July 1903, Marshall received a letter from Theodore Llewellyn Davies,[1] the principal private secretary to the Chancellor of the Exchequer, C.T. Ritchie, asking him to present his views on the 'fiscal problem' which had been engaging the attention of the British public and its government since the spring of that year.[2] Marshall's views were

[1] Theodore Llewellyn Davies (1870–1905) had been a student at Trinity College, Cambridge, from 1887, taking the two parts of the Classical Tripos in which he gained first class results in 1891 and 1892 respectively. In 1894 he joined the Treasury, and during 1898–1900 served as assistant secretary to the Royal Commission on Local Taxation. Marshall, who had contributed a Memorandum to this Commission, had probably first encountered Llewellyn Davies in this context (there is a Marshall letter to him on this subject dated 30 October 1901, reproduced in *Memorials of Alfred Marshall*, ed., Pigou, pp. 430–2). There is thus no truth in the unsubstantiated claim from J.C. Wood that Marshall and Llewellyn Davies were 'undergraduates together, and established a lasting friendship', an error based on confusing Theodore Llewellyn Davies with J. Llewellyn Davies, an earlier acquaintance of Marshall (J.C. Wood, 'Alfred Marshall and the Origins of his "Memorandum on the Fiscal Policy of International Trade" (1903): Some Unpublished Correspondence', *Australian Economic Papers* 21 (39), December 1982, p. 262 n. 8). Llewellyn Davies was principal private secretary to the Chancellor of the Exchequer from 1902 to 1904 (that is, to Ritchie and to his predecessor, Sir Michael Hicks-Beach), the capacity in which he wrote to Marshall on this occasion. From 1904 he served as secretary to the Income Tax Committee, until his death by drowning in July 1905 cut short a promising Treasury career.

[2] Relevant details are provided subsequently in this introduction. There is a huge literature on the subject of which the following references are particularly useful: A.W. Coats, 'Political Economy and the Tariff Reform Campaign of 1903', *Journal of Law and Economics* 11, April 1968, pp. 181–229; A. Gollin, *Balfour's Burden: Alfred Balfour and Imperial Preference*, London, Anthony Blond, 1965; J.C. Wood, 'Alfred Marshall and the Tariff Reform Campaign of 1903', *Journal of Law and Economics* 23(2), October 1980, pp. 481–95; Phyllis Deane, 'Alfred Marshall and Free Trade', in *Alfred Marshall in Retrospect*, ed. Rita McWilliams-Tullberg, Aldershot, Edward Elgar, 1990, pp. 113–32; Groenewegen, *A Soaring Eagle: Alfred Marshall 1842–1924*, pp. 376–89.

sought confidentially, for the eyes of the government only, though Llewellyn Davies indicated that there would be no problem for Marshall to publish this material later under his own name, if he so wished. Although Marshall was given *carte blanche* in what he could write, two issues were to be specifically addressed by him. To quote Llewellyn Davies, these were:

(1)   Imperial Preferential Tariffs – involving import duties in this country on Food and perhaps other more or less Raw materials

(2)   Retaliatory duties – adopted primarily perhaps for the purpose of Tariff negotiations, but involving most certainly permanent and systematic protection of Manufactures.[3]

Lewellyn Davies went on to indicate the 'endless issues arising out of these two main points'. Examples included possible alterations in the circumstances which had made free trade the best policy for England; the effects on free trade of development in business organisation such as trusts; the impact of the successful progress of protectionist Germany and the United States on the case for free trade; the problems of dumping by tariff-protected cartels for a free trade country's industries and means to remedy this situation; and some discussion of the incidence of import duties on corn, meat, dairy products, with, and without, preference for colonial products. Llewellyn Davies also invited Marshall to submit anything he had previously published on the subject and expressed the wish that if it could be arranged before the Marshalls went to the South Tirol for their summer holiday to discuss the matter personally at any place convenient to Marshall.[4]

Marshall only received this letter after he arrived at Stern in the South Tirol, his main holiday destination for 1903. In his reply[5] dated 14 July, Marshall proposed to send a Memorandum in a 'few days', a rash promise for a notoriously slow writer. In the meantime he undertook to send, or arrange to be sent, what little had appeared in print under his name on the subject. One of these publications was a 'comprehensive statement of [his] views as to the incidence of customs duties' in a letter to *The Times* reproduced in the *Economic Journal*,[6] the other his 1890

---

[3] T. Llewellyn Davies to Marshall, 2 July 1903, in Wood, 'Alfred Marshall and the Origins of his "Memorandum . . . Trade"', p. 263.   [4] *Ibid.*, pp. 263–4.

[5] Marshall to Llewellyn Davies, 14 July 1903, in *ibid.*, pp. 264–5.

[6] That is, Marshall to *The Times*, 22 April and 9 May 1901, reprinted in *Economic Journal* 11 (46) June 1901, pp. 265–8.

Presidential Address to Section F of the British Association on 'Aspects of Competition' which also dealt with some of the issues in which Llewellyn Davies had expressed in interest Although dated, this paper still had its uses, Marshall claimed, if only to demonstrate the rapid obsolescence of discussions on American trusts.[7]

By 12 August, that is within a month of the original invitation, Marshall wrote to Brentano, the German free trade economist, that he had despatched the second half of the Memorandum dealing with the effect on the basis of the fiscal system of changes in the last sixty years.[8] A letter from Llewellyn Davies on 13 August apologised to Marshall for his omission to thank him for receipt of the first part.[9] Marshall had sent this off a 'few days' before 20 July, as he told Brentano in a letter written on that day. Marshall described this first part as lengthy, and devoted to a discussion of 'the incidence of import duties'. It was explicitly opposed to views expressed in tracts in favour of tariff reform issued by Chamberlain's office and the false economic history on wheat prices contained in Hewins's articles in *The Times* which Marshall had been following with growing annoyance.[10] Apart from this general description of its contents which Brentano received, Llewellyn Davies contributed some specific detail on its contents by way of somewhat tempered criticism of one of Marshall's propositions. Given the difficulties associated with Wood's identification of the 1903 Marshall Memorandum among Treasury Papers in the Public Records Office, the relevant paragraphs need to be extensively quoted:

---

[7] Reproduced in *Memorials of Alfred Marshall*, ed. Pigou, pp. 256–91.

[8] Marshall to Lujo Brentano, 12 August 1903, substantially reproduced in H.W. McCready, 'Alfred Marshall and Tariff Reform', *Journal of Political Economy* 63(2), June 1955, pp. 264–5. The description of the contents of the parts comes from Marshall to Brentano, 20 July 1903, in *ibid.*, pp. 262–3. This conforms to the 1908 version but not to the identified 1903 text.

[9] Llewellyn Davies to Marshall, 13 August 1903, in Wood, 'Alfred Marshall and the Origins of his "Memorandum . . . Trade"', pp. 265–6.

[10] Marshall to Brentano, 20 July 1903, in McCready, 'Alfred Marshall and Tariff Reform', pp. 262–3. Hewins's articles on tariff reform for *The Times* commenced on 15 June 1903 under the by-line of an 'Economist'. By 20 July, they had reached seven, the article with which Marshall had been particularly incensed and which inspired the letter to Brentano. Marshall estimated that mail from Stern to Cambridge took three days if it reached its destination at all, a not unlikely event as Marshall himself was to experience (Marshall to Foxwell, 2 and 5 August 1903, Freeman Collection 13/244, 12/244).

Just one point occurs to me which I venture, with some diffidence, to suggest for your consideration. Is not paragraph 29 expressed in a way which might be capable of being misunderstood, and certainly might be unfairly quoted? I mean, especially, the statement that the price here would probably not rise by the full amount of the tax? In view of the fact that the increase in our Colonial Wheat supply would be gradual, and that the world's demand for Wheat is continually growing, it would appear that Foreign producers could have no difficulty in disposing of the produce of their existing plant and land and would merely be deterred from increasing the output by bringing new and less advantageous land under cultivation, or by cultivating more extensively. Consequently, it would be only the element of rent, would it not, that would not be borne by the consumer, namely, the element of representing the differential advantage of the worst land cultivated in Foreign countries after the imposition of the Duty, as compared with the worst that would have been cultivated had there been no Duty, and would not this be an almost negligible amount?

Again, I think your whole argument implies that the price in that country, though it need not be higher by the full amount of the tax than it would have been in the absence of the tax, is certainly higher by the full amount of the tax than the price in the free markets of the world. Consequently, in so far as we make the Foreign producer pay the tax we give a bounty to all other consumers who are our competitors? If this point is true, I think it would weigh so much with practical men that it might be worth stating.[11]

Llewellyn Davies enclosed three sets of printed proofs of Part I together with the original manuscript, one of which set of proofs was to be returned corrected as soon as possible. Neither copies of these early proofs, nor the original manuscript, appear to have been preserved among the Marshall papers.[12]

On 25 August, Llewellyn Davies acknowledged receipt of Part II of Marshall's Memorandum, an inordinate delay given the fact that Marshall had despatched it from Stern about a fortnight before. This suggests repetition on Llewellyn Davies's part of failure in immediately acknowledging receipt of Marshall's manuscript, a matter to be recollected when Marshall's authorship of the 1903 Treasury document on the fiscal problem is examined. Llewellyn Davies also indicated he

---

[11] Llewellyn Davies to Marshall, 13 August 1903, in J.C. Wood, 'Alfred Marshall and the Origins of his "Memorandum ... Trade"', pp. 165–6.   [12] *Ibid.*

would send proofs as soon as they were ready. More importantly, the letter indicated the initial fate of Marshall's papers which by then had been decided:

> the position should stand thus: that the Chancellor of the Exchequer asked you for your views: that you communicated to him a Memorandum which was and remains altogether your property: that he printed it for his own convenience, and for his private use: that he, incidentally, for your convenience, I hope, supplied you with some of the prints: but that the question of publication remains entirely in your own hands, except that he would prefer that, in case of publication, any reference to his intervention in the matter should be omitted. I needn't say that I hope you may manage to publish it soon.[13]

No further Marshall correspondence with Llewellyn Davies has been preserved, including possible messages which accompanied the proofs of Part II when they were sent. As subsequent correspondence with others shows, these proofs were received and corrected by Marshall during August, since the Marshalls' journey back to England was probably commenced in early September (to enable some factory inspections in European towns en route) and, judging from correspondence on 18 and 21 September, the Marshalls were back at Balliol Croft by, at the least, the first of these two dates.[14] On 19 September, thus, when the Marshalls were back in Cambridge, Marshall received a letter from Ritchie, the day after his resignation from the Cabinet as Chancellor of the Exchequer. This thanked Marshall for his paper and mentioned the fact that corrections of the proof of Part II, of which Marshall had kept no copy, had been lost in the post from Stern. Marshall's reply to Ritchie (dated 21 September) did not refer to this loss[15] but a letter to Brentano

[13] Llewellyn Davies to Marshall, 25 August 1903, in *ibid.*, pp. 267–8. Llewellyn Davies's advice on printing of the Memorandum contrasts with Marshall's later claim in a letter to *The Times* (21 November 1908) that his Memorandum was originally 'printed at the *Foreign Office* for private circulation' (my emphasis). Cf. Sydney Armitage Smith to Marshall, 20 June 1903, which referred to the Memorandum as 'in the Treasury', from which of course the invitation for Marshall to write it was originally issued. And see n. 20 below.
[14] Particularly correspondence with Helen Bosanquet and with Cannan, the last of which refers to the backlog of mail which greeted the Marshalls on their return to Cambridge. Marshall tended to use his return journeys from European holiday places for his 'economic inductions' of factories, social conditions of workers and so on (see Groenewegen, *A Soaring Eagle: Alfred Marshall 1842–1924*, pp. 187–9).
[15] C.T. Ritchie to Marshall, 19 September 1903, Marshall to C.T. Ritchie, 21 September 1903, in Wood, 'Alfred Marshall and the Origins of his "Memorandum . . . Trade"', p. 269.

ten days later explains the circumstances in some detail. It also indicates that these corrections of the proof had involved serious revision to his Memorandum, as printed for the Treasury in August 1903, given the time Marshall had devoted to it:

> I spent my last fortnight at Stern in rewriting that Memorandum of wh[ich] I told you. It was horribly confused & out of proportion: & I got it into fairly good order. But I had no rough copy of my second draft: and my letter containing it was *lost in the post*! Practically my Summer's work has been almost wasted. I shall however *perhaps* rewrite it again by aid of the original draft, expand it a little & publish it about Christmas. I am not sure at all. If I do, I will of course send you a copy.[16]

In line with Marshall's decision to publish, he communicated to Brentano in the letter just quoted, Marshall had started drafting that day a preface for a published Memorandum. This preface, unfinished though it was, has been preserved among Marshall's papers and has been reproduced on several occasions.[17] Like the preface, the Memorandum itself remained unfinished and unpublished business until events in the summer of 1908 brought it back to political debate and official publication.

Before examining the eventual publication of the Memorandum in August 1908, the document identified by Wood as the 1903 Memorandum, and here reprinted, needs some discussion. It is given fairly little discussion by its discoverer.[18] More surprisingly, Wood does not use it in his article reprinting the Llewellyn Davies and Ritchie correspondence which has been drawn upon so frequently in the discussion of this introduction so far.[19]

---

[16] Marshall to Brentano, 29 September 1903, in McCready, 'Alfred Marshall and Tariff Reform', pp. 266–7.

[17] It is preserved in the Marshall Library and was extensively quoted (not always quite accurately) in Wood, 'Alfred Marshall and the Tariff Reform Campaign of 1903', pp. 322–3.

[18] *Ibid.*, pp. 315–17 and esp. n. 3.

[19] See J.C. Wood, 'Alfred Marshall and the Origins of his "Memorandum . . . Trade"', p. 266 where references to the text of the Memorandum in correspondence from Llewellyn Davies are footnoted in terms of the 1908 version as reprinted by Keynes in *OP* whereas, if his attribution was non-problematical, the 1903 version ought to have been used. The 1908 version is the only reference to the Memorandum used in the article (*ibid.*, p. 261 n. 2) despite the fact that it was published well after Wood's 1980 *Journal of Law and Economics* article in which the original attribution was made, and which is mentioned in n. 3 of the *Australian Economic Papers* article.

The document itself is simply titled 'The Fiscal Problem', with no mention of an author. It is dated at the end of the text, 'Treasury, 25 August 1903'. It has a table of contents (not reproduced), which shows the text is divided into two major parts after a brief introductory of little over two pages. The paper includes a lengthy statistical appendix (not reproduced below) which on its final page mentions that it was printed at the Foreign Office on 6 October 1903.[20] The statistical appendix is not mentioned in the table of contents, but it is mentioned on several occasions in the text (below, pp. 319, 343). The two parts deal respectively with 'I. Preferential Treatment of the Colonies'; 'II. Retaliation'. They in turn are sub-divided into five and eight sub-sections respectively, which are separately numbered and titled. Individual paragraphs are not numbered but the sub-sections are. The text is printed in a single column with wide margins, suggesting that printing of the document had not gone beyond the proof stage. There are marginal summaries of the text, a number of footnotes, and references and paragraphing in the text on the whole tend to be relatively short, though in Part II in particular, there are some very long paragraphs,

Much of this physical description tallies with the Marshall–Llewellyn Davies correspondence quoted previously. The contents formally resemble precisely the two areas Marshall was explicitly asked to address, that is, on preferential treatment for the colonies and on retaliation. The first part also deals in some detail with the incidence of import duties on foodstuffs (with or without such preferential treatment) and with the effects of such import duties on wages. The publication date of 25 August for the completion fits in well with the last preserved letter of Llewellyn Davies to Marshall, acknowledging the receipt of Marshall's Part II in its initial version some time after its arrival, if the surmise on this is accepted. The 'proof' style of the printed 1903 text, and the anonymity of the Memorandum, also fits in with this letter. It allowed Marshall to correct the initial printing as he did (though with his corrections to the proofs of Part II lost in the mail) while for a 'private' document for restricted circulation among members of the Cabinet, reprinting in conventional double column form would have been an unnecessary expense given the very limited official status the paper was

---

[20] Cf. n. 13 above where Marshall recalled his Memorandum was printed at the Foreign Office though the document had originated within the Treasury.

to enjoy by the end of August. Circumstances such as these make it plausible to suggest that the document in question is indeed Marshall's 1903 Memorandum.

However, there are important reasons which cast very strong doubts on such a hypothesis. The first, and most important, relates to the specific reference to paragraph 29 in Llewellyn Davies's letter of 12 August, which was previously quoted in full. The paragraphs of the 1903 document are not numbered and if a 29th paragraph is identified by a separate count (not easily done unambiguously), its contents do not resemble that described in the letter. The text of Llewellyn Davies's letter does, however, conform to paragraph 29 of the 1908 Memorandum as reprinted by Keynes and almost verbatum matches some of its contents.[21] Secondly, as Whitaker[22] has argued, 'vocabulary and syntax of the 1903 document are decidedly un-Marshallian', so that to him Wood's attribution appears to be 'highly dubious'. Thirdly, Marshall's description to Brentano[23] of Part II matches the 1908 published version of the Memorandum but not the 1903 document. Fourthly, it is very hard to believe that Marshall could have constructed a statistical appendix to this document from the bibliographical resources he had taken to the Tirol. Finally, and also very significantly, contents of the 1903 and 1908 documents never match in specific wordings of text. Irrespective of the extent of the revisions Marshall was to make to the 1903 version prior to its publication in 1908 (and the evidence preserved among the Marshall papers, incomplete though this is, suggests these were quite substantial and prepared on more than one

---

[21] For example, Llewellyn Davies's statement (above, p. 302) that 'the price here would probably not rise by the full amount of the tax' matches 'the price here would probably not be raised at once by quite the full amount of the tax' (*OP*, pp. 384–5). It is presumably for reasons like this that Wood compared this part of the letter as reproduced in his 1982 article with the Keynes version of the Memorandum and not with the text of the 1903 document he had identified previously as Marshall's original text (see above, n. 19). The 1903 document at one stage actually suggests (in the vicinity of its twenty-ninth paragraph) that the consumer has 'to pay more by the amount of the tax [on] the imposition of import duties on foreign food' (below, p. 324).

[22] *The Correspondence of Alfred Marshall*, ed. Whitaker, Vol. III, Letter 962, n. 6: 'A purported copy of the initial 1903 printing of Marshall's Memorandum found by John C. Wood in the Achives of Treasury, seems to belie Marshall's claim that his alterations were minor. But the anonymous pamphlet identified by Wood is so un-Marshallian in vocabulary and syntax that Marshall's authorship seems highly dubious.'.

[23] Marshall to Brentano, 20 July 1903, as noted above, p. 301 and n. 8.

occasion),[24] there are no clear signs of that cannibalism of one document into another which is the hallmark of so much of Marshall's writing, particularly during this period.[25] It is in fact quite difficult to point to duplicate passages in the two texts, as is illustrated more fully in the summary comparison of subject matter between the two texts which follows.

Such a comparison reveals no duplicate passages whatsoever between the two documents and relatively little shared subject matter.[26] Paragraph 29 of the 1908 Memorandum in its discussion of supply responses to price changes in wheat from import duties resembles some of the argument on this subject in the 1903 document (pp. 324–6) but only in a general way. Paragraph 38 of the 1908 Memorandum on imports and unemployment covers a topic dealt with in the 1903 document (pp. 346–8) in quite a distinct way. An argument in paragraph 42 of the 1908 Memorandum on free trade problems in bilateral trade negotiations is covered in the 1903 paper (pp. 351–4); the economic progress of Germany and the United States as examples of the advantages of protection is likewise raised in both papers (1908, paragraphs 52–4, 1908, paragraph 68; 1903, pp. 334–5). A discussion about analine dyes as an example of failure in British industrial leadership and the supremacy of German chemical know-how occurs in 1908 (paragraph 70) and 1903 (pp. 349–50). The advantages of free trade policy to tax burdens on the poor likewise occurs in both papers (1908, paragraph 72; 1903, pp. 328–9). The papers share a similar outlook on remedies to the problems of dumping but not with respect to their detail (1908, paragraph 79; 1903, pp. 347–8, 351–4); and on losses to the British public from imperial preferences in import duties

---

[24] The documents on the revision preserved in the Marshall Library indicate Marshall's revisions went through several stages. For example, preserved proofs of the two parts of the document do not have continuous pagination. In addition, several new sections were added to these proofs in Marshall's handwriting towards the end of Part II, often from re-organised and drastically re-written material.

[25] On Marshall's cannibalistic proclivities see J.K. Whitaker, 'The Second Volume of the Principles . . .', in *Centenary Essays on Alfred Marshall*, ed. Whitaker, p. 201, and, for his earlier tendencies in this direction, J.K. Whitaker, *The Early Economic Writings of Alfred Marshall*, London, Macmillan for the Royal Economic Society, 1975, Vol. II, Appendix, esp. pp. 395–6.

[26] References are to the 1903 paper as printed below (frequently in brackets in the text) and the paragraphs of the 1908 Memorandum as published by Keynes in *OP*.

on foodstuffs (1908, paragraph 82; 1903, pp. 329–32). Such broad similarities are to be expected in papers devoted to the same issue; but analytically, as for example on the incidence of import duties, the tone of the two Memoranda could not be more different, despite general agreement on conclusions.

One other notable difference between the two documents is easily illustrated. The 1903 paper only cites a number of papers by Giffen (for example, pp. 332 n. 8, 334, 341–2), mentions a remark by Lowe on taxation and the loss of the American colonies (p. 330), refers once to Chamberlain's views (p. 337) and quotes a letter by Ernest E. Williams on the ambiguity in the term 'raw materials' for tariff regulation purposes (p. 352 n. 16). It makes no direct references to Hewins's letters in *The Times*, despite the fact that in July 1903 in his correspondence with Brentano[27] Marshall had declared this to be the case. In the context of the consequences of imperial preference for British food supplies in the event of war, there is, however, a striking similarity between the views expressed in the 1903 paper and some correspondence on the subject between Marshall and Henry Cunynghame the previous month.[28] None of these authorities are cited in the 1908 Memorandum, whose references to other authors are completely different. They open, characteristically for Marshall, with a general reference to the authoritative status of Ricardo on aspects of the subject of trade and the price level (p. 372); mention Cary and List as the great protectionist authors whose views ought to have been more carefully studied by free trade writers (paragraphs 35, 44); cite Jacob on the European wheat trade in the early part of the nineteenth century (paragraph 22)[29] and directly quote from Hewins's *Times* articles of 25 and 29 June 1903 (paragraphs 17, 27) on

---

[27] Marshall to Brentano, 20 July 1903, 'confidential P.S.', in McCready, 'Alfred Marshall and Tarif Reform', pp. 262–3.

[28] The relevant material in the 1903 paper is on p. 329; and see Marshall to Henry Cunynghame, June 1903, reprinted in *Memorials of Alfred Marshall*, ed. Pigou, pp. 447–8. This related to a public inquiry on food supply in case of war, of which Cunynghame was a member, so that Marshall's views may have become part of the public domain at an early stage. For a discussion, see J.K. Whitaker, 'The Economics of Defence in British Political Economy 1848–1914', in *Economics and National Security. A History of their Interaction*, ed. Craufurd D. Goodwin, Durham, NC, Duke University Press, 1991, pp. 51–2.

[29] Marshall to Brentano, 24 July 1903, mentions the authority of Jacob on these matters and his use of him in Part I of the Memorandum which he had just completed. In McCready, 'Alfred Marshall and Tariff Reform', p. 262.

matters associated with the wheat trade which had particularly annoyed Marshall when he first read them.[30]

It needs to be stated that Wood makes no observations of this nature on the 1903 and 1908 documents dealing with the fiscal problem. His comments on the differences between the two are confined to two sets of observations. He claims, without a great deal of evidence, that Marshall made 'substantial revisions to the original memorandum, altering both the format and content', an obvious inference from any comparison between the two documents if they are to be assigned to Marshall. For example, Wood argues that Part I of the 1903 document was a 'first draft' of Section O of the published version in 1908 which Marshall had prepared in the summer of that year.[31] Wood then explains in detail the change from the 1903 Part I to Section O of the 1908 version by appealing to shifts in Marshall's own thinking on colonial matters.[32] Footnotes[33] attribute the 1903 paper directly to Marshall on grounds which as argued here cannot really be accepted. The question that remains is, if the 1903 paper was not written by Marshall, as the evidence based on contemporary correspondence and textual comparison suggests, who did write it, particularly when, as Llewellyn Davies wrote to Marshall,[34] other economists were not to be generally consulted by the government on the matter. It seems perhaps most likely that the 1903 discussion of 'The Fiscal Problem' was an internal Treasury document, perhaps drafted by Llewellyn Davies himself and a version of the paper he sent to Marshall[35] for comment. Such a hypothesis conforms to the paper's substantial statistical base and, more importantly, to its use of recent diplomatic information to which Marshall would not have had access.[36] Other hypotheses about its authorship are possible.

The issues which had inspired Marshall's efforts in 1903 and the 1903 Memorandum on 'The Fiscal Problem' were tariff reform and imperial preference. These had been simmering in Britain from the late 1880s

---

[30] The part in which they were quoted was finished in the second half of July, as Marshall wrote to Brentano (24 July 1903), and since these letters had appeared in *The Times* during late June, they were easily accessible to Marshall at the time of writing this part.

[31] Wood, 'Alfred Marshall and the Tariff Reform Campaign of 1903', p. 315.

[32] *Ibid.*, pp. 315–17.   [33] *Ibid.*, p. 325 nn. 32–4.

[34] Llewellyn Davies to Marshall, 25 August 1903, in Wood, 'Alfred Marshall and the Origins of his "Memorandum . . . Trade"', pp. 267–8.   [35] *Ibid.*, p. 267.

[36] That is, 'The Fiscal Problem', below, pp. 346, 349.

with occasional minor eruptions. They came to a head in 1903 from the repeal of a fiscal measure introduced without a great deal of fuss in 1902 by Sir Michael Hicks-Beach, then Chancellor of the Exchequer. This introduced a duty of 1s. per quarter on corn and flour as a revenue measure designed to assist in financing the substantial cost of the Boer War. It was intended eventually to remit this duty on colonial produce, largely for the benefit of Canada, the revenue foregone by remission to be recouped by raising the duty on imported foreign produce. This strategy implied retention of the duty on corn and the in principle acceptance of imperial preference. It was also one for which Chamberlain had obtained provisional consent from the Cabinet. In April 1903, a new Chancellor of the Exchequer, C.T. Ritchie, supported by Sir Frances Mowatt, the permanent secretary to the Treasury and a staunch free trader, abolished the corn duty in the interest of free trade and, with it, the possibility of implementing imperial preference by this means. Taxes on food, and especially on corn like the now repealed duty, were regarded as particularly provocative fiscal measures by free traders given that repeal of the corn laws had ushered in Britain's period of free trade. A speech by Chamberlain to his Birmingham constituents on 15 May 1903 in favour of tariff reform, imperial preference, and with strong criticism of the dogmatic free traders such as Ritchie and Mowatt responsible for repealing the corn duty, is generally considered to be the direct starting point of the tariff reform controversy of 1903. Marshall's involvement has already been discussed in this introduction.

Four distinct tariff reform issues were on the agenda in the ensuing debate over the appropriate fiscal (taxation) policy for international trade policy. One concerned the justification of duties on imports for revenue reasons (revenue tariffs) of which Hicks-Beach's corn duty in 1902 was a perfect example. Free traders tended to see such revenue duties as the thin edge of the wedge in opening the door to genuine protectionist policies. Secondly, there were those desiring British tariffs to forge a retaliatory weapon against dumping (that is, selling below cost) foreign goods (especially those from the United States and Germany) on the British market. Dumping itself was associated with trusts and cartels which were known practitioners of such anti-competitive behaviour. Thirdly, the small but not insignificant band supporting imperial federation or an imperial free trade zone

needed tariffs in order to enable the British government to give preference to colonial imports by way of tariff exemptions in whole or in
part. Last, but not least, there were genuine protectionists who wished
to shelter an increasingly uncompetitive British industry against
German and United States imports thereby to protect the domestic
market and employment. All four of these issues were raised in the
1903 Treasury document 'The Fiscal Problem' here reprinted, and in
Marshall's 1903 Memorandum, at least in the form in which it was
published in 1908.

Marshall's intervention in the public arena of tariff reform debate
was that of a qualified free trader. He was able to condone temporary
protectionist measures for industrialising countries on infant industry
grounds but saw free trade as the best *British* trade policy for the start of
the twentieth century because it enabled maintenance of British competitiveness through cheap imported food and raw materials and even of
those manufactured goods required as inputs for British industry. This
policy stance, together with a strong dislike of Chamberlain and fear of
the corrupting impact of protection on the agencies of government,
made him accept the invitation to put his views to the government in the
manner already indicated. He had become even more receptive to this
from the *Times* articles by Hewins which had started to appear exactly a
month after Chamberlain's speech. These articles, with their implicit
claim to authority from being written by an economist, though never
explicitly supporting a specific protectionist scheme, were favourable to
Chamberlain-type views on tariff reform and highly critical of the
claims on economic consequences and benefits from British free trade
policy as presented by most economists. By mid-August, Marshall was
sufficiently aroused by the issue, especially as it was presented by
Chamberlain and his supporters, to affix his name together with thirteen
other academic economists to a letter to *The Times* in favour of free
trade principles and against duties on food. Marshall's subsequent
doubts about the wisdom of that decision, plus an intention to explain
himself better by presenting a lengthy, reasoned and dispassionate
examination of the subject in a book to be called *National Industries and
International Trade*, explain why he failed to do anything in late 1903
about publishing the Memorandum. This was despite his initial enthusiasm which he had communicated to Brentano in late September 1903,
tempered though it was by his self-confessed inability to be sufficiently

crude and unscientific to rebut effectively Chamberlain's selfish and ignorant appeals.[37]

In the event, fortuitous circumstances led to official publication of Marshall's 1903 Memorandum in revised form exactly five years later. The circumstances can be briefly recounted. In the 1908 budget debate, David Lloyd George as Chancellor of the Exchequer had quoted Marshall's views on the effects of protection on German workers from the 1903 Memorandum, which he had found in the Treasury. This led to the demand from the Opposition that the source of this quotation be published by the government. Marshall consented to this request, on the condition he could make revisions to improve the style of the 1903 document which had been written in haste and in which, for reasons recounted earlier, the second part had not even been properly corrected by him. The ensuing Parliamentary Paper was reprinted by Keynes in his *Official Papers of Alfred Marshall*.[38]

Given the fact that the 1903 Memorandum, the text of which follows, was not written by Alfred Marshall on the available evidence, reasons for reprinting it here need to be briefly reiterated. Its attribution to Marshall in a well-known source on Marshall's role in the tariff controversy inspired the original decision to reprint, and thereby make the 1903 paper more accessible to Marshall scholars and to those more generally interested in the 1903 tariff debate. It may be added that, despite the evidence here presented, which in my view makes it difficult, if not impossible, to attribute the 1903 paper to Marshall, the possibility that Marshall did contribute to it cannot be totally dismissed. If it is the paper written for the Treasury by Llewellyn Davies, of which he sent a draft to Marshall for comment in August 1903, then Marshall may have had some input into its final form. But even if it has no direct or indirect connection with Marshall whatsoever, it is worthwhile reprinting as useful background to a controversy in which Marshall did become officially and unofficially involved in an important way. Moreover, making it available in this way allows those who wish to assign it to Marshall's pen easier access to some of the evidence on which such a claim has to be based. In any case, its reprinting usefully

---

[37] Marshall to Brentano, 29 September 1903, in McCready, 'Alfred Marshall and Tariff Reform', pp. 166–7. The contents of this, and the preceding three paragraphs, draw extensively on the references cited in n. 2 above.

[38] See Groenewegen, *A Soaring Eagle: Alfred Marshall 1842–1924*, pp. 385–8.

supplements the version of Marshall's last official paper reprinted by Keynes.

The paper is not completely reprinted; its statistical appendix has been omitted. Editorial notes have been kept to a minimum because no attempt has been made, despite earlier intentions to do so, to cross-reference it to Marshall's 1908 memorandum as reprinted in *Official Papers*. Detailed comparison of the contents of both, reported earlier in this introduction, would have made that a rather worthless enterprise in any case.

TEXT

The two principal questions which have been recently discussed in connection with the fiscal problem are: (1) Whether preferential treatment should not be accorded to our Colonies, in order that British trade may be more independent of foreign countries, and that the ties binding together the British Empire may be strengthened; and (2) whether we ought not to arm ourselves with some retaliatory weapons, both against high Tariffs generally, and specially in case foreign countries either unload upon us their surplus goods below cost price, or bully any of our Colonies which may trade with us on favoured terms.

It is asserted that on the answer returned to the first question the fate of the Empire depends, and that the second question is put forward in the interests of real free trade. Though there may not be any idea of protecting and thus bolstering up any particular interest or interests, both questions involve a revival of protective Tariffs, and a serious departure from our present fiscal system, under which the British market is open to the whole world – an all-important consideration to a country like ours that cannot feed itself, and is largely dependent on other countries for the raw materials required for its manufactures; and under which taxes are imposed for revenue purposes only.

But, though the questions which are now being raised were fought out and settled over fifty years ago, yet it will be admitted that they deserve to be very carefully re-examined in the light of present economic conditions. We are no longer the workshop of the world, without a rival: we have formidable competitors. Germany and the United States have sprung into great manufacturing countries, and Russia is becoming an industrial Power to reckon with. Other countries have been developed, and none have followed our example. On the contrary, in almost all countries walls of Tariffs of a highly protective character are being built up which impede trade with the United Kingdom. Owing to a fall in prices and an increase of population, we have become more than ever dependent on sea-borne food and raw materials. Keen competition being the order of the day returns must be small, and, in order that they may not be still smaller, economy of production is more and more of a necessity – economy which takes the form of combinations, like Joint-Stock companies in our country, trusts in America, and cartels in European countries. The whole idea of the relations of the Colonies to the mother country has undergone a great change. It is no longer the United Kingdom and her dependencies; it is the British Empire which, scattered all over the world, has to be consolidated.

Preferential treatment and retaliation appear, at first sight, to be intimately connected with one another. Both involve protective duties, either intentionally or unintentionally; both prejudicially affect the interest of the consumer. But, on closer inspection, they will be found to be inconsistent with one another. In the first place, the duties to be imposed which would best lend themselves to be applied to preferential treatment would probably not be, and hardly could be, suitable to retaliation. In the second place, the object of retaliation is to increase trade with the foreigner; whilst, by preferential treatment, the object is to dispense with foreign trade. In the third place, the two policies are supported on different grounds and by different people.

It is proposed to discuss both these policies, and to discuss them from a practical point of view, excluding from the discussion, as far as is possible, theories of political economy.[1] Before, however, they are separately considered, two general observations which apply as pertinently as retaliation as to preferential treatment may be made. By both, great changes in taxation are involved, and this of itself is a very serious matter; for, with a case of so difficult and abstruse a problem as the incidence of taxation, it is certain there is much truth in the old maxim that 'an old tax is no tax,' and in the saying that, 'sooner or later, taxation, if undisturbed, finds its own level.' A great authority on such a subject used to declare that, in moments of scepticism, he doubted 'whether

---

[1] This statement by itself would almost be sufficient to say this paper could not have been written by Marshall.

there is any injustice in taxation and changes.' Another general but very important consideration is that the expressed object of the proposed changes of taxation is to bring about a change of trade. Now, anything that tends to divert trade from its natural channel and to disturb its settled course is 'a leap in the dark,' and, consequently, attended with danger; for trade, like credit, is a very sensitive plant, of slow growth. It is easy to disorganize and lose trade; it is most difficult to organize and make it.

I.   Preferential treatment of the colonies

1.   *Application of Preference*

Preferential treatment can be given in various ways:

1.   We can impose a duty on everything imported into this country from foreign countries, and exempt from it imports coming from the Colonies.
2.   We can impose comparatively high duties on certain selected articles sent to us by foreign countries, and lower duties on these articles sent to us by the Colonies.
3.   We can select certain articles largely produced in the Colonies, and we can then tax those articles when they come from foreign countries and let them in free when they come from the Colonies.

No specific plan has been compounded with any authority; but it has been distinctly stated that raw materials are not to be taxed; and, as very few manufactured articles come to this country from the Colonies, the object sought would not be attained by imposing a duty on such articles. Therefore, by a process of exhaustion, the foreign articles to be taxed, for preferential purposes, must be articles of food which are produced in large quantities in the Colonies; and, presumably, in order that the sum to be raised may be worth raising and that the preference given to the colonies may be worth having, the tax must be an appreciable tax.

In the absence of a formulated plan, one must be assumed; otherwise, it will not be possible to see how preferential treatment will work. For illustrative purposes, one plan is as good as another, and the assumed plan proposed to be taken is a 10 per cent. *ad valorem* duty on all articles of food coming from foreign countries, and foreign countries only.

There is an advantage in taking 10 per cent. (which on grain is about equal to 3*s*. a quarter), because it is very simple to work and follow, and because it would initially produce about the amount which has often been talked about.

The first problem that has to be faced is, what would be the effect of an import duty on food-stuffs coming from foreign countries.

It will not be questioned that the imposition of a duty increases by the amount of the duty – and it may be something more – the out-of-pocket expenses of the final seller. In these circumstances he may resort to one or other of three courses, or in part to all three: (1) He may increase his price to the buyer; (2) he may reduce the out-of-pocket expenses in other directions; (3) he may accept a smaller profit. There may be special circumstances, in which he may be able to make the necessary adjustment by reducing his expenses, without increasing his price. But, as a rule, the method of adjustment has to be recourse to an augmentation of the price which the consumer is charged; and this is particularly the case with unmanufactured articles, like bread and meat, which are universally consumed and almost universally produced; for, with such articles, the play of competition is unimpeded among both producers and consumers, and, in consequence, expenses and profit are necessarily cut very fine.

It is submitted, then, that in the normal state of things – especially in cases where the article taxed is more or less a necessary of life – the tax falls on the consumer; and it may equally fall upon him, though the burthen need not be apparent, for there may be other causes at work which may be contemporaneously forcing down the price of the article, and which thus conceal the effect of the tax from the purchaser.

Therefore, *primâ facie*, food-stuffs will, on their being subjected to an import duty, be dearer; and, indeed, it is surely of the essence of the scheme that they should be so; otherwise, what would be the gain to the colonies? Moreover, if a tax does not raise the price, why should objection be taken to taxing raw materials?

It has been stated, however, that, granted that there will be a rise in the price of food, there will be a compensating rise in wages. There is certainly no economic law which raises wages on the imposition of a tax on food-stuffs; nor does experience suggest that high wages go with dear food – rather the contrary. But, if there were a rise of wages in the labour markets generally, it would probably be the result of the action of Trades Unions, which are now highly organized in every branch of trade; and a rise by such action would probably not be brought about without a severe and prolonged struggle, leading to disastrous strikes and temporary paralysis of industry; nor would it follow that the rise, if one occurred, would be proportionate to the increased price of food, or (in other words) that the increased wages would go as far as the lower wages when food was cheaper.

Even if it were granted that a rise of wages would be tolerably general among the wage-earning classes, it must be remembered that an enormous number of employés gain their livelihood on fixed salaries or are dependent upon fixed pensions – soldiers, sailors, all civil servants of the State, as well as all those employed by local authorities, public bodies, and private Companies. The whole of this class must either face a more expensive cost of living, and have less to spend on things which are not necessaries of life, or else they would agitate for an increase of pay, with the necessary alternative results – dissatisfaction and impoverishment if their demand is refused, or a heavy increased burden on their employers if their demand is granted.

Perhaps the material point connected with the taxation of food to be borne in mind may best be summarized in this way: The increased cost of living is either going to be made up to persons of slender means (or, rather, to those who earn fluctuating wages), or it is not. If, on the one hand, it is going to be made up to them, every employer in the United Kingdom will have a larger wages-bill to pay, and our manufacturers will all have to carry a heavier weight in the industrial handicap which is open to all the world. For, the cost of production will be increased just as much by their having a heavier wages-bill to pay as by their having to pay more for their raw materials, which are not to be taxed in connection with the proposed preferential arrangements. If, on the other hand, the cost of living is not going to be made up – and it cannot be made up to those dependent on fixed salaries – the struggle for life will be sensibly aggravated, and an ascertained loss will be incurred for an unascertained and unascertainable gain. Surely this is calculated to prejudice the ideas of Imperial unity in the eyes of the working classes, and to make the Colonies odious to them.

But it is intended that an increased, and an appreciably increased, cost of food must come sooner or later; it is merely a question of time. The foreign country that sends us the most corn is the United States, and if the United States go on increasing at its present rapid rate it will, it is said, need all its corn for its own people; we shall, then, whether we like it or not, be compelled to seek other sources of supply. The most natural "other sources of supply" are our Colonies, and we should therefore do all in our power meanwhile to encourage and tempt them to get ready to supply us. This argument seems to leave out of account the rapidly-growing resources of other parts of the globe, like South America; but in any case, if the evil day must come, why should we anticipate it? – Why should we make food dearer before we need? It is quite certain that, if our foreign supplies of corn fall off, the colonies which could grow corn in abundance will set to work of their own accord.

2. *Value of Foreign and Colonial Trade*

In the Appendix,[2] there will be found some Tables, framed on a simple basis, which purport to show the respective values of our trade with foreign countries and Colonies.

The total trade in merchandise of the United Kingdom may be summarized as follows: [Table 4.1]

The main conclusions to be drawn from this summary are –

(1) That of the goods we import, four-fifths come from foreign countries, and one-fifth from the Colonies;

(2) That of the goods we export and re-export, about two-thirds go to foreign countries, and one-third goes to the colonies;

(3) That of the aggregate sea-borne trade, three-fourths is done with foreign countries, and one-fourth with the Colonies.

There is a third table in the Appendix,[3] which purports similarly to show how much trade the self-governing and other Colonies do with the British Empire, and how much with foreign countries. It may be briefly summarized as follows – [Table 4.2].

A very important point is what commercial advantage this country is to obtain in return for the grant of preferential treatment. Is there to be a *quid pro quo*? If the country is to tax all food-stuffs which are imported

---

[2] The Appendix is not reproduced. The subsequent two paragraphs discussing these tables are deleted.   [3] Not reproduced here.

[Table 4.1] UNITED KINGDOM TRADE, 1902

	Foreign Countries		Colonies		Total	
	Value £	Per cent.	Value £	Per cent.	Value £	Per cent.
1. Total imports (exclusive of coin and bullion) from	421,598,000	80	106,793,000	20	528,391,000	100
2. Total exports (exclusive of coin and bullion) to –						
(a) British and Irish produce	174,396,000	62	109,028,000	38	283,424,000	100
(b) Foreign and colonial produce (re-exported)	57,332,000	87	8,482,000	13	65,814,000	100
	231,728,000	66	117,510,000	34	349,238,000	100
3. Aggregate of imports and exports	653,326,000	75	224,303,000	25	877,629,000	100

[Table 4.2] COLONIAL TRADE, 1901

	British Empire				Foreign Countries		Total	
	United Kingdom £	Other Parts £	Total £	Per cent.	£	Per cent.	£	Per cent.
Imports								
Self-governing Colonies	62,235,000	15,669,000	77,904,000	61.6	48,478,000	38.4	126,382,000	100.0
Other Colonies	56,881,000	17,596,000	74,477,000	63.9	42,127,000	36.1	116,604,000	100.0
Total	119,116,000	33,265,000	152,381,000	62.7	90,605,000	37.3	242,986,000	100.0
Exports								
Self-governing colonies	67,513,000	16,900,000	84,413,000	72.2	32,431,000	27.8	116,344,000	100.0
Other Colonies	39,957,000	18,249,000	58,206,000	48.5	61,929,000	51.5	120,135,000	100.0
Total	107,470,000	35,149,000	142,619,000	60.2	94,360,000	39.8	236,979,000	100.0

from foreign countries and allow the food-stuffs imported from Colonies to come in free, in order to increase our trade with them, we may expect, and reasonably expect, that the Colonies will admit our goods on terms more favourable than those accorded to foreign countries. But a preference can be given to this country in two ways: A Colony may retain the present Tariff rates on goods which come from foreign countries, and reduce the rates on British goods in our favour. A Colony may retain the present Tariff rates on goods which come from the United Kingdom, and increase the rates on foreign goods. Both arrangements are preferential; but, while the first alternative might possibly prove to be of real value to us, it is probable that the second alternative would be of little use.

3. Probable Operation of a Preferential Arrangement

Let it, however, be assumed that a reasonable reciprocation has been arrived at, and that a preferential agreement on those lines is in force in the self-governing colonies. Let us see how such an agreement might operate in practice.

It is supposed that Canada, for instance, is supplying us with more wheat, and is in return taking more of our manufactured goods. But what guarantee have we that the arrangement will work as it is intended to work? It is understood that in summer a great deal of corn grown in the United States is shipped to England from Montreal in Canada because it is the cheapest shipping port, and that in winter a great deal of corn grown in Canada is shipped to England from Portland in the State of Maine, because the navigation of the St. Lawrence is impeded by ice. It is hardly conceivable that, even if certificates of origin are enforced as strictly as they can be, some American corn will not find its way into this country on preferential terms, entailing free entry which is not intended, and a consequent loss of revenue.[4]

But the United States' Government might prefer to take a more decided line of its own. It might decline to allow Canadian corn to be shipped in American ports any longer, or else it might make the use of

[4] There is a duty on foreign grain entering Canada; but this duty would, when the American grain passing through Canada reached the United Kingdom, be counterbalanced by the immunity of the article from taxation in Great Britain. (Original note.)

American ports conditional upon the payment of a duty, so as to place Canadian corn on an equality with corn coming from the United States.

This does not exhaust the awkwardness resulting from a preferential agreement between Canada and the mother country. The United States' Government might offer to make a Commercial Treaty with us which was favourable to the admission of our manufactured goods, on condition that American wheat was allowed to come into this country free. The hands of His Majesty's Government would be tied by the agreement arrived at with Canada on a preferential basis. The American offer would have to be declined on account of the engagements we had entered into with our Colonies; and the interests of our own manufacturers would have to be sacrificed to the interests of our Colonies. This loss of freedom is one of the most serious features of any preferential arrangements.

Nor might we be the only country that would feel the awkwardness of having our hands tied. The Dominion of Canada might be subject to similar inconvenient experiences. Her big next-door neighbour might make her a most attractive commercial offer, entailing, however, the grant of most-favoured-nation treatment; but to this she would be unable to accede owing to the preferential treatment she had accorded to the mother country.

In Australia, as well as Canada, there are two different interests to be reckoned with – the agricultural and the industrial. Any concession of a preferential kind coming from the Colonies must be made by the industrial interest; but it will be the agricultural interest that will benefit from any preferential treatment accorded to the Colonies by Great Britain. Therefore, is not the principle of preferential treatment calculated to incite directly the hostile feeling of one class towards the other, if indeed it does not prevent the conclusion of any arrangement for which it is worth the while of the mother country to make a sacrifice?

Another difficulty might easily arise, after some experience of the preferential treatment had been made. Suppose that a Colony, like New Zealand, had offered to lower its Tariff appreciably in favour of this country, and that the result had been to increase considerably the import of Colonial mutton into this country, and the exports of British manufactures into the Colony. But a further result had been that, as British goods came into New Zealand at a comparatively low rate, the Colonial revenue appreciably suffered. The Colony, in fact, finds that her financial needs do not enable her to submit to these inroads upon her revenue; what conceivably would happen is that the choice of the Colonial Government would lie between financial straits on the one hand, combined with the partial surrender of the Colony's fiscal independence, and an abandonment, on the other hand, of the commercial Agreement with the mother country which had been made at so much cost to ourselves.

But now let it be seen, from the point of view of the British taxpayer, how the assumed plan for preferential treatment would work.

The first thing to be ascertained is the amount of revenue derivable from the tax of 10 per cent. The imports of non-dutiable food-stuffs stand as follows for 1902:

From Foreign Countries	From Colonies	Total
£	£	£
144,267,000	32,192,000	176,459,000

But it is clear that, if the yield of this tax is taken to be 10 per cent. on 144,267,000*l.* or 14,426,000*l.*, the amount is exaggerated, for the value as given includes the foreign and colonial produce re-exported, on which, as it will be entitled to a drawback, no revenue will be realized.

Accordingly the re-exports must be deducted, and the net imports taken. Thus:

	From Foreign Countries	Per Cent.	From Colonies	Per Cent.	Total
	£		£		£
Imports of non-dutiable foodstuffs	144,267,000	82	32,192,000	18	176,459,000
Re-exports*	3,533,000	62	1,443,000	38	4,976,000
Total	140,734,000	82	30,749,000	18	171,483,000

* The published Returns do not show how much of the re-exports is of foreign, and how much of colonial origin. The proportions used in this Table have been specially computed by the Customs.[5]

The revenue then to be raised would be 14,073,000*l.*; but this does not represent the full extent of the burthen which the tax will entail on the consumers.

[5] A further reason why the Memorandum could not have been written by Marshall.

This is true absolutely when the character of the competing articles is indistinguishable or nearly so, as is the case with most raw materials, corn, meat, bacon, hams, butter and eggs.[6] If on the other hand there is a considerable difference of quality between the imported and the home-produced articles, and the competition is accordingly only indirect – as in the case of dead meat – a rise in the price of the imported article may not act directly on the price of the home-produced article. As, however, the difference of price before the rise represents the market estimation of a real difference in value, it is clear that, if the difference in price becomes less, through a rise in the price of the imported article, the home-produced article will, if its price remains unaltered, become relatively 'better value', and, therefore, more in demand. The result will be that prices will so adjust themselves that the original difference in price will be restored.

In the event, therefore, of the imposition of import duties on foreign food-stuffs, it may be taken that the consumer would have to pay more by the amount of the tax, not only for the foreign produce, but also for the whole of the colonial produce and home-produce which enter into competition with it.

The figures of the Colonial imports have already been given; the amount of home produce which would be affected is more difficult to estimate. Of dairy produce, vegetables, fruit, &c. – a most important part of it – there are no statistics. But if we take the best figures that can be obtained of corn and meat only, the home production of these commodities stands to the total imports of foreign and colonial food-stuffs of all kinds in the proportion of about 2 to 3.

On these assumptions, then, the burthen imposed by the assumed *ad valorem* duty will approximately be as follows:

	£
10 per cent, on the total sea-borne supply amounting as above to 171,483,000*l*.	17,148,000
Plus two-thirds of that sum to represent the estimated rise in price of the competing home produce, which would be	11,432,000
Total	28,580,000

[6] Apart from 'fresh' butter and 'new-laid' eggs, which stand in a similar relation to the rest of the supply – largely of English and Irish origin – as British meat does to foreign and colonial. (Original note.)

[Table 4.3]

	Food-stuffs Imported from Foreign Countries and consumed in the United Kingdom		Foodstuffs Imported from colonies and consumed in the United Kingdom	
	Value	Amount by which 10% Import Duty Raises Price, and which is Payable to Exchequer	Value	Amount by which 10% Import duty raises Price but which is not Payable to Exchequer
	£	£	£	£
1. On the inauguration of the Preferential Scheme	140,734,000	14,073,000	30,749,000	3,075,000
2. When the Scheme is in operation	110,734,000	11,073,000	60,749,000	6,075,000

The Exchequer, however, would only receive 10 per cent. on the foreign imports (140,734,000*l.*) or 14,073,000*l.*, which is less than one-half of the increased burthen. In other words, of the remaining 14½ millions about 11½ millions would go into the pockets of the home producer, and 3 millions odd would, on the inauguration of the preferential scheme, constitute the tax-payers' contribution to the Colonies or disguised grants-in-aid of them.

But, if in consequence of the immunity of colonial produce from taxation, the preferential plan has the effect which it is intended to have, these 3 millions will not represent by any means the whole of the contribution to the colonies: for the foreign taxed articles will be gradually displaced by colonial untaxed articles. It is fair to assume that the displacement will be considerable; otherwise, there would be no justification for making such a radical change in our fiscal system. On the other hand, let it be assumed that the rise in price will not be sufficient to bring about any appreciable increase in the home production.

Let it then be supposed that foreign (taxed) articles will, in the course of a few years, be diminished by 30,000,000*l.* and colonial (untaxed) articles *pro tanto* increased. The consequences of this change in the supply of food-stuffs are shown in the following table: [Table 4.3]

What follows, then, from the assumed operation of the preferential scheme is that the revenue payable into the Exchequer decreases from 14 to 11 millions, or by 3 millions, and that the wasteful portion of the burthen, or the price of the untaxed imported articles, is increased by the same amount.

The sum of 14 millions would, it may be assumed, have been devoted either to reducing existing taxation or to meet some new public charge, like old-age pensions, and the dwindling of that sum to 11 millions will have to be made good by the revival of part of the taxation which has been remitted, or, if no taxation has been remitted, by some form of new taxation. An early change of taxation will thus again be necessitated, and of all things to be avoided are frequent fiscal changes. Of course, if the preferential scheme succeeded decisively, there would be a much larger deficiency of revenue to be made good. It may be said that no allowance is made for the automatic growth of revenue, but this cannot be depended upon. There may be a falling-off instead of a growth; and the outside that sound finance permits us to do, is to set the automatic growth of revenue against the automatic and more certain growth of expenditure.

The whole of the contribution to the Colonies will be given in the worst form, because it will not only be an unascertainable sum, but it will be a disguised grant, the amount of which will grow in proportion to the success attained by the preferential scheme – a growth which must be insidious, because it will not be able to be detected.

Further the inequalities of the assumed scheme (or of any other scheme) deserve special attention. It has been shown that the imports of food-stuffs from the Colonies which are retained here for home consumption are estimated to be worth 30,749,000l. It is proposed, for present purposes, to take the estimate at 30,000,000l., because, as, according to the further assumption of the working of the preferential scheme, these colonial imports are to increase by 30 millions, they would exactly double. It is further proposed to test the working of the scheme by ascertaining how the supposed contribution of the British consumers would work out per head of the population of the self-governing Colonies. The illustration will, it is thought, be made clear by the following statement:

	Present Imports	Assumed Imports, after Preferential Scheme is in Working Order	Contribution of United Kingdom to Colonies on assumption that Price of Colonial Produce is enhanced by tax on foreign Produce	Population	
				Number	Per Capita
	£	£	£		£ s. d.
Self-governing Colonies					
Canada	14,774,000	29,548,000	2,954,800	5,388,000	0 11 0
Newfoundland	150,000	300,000	30,000	221,000	0 2 9
South Africa	14,000	28,000	2,800	1,000,000*	0 0 0¼
Australia	3,171,000	6,342,000	634,000	3,858,000	0 3 3
New Zealand	4,573,000	9,146,000	914,600	843,000	1 10 8
	22,682,000	45,364,000	4,436,400	—	—
Other Colonies	7,318,000	14,636,000	1,463,000		
Total	30,000,000	60,000,000	6,000,000		

Note:
* Estimate of white population only.

The inequalities of the preferential scheme will be seen at a glance. New Zealand would gain immensely, Canada would be benefited appreciably, and Australia would get comparatively little; while South Africa, whose Tariff is not a highly protective one, would, for no fault of her own, receive next to nothing. It is difficult to imagine that such glaring inequalities, resulting from pure accident, would be tolerated; indeed, how could they be defended? They must give rise either to grievances and soreness, or to a demand accompanied with wrangling, that other articles besides food-stuffs, which must be raw material, shall be the subject of preferential treatment.

What has to be specially borne in mind is that, if the taxes are taken off tea and sugar and put on bread and meat, the alteration is not, and cannot be, an adjustment of taxation (in the ordinary sense of the word), which is to shift the burthen from one shoulder to another, and to leave it the same. If the people of this country are told that what is proposed is to sub-

stitute half-a-dozen for six, to which no objection can be taken, it is submitted that they will be unintentionally misled, because the substitution
cannot be made. The half-a-dozen is not really six; in the first instance, it
will be twelve, and it will become some still higher figure if the preferential scheme works as it is intended to work. In other words, suppose that
the taxes on tea and sugar, which produce about 12 millions of revenue,
are taken off and that taxes are imposed on food-stuffs, the process must
involve an economic waste; for import duties are being imposed on articles which are produced at home as well as abroad, and import duties on
articles which are only produced abroad are being taken off. The burthen
of the tax-payers, therefore, will have to be increased by a great deal more
than 12 millions in order to pay into the exchequer the same amount,
because a large part – the colonial and home-produced part, equal to at
least one-half of the whole supply – of the food-stuffs whose price is
enhanced will escape the tax, and eventually, if the preferential scheme
answers, the burthen will have to be increased by a still larger amount.

It is to be remembered, too, that what is contemplated is an increase
of the burthens which, however concealed they may be, fall on the community at large, and which are thus specially felt by the poorest classes.
This is in direct opposition to the trend of the policy steadily pursued
for over half a century, which has been to reduce the taxes levied on
commodities of general consumption, and to raise relatively more
revenue by means of taxation which affects the better-to-do. In fact, the
proportions between indirect and direct taxation, which have gradually
become nearly even, will be upset, and what has been done by successive Chancellors of the Exchequer for more than fifty years will be
undone. Moreover, in these days, when the tendency to spend freely –
too freely – is so marked, any steps taken in the direction of raising
revenue without strict regard to the needs of the State cannot be
regarded with indifference. Indeed, there can hardly be imagined anything less likely to make for economical administration.

There is another administrative inconvenience which must appeal
strongly to the Treasury. The Budget Estimates would be liable to be
deranged any year, inasmuch as a considerable portion of it would be
dependent on the state of the harvest in the colonies. If it were a bounti-
ful harvest in the Colonies, a sudden impulse would probably be given
to the import of Colonial untaxed grain, which would take the place of
foreign grain, and from that grain the Chancellor of the Exchequer

would have counted upon receiving a given amount of revenue. If, on the other hand, the Colonial harvest failed, there would be an abnormal inrush of foreign taxed grain which would give him more revenue than he wanted. The inconvenience resulting from the derangement of his calculations can hardly be properly appreciated beforehand, or by other than those who are concerned with Budget-making.

4.   Other Consequences

One of the common arguments used against the present system and in favour of Colonial preference, is that we are not self-contained enough – that we are too dependent on foreign countries for our food and raw materials, and that we are too much at their mercy in time of war. These objections, it is said, would be obviated if we drew more supplies of necessaries from our Colonies. Canada can well be made the granary of the Empire; India could grow more cotton; Australia and South Africa could provide us with all the wool we want; New Zealand could furnish us with more mutton. But the ships which bring in these articles from the colonies will be British, and would be more liable to capture than those coming from foreign ports. In time of war, the tendency is to transfer the carriage of food supplies to neutral flags; and so long as the United States are our principal purveyors of wheat, we shall have a powerful nation whose interest it will be to see that the movement of grain under her flag is not interfered with.

When the principle of preferential treatment has once been admitted in connection with taxation on food, it will, it is conceived, be very difficult, if not impossible, to decline to extend the treatment to taxation on alcoholic drinks. Indeed, past experience makes it certain that the Australian and South African colonies will press for a preference on wines, and that the West Indies will demand a reduction of the duty on rum. But, if the spirit duties are lowered in favour of a Colony, how will it be possible to retain the present excise duty, which corresponds to the Customs duty, without giving the Colonial producer of spirits a 'pull' over the home producer of spirits?

One thing to be feared from the admission of the principle of differential treatment and from its inevitable consequences – the revival of protection and the imposition of a burden on the people of this country for the benefit of the Colonies – is pretty certain. Protection, which affects the interests of the producer, died hard last century. Free trade, which directly affects the interests of the community at large, will die still harder in the twentieth century. The supporters of free trade may be beaten in one of the early fights; but even if they are, they are not likely to accept defeat. There will probably be a prolonged series of struggles. Possibly the forces may be unequal, but there will be arrayed against one another in fierce combat for years and years to come all the Free Traders and all the Protectionists, which will constitute the political parties dividing the country – the 'outs' and the 'ins'. Into the fight colonial questions, which have hitherto been carefully kept out of party conflict, will inevitably and most unfortunately be dragged; and for the first time they will form a prominent shuttlecock between the political battledores of the State.

These are some of the difficulties which beset a change in our fiscal system, the object of which, being to unite the Empire, must commend itself to every right-minded British citizen; but they do not pretend to be exhaustive. The fact is, it is impossible to foresee all the difficulties that may arise in connection with so fundamental a change. The whole of them cannot be realized until the time comes for giving legislative effect to them. The test of their being surmountable is the draftsman's ability to comply with the instructions given to him and the view formed of the bill when drafted by the House of Commons.

5.   Concluding Remarks

Regard being had to the possible risks and dangers attending preferential treatment, it may perhaps be well to bear in mind some remarkable words spoken by Mr. Lowe some forty years ago, lest a prophetic character is given to them. 'In the time of the American revolution', he said, 'the Colonies separated from England because she insisted on taxing them. What I apprehend as likely to happen now is that England will separate from her Colonies because they insist on taxing her.'[7] And to accord Colonies preferential treatment *is* taxing her. No one now-a-days is likely to take such a gloomy view of possible results; but it

---

[7] I have been unable to trace the source of this remark here attributed to Robert Lowe, later Viscount Sherbrooke (1811–92), and Chancellor of the Exchequer in the first Gladstone government.

cannot be denied that a severe strain upon the present feeling in favour of the Colonies might be produced.

It is said that there must be some business-tie between the Colonies and the mother country; but are there not business ties already? Are not the Colonies provided with unlimited capital, and are not their loans treated preferentially by being included in the category of trust securities? and are they not almost entirely dependent on us to defend them in times of danger? Had not these practical ties be better relied on? If regard is to be had to sentiment, is not the best of all ties mutual pride? Has not the pride of England's power and might appealed to the Colonies of late? and will it not continue to do so? Let it be remembered, then, that by altering the system on which we have so long thriven, we shall quite possibly make the country poorer; if we make it poorer, we shall make it less powerful; and if we make it less powerful, we shall weaken the tie.

If, however, the existing practical ties, together with the sentimental one, are deemed to be inadequate for the purpose of holding the Empire together – if there must be 'a greater continuity of national interests and Imperial effort', and if there must be more settled business relations between the Colonies and the mother country, which can only be secured at the expense of the latter – if, in short, political considerations really outweigh economic ones, had it not better be done, in the interests of the tax-payer at home, in the least costly way? Instead of a preferential tariff, under which the taxation on the community must be greater than the benefit to the Imperial Exchequer, and which, therefore, must entail an unnecessary burthen, it might be better to resort to the system of direct grants. At any rate, such a system would be all above-board, and under it we should all know how we stood, the Imperial Government knowing the exact cost of encouraging the development of Colonial food supplies and of enlarging the Colonial custom for our manufactures, and the Colonial Governments knowing the exact amount of encouragement and reciprocity which each of them received. Under this system, too, there would result further advantages. In the first place, the price of food-stuffs, whether coming from foreign countries or the Colonies, or supplied at home, would not be raised, except so far as they might be affected by the additional amount of general taxation which would have to be levied in consequence of the new Colonial grants. In the second place, the assistance to the Colonies ought to admit of being meted out with some better regard to equality and fairness, without merely benefiting the Colonial producers; Colonial questions would not be dragged into the arena of economic partisanship; and foreign countries could not take offence at our action.

II.   Retaliation

Under this head, it is proposed to deal not only with the possible measures of a retaliatory kind, which may be in contemplation for putting down 'dumps' and 'bullying', but also with some of the arguments which are used in the present discussion in favour of a more general revival of protection.

Some very simple statistics will show how we are doing under our present system. It is unreasonable to compare the present order of things with that which prevailed before free trade was adopted, and to attribute the leaps and bounds we have made exclusively to the adoption of that policy. There have been many contributory causes at work, all conducing to the prosperity and well-being of the community – causes which it is unnecessary to analyze here. But if a period which is neither too long nor too short be reviewed, and if it be found that, on the whole, during that period, we have not done badly, it may be inferred that there is nothing seriously amiss, and that the chances are that, by instituting a great change, we may make matters worse instead of better.

1.   Comparison of 1882 and 1902

A period of twenty years is taken; that is, the year 1902, which was a fairly prosperous year, is compared with the year 1882, which was a very similar year.

The first figures which are adduced in the comparison relate to our foreign trade, consisting of imports and exports, because it is the condition of our sea-borne trade which has brought the fiscal question to the front, but to which an exaggerated importance is apparently attached, at least as compared with our home trade.[8]

---

[8] It is not possible to appraise with any accuracy the value of internal trade; but some years ago Sir Robert Giffen estimated that it was eight times as valuable as the external trade. He took the total earnings of the United Kingdom, which he believed could be computed, and from these he deducted the value of the exports of home produce, after taking off from it 30 per

The following statement compares the imports and exports in 1902 with those in 1892, and it should be borne in mind that the population has increased during that period a little over 19 per cent. –

	1882	1902	Increase	Percentage of Increase
	£	£	£	
1. Imports (exclusive of coin and bullion)	413,020,000	528,391,000	115,371,000	28
2. Exports (exclusive of coin and bullion) (a) British and Irish produce	241,467,000	283,424,000	—	17
(b) Foreign and Colonial produce	63,194,000	65,814,000	—	—
	306,661,000	349,238,000	42,577,000	14
3. Aggregate amount of foreign trade	719,681,000	877,629,000	157,948,000	22

Our imports, then, have increased substantially faster than our population. The growth of our total foreign trade is also proportionally larger. Our exports only have rather lagged: and they would appear to lag a good deal more if coal were excluded from the comparison, as some people contend; the ground of this contention being that coal is an exhaustible product of the earth which cannot be replaced by labour, and therefore represents national capital, and not an annual output of trade.

It is proposed to examine the consequences of this argument. If it is true of coal, it is true of iron ore, which is believed to be much nearer exhaustion than coal; and it applies as much to coal and iron imported into this country as to that produced at home. It must also be true of all products of coal and iron ore, i.e., of the entire iron trade of the nation, from pig-iron to the most finished machinery: and of the entire metal industries – lead, copper, brass, tin, also of all bye-products of coal, such as dyes, aniline, and others.

cent., which he considered represented the amount of foreign raw material in the goods exported. If we take the present earnings of the United Kingdom at 1,700,000,000l., and take 30 per cent. off the present exports of British and Irish produce, thus reducing them from 284,000,000l. to 200,000,000l., we arrive at about the same value of the internal trade relatively to the external trade, viz., as eight to one. This escalation is probably the nearest approximation to facts that is ascertainable. (Original note.)

Further than this. It may be said that what is true of coal and metal is true of every trade-product of which they, or either of them, are an essential element. Combing, spinning, and weaving of textile products, for instance, are impossible without brick-furnaces (an exhaustible product of the earth), from boilers, and steel machinery. Cotton and wool, again, are the mere raw materials to which brick, coal, and iron, give a market value.

But coal and iron ore are by no means the only exhaustible products of the earth which cannot be replaced by labour, and *ex hypothesi*, all such products are also national capital, as distinguished from trade output. There is mineral oil which is an earth product, and forms a very large item in the United States exports. As speculators know to their cost, it is very liable to exhaustion. Then porcelain, china, and earthenware, are other good examples. They are the product of factory buildings, brick furnaces, iron boilers, machinery, refined clay, mineral glaze, and mineral colours. The whole process deals with exhaustible earth-products, *plus* labour; but labour is an element common to them and to coal and iron. Indeed, labour is 80 per cent. of the cost of coal production.

Lastly, there is land and sea carriage – the railway, the locomotive, and the ship – without which there is no such thing as importing or exporting. All these are compounded of exhaustible earth-products, the capital of the nation.

These examples might be multiplied; but it is enough to say, and it can be said with safety, that there is no export of a manufactured article from this country into the production of which there does not enter an element of coal, iron, or some exhaustible product of the earth, which cannot be replaced by labour.

To return to exports generally – whether coal is or is not included – it must be admitted that they are not as buoyant as they might be; but it is well to remember what Sir R. Giffen told the Statistical Society on the 17th January 1899. 'The assumption,' he said, 'that in diminishing our transactions with foreigners we necessarily diminish our transactions altogether is utterly unwarranted, both theoretically and practically. We see even in our foreign trade how much the description of goods which we produce for export change from period to period. It is no violent assumption that the change may go further, and that instead of certain of our producers making articles for export with which to buy abroad

[Table 4.4]

	1882	1902 (At prices of 1882)	Increase	Percentage of Increase
	£	£	£	
1. *Imports* (exclusive of coin and bullion)	413,020,000	646,782,000	233,762,000	56.6
2. *Exports* (exclusive of coin and bullion) – (a) British and Irish produce	241,467,000	346,928,000	105,561,000	43.7
(b) Foreign and Colonial produce	65,194,000	80,562,000	15,368,000	23.6
	306,661,000	427,490,000	120,829,000	39.4
3. *Aggregate amount of foreign trade*	719,681,000	1,074,272,000	354,591,000	49.3

something we require, they may produce directly something we require at home.'[9]

Indeed, it may be questioned whether a want of elasticity of our exports is a sign of lack of prosperity, and, much less, of national decadence. It depends upon whether foreign trade or home trade happens, at any given moment, to be the more profitable; and provided we get enough imports (as by all admissions we do), we need not be concerned about the ups and downs of exports.

But generally as regards our foreign trade during the last twenty years, it should be borne in mind that the expansion of it would be considerably greater, had there not been an appreciable fall in prices – a fall, represented by the 'index numbers,' of 2,442 to 1,995. [Table 4.4] shows what the value of merchandise imported into and exported out of the United Kingdom would have been in 1902, had prices kept steady during the time under comparison.

To proceed with the rest of the comparison, the following terse statement adducing the most obvious tests of internal wealth, shows that, in the twenty years compared, there has been an increase in excess of the proportionate increase of population under every head.

[9] That is, Sir Robert Giffen, 'The Excess of Imports', read before the Royal Statistical Society, 17 January 1899, *Journal of the Royal Statistical Society* 62, Part I, March 1899, p. 28.

[Table 4.5]

	1882	1902	Percentage of Increase (+) Decrease (-) 1902 with 1882
	No.	No.	
Population of the United Kingdom	35,207,000	41,961,000	+ 19.18
Paupers of the United Kingdom	1,012,000	1,016,000	
Paupers per cent. of population	2.87	2.42	− .45
Savings Banks	£	£	
Due to depositors (cash and stock)	85,037,000	213,279,000	+ 150.81
	No.	No.	
Accounts remaining open	4,412,000	10,780,000	+ 144.33
	£	£	
Life Assurance Companies' premiums	14,766,000	32,070,000 (1901)	+ 117.19
Banking deposits: Estimated total deposits and current accounts held in the United Kingdom (say)	⎰ 550,000,000 to 560,000,000	699,000,000 to 700,000,000 ⎱	+ 25.3
Total amounts cleared at the London Bankers' Clearing House in the year	6,221,000,000	10,029,000,000	+ 61.21
Shipping – Registered sailing- and steam-vessels belonging to the United Kingdom employed in home and foreign trade	Tons 6,715,000	Tons 9,806,000	+ 46
Ships built in United Kingdom (a year's average)	568,000	954,000	+ 68
Railways – Passengers conveyed (exclusive of season ticket holders)	No. 654,838,000	No. 1,188,568,000	+ 81.51
Weight of goods and minerals conveyed	Tons 256,216,000	Tons 437,055,000	+ 70.58
Coal consumed in the United Kingdom	135,566,000	182,199,000	+ 34
Gross amount of annual value of property and profits assessed to the income tax	£ 560,064,000	(1901) £ 866,993,000	+ 54.8
Power of consumption of dutiable articles, as represented by duty collected, adjusted for comparison*	(1882–1883) £ 41,739,000	(1902–1903) £ 55,083,000	+ 31.97
Workmen's Co-operative Societies – Number of members	No. 680,252	No. 1,871,040	+ 200
Amount of sales	£ 24,137,000	£ 81,199,000	+ 235

*   This comprises only the articles which were subject to duty in both years. Where the duty has been altered since 1882, the actual yield in 1902–1903 has been adjusted proportionately to the alteration in rate of duty.

It will be admitted, even by those who are dissatisfied with our present system, that in spite of it the statistics point to a tolerably satisfactory state of things. But, notwithstanding, they seriously advocate a change, and they support it on many grounds.

2. *Allegation against Free Imports*

A common argument used is that the importation of foreign manufactured goods displaces native labour. Indeed, Mr. Chamberlain went so far as to say: 'It is a mathematical truth that if imports come into the country of manufactured goods which we can make as well as any other nation, they must displace labour.' But is this assertion correct? Every foreign import, not sent to us in payment of outstanding debts, or in respect of interest on British capital invested abroad – and these must come in under any fiscal system, so long as the debts exist – is paid for by an equivalent British product or service, and that product or service almost certainly employs an equivalent amount of British labour, probably a great deal more. If there were want of employment in this country, we might, it is true, produce the foreign-made article as well as the home-made article; but there is no evidence of this. On the contrary, there is good proof that our people, on the whole, are well employed. The fact is, we export what pays us best and import what pays us least well to make at home.

Again, it is common to take certain manufactured articles, like boots and shoes, cotton goods, hardware, or agricultural implements, and to point to the increase of their importation, resulting in an expenditure of millions a year more on foreign goods, and in the reduced employment of our own operatives. If the amount paid in wages, it is said, went to British workmen, we should be much better off than we now are. But are these not rather random statements? – If they are followed up, it will probably be found that one of two things has happened. It may be that the makers of these selected articles are as busily employed as ever; only the consumption of them has so increased at home that our own producers cannot keep pace with the demand, which would, if foreign competing goods were excluded, have to go in part unsatisfied. Or it may be that these foreign articles are really ousting the home-made goods owing to their cheapness; but, as it is certain they are not sent here for nothing, there must be a corresponding export of our goods; and if the

British makers of boots and shoes, of cotton goods, of hardware, and agricultural implements are doing badly, the British makers of some other goods must be doing well. It cannot be too prominently borne in mind that those who are hurt are those who cry out; while those who are doing well don't shout for joy over their prosperity.

Our policy of free imports is, no doubt, primarily for the advantage of the consumer; and the question frequently raised in the fiscal discussion is whether our policy ought not rather to be practically framed in the interests of the producer. It is alleged that British capital and labour cannot hold their own against foreign competition, unless they are protected in the enjoyment of the home market, even though such protection can only be provided at the expense of the British consumer.

In the first place, it is argued that the maintenance of our own great industries is a national object of sufficient importance to warrant a considerable self-sacrifice on the part of the community. To this argument the reply of economic theory is that an industry which requires bolstering up in any particular place is not the industry best suited to that place, that it should give way and make room for another. There is still an abundance of force in this reasoning. But it may be admitted that the progress of science and invention tends to make its application more difficult. The amount of capital sunk, in the highly specialized plant and machinery of a modern industry, makes it every day a more serious step for either capital or labour to abandon one form of industry for another. Whether this consideration should in any given case be allowed to outweigh the economic evils of protection is a question which can only be decided by those upon whom the cost would fall. If the mass of the people are prepared to bear the expense of saving a particular industry from perishing under competition, nobody is entitled to gainsay them. The community may take this burden upon itself just as it does that of a subsidy to any other unremunerative undertaking which is considered to be for the national advantage, or which suits the national taste. Only it is incumbent upon those who advocate it to make clear the nature and purpose of the proposal. In particular it should be shown whether the protection is intended to be temporary or permanent. If the causes which place the industry at a disadvantage are of a temporary character, so that their effects can be outlived by a few years of artificial support, this fact should be capable of demonstration. When this cannot be demonstrated, it must be recognized that there can be no drawing back from protection when once it has been granted. The need for it must indeed tend to increase. An industry which could not improve sufficiently under the stimulus of unlimited competition to hold its own will certainly not improve more, when deprived of some of that stimulus. And the evils attendant upon the extinction of an industry from natural causes are intensified, when its extinction is brought about by the withdrawal of artificial support.

In the second place, it is argued that, because protection of a single industry benefits that industry at the expense of the rest of the community, therefore, protection of all industries benefits everybody at nobody's expense; and this is an arrangement that makes a strong appeal to many minds. It is not true that all consumers are producers in the sense that they ply an industry which can be directly injured by foreign competition, or which can directly benefit by the exclusion of such competition. But assuming, for the purposes of argument, that such were the case, the result of uniform protection all round would not be for the benefit of any industry. What a person engaged in a particular industry would gain as a producer by its protection, he would lose as a consumer by the protection of other industries. Only, when that is the case would the benefits of protection be equitably distributed. And when that uniformity had been attained no person or industry would be better off than before; while all would be the worse for the economic waste involved in an artificial production, as well as the expense and the hindrances incidental to the protective system. Superhuman powers would need to be possessed by any Government undertaking to secure such uniformity; but, in so far as their dispositions failed to secure it, injustice would be done. The only benefit that could accrue to protected industries on this ideal system would be at the expense of those classes whose incomes are not directly dependent upon commercial undertakings, such as professional men, those who minister to the instruction, comfort, or amusement of others, Government servants of all grades, annuitants, and so on. In the long run the majority of these would succeed in making good their claim to a share in the benefits enjoyed by the protected classes. For their rates of remuneration depend ultimately upon those which the same qualities can command in other employments. In so far as they succeed, the result is the same as before, namely, that the benefit, when diffused universally, ceases to be a benefit at all. In so far as they may fail, the benefit enjoyed by the protected industries consists only of what they are enabled to obtain from the classes least able to enlist State intervention on their behalf.

It is often asserted that one of the results of our fiscal system which has done us most harm is that, having depressed our agricultural industry, it has drawn a great number of people from the rural districts to the towns, with the consequences that they lead more unhealthy lives, and that their physical standard has declined and is declining. Granted that this assertion is true, nobody can deny the importance of the question which it raises; but in none of the proposals which have been seriously put forward of late is there any inducement to people to go back to the land. Indeed, import duties of a truly protective character, which might give an impetus to agriculture, are disclaimed; and our corn and meat are not to be supplied by the British farmer. The supply is to come from our Colonies, and to be encouraged to come thence. The British farmer may be less undersold by foreign countries; but he will be as much undersold by the Colonies. It will make no difference to him whether the wheat and mutton come from one or the other. In any case, there is nothing contemplated which will revive agriculture. But even if the corn-producing powers of this country were rehabilitated by an appreciable rise in the price of the article, would the rehabilitation really be welcomed by those who are intended to be benefited? Have not the agricultural conditions of the country already undergone too great a change? Is not the cheapness of grain for feeding cattle of more importance to many farmers than the dearness of grain for feeding the people?

3. Excess of Imports over Exports

The enormous sum of about 180,000,000*l.* represents the present annual excess of imports over exports, which is said to be the balance of trade against us; and this excess, which, though the amount has grown, has been an uniform characteristic of our international trade, exercises the minds of many people. It is contended that this must be an unhealthy state of things; for, as we are buying more than we are selling, we must be living on our capital, and living on it to the extent of over 1,800,000*l.* in ten years.

However the difference is to be accounted for, one thing is certain, and that is, that commodities do not pass into this country *gratis*. The fact, which people forget, we are bound to reckon not only what we receive in exchange for goods, but what we receive in exchange for services, such as those of lenders of capital, shipowners, under-writers, and mercantile agents of every kind, all of which have to be paid for just as much as goods.[10] In fact, before this country has to exchange a pound's worth of her own goods for a pound's worth of foreign products, it has to receive 180,000,000*l.* of goods from abroad.

Some people are under the impression that these excess imports represent repayment of British capital; but if the repayments were a considerable quantity, there would necessarily be a shrinkage of income derived from investments abroad; and so far from there being a tendency in that direction, such income has, as the income tax figures show, continuously and steadily increased. In fact, in less than twenty years, it has almost doubled, having risen from 31,890,000*l.* in 1882–83 to 62,550,000*l.* in 1901–1902. But this amount, large as it is, does not include income derived from operations abroad, such as the profits of business carried on by numbers of foreign and colonial Banking and Industrial Companies and firms, which are domiciled here, and which, in their statements of profits and gains, do not distinguish between those that are earned abroad and those that are earned at home. What the total of such income may be it is impossible to state with any approach to accuracy. But it has been estimated to be as large as the income from foreign investments proper, and therefore, if it be put at half that amount, or 30,000,000*l.*, we should probably be well within the mark. Half the difference, namely, 90,000,000*l.* is thus accounted for.

The rest of the excess imports (amounting also to 90,000,000*l.*) is due to the freights and insurance premiums which we earn by carrying goods, not merely between the United Kingdom and foreign countries, but between one foreign country and another foreign country. The authority who has devoted most attention to this point is Sir R. Giffen; and in the lecture which he delivered in 1882,[11] when the excess imports amounted to 120,000,000*l.*, he gave some elaborate calculations,

---

[10] Imports are entered at our custom-house at 'c.i.f.' values, as they are termed, which stand for 'cost', 'insurance', and 'freight', whereas exports are entered at 'f.o.b.' values, which mean 'free on board'. (Original note.)

[11] Sir Robert Giffen, 'The Use of Import and Export Statistics', read before the Statistical Society, 21 March 1882, *Journal of the Statistical Society* 45, Part II, June 1882, pp. 181–284.

according to which he estimated the services connected with shipping at 76,000,000*l*., namely, earnings for freight at 60,000,000*l*., and commissions and other charges at 16,000,000*l*. In 1899 he read another paper before the Society on the same subject.[12] Though his method of calculation had been much discussed in the meanwhile, he saw no reason to depart from it, and applying it to the current state of affairs, when the excess of imports amounted to 160,000,000*l*. the corresponding figure he arrived at was 88,000,000*l*.

These calculations made by Sir R. Giffen involved data as to shipping freights which are not readily available now, and which, if available, would have to be used with even greater discrimination, owing to temporary variations caused by the war in South Africa[13] and by competitive struggles.

Another factor which he used was the excess of imports into all the countries of the world over the exports from all countries. This excess, which he reckoned in 1882 at 162,000,000*l*, could represent nothing but the cost of carrying products from one country to another. If the available particulars of imports and exports for the whole world are taken, the excess may be confidently reckoned now at over 200,000,000*l*.; and as the British share of this difference can be calculated according to the British proportion of the world's shipping, there is no reason to doubt that the estimate of 90,000,000*l*., made by the Board of Trade this summer, for freight (including commissions) is as near the mark as anything that can be got.

If to this sum of 90,000,000*l*. there be added the estimate of income from investments and operations outside the United Kingdom – namely, another 90,000,000*l*. – the whole excess of imports over exports is accounted for. It is true that the imports are not exceeded by the goods exported *plus* the services rendered, which would indicate that we are not just now sending fresh capital abroad; but this is not surprising if regard is had to the absorption of our own capital for the war.

It may, however, be said that, though the aggregate excess of

[12] Sir Robert Giffen, 'The Excess of Imports', this was quoted previously in the Memorandum, above, p. 335 and n. 9.

[13] The Boer War (1899–1901) had, of course, also been indirectly responsible for the controversy over fiscal policy since the corn duty which had started the fracas had been imposed to help to defray the costs of that war. See above, introduction, pp. 309–10.

imports may be satisfactorily accounted for, yet in individual cases the difference is much more marked. For example, the imports into this country from the United States are (according to the Tables in the appendix) nearly 127,000,000*l.*, and the exports from this country to the United States are only 24,000,000*l.* Investments and freight will not, it will be said, account for this enormous difference. Some additional explanation is required, and it is not difficult to furnish it. In the first place, large remittances are made by the United States to cover the expenses which Americans in such large numbers incur on European travel. In the second place, there has to be taken into account the large trade with the United States which we do by means of (what are called) triangular routes. Our imports of food and raw material from America, as a matter of fact, are largely paid for in tropical produce. For, a common form of settling the Anglo-American account is this – We are indebted to the United States for raw materials imported from them; at the same time tropical countries are indebted to us for manufactures exported hence to them; the United States have a large demand for tropical produce; and the tropical countries, in complying with that demand, liquidate both their indebtedness to us and our indebtedness to the United States. Thus, we are enabled to export our manufactures in payment of the raw materials which we require from the United States, without coming into collision with the American Tariff. As regards this three-cornered trade, which is, of course, often still more roundabout, it is worth noticing that many tropical countries (e.g., India), receive from us more than they send to us.

On the subject of imports and exports there is a common belief that a nation profits by exporting, and loses by importing goods. This belief is surely the result of a confusion of thought, which could scarcely have arisen, were it not that the use of money tends to obscure the real course of commercial transactions. The individual trader is accustomed to regard his bargain as completed when he has received money in exchange for his goods, and to estimate his profit according to the money so received. He is justified in doing that, only because the possession of the money enables him to command other goods or services which he may desire. His bargain is not really complete until the money has been further exchanged for these commodities, and it is in the shape of these commodities that he finally receives the equivalent of the goods which he has sold and his profit on the transaction as well.

Exactly the same is true of international trade. In that case, the working of the transaction is apt to mislead people, because no exchange of money intervenes. Between nations, commodities and services are exchanged for commodities and services; it is only for settlement of the margins arising on balance of these transactions that the transport of specie from one country to another is required. There cannot, it is true, even in the case of foreign commerce, be obtained statistics to show the quantities of goods received by a country in return for the goods in payment for shipping and other services and in connection with international indebtedness. If it were possible to eliminate these items from the import and export Returns, the remaining totals would represent the goods imported in payment for the goods exported. It would then be obvious that, the more imports a country received in exchange for its exports, the greater its benefit from the exchange. Although the means do not exist for making this analysis of the Returns with anything like precision, and only the roughest approximations can be made to the amounts representing payments in respect of services or debt, none the less it remains true that, so far as the exchange of goods for goods is concerned, a country's wealth is increased by what it imports, and not by what it exports.

4.   The Examples of the United States and Germany

The advocates of a fiscal change very naturally adduce, in favour of their policy, the examples of the United States and Germany. 'You tell us,' they say, 'that anything to do with protective Tariffs has a blighting effect on the general condition of a country; yet there are no two countries which have so overhauled us in the commercial race, and which are themselves so prosperous, as the United States and Germany, and they have deliberately adopted Protection as their creed. How do you account for that?'

In the first place, the nature of our trade is different to that of the United States and Germany. We cannot feed ourselves; we have to depend on other countries for the raw materials which we work up into manufactures. Germany, no doubt, imports some corn; but her chief imports, and almost the entire imports of the United States (except those which are the produce of tropical countries) consist of manufactures, semi-manufactures, and luxuries. Such articles can better stand import duties than necessaries of life. In fact, other countries are mostly self-supporting.

In the second place, population is an important factor, and the populations of the United States and Germany and the population of this country have very different totals. There are to-day 78 millions of people in the American Union, and in Germany there are 56 millions, while in the United Kingdom the population is about 42 millions.

In the third place, the geographical conditions are quite different. Unlike the British Empire, the United States and Germany lie, as it were, within a ring-fence, and they have so much Free Trade at home that the conditions of each individual industry approximate those which would exist, were the competition with all the world unrestricted. This is specially the case with the United States, which has an enormous territory, equal to that of all Europe, indeed the largest Free Trade area in the world, and which has already 'to hand' (so to speak) unlimited supplies of all principal raw materials – coal, timber, iron, and corn.

In the fourth place, Protection, when it is once implanted, takes firm root. It creates vested interests. The influence of those who enjoy the vested interests is strong in the legislature. Even, therefore, were it condemned, (which it certainly is not), either in the United States or Germany, it would be difficult and invidious to remove, because an alteration inevitably means an infliction, for the time being, of considerable loss on a number of employers and employed. This consideration is a strong inducement to retain Protection. Indeed, it is almost certain that its knell would not have been sounded in this country which it was, had it not been that what remained of Protection affected the food of the people, and that famine stared part of the United Kingdom in the face.

The United States can afford to indulge in an uneconomic and expensive fiscal system. They have such natural and boundless resources, and so huge a population, far exceeding our own, that the wonder is that they have not cut us out, and, relatively, have forged ahead of us, more than they have. They have, no doubt, vastly expanded, but they have had, and have, their anxieties, such as an increased cost of living, the reaction of the Trusts, the absence of healthy competition, the troubles of big financial houses and combinations.

As regards Germany, it may be questioned whether it has really been so flourishing as it is often represented to be. Trade has certainly been stimulated ever since the Franco-German war; but has it not been over-stimulated? There has been an increase of production and in exports on a vast scale; but has it been on a sound basis? Production has far exceeded legitimate demand, and the result has been periodical very severe depressions. What is a recent picture of Germany painted by Consul-General Schwabach in the Consular Report? Depression in trade and industry; want of employment; the lowering of wages, which has crippled the purchasing power of the masses; industrial undertakings finding no home market for their output; the export trade forced to the utmost, and in many cases unremunerative; the home iron and electrical industries dull; the paper trade and leather trade depressed. This painting is hardly indicative of the success of Tariffs in Germany.[14]

5   Germany's Action towards Canada

However that may be, the recent action of that country towards Canada, in penalizing a British Colony for granting commercial preference to the mother country, has, no doubt, been much resented. Every British citizen considers that the commercial relations between Great Britain and her Colonies are a matter of purely domestic concern, and that interference therewith is not to be tolerated. But it must be remembered that the conception of those relations has, until lately, been very different to what it now is. As a matter of fact, commercial arrangements with foreign Powers have been separately made by self-governing Colonies, in pursuance of their valued fiscal independence; and, in return, the right to revise with the Colonies those arrangements, when prejudicially effected, is naturally claimed and exercised by the Powers. Therefore, the present action of Germany is easily understood, and cannot be said to be unreasonable. At the conference with the Colonial Premiers, it was agreed that a Colony, if it gave a preference to us in trade, and was in consequence discriminated against by a foreign Power, would, with its tariff, have an effective remedy in its own hands; and this view has been acted upon up to the present time. If, contrary to expectation, the remedy proves inadequate, the only alternative may be a tariff war waged by the mother country. But surely, before we take so serious a step, we had better wait and see whether the example of

---

[14]   Cf. Diplomatic and Consumer Reports. Parliamentary Paper No. 2959. (Original note.)

Canada is going to be followed by the rest of our self-governing Colonies? It is one thing to embark on a tariff war for the sake of a great principle – the principle of vindicating the right of the constituent parts of the Empire to arrange their mutual trade relations as they please; it is another thing to embark in it for the sake of improving our trade with a single Colony.

6. *The Conditions and Effects of 'Dumping'*

Some reference is called for to the important question of 'dumping', of which so much is heard. It is understood that 'dumping' is the export of home products at prices unremunerative to the exporter, and that 'dumping ground' is the market on which such products are unloaded.

'Dumping' is of two kinds: It may proceed from weakness. It may proceed from strength.

It proceeds from weakness when the exporting country has a surplus of production which it cannot dispose of in its home market, which it cannot afford to hold over till its home demand increases, and which it cannot put upon foreign markets at a profit. It is thus forced to put its surplus upon the foreign market at a price below the cost of production in that market. Such an export will probably be, and in the case of both the United States and Germany is, a loss to the exporter.

'Dumping' proceeds from strength when the producer in one market attempts to destroy his rival in another, by furnishing supplies below cost price, until the producer in the rival market is ruined or driven into other trades. The importer, it is contended, may then put up his prices to a very remunerative point, and monopolize the foreign market from which he has driven his rival.

It is important to examine the effects of each of these dumping theories.

First, as to dumping from weakness. It must be assumed that the American or German dumper is a person of ordinary intelligence. He does not willingly produce goods in order that he may dump them down in our markets at a price below the cost of production. He will, therefore, prefer to limit his output to the amount which he can dispose of at a profit, and will extend or contract it, according as he anticipates good or bad times in his remunerative markets. Of course, at intervals, he may be caught by a sudden slump, when he has a surplus on his hands larger than his home market can absorb, or is unable at once to slacken his output, and he will then have to face the alternatives of holding up his surplus (which he will do if he anticipates a speedy revival), or of selling it for what it will fetch in England.

But, if his weak financial position drives him to the latter alternative, it is subject to one serious limitation. He can only dump such manufactured products as he can find a ready market for. If, for instance, the American Steel Trust – the body whose prospective action causes great alarm in this country – be taken, it will be found that the standardized railway engines of that Trust cannot run on our lines; their marine engines do not suit our ships, and the Trust can, therefore, only dump pig-iron, billets, &c. It would seem, then, to follow that in America dumping can only be occasional, and in comparatively small quantities.

Moreover, the benefit will not be all on the side of the dumper. He must first employ and pay British shipping to carry his surplus to England; he must then offer his goods for sale in England at an unremunerative price; while the English merchant, if he buys them, presumably does so because he sees his way to make a profit by them.

As regards our iron trade, the immense extent of it, as compared with the limited amount of the dump, its elasticity, the increased demand, and the new channels of production which a cheap supply always creates, will combine to mitigate the ironmaster's loss by directing his energy and capital into new paths, such as a combine of his raw material trade with that of the maker of the finished product. It must not be forgotten, too, that the United States are still importing pig and manufactured iron for their home market; that, as a matter of fact, they have not dumped, and are not dumping in any appreciable degree.

As to the German dumper, his case is different. His weakness, and, consequently, his dumping is as permanent as his present Tariff. The German Government has deliberately fostered over-production in that country, and, owing to the protection from competition afforded by the Tariff, that production is costly. The natural restriction of its home trade has followed, and the German producer is thus compelled to export a continually-increasing surplus at unremunerative rates. Another cause may have contributed to this result. It is understood that Germany, speaking generally, trades not on accumulated capital, as is the case with this country, but on money borrowed from the banks. As soon, therefore, as the commercial prospects become overclouded, the banks call in a portion of their advance, and the manufacturer has no other means of meeting this demand than by exporting, at a serious loss, the surplus on his hands.

The general condition of the iron and steel market in Germany have been so depressed that the result is that the dumping in that country from weakness has become permanent and increasing. It is now a regular source of cheap supply to which our manufacturers look as a normal source of profit. The recent Reports of Consul-General Ward, of Hamburg, supply a remarkable illustration of this tendency. The state of their home trade compels the Germans to dump steel plates for shipping in England at the prices of bankrupts' stock. Our shipbuilders are thus enabled to build ships at a very low price, and these they sell to the Germans.

As to our own iron works, the Commissioners of Inland Revenue in their Annual Report show that the gross income assessed on iron-work ore was increased from 1,840,350*l.* in 1896–97 to 5,380,418*l.* in 1900–1901. Thus in four years the income from this trade increased about 300 per cent. In the face of these figures, it is submitted that the German dump has not materially injured our trade.

In considering this question, however, it is extremely important that a distinction should be drawn between the dumping below cost price of goods which we can equally well supply ourselves, and the imports of goods which we have lost the power to supply, and of which the Germans have secured the monopoly by technical education, closer study, and improved methods.

Here perhaps, a digression is permissible, in order to quote an instance of the loss of a trade due to these causes – the coal tar colour trade. The story is humiliating to this country.

The secret of aniline dyes was first discovered by English chemists. They took out patents for their invention, and so long as those patents ran their discovery was of great benefit to our cotton trade. But the ignorance of the manufacturers who used these dyes for their cottons was so great, and in this country the study of science applied to manufactures was, and remains, in such an infantile state that the discovery was never developed or improved by our chemists at home, and it is believed that, so far as we are concerned, the dye of to-day is the dye of 1884.

Meanwhile in Germany the Charlottenburg University and the

Central Stelle were yearly turning out a large staff of young chemists whose mission was to study the application of science to every species of manufacture. They took up the question of these dyes and developed them to a point at which they drive the old English mixture out of all markets. They obtained patents in this country and Germany for each step in the invention as they took it, and the German manufactures, to whom the whole trade passed, have purchased the patents, and refused to issue licences for the manufacture of the dyes in this country.

Meanwhile we could have done the same thing as regards the German market if we had had chemists 'of commerce' who were sufficiently educated to make discoveries in the improvement of dyes which were worth protecting by patent. Unfortunately we had none, and we have lost the trade.

Nor is this the only industry which we have lost for the same reason. The making of surgical and other scientific instruments, the working up and application of bye-products in manufacture are gone or are going from us. But it is obvious that this is no question of tariff. What we do not produce, no import duty can protect; and, if the duty were raised to the prohibition point, we should lose not only the manufacture, but even the use of the articles themselves in our own industries.

To return from this digression to the question of 'dumping'. Dumping from strength has still to be examined. Such dumping does not exist in Germany. Therefore, it is only in the United States where it is to be found.

It is generally assumed that the Iron and Steel Trust must be the principal culprit. What are the facts? Various separate interests were acquired at an extravagant price. It was, indeed, so over-capitalized that its ordinary shares and its preference shares have now fallen to so great a discount, that they are practically unsaleable. In a year of extraordinary prosperity in the United States, there is a decrease in the earnings of the Trust in the last quarter of 1,163,000 dollars, and in the last half-year of 2,809,000 dollars; while in its advance orders there has been a decline of 75,415 tons compared with last year.

These figures are evidence that the Trust can only keep its head above water by producing as cheaply as possible, and by selling in the dearest market. Its immediate object is, therefore, to secure its home market, in which, by aid of the protective Tariff, the consumer is forced to purchase at a greatly enhanced price. It is to this home market of

80,000,000 people that the American manufacturer looks first; his foreign exports are a matter of quite minor importance to him.

Now, the total output of the English iron trade is computed at 139,441,000*l.*, and it is not disputed that its production on the spot is as cheap as the price at which the American Trust can put down its products in England. It follows that if the Trust is to succeed in seriously crippling such a trade, it must do one of two things.

Either it must forego for many years any prospect of a dividend – a course which may reasonably be supposed to lead to a revolt of its shareholders; or it must raise its prices still higher against the American consumer, in order that the means for the attack upon British trade may be supplied – not an easy matter to do, because the Trust's output is less than half the total production of the States, and its rivals will annex more and more of the home market as the prices rise.

There are American writers who hold that, although the Trust could not succeed in injuring our market as a whole, it might concentrate its attack upon one section at a time, and, when that had been crushed, might move on to the next, and thus, by degrees cover the whole ground. And with what result? If our home production were destroyed, the Trust would find itself in direct competition with the Germans for supplying our market, and this competition would secure us a cheap supply of raw and semi-manufactured iron at dumping prices, until the German dumper was destroyed. The trade and the consumer would absorb and profit by the cheap imports dumped on the particular section, and that section, after a short period, of dislocation, would turn its attention to other and more profitable business. The evidence appears to show that the English trade is much stronger than the dumper, and would crush him in the struggle. So much for dumping.

7. Retaliatory Weapons

It is urged, however, that, apart from dumping, we ought to have something to offer to other countries, in order to be able to bargain with them; that we are now placed at a disadvantage in negotiations as compared with our protective neighbours; that, in short, the only effective diplomatic weapon is a tariff with which we could threaten foreign Powers. Let it be first remembered that foreign tariffs are not specially aimed against this country, and that, so long as they mete out one and the same treatment to everybody alike, they cannot be said to be 'hostile'. That is to say, if foreign countries, having two scales of duty for their tariff – a maximum or general tariff for those who treat them ill, and a minimum or Conventional for those who treat them well – accord us, as they almost universally do, the minimum scale, their action is certainly not unfriendly, though it may be, and is, an obstacle to our trade relations, as all tariffs must be.

But, if we take power to arm ourselves with weapons which consti-tute discriminating protection, and by which we deliberately intend to exclude some specific articles of a particular country, or to penalize their entrance at our ports, that will really be erecting a hostile tariff – we shall be issuing a declaration of commercial war. The first effect will be that we shall automatically lose, for what it is worth, the most-favoured-nation treatment[15] in the country against which our retalia-tory weapon is specially directed, and our export trade, which was handicapped before, will be more than ever handicapped now, because it will be subject to the maximum scale of the tariff instead of the minimum scale. But more than this: a war of tariffs is what two can play at; and, though it is generally assumed that the country which we intend to fight will, as soon as it sees the muzzles of our guns pointed at her, cease to do what we object to her doing, is it not quite possible, if not probable, that we shall come off worsted in the fight? For, while foreign countries might penalize the whole of our exports to them, amounting to 174,000,000*l.*, we could only penalize the import of (what are called) 'manufactured articles', amounting to 119,000,000*l.* and not nearly the whole of them, for much of that which is the manu-factured article of one trade is the raw material of another.[16] It is the

---

[15] The most-favoured-nation treatment will probably have been forfeited by the preferential arrangement. (Original note.)

[16] The difficulty of drawing the line between raw materials and manufactured articles is explained in the following letter written by Mr. Ernest E. Williams: – 'What are raw materi-als? – flour, eggs, pig-iron, woollen yarn, sawn timber, ropes, sugar, ship-plates, fishing tackle, copper ingots, jam, paper. That is as varied an assortment as one can desire, and all the articles named are of more or less considerable commerce, sufficient to demand their being placed on one side or the other of the dividing line between dutiable and duty free. Now, see the confusion and the illogicality which must result if the line be drawn as some of our tariff novices would draw it. Flour is a food-stuff, a raw material (of the biscuit trade) and a manu-facture (the fully manufactured article of the milling industry). Eggs are both food-stuffs and the raw material of manufacturing industries. Pig-iron is a manufacture and the raw material

same both with Germany and the United States individually. What we could tax of theirs is less than what they could tax of ours. In short, we present a wider front that is assailable, owing to the nature of our imports and exports. Moreover, we are in another respect different to any other Power; we are carriers for the world, and consequently our shipping trade supplies a huge target which is exposed to most damaging shots. While, therefore, we might succeed in keeping out of this country certain foreign articles, which, if they were semi-manufactured articles must benefit some industry or another, and which, if they were wholly manufactured articles must benefit the consumer, we could easily provoke a heavier fire on ourselves than we could inflict on others; and so with our retaliatory blunderbusses we should stand to lose more than we gained.

If, however, notwithstanding, there is to be established a Tariff for retaliatory purposes, a difficulty would present itself of a formidable and practical kind. To serve as a weapon of retaliation, the Tariff must be of a 'give-and-take' character; and then we become confronted with a Parliamentary difficulty. The Government would have a choice of evils. They must either obtain from Parliament a general power – a sort of *carte blanche* – to impose duties, and to alter duties, on articles coming here from foreign countries, which have prohibitory Tariffs against us; or else they must be able to give an undertaking that Parliament shall be immediately asked to impose or alter taxes on specific articles, and this irrespectively of the financial needs of the State. Considering the jealousy with which the House of Commons regards its taxing rights, could they be asked to give, or, if asked, would they be likely to give, the Government a power to tax at its discretion manufactured articles

of the iron and steel trades. Yarn and timber are also both manufactures and raw materials of other manufacturing industries. Even an apparently fully manufactured article, such as is a rope, is also raw material (*vide*, the shipbuilding industry). Sugar, whether raw or refined, may be regarded in any of the three categories; ship-plates, fishing tackle, copper ingots in two of these; jam in two; paper in two also, for it is the raw material of the printing trades.

If the gentlemen who announce their desire to put import duties upon food-stuffs and manufactures, leaving to imported raw materials free entry, get the opportunity of constructing a tariff in accordance with their division, they will have before them a task whose difficulty – nay, impossibility – they have not yet realised. In the meantime, by advocating such an impracticable arrangement, they will put into the hands of their opponents an argument of real, logical force, of which the said opponents may be trusted to make full use.' (Original note.)

specified in a list, which would have to be a very comprehensive one, especially when the tax might be the outcome of pressure brought to bear by a special industry? Such a proposal would raise crucial constitutional points. But what is the alternative? The alternative is to propose to Parliament, as often as the Government has need, a particular weapon in the shape of a tax on a particular article; and it is pretty certain that the Parliamentary difficulties which are now experienced would be nothing in comparison with those attending the insertion of new articles in the Customs tariff, every one of which would excite competing interests and would be reviving the fight of Free Trade *versus* Protection. Indeed, it may be very much doubted whether an effective Customs Tariff, and frequent need of altering it, is compatible with our present Parliamentary machinery.

Another and very serious difficulty arising out of a Tariff and its changes would be the difficulty of dealing equitably with existing contracts. Under modern conditions of business, the supply of goods is largely regulated by contracts, which run for months, and, in many cases, for years ahead. Such contracts may, of course, be gravely affected by that imposition or abolition, and by the increase or reduction of duties on the articles concerned. When the change in the Tariff would make the exact fulfilment of the terms of the contract manifestly inequitable, there are two courses open: One is that the duty on the particular article covered by the contracts should be removed; the other is that the contract may be varied as between the parties to it, so as to draw the burthens imposed by the Tariff on the party best able to bear it. Resort has been had to both of these courses in connection with the duties recently imposed on coal, sugar, and corn, and experience has shown that they entail immense labour upon the traders concerned, upon representatives in Parliament and upon public Departments. But labour, however great, can be got through. What is a real difficulty is that the complication and variety of industrial processes and contractual obligations make many cases very doubtful, and constantly lead to cases of indisputable hardship. Moreover, that the goods passing under contract are the identical goods which have paid duty is very difficult of proof, and thus most conducive to litigation. There is great truth in the saying that 'the trade will stand being taxed, but won't stand being teased', and a Tariff is almost as certain to 'tease' as it is certain to 'tax'.

8. Conclusions

But, while the expediency, and even the practicability of altering our fiscal system in the direction of protection, however limited or discretionary, whether intentionally or unintentionally, is questionable, and while it is believed that an alteration were it even expedient as well as practicable, would do more harm than good, it is not contended that everything is for the best in the best of all fiscal systems – that commercial things are so well that they could not be bettered, or that the condition of trade is so satisfactory that there is no need for improvement.

Though there is no indication of general depression, it would be absurd to say that no single market is depressed. On the contrary there is no doubt that an industry here and an industry there is languishing; and there is certainly one market in which everything is stagnant and dull, and everybody is downcast and complaining – the money market. It is believed, however, that the causes of this stagnation and dullness are transient, being in great measure due to an enormous expenditure of an economically wasteful character in South Africa, and a very large absorption of capital which was required to meet that expenditure. As usual, the war, while it was going on, stimulated many industries – all those indirectly as well as directly connected with munitions, supplies, equipment, and transit; and it also led to an exceptional demand for labour, owing to the numbers of men drawn off to the seat of war. Artificial stimulation is invariably followed by a reaction; and, as the activity in trade created by war is necessarily followed by depression, we cannot be otherwise than feeling the enormous loss caused by the war, the only economic remains of which are debt and increased taxation. The wonder is not that we are experiencing the feeling of this great loss, but that we have not felt the shock more severely. The fact is that, while formerly inflation was followed by a crisis, 'the city' now exercises more caution, and guards against the more violent forms of collapse, depressions being substituted for panics. Wealth expended in a form which leaves no permanent economic advantage must produce prostration; and we must wait patiently the natural process of repair, remembering that of all markets, the money market is the most sensitive, affected as it is by the sanguine and pessimistic views of investors and speculators.

But is it possible to imagine that a change of taxation, which any scheme of preferential treatment or retaliation must entail, is likely to hasten the return of good times in the city? On the contrary, nothing is more calculated to unsettle trade than fiscal changes, or even the prospect of them; and the unsettling of trade may have disastrous effects on our leading industries – effects which are bound to tell on the money market.

Another rather disquieting consideration to be taken into account is the recent falling off in the amounts deposited in the Savings Banks. No satisfactory explanation of the decline is forthcoming, unless it be that the low price of gilt-edged securities is proving very attractive. But, if the decline should indicate a diminished saving power on the part of the wage-earning classes, it is difficult to believe that that tendency will be arrested by proposals involving a certain increase in the cost of living and a very uncertain increase of wages.

In short, State interference in Tariff matters, in however mild and unobtrusive a form, must tend to make commodities dearer. If you make commodities dearer, whether they are food-stuffs, or apparel, or less necessaries of life, you make wages less effective: the sovereign, which will lose part of its purchasing power, won't go so far as it does now. A reduction in the value of wages means either that the wage-earner has less to spend and thus is obliged to curtail his wants, or else that there must be a rise in wages. It is uncertain, therefore, whether the wage-earner will lose or not. It is certain that the manufacturer will suffer in both cases; for, either the demand for his goods will fall off, or the cost of his production will be enhanced.

Treasury, 25 August 1903.

INDEX

Aberdare, Lord 9–10, 14
abstinence, and interest 271–2
adjustment time, and monetary equilibrium 77n
adult education, problems of 29–30
aggregate demand, and reduced working hours
161, 162, 163, 164, 165, 166, 167, 168
American statistical methods 256, 258–61
American statistics, Giffen's criticism of 87,
243–4, 259–66
analine dyes, and British industrial leadership
307, 349–50
'angel of the hearth' model, and Marshall's
Bristol evidence 12
Applegarth, Robert 131 and n.
arbitration bureaus 236–8; see also conciliation
and arbitration
Armitage-Smith, Sydney 303n
articled pupils, at Bristol University College
16–17
Australia, minimum wage legislation in 85n

balance of trade, and international specie
movements 71
Balfour, Arthur 2, 81
Balfour, Gerald 88n, 143, 172, 173n, 178n, 183 and
n., 185, 186n, 213n, 220, 225, 238, 266, 274
Beernaert, A.M.F. 231–2 and n.
Berry, Arthur 20n
Birt, Colonel 105, 138–41, 284
Board of Trade 116, 235–8; and employment
statistics 242, 257; and production statistics
246–7, 249–51; and statistical method 241; and
statistics on residuum 245–6; and wage
statistics 239, 240, 242–3, 256
Boer War: and balance of trade 342; and wasteful
expenditure 355–6
Boer War finance, and tariff reform 310
Booth Charles 5, 87, 89, 102n, 106, 107n, 110, 136
and n., 137 and n., 214n, 215n, 216n, 217n,
219n, 246n
Bosanquet, Helen 303n

Bowley, Arthur 20n
bread prices, and their income effect 76
Brentano, Lujo 301 and n., 303n, 304 and n., 306
and n., 308 and n., 311, 312n
Bridel, Pascal 69n
Bright, John 192, 193
Bristol University College: building programme
of 36–7, 59; financial position of 24–5, 26, 37;
and management of student lodgings 23–4;
nature of its students 21–2; origins of 14–15;
and religious education 22–3; scholarships at
19, 59–60; staffing position of 26, 30, 31, 37;
student sources of 18–19, 19–20, 61
British foreign trade, characteristics of 319–21
bureaucracy, and socialism 195–6
Burns, John 131 and n.
business education 4, 11, 12; and evening classes
at Bristol 18, 21n, 25, 28, 37

Caldicott, John 15
Cambridge University 15, 20, 26, 31, 33, 34,
35,36, 38, 43, 44, 45, 46, 50, 52, 57, 59;
economics and politics tripos of 11; and
women's degrees 11
Cannan, E. 82n, 303n
capital accumulation; and municipal socialism
126; and public enterprise 122–3
capital costs, of municipal socialism 125
censorship, as state function 135, 136
census work: and labour bureau 227–9; and
labour research 222, 223
Chamberlain, Joseph 301, 310, 311, 337
Clifton College 15, 30–1, 41, 48
Committee on Higher Education in Wales and
Monmouthshire: recommendations of 10–11;
terms of reference of 9
community interests, and trade unions 96
competition: and irregular employment 108, 118;
and productivity 89, 289, 293; and public
enterprise 124, 126; and trade union strength
97

357

hoarding, and price level 74
hours of work: for dock labour 283–4, 285; and
    irregular employment 109; and organisation
    of industry 152–3; and output reduction
    109–10; and productivity 163; versus hours of
    duty 148, 149, 150; *see also* eight-hour day
housing policy 89, 272–4
Hubbard, W.E. 136 and n
Hyndman, H.M. 5, 89, 107n, 118n, 266 and n.,
    268n, 270n, 272n

imperial interests, and imperial preference
    330–2
imperial preference 300, 305, 307–8, 309–11, 314,
    315, 320–1; and differential colonial gain
    326–8; exclusion of raw materials from 316;
    and German retaliation 346–7; and growth of
    protection 329–30; methods of
    implementation 316; possible operation of
    321–9; and potential conflict within colonies
    322–3; and retaliation 352–3; United States
    reactions to 321–2
import duties: and food supply 317–18, 319;
    incidence of 300, 301, 302, 307, 317
imports, and population growth 333–4
Inama-Sternegg, C.T. von 231 and n.
income for university teachers 29–30
income tax data, as statistical source 258–9, 269
industrial census 217–18, 219
industrial disputes, and tariff reform 318
industrial fluctuations 108; and capital goods
    sector 100; causes of 99–100; and fashion
    changes 100–1, 154; and irregularity of
    employment 98, 99, 100; and seasonal factors
    154; and speculation 109; and state enterprises
    121–2; and statistical inquiries 248–50; and
    uncertainty 154, 155
information: and labour mobility 103–4; as
    remedy for irregular employment 108
Ingram, J.K. 173 and n.
innovation: and reduced unemployment 145; and
    socialism 134, 185; and state enterprise 135; and
    trade union activity 294–5
interest of capital, legitimacy of 272–2
international competition, and irregularity of
    employment 101
international competitiveness 314–15
international specie distribution 70, 71, 72
international trade: and industrial fluctuations
    99–100; and relative price levels 68
investment earnings, legitimacy of 270–2
invisible exports 340–1, 342
irregularity of employment, 2, 4, 83, 85, 86–7;
    causes of 98–104, 152–3; in iron industry
    155–6; origins of 155; remedies for 107–28; *see
    also* unemployment

Jacob, William 308
joint stock companies, and J.S. Mill 178–9

Jones, Lloyd 129
Jowett, Benjamin 4n, 15, 56n, 82n, 88n

Kadish, Alon 12n, 20n
Keynes, J.M. 1, 2, 3, 4, 5, 11, 66, 67n, 83, 84, 85,
    306, 307n, 312
Keynes, J.N. 31n, 50n, 65, 66
Kiaer, A.N. 231 and n

labour, and non-material incentives 194 and n.
Labour Commission 1, 2–3; balanced
    membership of 82; as educational experience
    for Marshall 5; *Final Report* of 3, 4, 81, 83–4,
    84–7, 90, 287, 288n; Group B 4; preparation of
    its *Final Report* 84; role of chairman in 88;
    sub-division of its *Final Report* 84; terms of
    reference of 81
Labour Department 116
labour disputes 91, 93, 108, 123–4, 234, 288–9,
    290–1, 292
labour exchanges 116–17; in Paris 117
labour mobility, and structural change 102–3
Laidler, David 69n
Le Play, M.F. 228n
level of prices, determination of 75
living standards, and productivity 267–8, 269
Lloyd George, David 312
London County Council: and irregular
    employment 111–12; and worker
    representation 132; and working conditions
    128
London University 18, 32, 34, 44, 52, 59
low wages, not economic wages 128
Lowe, Robert 308, 330 and n.
Ludlow, J.M. 5, 87, 89, 129–32

McCulloch, J.R. 175, 178
Macgregor, D.H. 20n
machinery: and shift work 196–7, 294; and
    unemployment 156–7
McWilliams-Tullberg, Rita 12, 46n
Maloney, John 12n
Malthus, T.R. 212n
Malthusianism, and wage effects of reduced
    hours 202–3, 204
Mann, Tom 5, 84, 87, 88n, 89, 104n, 107 and n.,
    109n, 131 and n., 202, 275
Mansion House relief, and unemployment 277–8
Marshall, Alfred 4; as author of 1903
    memorandum on Fiscal Policy 5, 303–7; on
    educational value of Labour Commission 82;
    on examinations 35–6; as examiner 32–3, 34,
    43n; and *Final Report* of Labour Commission
    83–7; and Higher Education Committee
    11–12; and intimidation of working-class
    witnesses 88; and Labour Commission 2–3; on
    minimum wage 85; as political economy
    teacher 37n, 39n; as Principal of Bristol
    University College 10, 12–13; and Royal